NASP

School Crisis Prevention and Intervention

The PREPaRE Model

Stephen E. Brock
California State University, Sacramento

Amanda B. Nickerson
University at Albany, State University of New York

Melissa A. Reeves
Winthrop University, South Carolina

Shane R. Jimerson
University of California, Santa Barbara

Richard A. Lieberman
Los Angeles Unified School District

Theodore A. Feinberg
National Association of School Psychologists

P | R | E | PaR | E
Prevent | Reaffirm | Evaluate | Provide and Respond | Examine

From the NASP Publications Board Operations Manual
The content of this document reflects the ideas and positions of the authors. The responsibility lies solely with the authors and does not necessarily reflect the position or ideas of the National Association of School Psychologists.

Published by the National Association of School Psychologists

Copies may be ordered from:
NASP Publications
4340 East West Highway, Suite 402
Bethesda, MD 20814
(301) 657-0270
(301) 657-0275, fax
(866) 331-NASP, Toll Free
e-mail: *publications@naspweb.org*
www.nasponline.org

ISBN 978-0-932955-67-8

Printed in the United States of America

10 11 12 10 9 8 7 6 5 4 3 2

Dedication

This book is dedicated to school-based mental health professionals who engage in crisis prevention, preparedness, response, and recovery efforts to support the students they serve. Having been in your shoes, we want you to know how much we appreciate your efforts. It is our hope that this book contributes to your important efforts and helps to make this most difficult work a more manageable task.

For Christine Jane *(Stephen E. Brock)*

For Arlene and Stanley Nickerson, providers of eternal social support *(Amanda B. Nickerson)*

For my resiliency builders, Shawn, Austin, and Taylor; Gary and Kathy Louvar; and Shirley Reeves; to crisis team colleagues in Colorado whose work served as a foundation for this project *(Melissa A. Reeves)*

For Kathryn, Gavin, and Taite *(Shane R. Jimerson)*

For Jill (*my* crisis responder) and Ruth and Morton, for their eternal love and support *(Richard A. Lieberman)*

For the love of my life, Fran *(Ted Feinberg)*

Table of Contents

Preface

This book has been written to complement and reinforce the *PREPaRE School Crisis Prevention & Intervention Training Curriculum* (Brock, 2006a; Reeves, Nickerson, & Jimerson, 2006a). PREPaRE was developed through the collaborative efforts of workgroups sponsored by the National Association of School Psychologists (NASP), that is, the Crisis Prevention & Intervention and the PREPaRE Workgroups. This endeavor further extends NASP's decade-long leadership in providing evidence-informed resources and consultation services related to school crisis prevention, preparedness, response, and recovery. PREPaRE training is designed for educators and other school-based mental health professionals committed to improving and strengthening their school crisis prevention activities and crisis response procedures. Pilot testing of this curriculum revealed that the PREPaRE workshops have a high degree of consumer satisfaction, have a positive effect on participants' attitudes regarding their involvement on a school crisis team, and result in significant changes in crisis prevention and intervention knowledge (Brock, 2006b; Nickerson, 2006).

The need for the PREPaRE curriculum is emphasized by the fact that schools play a critical role in crisis prevention and intervention, meeting the needs not only of students but also of staff, families, and often the local community. As evidenced by recent crisis events, schools are integral to an overall community crisis response in terms of providing a safe haven, disseminating information, identifying individuals at risk, providing mental health services, linking individuals with community services, tracking displaced families, supporting long-term recovery, and generally serving as a model of control and normalcy in the face of trauma. To serve these functions, schools must have crisis plans and teams in place that encompass prevention, preparedness, response, and recovery. School crisis teams must be adequately trained to address a range of crisis events, to understand the systems and procedures that need to be in place to respond to crises, and to address the unique mental health needs generated by crisis exposure. School crisis plans and procedures must be fully integrated into community emergency response efforts, including law enforcement, fire and rescue, and community-based mental health service providers. These procedures must also be clearly communicated to staff, parents, and community leaders.

In preventing, preparing for, responding to, and recovering from crises, school crisis teams can emphasize (a) the promotion of the mental health, risk and resiliency, and coping capacity of the individuals affected by a crisis, particularly students, and (b) the unique opportunities and challenges presented to schools when preventing and responding to crises. Training for school crisis teams therefore must address crises as mental health risks as well as physical health and safety risks within the context of the school culture. Finally, an important goal of successful crisis prevention, preparedness, response, and recovery is to support academic functioning.

PREPaRE provides school-based mental health professionals and other educators with training on how best to fill the roles and responsibilities generated by their membership on school crisis teams. It is the only comprehensive, internationally disseminated training curriculum developed by school-based mental health professionals (each of whom has firsthand school crisis experience and formal training) specifically for school-based professionals. The curriculum is based on the following three assumptions:

1. Preparation for addressing the crisis-related needs and issues of children is critical. Children represent an especially vulnerable population, and their crisis reactions or symptoms are often more significant than those observed among adults (Brymer et al., 2006). In addition, it is commonly accepted that childhood trauma can have an impact on the child's cognitive, moral, and personality development and on coping abilities (Barenbaum, Ruchkin, & Schwab-Stone, 2004). In other words, the stakes can be quite high when it comes to school crisis response, and the need for a crisis intervention model, such as that offered by PREPaRE, is great.
2. The skill sets of school-based professionals are best utilized when they are embedded within a multidisciplinary team that engages in crisis prevention, preparedness, response, and recovery. Such school crisis teams allow each discipline to make optimal use of their unique professional skills and talents for preventing, preparing for, and responding to crisis events. For example, by virtue of their professional training and job functions, school-based mental health professionals are best prepared to address the psychological issues associated with school crises.
3. Schools have their own unique structures and cultures. Given this reality, without an understanding of schools and how they function, even the most skilled of crisis interveners will be at a distinct disadvantage when it comes to providing crisis prevention, preparedness, response, and recovery services in the school setting. In the words of Brown and Bobrow (2004): "As outside providers enter the school setting specifically to provide mental health services, a clear understanding of the school structure and culture is warranted" (p. 212). Thus, there is a clear need for schools to have their own crisis team models, such as the model offered by PREPaRE, which take into account schools and how they function.

It was within these assumptions that PREPaRE was conceived and developed. Using the guidance offered by this curriculum, schools can become better prepared to develop their own crisis prevention, preparedness, response, and recovery resources and respond promptly and appropriately to the unique crisis-intervention needs of the students they serve.

The PREPaRE model emphasizes how school-based mental health providers, as members of a school crisis team, must be involved in a hierarchical and sequential set of activities (Figure P.1). The model also incorporates foundational knowledge provided by the U.S. Departments of Education (2003, May) and Homeland Security (2004). Specifically, PREPaRE describes crisis team activities occurring across the phases of crisis prevention, preparedness, response, and recovery, including the Department of Education's Readiness and Emergency Management for

Figure P.1. The PREPaRE acronym represents a sequential and hierarchical set of crisis interventions.

P	**P**revent and prepare for psychological trauma
R	**R**eaffirm physical health and perceptions of security and safety
E	**E**valuate psychological trauma risk
P	**P**rovide interventions
a	**a**nd
R	**R**espond to psychological needs
E	**E**xamine the effectiveness of crisis prevention and intervention

Schools (REMS) guidance, and the Incident Command System (ICS) as delineated by the National Incident Management System (NIMS) of the Department of Homeland Security.

ABOUT PREPARE WORKSHOPS

PREPaRE includes two workshops, which can be conducted together or separately (as well as two corresponding "training of trainers" presentations).

Workshop 1, Crisis Prevention and Preparedness: The Comprehensive School Crisis Team (Reeves, Nickerson, & Jimerson, 2006a), is designed for groups as large as 100. This 1-day workshop reviews the crisis prevention and preparedness element of PREPaRE. The workshop is designed to give school-based mental health professionals and other educators a basic understanding of the comprehensive school crisis team and their role or roles on these teams. The workshop emphasizes the systems issues relevant to the prevention and preparedness element of PREPaRE. The importance of preventing and responding to crises within the structure of a comprehensive, multidisciplinary school crisis team is highlighted using the Incident Command System (ICS). The workshop also reviews steps to create safe, effective, and responsive school environments to prevent crises. Finally, the workshop discusses how schools can prepare for crises by developing, exercising, and evaluating plans. Activities and tabletop exercises are conducted within the workshop to reinforce workshop objectives.

This PREPaRE workshop is appropriate for all school personnel who need to understand how the comprehensive school crisis team is organized and how it functions. Crisis team participants can include, but are not limited to, school-based mental health professionals, administrators, teachers, other pupil services personnel, security officers, front office staff, transportation directors, and before- and after-school activities coordinators.

Training of Trainers (ToT) for Workshop 1, Crisis Prevention and Preparedness: The Comprehensive School Crisis Team, is a 4.5 hour training designed to provide the information and practice needed to become a Crisis Prevention and Preparedness workshop trainer. A prerequisite for this training session is completion of the Crisis Prevention and Preparedness workshop. The trainers' workshop reviews the logistics of workshop presentation and specific guidance on how to present the workshop (with a special emphasis on a standardized delivery). Participants are given the information they need to independently offer the Crisis Prevention and Preparedness workshop.

Workshop 2, Crisis Intervention and Recovery: The Roles of School-Based Mental Health Professionals (Brock, 2006a), is designed for 15 to 40 participants. The 2-day workshop reviews the elements of the PREPaRE model related to school-based mental health crisis intervention and recovery. Although specific mental health protocols for immediate intervention have not yet been validated (Vernberg et al., 2008), sufficient evidence supports the basic principles put forward by this workshop. The workshop is designed to give school-based mental health professionals evidence-informed knowledge that will help them develop the skills they will need to aid students and staff following a school-associated crisis event. Activities and role plays are embedded to reinforce workshop objectives.

Workshop 2 is based upon the assumption that, as members of a school crisis team, school-based mental health professionals must be involved in the following hierarchical and sequential set of activities. First, the school-based mental health professional strives to prevent those psychological traumas that can be avoided and prepare for those that cannot. Second, once a crisis event has occurred, all school staff members, including school-based mental health professionals, initially focus on helping to reaffirm physical health and students' perception that they are safe. Third, school-based mental health professionals evaluate the degree to which individuals have suffered psychological trauma. Fourth, using evaluation data and evidence-informed interventions, school-based mental health professionals provide crisis interventions and respond to the psychological needs of school community members. Finally, the professional examines the effectiveness of the school crisis intervention and recovery efforts.

This second PREPaRE workshop is appropriate for any individual filling the ICS role of crisis intervention specialist. Participants could include school-based mental health professionals (e.g., school psychologists, social workers, counselors, and nurses), administrators, and other individuals whom the team has identified as appropriate providers of crisis intervention. Additionally, this workshop can be helpful for community-based mental health professionals who may work with the school crisis team or be brought in to the school to assist in crisis response.

Training of Trainers (ToT) for Workshop 2, Crisis Intervention and Recovery: The Roles of School-Based Mental Health Professionals, is a 12-hour session designed to provide the information and practice needed to become a workshop trainer. A prerequisite for this session is completion of the Crisis Intervention and Recovery workshop. This session includes a review of the logistics of workshop presentation and specific guidance on how to present the workshop (with a special emphasis on a standardized delivery). Participants will receive the information needed to independently offer the Crisis Intervention and Recovery workshop.

All individuals who receive PREPaRE training through the two workshops will gain a better understanding of the organization and function of a comprehensive school crisis team (crisis prevention and preparedness) and the knowledge and skills necessary to meet the mental health needs of students and staff in the aftermath of a crisis (crisis intervention and recovery). This understanding will include knowledge about crisis reactions, how to prevent psychological trauma, assessment of risk for psychological trauma, crisis intervention, and evaluation of the effectiveness of the school crisis response. In addition, it is anticipated that school-based professionals will better understand their roles within the comprehensive team.

CONCLUSION

This book offers a review of the PREPaRE model and, perhaps most importantly, the science and scholarship that serve as its foundation. The chapters of this book both complement the experiences of PREPaRE workshop participation and provide access to its curriculum for individuals who have not been able to participate in the workshops.

As this book was being written, NASP was informed by the American Red Cross that crisis-trained school psychologists and counselors will now be invited to become members of the American Red Cross Disaster Mental Health Network. This decision represents further affirmation of the importance of school-based mental health professionals in crisis prevention, preparedness, response, and recovery.

Acknowledgments

As with any project of this magnitude, development of the PREPaRE training model was significantly influenced by a number of organizations and individuals. Specifically, the authors of this book would like to acknowledge the contributions of the California Association of School Psychologists' (CASP) Crisis Specialty Group (whose members included past NASP president Lee Huff and the late Ross Zatlin, Sweetwater Union High School District, Chula Vista, CA); and the Colorado Society of School Psychologists' (CSSP) State-Wide Crisis Response Team (members included past CSSP president Susan Compton, Susy Ruof, and Char Armstrong). We would also like to thank PREPaRE Workgroup members Christina Conolly-Wilson, Brian Lazzaro, Leslie Paige, and Melinda Susan for their ongoing commitment to this project and contributions to this book.

In addition, we acknowledge the following Crisis Prevention and Preparedness Topic Group members for their contributions: Leob Aronin, Woodland Hills, CA; Carol Benroth, Grand Junction School District, CO, and Anchorage, AK; Alan Cohen, Community Stress Prevention Center of Tel Hai College, Kiryat Shmona, Isreal; Cindy Dickinson, Fairfax County Schools, VA; Corrina Duvall, University at Albany, NY; Ken Greff, Bothell, WA; Leslie Paige, Ft. Hays State University, KS; Susy Ruof, Johnstown, CO; Donna Smith, ARIN Intermediate Unit 28, Indiana, PA; Amber Warrell, University at Albany, NY; Sarah Wilke, Aurora Public Schools and Colorado Department of Education; and Elizabeth Zhe, University at Albany, NY.

The following Crisis Intervention Topic Group members are acknowledged for their contributions: Melissa Allen Heath, Brigham Young University, UT; Servio A. Carroll, Sheridan County School District #2, WY; Ray W. Christner, Philadelphia College of Osteopathic Medicine, PA; Alan Cohen, Tel Hai College, Kiryat Shmona, Israel; Sylvia Cohen, Scottsdale Unified School District, AZ; Rose DuMond, Campbell Union School District, CA; Lillie Haynes, Dallas Independent School District, TX; Ellen Krumm, Gallup-McKinley School District, Gallup, NM; Sharon Lewis, Lodi Unified School District, Lodi, CA; Michael Pines, Los Angeles County Office of Education, CA; Doug Siembieda, Long Beach Unified School District, CA; and Philip Saigh, Columbia University, NY.

Special Topics Group members are also acknowledged for their contributions. On the topic of Threat Assessment: Jill Sharkey (chair), University of California, Santa Barbara; Dewey Cornell, University of Virginia; Sally Dorman, Charles County Public Schools, MD; Gina Hurley, Barnstable High School, MA; Linda Kanan, Cherry Creek School District, CO; Kathy Sievering, Jefferson County School District, CO; Melinda Susan, Sonoma County Office of

Education, CA; Paul Webb, Clark County School District, NV; and Diana Browning Wright, California Department of Education's Diagnostic Center, Southern California. On the topic of Grief: Melissa Allen Heath (chair), Deon Leavy, and Kristy Money, Brigham Young University, UT; Rona Leitner, Anna Kirchgater Elementary School, Sacramento, CA; Rosario Pesce, J. Sterling Morton High School District, Cicero, IL; Joelene Goodover, Great Falls High School, MT; Dana Chmiel Doré, Hopewell Public Schools, VA; Nadine Larson Woodle, Naperville Community Unit School District, IL; and Christie Cremeens, Madison County Schools, KY. On the topic of Bullying: Susan Swearer (chair), University of Nebraska, Lincoln; Preston Bodison, Baltimore School District, MD; Carly Cornelius, Madison County Schools, KY; Susan Eldred, Chapman University, CA; Marolyn Freedman, Santa Monica/Malibu Unified School District, CA; Lillie Haynes, Dallas Independent School District, TX; Ian MacLeod, Amos Alonzo Stagg High School, IL; Elizabeth Rivelli, Hingham Public Schools, MA; Bryony Rowe, University of Kentucky; Peter Sheras, University of Virginia; and Karen Sternat, Colonial Intermediate, PA. On the topic of Terrorism: Cathy Kennedy Paine (chair), Springfield School District, Springfield, OR; Craig Apperson, Washington State Office of Superintendent of Public Instruction; Jenny Wildy, Eastern Kentucky University; and Ralph E. "Gene" Cash, PhD, Nova Southeastern University, FL. On the topic of Suicide: Richard Lieberman, Los Angeles Unified School District, CA (cochair), and David Miller (cochair), University at Albany, NY. On the topic of Natural Disasters: Judy Oehler-Stinnett (chair), Oklahoma State University; Carla Cruise, San Bernardino City Unified School District, CA; and Keith Marcantel, Woodland Park School District, CO.

Other Crisis Prevention and Preparedness Topic Group members who participated in this project include Jennifer Kitson, Safe Schools/Healthy Students and Education Development Center, Newton, MA; Linda Kanan and Cathy Lines, Cherry Creek School District, CO; and the following students from the University at Albany, NY: David Halta, Natasha Little, and Robin Roberts.

Other Crisis Intervention Topic Group members who participated in this project included Wendy Carria, Arlington Public Schools, VA; Deborah Crockett, Fayette County Board of Education, GA; Elliot Davis, Brandywine School District, DE; Michelle Demaray, Northern Illinois University; Kimberly Knesting, University of Northern Iowa; Stephanie Livesay, Montgomery County Public Schools, MD; Christine Malecki, Northern Illinois University; Joe Nail, Clayton County Public Schools, GA; Kris Rodriguez, San Joaquin County Office of Education, CA; Denise Snow, Woodinville High School, WA; and Rosemary Virtuoso, Clark County School District, NV.

Finally, we are indebted to Linda Morgan, Kathy Cowan, and Brieann Kinsey at the National Association of School Psychologists, whose attention to detail, responsiveness, and dedication made the publication of this book a reality. We also thank our copyeditor, Kathy Kelly, for her careful work.

Chapter 1

BASIC ASSUMPTIONS

This chapter provides a review of information prerequisite to school crisis prevention, preparedness, response, and recovery and the PREPaRE model. Specifically, it addresses the following questions:

1. What are the crisis *events* that school crisis teams strive to prevent, prepare for, and respond to? What are the defining characteristics of these events, and how do these characteristics help to suggest the level of crisis response?
2. What are the crisis *reactions* seen among students (as well as parents and school staff members) that school crisis teams strive to prevent, prepare for, and respond to, and what might be considered the personal consequences of crisis event exposure?
3. What is the primary focus and the range of school crisis teams' *responses* to prevent, prepare for, respond to, and recover from crisis exposure, and how do these elements fit into the PREPaRE model?

After addressing these questions, the chapter concludes with a brief overview of this book.

THE CHARACTERISTICS OF CRISIS EVENTS

Before considering specific crisis prevention, preparedness, response, and recovery strategies, all crisis team members must understand the essential characteristics of a crisis event. In other words, they should know exactly what those situations are that school crisis teams strive to prevent, prepare for, respond to, and recover from and what situations may require the use of specific school crisis interventions. Brock (2002a, 2006a, 2006b) suggested that the types of events that may require a school crisis response are extremely negative, uncontrollable, and unpredictable.

The first and perhaps most fundamental characteristic of a crisis event is that it is perceived as being extremely negative (Carlson, 1997). Crises have the potential to generate extreme pain. These events may cause physical pain or emotional pain, or be viewed as having the potential to cause such. For example, according to the American Psychiatric Association's *Diagnostic and Statistical Manual of Mental Disorders, Fourth Edition-Text Revision* (DSM-IV-TR; APA, 2000), the types of events capable of generating posttraumatic stress disorder (PTSD) reactions involve "actual or threatened death or serious injury, or other threat to one's physical integrity" (p. 462). Section 3 of this book discusses the fact that the student's perception of the crisis event is critical, and the more negative the individual's view of the event and its impact, the more significant the personal crisis becomes (Bryant, Salmon, Sinclair, & Davidson, 2007; Shaw, 2003).

The second characteristic is that these events *generate feelings of helplessness, powerlessness, and/or entrapment* (APA, 2000). Crisis events often result in individuals feeling they have lost control over their lives. The degree to which an event generates these feelings has a significant effect on how the event is perceived. For example, students who have not been provided with earthquake preparedness training will likely judge an event such as an earthquake to be more uncontrollable, and thus more frightening, than students with such training who know how to respond to these events.

Finally, crisis events typically *occur suddenly, unexpectedly, and without warning.* A key factor that makes the event traumatic is the relative lack of time to adjust or adapt to crisis-generated problems (Carlson, 1997). Regarding event predictability, it has been suggested that relatively gradual and predictable events (e.g., death following a long-term terminal illness) generate less traumatic stress than those that are very sudden and unpredictable (e.g., accidental death, random shootings). If a crisis is more predictable, there is more likely to have been an

Table 1.1. Events That May Require Crisis Intervention

Life-threatening illnesses	Disfigurement and dismemberment
Assaults	Road, train, and maritime accidents
Fires or arson	Suicide attempts
Explosions	Fatal accidents
Sudden fatal illnesses	Suicides
Homicides	Human aggression
Domestic violence	Kidnappings
Terrorist attacks	Invasions
Prisoners of war	Hostage taking
Hijackings	Torture
Hurricanes	Floods
Fires	Earthquakes
Tornadoes	Avalanches or landslides
Volcanic eruptions	Lightning strikes
Tsunamis	Airline crashes
Nuclear accidents	Dam failures
Exposure to noxious agents or toxic waste	Construction or plant accidents

Table 1.2. Crisis Event Classifications

1. Acts of war and/or terrorism
2. Violent and/or unexpected death
3. Threatened death and/or injury
4. Human-caused disasters
5. Natural disasters
6. Severe illness or injury

Note. From *Preparing for Crises in the Schools: A Manual for Building School Crisis Response Teams* (2nd ed.), p. 14, by S. E. Brock, J. Sandoval, & S. Lewis, 2001, New York: Wiley. Copyright 2001 by John Wiley & Sons. Adapted with permission.

opportunity to prepare and to make cognitive and emotional adjustments (Saylor, Belter, & Stokes, 1997).

To clarify the types of events that school crisis teams address, and to begin to make the point that not all crisis events have equivalent traumatic potential, Table 1.1 offers specific examples of events that possess the crisis characteristics just described, and Table 1.2 offers more general crisis event classifications. Members of the school community (i.e., students, staff, and parents) who experience or witness one of these events, or learn about a significant other being exposed to such an event, are *potential* psychological trauma victims and *may* require one or more of the PREPaRE elements to be discussed in the chapters that follow.

Crisis Event Variables

The types of crisis events listed in Tables 1.1 and 1.2 clearly are not equally distressing. Some of these events are more traumatic than others. Supporting this observation, Saigh, Yasik, Sack, and Koplewicz (1999), in a review of the literature, reported that rates of psychological trauma among children and adolescents (as indicated by the presence of PTSD) vary considerably both within and between crisis event types (with PTSD rates ranging from 0% to 95%). Thus, it is important to consider the varying potential of a given event to generate psychological trauma. Brock (2002b, 2006a, 2006b) referred to the variables that make some crisis events more traumatic than others as "crisis event variables." As illustrated in Figure 1.1, relative event predictability, consequences, duration, and intensity interact with the crisis itself and make some events more devastating than others.

Generally, human-caused events (in particular, those that involve personal assault by someone who is familiar) are more distressing than are natural disasters (or "acts of god"; Charuvastra & Cloitre, 2008). For example, though only 5% to 10% of children and adolescents might be considered as meeting full PTSD criteria following exposure to natural disasters (La Greca & Prinstein, 2002), studies of children exposed to war-related stressors typically find PTSD rates above 30% (Saigh et al., 1999). Similarly, it can be concluded that events that are intentional are more distressing than events that are considered to be accidents (Charuvastra & Cloitre, 2008). For example, among a sample of eighth graders, lifetime prevalence estimates suggested that whereas only 11.5% of females and 10.3% of males involved in a traffic or other serious accident had PTSD, 37.5% of females and 16.7% of males who had been physically abused had this

Figure 1.1. How crisis event variables make some crisis events more traumatic than others.

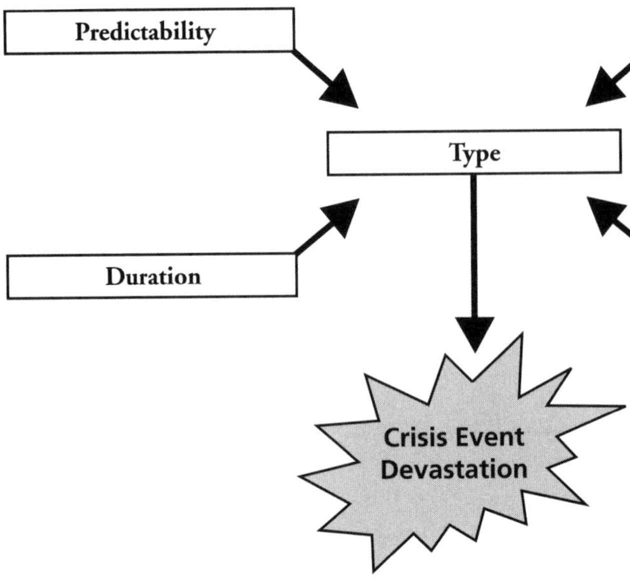

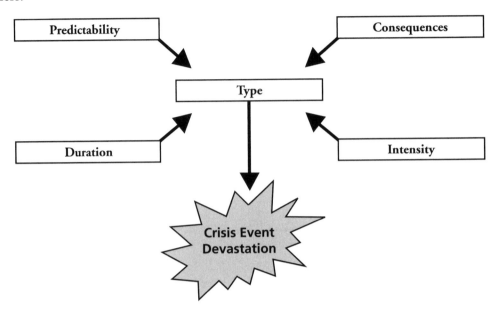

anxiety disorder (Elkit, 2002). However, this does not mean that natural disasters and accidents cannot become highly traumatic; there is clear evidence that they can.

Natural disasters that occurred suddenly, unexpectedly, and without warning (i.e., were not predictable); resulted in multiple fatalities and severe property destruction (i.e., had particularly devastating consequences); were associated with longer crisis event exposure (i.e., were of longer duration); and/or involved exposure to gruesome aspects of the crisis (i.e., had exposures that were especially intense) can be highly traumatic. The potential for natural disasters to become highly traumatic is clearly illustrated by Pynoos et al.'s (1993) study of youth following a particularly destructive Armenian earthquake that occurred on December 7, 1988. The earthquake—a type of natural disaster that is especially unpredictable—resulted in 55,000 fatalities. The earthquake's effects can also be considered to have had a long duration, given that the associated damage to local housing infrastructure (particularly schools and hospitals) resulted in long-term survival challenges during the freezing winter months. Finally, this crisis event resulted in youth being exposed to particularly gruesome aspects of the earthquake's aftermath. At the time of the earthquake, most youth were in inadequately designed schools, and as a result, two-thirds of the total deaths were children and adolescents (Azarian & Skriptchenko-Gregorian, 1998a). Given the interaction of these variables—predictability, consequence, duration, and intensity—with this type of natural disaster, it is not surprising to find that just over 90% of youth reported severe PTSD symptoms (Pynoos et al., 1993).

As might be expected, in the United States, Hurricane Katrina had similarly dramatic consequences. Although this event was relatively predictable, its consequences were dramatic. Katrina resulted in over 1,000 deaths, more than 500,000 people were displaced, and over $100 billion in damage occurred (Rosenbaum, 2006). Furthermore, the duration of crisis challenges and the intensity of crisis experiences were especially high for those who lived in New Orleans. Natural disasters typically do not generate significant psychopathology (La Greca & Prinstein, 2002; Saigh et al., 1999), but given these facts, it is not surprising to find that almost half (49.1%) of a sample of adult residents of the New Orleans metropolitan area had a 30-day prevalence of a DSM-IV-TR anxiety or mood disorder, and almost a third (30.3%) were estimated to have PTSD (Galea et al., 2007). Given that children are an especially vulnerable population (Brymer et al., 2006), it might be expected that the prevalence of Katrina-related psychopathology was even greater among children.

Levels of School Crisis Response

Knowledge of the traumatic potential of crisis events (the "crisis event variables") is critical given that different combinations of these variables will call for different levels of school crisis response. Obtaining an accurate estimate of the required level of crisis response is important because of the dangers associated with both over- and underreacting to a crisis event. More extreme caregiver reactions to a crisis event are associated with an increase in PTSD risk (Eksi et al., 2007); overreacting may increase students' threat perceptions and associated risk for psychological injury. On the other hand, underreacting may result in students' needs not being met and valuable resources being wasted. The four levels of school crisis response found within PREPaRE are listed in Table 1.3 (Brock, Sandoval, & Lewis, 1996, 2001).

The first level of school crisis response is the *minimal response*. This level implies that the given crisis event was not highly traumatic and that available school resources can manage the crisis without being required to leave their traditional school roles (i.e., there is no need for school crisis team members to clear their calendars) when responding to the crisis event. The provision of

Table 1.3. Levels of School Crisis Response

1. Minimal response
   - Few school community members are affected by the event, and school resources can manage the response without leaving traditional roles.
2. Building-level response
   - Many school community members are affected by the event. However, by clearing calendars, school-site resources can independently manage the response.
3. District-level response
   - Many school community members are significantly affected by the event and even after clearing their calendars, school-site resources cannot independently manage the response. Additional district resources are required to manage the response.
4. Regional-level response
   - A large number of school community members are significantly affected by the event, and even with district resources the response cannot be managed independently. Additional regionally based staff and resources are required to manage the response.

any necessary crisis response can be fit into the normal daily schedule of the providers of these services. Crisis events that might require this level of response include nonfatal accidental injuries that are not considered to be human caused or intentionally inflicted. Events of this type are not likely to adversely affect many school community members, so the need for crisis response is minimal.

The second level of school crisis response, *building level*, implies that although the crisis event is potentially traumatic, available school resources can manage the crisis. However, when responding to the event, team members are required to leave their traditional roles (i.e., to clear their calendars). Crisis events that might require this level of response include nonfatal accidental injuries that are human caused or the result of natural disasters that are not associated with fatalities or long-term coping challenges.

The third and fourth levels of school crisis response are *district level* and or *regional level.* These levels imply that the crisis event has the potential to be highly traumatic, and not only are building-level personnel required to leave their traditional roles, but the number of school community members affected will likely overwhelm building-level crisis resources. The affected school will need to call in resources from outside of the school or school district and will include crisis interveners who are not typically assigned to the school affected by the crisis event.

Whether a response is district or regional level is determined by the availability of local resources. This means, for example, that a small school district with relatively few crisis team members would need support from a regional response much sooner than a larger school district would. Crisis events that might require this level of response typically include those that are caused by human aggression, have one or more fatalities or significant property destruction, occurred with relatively little warning, presented ongoing coping challenges for a relatively long period of time, or resulted in exposure to intense crisis images and actions. Events of this type are likely to have adversely affected a large number of school community members; therefore the need for crisis response is significant (and for some schools and in some situations overwhelming).

Table 1.4 provides additional examples of possible matches between a crisis event and the appropriate level of crisis response. In these examples, in addition to crisis event variables, other factors will also be important in determining crisis response level, such as the size of the school or school district, available resources, and idiosyncratic threat perceptions. In other words, Table 1.4 is not intended to be prescriptive, but rather to illustrate how event variables may influence the level of crisis response.

CRISIS REACTIONS: THE PERSONAL CONSEQUENCES OF CRISIS EVENT EXPOSURE

Before considering specific crisis prevention, preparedness, response, and recovery strategies, crisis team members must be knowledgeable about crisis reactions. In other words, exactly what are the personal consequences of crisis event exposure that school crisis teams strive to prevent, prepare for, respond to, and recover from and that may require the use of specific school crisis interventions? As with other models of crisis response (e.g., Brymer et al., 2006), PREPaRE does not assume that all trauma-exposed students will develop severe mental health challenges or have

Table 1.4. Matching Level of Crisis Response With Crisis Event Variables

		Crisis Event Variable Examples				
Crisis Event Example	*Estimated Crisis Response Level*[a]	*Type*	*Consequence*	*Predictability*	*Duration*	*Intensity*
Student falls and breaks leg on playground while playing kickball	**Minimal** Crisis response	Accident (not human caused)	Nonfatal injury	School staff expect playground accidents	Minutes	Others see the student falling and crying
Rain causes local flooding and damages playground equipment, one classroom; no injuries	**Building** Crisis response	Natural disaster (an "act of God")	No fatalities or injuries	Flooding was forecast 2 days in advance	Days	Students see the damage
A gang fight takes place off campus and involves students at your school	**District** Crisis response	Human caused (violent assault)	One fatal injury	Students predicted the fight	Minutes	No students witnessed the event
A gunman attacks on a crowded playground; some students are in lockdown all day	**Community/ Regional** Crisis response	Human caused (violent assault)	Multiple fatalities	Sudden and unexpected	Hours	Students are expose to gruesome sights

Note. [a]These estimated crisis response levels are not prescriptive. Rather, they are intended to illustrate how crisis event variables may influence response levels. For example, relative to larger schools and school districts, smaller schools and school districts will require a greater level of response for the same crisis event.

significant long-term coping difficulties. Rather, the model is based on an understanding that trauma-exposed students will display a range of crisis reactions, some of which will necessitate very little school- or community-based mental health assistance and others that will require more intense crisis intervention. Slaikeu's (1990) definition of the crisis state provides a framework through which to understand the types of crisis reactions that will require more involved crisis intervention assistance.

The Crisis State

According to Slaikeu (1990) the crisis state is "a temporary state of upset and disorganization, characterized chiefly by an individual's inability to cope with a particular situation using customary methods of problem solving, and by the potential for either a radically positive or negative outcome" (p. 15). The need for school crisis intervention services will depend on the extent to which school community members enter into the crisis state. The following paragraphs discuss the key elements of this definition. The importance of crisis teams understanding these elements is underscored by the fact that whereas the occurrence of a crisis event should prompt *consideration* of the need to provide a school crisis response, an event itself is insufficient to justify *provision* of the response. Rather it is the personal consequences of the crisis event for school community members that provide the rationale for provision of crisis intervention. Thus, it is essential that school crisis team members understand the consequences of crises that signal the need for crisis services.

Perhaps the most obvious manifestation of the crisis state is "upset and disorganization." Among more severely traumatized students and staff members these reactions "involve intense fear, helplessness, or horror (or in children, ... disorganized or agitated behavior)" (APA, 2000, p. 463). A more detailed examination of the specific ways in which upset and disorganization can be manifested is offered in chapter 10's discussion of the warning signs of psychological trauma. For now, it is sufficient to mention that these consequences include emotional, cognitive, behavioral, and physical reactions (Brymer et al., 2006).

The next element of Slaikeu's (1990) definition, an inability to cope, is a consequence of the fact that crises are events that are not a part of the usual range of school experience. They are, in fact, so far from the ordinary that they have the potential to overwhelm previously developed problem-solving or coping strategies. In other words, they present students with problems that (at least initially) appear to be without solution. For example, when confronted with typical school yard aggression (e.g., a fight with a peer), a student might choose from several previously developed coping options (e.g., fight back, ignore the peer, tell a teacher, or run away). While likely effective for relatively minor and more typical school yard fights, these problem-solving strategies do not work when confronted with a school yard shooting. In this case, typical coping options would likely not be viewed as effective. Thus, the problem would appear to be without a solution, and the student would consequently experience upset and disorganization.

The final element of Slaikeu's (1990) definition, the potential for a radically positive or negative outcome, is a consequence of the fact that crises redefine how individuals perceive the world. They are situations in which the potential for change is great, and the changes mandated by the crisis present the individual with both opportunity and danger. Those who adaptively cope with a crisis not only are no longer upset and disorganized, but have also developed new problem-solving strategies. Developing these new strategies not only allows the individual to return to precrisis functioning levels, but can also result in greater psychological resilience. For example, students may cope with a natural disaster by acknowledging that such events are relatively rare and that the danger they present can be minimized by taking protective actions. These students are able to return to their precrisis functioning with new adaptive coping strategies (considered a radically positive outcome). On the other hand, other students may cope with the same disaster by deciding not to leave their homes (a radically negative outcome). It is important to acknowledge that the danger and opportunity that trauma exposure presents to students (and schools) makes school crisis intervention very consistent with the general purpose of schooling (i.e., to promote the development of skills that allow the student to be a more productive member of society).

Other characteristics of the crisis state are that it represents more than simple stress and is not necessarily a sign of mental illness. Responses following crises differ from stress in several ways. First, people in crisis have lowered defenses and are open to suggestion. In contrast, individuals who are "stressed" are typically defensive. Second, a crisis has the potential for a radically positive or radically negative outcome. On the other hand, the typical outcome for the individual experiencing simple stress is either adaptation and survival or a return to the status quo. Finally, although the crisis state has a sudden onset and is of fairly short duration, the stress state usually builds up gradually and is in many cases a chronic problem.

Although the symptoms of the crisis state may be similar to those of psychopathologies, they are not necessarily signs of mental illness. Given sufficient stress, anyone, regardless of how psychologically ill or healthy, can enter into a crisis state. Simply put, it is a common reaction to abnormal circumstances. This is not to say that mental illness cannot evolve out of, or be exacerbated by, the crisis state. Although the crisis state typically resolves itself within several weeks, in some cases it may evolve into mental illness.

Mental Illness

For all but the most extreme of crisis events, it is expected that most people will recover from the psychological trauma generated by event exposure (National Institute of Mental Health [NIMH], 2001). However, mental illness is a possibility, and to the extent these disorders are present, there clearly is a critical need for immediate and highly directive school crisis intervention. Thus, it is important for all school crisis team members to be aware of the psychopathologies that are a potential consequence of crisis exposure.

Anxiety disorders, in general, and PTSD, in particular, are the most common psychopathologies associated with exposure to a crisis event (Green, 1994). Of particular interest to educators is the finding that PTSD symptom severity has been linked to school performance. For example, it has been documented that in a sample of 11- to 14-year-olds, students with severe to very severe PTSD had significantly lower grade point averages (GPAs) than students whose PTSD was described as moderate. Furthermore, following a group intervention designed to

Table 1.5. Possible Psychopathological Consequences Associated With Crisis Exposure

- Anxiety disorders (e.g., acute and posttraumatic stress disorders, panic disorder, specific phobia)
- Substance-related disorders (e.g., substance abuse)
- Dissociative disorders (e.g., dissociative amnesia)
- Mood disorders (e.g., major depressive episode/disorder)
- Disorders of infancy, childhood, or adolescence (e.g., separation anxiety disorder)
- Sleep disorders (e.g., insomnia, sleep terror disorder)
- Adjustment disorders (e.g., adjustment disorder with depressed mood)

address traumatic stress consequences, reductions in PTSD symptoms were associated with improvements in students' GPAs (Saltzman, Pynoos, Layne, Steinberg, & Aisenberg, 2001). Additional research indicates that when adolescents with this disorder are compared with those without PTSD (including those who have been exposed to crisis events but do not have PTSD); they score significantly lower on measures of academic achievement (Saigh, Mroueh, & Bremner, 1997).[1]

Despite the frequency and consequences of PTSD, it is not the only diagnosis linked with crisis exposure (APA, 2000; Berkowitz, 2003; Green, 1994; Hoven et al., 2004; Ritchie, 2003). Table 1.5 provides a list of other psychopathologies that may afflict individuals following exposure to a crisis event.

Although psychopathological outcomes typically are found among a minority of those exposed to a crisis event, the exact percentage of the population who will have such outcomes will vary. Some events are more traumatic than others. In addition, whether an individual will develop a psychopathology will depend on the complex interaction between the nature of the crisis event, the crisis victim's unique crisis experiences, and his or her external environmental resources and internal personal vulnerabilities (Berkowitz, 2003; Brock, 2002c). Again, although exposure to a crisis event is necessary to trigger postcrisis psychopathology, it is not sufficient to explain its onset (Berkowitz; McFarlane, 1988; Saigh et al., 1999).

School-Associated Crisis Consequences

In addition to the effects already mentioned, other consequences of crisis events occur that are relatively unique to the school setting. In fact, it has been suggested that disruptive behavior at school may be the primary outcome of student exposure to a crisis event (March, Amaya-Jackson, Terry, & Costanzo, 1997). These unique crisis effects are listed in Table 1.6. They include school behavior problems such as aggressive, delinquent, and/or criminal behavior (Azarian & Skriptchenko-Gregorian, 1998a; Carlson, 1997; Monahon, 1993; Nader & Muni, 2002); school absenteeism (Azarian & Skriptchenko-Gregorian, 1998a; Silverman, & La Greca, 2002);

[1] See Nickerson, Reeves, Brock, and Jimerson (2008) for a contemporary review of literature and best practices regarding the identification, assessment, and treatment of students with PTSD at school.

Table 1.6. The Consequences of Crises on School Functioning

- School behavior problems, such as aggressive, delinquent, and criminal behavior
- School absenteeism
- Academic decline
- Exacerbation of preexisting educational problems

academic decline[2] (Cook-Cattone, 2004; Nader & Muni, 2002; Silverman & La Greca, 2002; Yule, 1998); and exacerbation of preexisting educational problems (Vogel & Vernberg, 1993). Clearly, if these consequences are observed subsequent to a crisis event, a crisis response is warranted. Furthermore, assessment of these crisis consequences can be helpful in evaluating the effectiveness of a school crisis response (see chapter 17).

Positive Consequences of Crises

Crises are not only times of danger, but also times of opportunity. Thus, it is important for school crisis teams to consider some of the outcomes they hope their crisis response will achieve. For example, positive outcomes for schools and school districts might include the following: (a) administrators and the public recognize the need for programs for prevention, preparedness, response, and recovery; (b) more school-based mental health professionals and other staff members obtain prevention, preparedness, response, and recovery training; (c) more assistance is available to schools in the form of grants, emergency aid, and other additional funds to increase prevention, preparedness, response, and recovery services; and (d) more student support resources (e.g., school psychologists) become available. Similarly, positive outcomes for individual students and staff members might include the following: (a) some survivors become better able to cope with crisis problems, and (b) some change their lives in a positive direction (e.g., becoming helpers or advocates for others who later may be a victim or survivor). Evidence that these positive outcomes have been obtained can help to document that a given school crisis response has been successful.

THE CRISIS RESPONSE

Finally, before crisis team members consider specific crisis prevention, preparedness, response, and recovery strategies, they must understand the primary goals of crisis intervention and be knowledgeable about the range of crisis responses that school crisis teams provide.

The Primary Goal of Crisis Intervention

The primary goal of school crisis intervention is to help restore the crisis-exposed student's basic problem-solving abilities and in doing so to return them to their precrisis levels of functioning

[2] Regarding academic impairment following crises, it is traumatic stress reactions (i.e., PTSD) and not simple crisis exposure that puts students at risk for serious academic decline subsequent to crisis event exposure (Saigh et al., 1997).

(Sandoval & Brock, in press). Given this perspective, it is important for crisis team members to understand the basic elements of so-called normal coping. A useful framework for understanding what normal coping is has been offered by Moos and Billings (1984), who offer a taxonomy of coping skills organized into three domains, each with three skills (see Table 1.7).

The first coping domain, *appraisal-focused*, involves the crisis-exposed individual rationally thinking through and preparing for crisis event consequences (logical analysis and mental preparation), possibly reframing the event (cognitive redefinition), and in some cases, mentally maintaining the event at a distance until he or she is physically and emotionally ready to address it (cognitive avoidance or denial). It is important to acknowledge that this last appraisal-focused skill has important implications for crisis intervention. Specifically, it suggests that such intervention must be sensitive to the possibility that not all school community members will be immediately ready to confront crisis facts.

The second coping domain, *problem-focused*, involves the crisis-exposed individual assertively striving to identify crisis facts and support systems (seeking information and support), initiating efforts to address crisis-generated problems (taking problem-solving action), and adjusting relationships and activities so that there are substitutes for resources removed by the crisis event (identifying alternative rewards).

The third and final domain, *emotion-focused*, involves the crisis-exposed individual managing the emotions generated by the crisis event (affective regulation), venting feelings in a way that brings some relief (emotional discharge), and cognitively attempting to respond to the problem by accepting it (resigned acceptance).

The Range of Crisis Responses and PREPaRE

The acronym PREPaRE refers to the range of crisis response activities that school crisis teams need to be prepared to provide. As illustrated in Figure 1.2, PREPaRE stands for prevent and

Table 1.7. A Taxonomy of Normal Coping

Coping Domain	*Coping Skill*
Appraisal-focused: Understand the crisis in a productive manner	1. Logical analysis and mental preparation 2. Cognitive redefinition 3. Cognitive avoidance or denial
Problem-focused: Confront the crisis reality	1. Information and support seeking 2. Problem-solving action 3. Identification of alternative rewards
Emotion-focused: Manage crisis reactions and regulate emotions	1. Affective regulation 2. Emotional discharge 3. Resigned acceptance

Note. Source "Conceptualizing and Measuring Coping Resources and Processes," by R. Moos & A. Billings, 1984, in L. Goldberger & S. Breznitz (Eds.), *Handbook of Stress: Theoretical and Clinical Aspects,* pp. 109–145, New York: Macmillan.

Figure 1.2. The relationship between phases of a crisis, the specific PREPaRE school crisis interventions, levels of prevention/intervention, and comprehensive school crisis team elements.

<table>
<tr><td rowspan="2">Crisis Phase
(Raphael & Newman, 2000; Valent, 2000)</td><td colspan="2">Preimpact
The period before crisis</td><td rowspan="2">Impact
When crisis occurs</td><td rowspan="2">Recoil
Immediately after crisis threats end</td><td rowspan="2">Postimpact
Days/weeks after the crisis</td><td rowspan="2">Recovery/Reconstruction
Months/years after crisis</td></tr>
<tr><td>Preparation and planning</td><td>Threat and warning</td></tr>
<tr><td rowspan="11">PREPaRE:
School Crisis
Prevention and
Intervention Training
Curriculum</td><td colspan="4">Prevent and prepare for psychological trauma risk</td><td></td><td></td></tr>
<tr><td colspan="2">• Prevent and prepare for crisis
• Foster student resiliency</td><td colspan="2">• Keep students safe
• Avoid crisis scenes and images</td><td colspan="2"></td></tr>
<tr><td colspan="2"></td><td colspan="3">Reaffirm physical health, and ensure perceptions of security and safety</td><td></td></tr>
<tr><td colspan="2"></td><td colspan="3">• Meet basic physical needs (water, shelter, food, clothing)
• Foster perceptions of safety</td><td></td></tr>
<tr><td colspan="2"></td><td></td><td colspan="3">Evaluate psychological trauma</td></tr>
<tr><td colspan="2"></td><td></td><td colspan="3">• Evaluate crisis exposure and reactions
• Evaluate internal and external resources</td></tr>
<tr><td colspan="2"></td><td></td><td></td><td colspan="2">• Make psychotherapeutic treatment referrals</td></tr>
<tr><td colspan="2"></td><td></td><td colspan="3">Provide interventions And Respond to psychological needs</td></tr>
<tr><td colspan="2"></td><td></td><td colspan="3">• Reestablish social support systems
• Provide psychoeducation: Empower survivors and their caregivers</td></tr>
<tr><td colspan="2"></td><td></td><td></td><td colspan="2">• Provide classroom-based or individual crisis intervention or both
• Provide or refer for longer-term crisis intervention</td></tr>
<tr><td colspan="6">Examine the effectiveness of crisis prevention and intervention</td></tr>
<tr><td>Level of prevention (Caplan, 1964)</td><td colspan="2">Primary</td><td>Primary</td><td>Primary and secondary</td><td>Secondary</td><td>Tertiary</td></tr>
<tr><td>Level of preventive intervention (Gordon, 1983)</td><td colspan="2">Universal</td><td>Universal</td><td>Universal and selected</td><td>Universal, selected, and indicated</td><td>Selected and indicated</td></tr>
<tr><td>U.S. Department of Education (2003)</td><td colspan="2">Crisis prevention/mitigation and preparedness</td><td colspan="4">Crisis response and recovery</td></tr>
</table>

Note. From "Best Practices for School Psychologists as Members of Crisis Teams: The PREPaRE Model" (p. 1488), by S. E. Brock, A. B. Nickerson, M. A. Reeves, and S. R. Jimerson. In A. Thomas and J. Grimes (Eds.), *Best Practices in School Psychology V*, 2008, Bethesda, MD: NASP. Copyright 2008 by the National Association of School Psychologists. Reprinted with permission.

prepare, reaffirm, evaluate, provide intervention and respond, and examine. Specifically, the PREPaRE model emphasizes that members of a school crisis team must be involved in the following hierarchical and sequential set of activities. First, team members strive to prevent those crises that can be avoided and to prepare for trauma that cannot be prevented. Second, once a crisis event has occurred, all crisis team members initially focus on helping to ensure physical health and perceptions of security and safety. This immediate reaction to a crisis event is based on the assumption that for recovery to begin, school community members must have their basic needs met, and not only be safe but also believe that crisis-related danger has passed. Third, team members evaluate the degree to which individuals have suffered psychological trauma. Fourth, from assessment data, team members respond to the psychological needs of school community members. Finally, the model calls for an examination of the effectiveness of crisis prevention and intervention efforts.

This model is consistent with guidance and direction offered by the U.S. Departments of Education (2003) and Homeland Security (2004). According to the Department of Education, crisis response has four phases: (a) prevention and mitigation, (b) preparedness, (c) response, and (d) recovery. Thus, in the PREPaRE model, school crisis team members do more than simply react to immediate crisis circumstances (crisis response). They are also involved in activities designed to reduce or eliminate crises (crisis prevention and mitigation), prepare for those events that cannot or are not prevented (crisis preparedness), and have protocols in place to address the long-term consequences of school crises (crisis recovery).

Though crisis events clearly have the potential to generate significant psychological injury, the PREPaRE model also acknowledges that—with the exception of the most extraordinary crisis circumstances and with the support of naturally occurring family, school, and community resources—the majority of school community members will recover from their exposure to crisis events. Given this reality, most of the school crisis intervention services included in PREPaRE are considered to be indirect services. Often when crisis team members are implementing the elements of this model, they will be working behind the scenes, ensuring that students, staff, and parents are well positioned to realize their natural potential to overcome crisis. Of course these naturally occurring resources do have their limits, and this is where the assessment and response elements of PREPaRE come into play. Overall, PREPaRE aims at fostering natural recovery from psychologically traumatic events, while at the same time identifying the most severely distressed and providing them with an appropriate crisis intervention response.

THE PURPOSE AND PLAN OF THIS BOOK

This book provides a detailed examination of the rationale for and science of the PREPaRE model, and in so doing highlights best practices in school crisis prevention, preparedness, response, and recovery. It is intended to supplement and make more accessible the contents of the PREPaRE workshops. It is not a substitute for actual workshop participation and the many skill-building activities contained within these sessions.

Its five sections correspond to each element of the PREPaRE School Crisis Prevention & Intervention Training Curriculum. Section 1 contains a discussion of preventing and preparing for crisis events. This begins with a discussion of the rationale and goals of school crisis prevention and preparedness, and obstacles to preparation (chapter 2). It then examines school crisis teams (chapter 3), general and specific school crisis planning issues (chapters 4 and 5), and methods for exercising, or practicing, these plans (chapter 6). It concludes with an examination of strategies designed to prevent or mitigate the circumstances that would necessitate psychological crisis interventions (chapter 7).

Section 2 reviews strategies designed to reaffirm physical health (chapter 8) and perceptions of security and safety (chapter 9). Section 3 reviews strategies for evaluating psychological trauma. It addresses the rationale and theoretical foundations for the evaluation of psychological injury (chapter 10) and examines practical issues relevant to actually conducting psychological triage (chapter 11).

Section 4 examines approaches to providing crisis interventions in response to individual psychological needs. Specifically, it examines the primary importance of reestablishing social support systems (chapter 12), psychological education (chapter 13), classroom-based crisis intervention (chapter 14), and individual crisis intervention (chapter 15). This section concludes with an overview of the psychotherapeutic treatments that some of the more severely traumatized students and staff will require (chapter 16).

Section 5 reviews strategies designed to examine the effectiveness of crisis prevention and preparedness and intervention activities (chapter 17). Finally, section 6 presents some important final considerations. First, a chapter on caring for the caregiver acknowledges the difficulty of school crisis intervention (chapter 18). In the final chapter the authors' concluding comments also discuss the need for empirical research to validate the elements of the PREPaRE model (chapter 19).

Section 1

PREVENT AND PREPARE

Consistent with guidance offered by the U.S. Department of Education (2003), PREPaRE emphasizes that school crisis teams do more than simply respond to crisis events. Ideally, school crisis teams are active well before crisis events occur, because they simultaneously engage in both crisis prevention and crisis preparedness activities. As illustrated in Figure 1.2, the majority of prevention and preparedness activities take place before a crisis occurs, during what Valent (2000) has identified as the *preimpact* phase, or what Raphael and Newman (2000) have identified as the *planning and preparation/threat* and *warning* phases. However, some prevention activities may take place during the *impact and recoil* phases (Raphael & Newman; Valent), when school crisis teams strive to keep students safe and to avoid exposure to potentially traumatizing crisis scenes and images.

The six chapters in this section review essential information considered to be prerequisite or complementary to the school-based mental health response to school-associated crisis events. The section begins with an overview of school crisis prevention and preparedness (chapter 2) and then explores how the Incident Command System (ICS) of the National Incident Management System (NIMS) can be used to structure school crisis teams (chapter 3). Chapters 4 and 5 then examine the general and specific planning aspects of a school crisis plan. Chapter 6 discusses strategies for exercising school crisis teams and plans to ensure that they are operational. Finally, the section concludes with a discussion of preventing and preparing for the psychological injuries that can be precipitated by exposure to a school-associated crisis event (chapter 7).

Chapter 2

SCHOOL CRISIS PREVENTION AND PREPAREDNESS RATIONALE, GOALS, AND OBSTACLES

Preventing and preparing for school crisis events are essential elements of the PREPaRE model. This chapter begins to explore these elements by offering a discussion of the rationale and goals of school crisis prevention and preparedness, as well as the common obstacles that often interfere with the development of school crisis prevention and preparedness protocols.

RATIONALE FOR CRISIS PREVENTION AND PREPAREDNESS PLANNING

Many researchers in the field have suggested that it is essential for educators to have established crisis prevention and preparedness protocols and plans (Brock & Poland, 2002; Brock, Sandoval, & Lewis, 2001; Capewell, 2000; Dwyer & Jimerson, 2002; Jimerson & Huff, 2002; Nickerson & Heath, 2008; Osher, Dwyer, & Jimerson, 2006). Although large-scale disasters such as fatal school shootings are rare, many other crises that have the potential to significantly affect schools and their surrounding communities occur with relative frequency (e.g., accidental deaths and acts or threats of violence). For instance, during the 2005–2006 academic year in the United States, 78% of schools experienced one or more violent crimes, 17% experienced one or more other serious violent incidents, approximately 6% of students ages 12 to 18 reported that they avoided school activities or one or more places in school because they thought someone might attack or harm them, and students ages 12 to 18 were victims of about 1.5 million nonfatal crimes of violence or theft at school (Dinkes, Cataldi, & Lin-Kelly, 2007). Furthermore, crises are associated with a range of student reactions that have the potential to negatively affect their behavior, adjustment, and education. Given these observations, it is clear that there are important reasons for crisis prevention efforts.

Although crisis prevention is necessary, it is not sufficient. Even the best of prevention programs will not be able to stop all crisis events from occurring. Thus, crisis preparedness planning is also required. Such planning helps to ensure that all crisis response and recovery needs are met and available resources are effectively deployed. Foremost, crisis preparedness is important because crises typically result in an overwhelming requirement to attend immediately to multiple demands that are outside of normal routines. Without a crisis preparedness plan, important crisis response and recovery activities and needs may be overlooked.

The need for crisis preparedness is reinforced by the results of research, which suggested that it is not a matter of *if* a school will face a crisis, it is a matter of *when*. In a survey of 228 school psychologists, 93% reported that their schools had experienced and responded to serious crises (Adamson & Peacock, 2007). It is safe to say that all schools need crisis teams and plans. Without plans in place, schools facing a crisis can neglect important tasks during and following a crisis event, which can lead to unnecessary chaos, trauma, and panic.

Legal Rationale for Preparedness Plans

An additional reason for crisis prevention and preparedness efforts is that the failure to address these issues can result in litigation (Bailey, 2006). Although it has been argued that schools are exempt from litigation because of local governmental immunity, the financial cost of defending these lawsuits (Brickman, Jones, & Groom, 2004) and the potential negative public relations can be very damaging. Conversely, with the relative calm and control generated by having school crisis teams and plans in place, schools are in a much better position to help school communities recover from crises. For example, following a crisis, the school that presents itself as having and following a crisis plan will foster perceptions among crisis survivors that the crisis can be managed and thereby increase the belief that crisis-associated challenges can be solved. These schools also will be better able to reduce the level of chaos that occurs during an emergency, to aid in the identification of individuals in need, and to help school communities return to normalcy more quickly.

Legislation Supporting Crisis Prevention and Preparedness

In addition to the motivations described above, some legislative initiatives provide additional reasons for school districts to engage in school crisis prevention and preparedness efforts. Federal acts that have provided funding for crisis preparedness efforts include the Improving America's Schools Act of 1994, the Schools Safety Enhancement Act of 1999, the Goals 2000 Educate America Act, and the School Anti-Violence Empowerment Act of 2000. Although primarily concerned with academic progress, the No Child Left Behind Act of 2001 also requires local school systems that receive federal funding (under Title IV, Part A, Safe and Drug-Free Schools and Communities) to provide assurances that they have a crisis plan. Furthermore, in July 2004, President George W. Bush signed Executive Order 13347 (Individuals with Disabilities in Emergency Preparedness), which requires public entities to include people with disabilities in their emergency preparedness efforts (U.S. Department of Education, 2006b).

Local and state laws and regulations also affect a school district's prevention and preparedness efforts (National Education Association, 2007b). For example, some individual states have passed laws that require prevention programming, yearly crisis response training, regular practice of safety drills, or submission and practice of building- or district-level crisis plans. According to the School Health Policy and Programs Study (SHPPS, 2007), 92% of states require districts or schools to have a crisis plan. However, many federal and state laws lack specific guidelines or definitions, which results in great variability in how the laws are interpreted and implemented.

Other legislation that is relevant to crisis prevention and preparedness is the Family Education Rights and Privacy Act of 1974 (FERPA). FERPA allows schools to disclose otherwise confidential student records to appropriate officials without parental consent under certain circumstances, such as in cases of health and safety emergencies (Bailey, 2006; U.S. Department of Education, 2007).

GOALS OF CRISIS PREVENTION AND PREPAREDNESS

The primary goal of school crisis prevention and preparedness efforts is to develop school crisis teams and plans. In turn, these teams and plans work to develop procedures and protocols that (a) reduce the likelihood of crisis events occurring; (b) ensure response readiness for crises that are not, or cannot be, prevented; (c) provide direction immediately after a crisis event to minimize crisis impact and restore equilibrium; and (d) help repair crisis damage and return to precrisis (or baseline) operation and functioning (U.S. Department of Education, 2003). In other words, school crisis teams should be engaged in crisis prevention, preparedness, response, and recovery.

School crisis teams and plans provide leadership and guidance relevant to each of Raphael and Newman's (2000) and Valent's (2000) phases of crisis (see chapters 3, 4, and 5). PREPaRE articulates additional goals of these activities, including that all school districts and schools have *comprehensive* crisis teams and plans that (a) take an "all hazards" approach to address likely events, (b) are developed collaboratively with community-based partners, (c) are based upon data and information, (d) are practiced on a regular basis, (e) are continually reviewed and updated, (f) make use of the National Incident Management System's (NIMS) Incident Command System (ICS), and (g) are tailored to the needs of individual schools (Reeves et al., 2006a).

OBSTACLES TO CRISIS PREVENTION AND PREPAREDNESS

The literature suggests that common obstacles to crisis prevention and preparedness include problems with crisis plans. Specifically, plans are not (a) comprehensive; (b) practiced regularly; (c) coordinated with community-based emergency response agencies; (d) discussed with families, staff, and students; (e) attentive to the unique considerations of students with special needs; (f) based on factual data and circumstances; or (g) regularly updated and used (Burling & Hyle, 1997; Graham, Shirm, Liggin, Aitken, & Dick, 2006; Kano & Bourke, 2007; Phinney, 2004; Trump, 2000). Additional obstacles to crisis prevention and preparedness were previously described by McIntyre and Reid (1989). Unfortunately, almost 20 years later, many of the following obstacles are still prevalent.

Myths

The first obstacle is the belief that "it won't happen here." Consequently, many schools wait until a crisis has occurred before engaging in crisis preparedness and planning (Brock, Sandoval, & Lewis, 2001).

Territorial Issues

A second common obstacle is territorial, or "turf," issues, which include disagreement regarding who will initiate and/or lead crisis prevention and preparedness efforts, who pays for needed training and supplies, who pays for long-term support services, and who is the incident commander when multiple agencies are involved. These issues emphasize the importance of collaborating with key stakeholders, such as school boards, administrators, and other community-based response agency personnel.

To facilitate collaboration and thus avoid such turf issues, school boards and educational leaders need to take a leadership role in crisis team development and planning. An example of such leadership is provided by the Virginia Department of Education, which advocates that school boards establish a policy foundation and framework conveying the seriousness of crisis prevention and planning (Black, 2004; Virginia Board of Education, 1999). These policies need to reflect various aspects of crisis prevention and preparedness, from designing, updating, and implementing prevention efforts and preparedness plans, to rehearsing drills, developing a school board policy statement, and integrating crisis roles and responsibilities into job descriptions.

Limited Resources

A final common obstacle is limited resources, such as time for planning, training professionals, and securing funding (Bischof, 2007; Nickerson & Zhe, 2004). Financial constraints are prevalent in today's schools as funding for federal and state planning becomes less available. Furthermore, because of the recent focus on academic achievement and associated consequences of not demonstrating academic growth (e.g., those generated by the No Child Left Behind Act), principals have to make difficult monetary decisions, with crisis prevention and preparedness often taking a back seat to academic initiatives.

CONCLUSION

Crisis prevention and preparedness can be overwhelming when considering all that is involved. To make these activities more manageable, school districts must develop a multidisciplinary school crisis team to help with preparedness and follow best practice crisis planning guidelines. A successful approach is to begin with two or three crisis goals to improve the school's or district's plan, and to implement these well, rather than to try to do too much at once. Once those goals are met, another two to three goals should be chosen to continue working toward comprehensive plans that encompass prevention, preparedness, response, and recovery, while addressing the unique needs of the school setting. Ultimately, the objective is to develop comprehensive school crisis teams and plans that include protocols and procedures for prevention, preparedness, response, and recovery.

Chapter 3

SCHOOL CRISIS TEAMS

The U.S. Department of Homeland Security's (2004) National Incident Management System (NIMS) and its Incident Command System (ICS) provide a standardized structure for school crisis teams. A basic premise of PREPaRE is that school-based mental health professionals are most effective when they fill a specific ICS role and are surrounded by a multidisciplinary team whose members fill all other ICS roles. This chapter reviews the elements of the ICS and the activities of the school crisis team, with a special emphasis on crisis response and the role of the school-based mental health professional. Also discussed is the concept of multiple crisis response levels, and the initiation, implementation, and maintenance of school crisis teams (with suggestions for collaboration with community-based crisis response partners).

ICS ACTIVITIES OF THE SCHOOL CRISIS TEAM

Homeland Security Presidential Directive 5 required state, tribal, and local agencies to use NIMS as a condition for federal preparedness assistance beginning in 2005 (U.S. Department of Homeland Security [DHS], 2004). NIMS provides a common set of concepts, principles, terminology, and organizational processes to be used in planning and preparing for, responding to, and recovering from crises. All federally funded entities are required to adopt NIMS and the ICS.

According to the U.S. Department of Education (2003), all phases of crisis prevention, preparedness, response, and recovery are interconnected. Consequently, developing a school crisis team requires partnerships between public health, mental health, law enforcement, public safety, and local government. The ICS is a structure designed to delineate roles to manage crises. When schools use this system, communication with other agencies and overall crisis team organization are improved. The basic premise of ICS is that, in a crisis situation, staff members make transitions from their day-to-day jobs to perform similar functions within the crisis team. For example, the school psychologist would transition from traditional assessment, consultation, and counseling activities to the crisis team activities of psychological trauma risk screening, crisis-related psychoeducation, and crisis intervention.

Two key concepts in the ICS include division of labor and span of control. *Division of labor* refers to the fact that, in every crisis, no matter how large or small, there are certain required functions or tasks. During planning, it is important to preassign team members to functions based on their job assignments and expertise. The concept of *span of control* emphasizes that no one person should be in charge of more than seven other team members; the optimum number is five, unless a large number are performing the same crisis team function.

The ICS can be used for a broad spectrum of crises, across all levels of government and nongovernmental agencies, and across disciplines. Figure 3.1 illustrates the five major ICS functions and provides examples of school staff members who may fill the roles under each of these functions. School-based mental health professionals must be familiar with the terminology and concepts used in this approach to understand the multidisciplinary nature of crisis teams and

Figure 3.1. Elements of the ICS, their hierarchical relationships, and ICS roles filled by school crisis team members and school personnel.

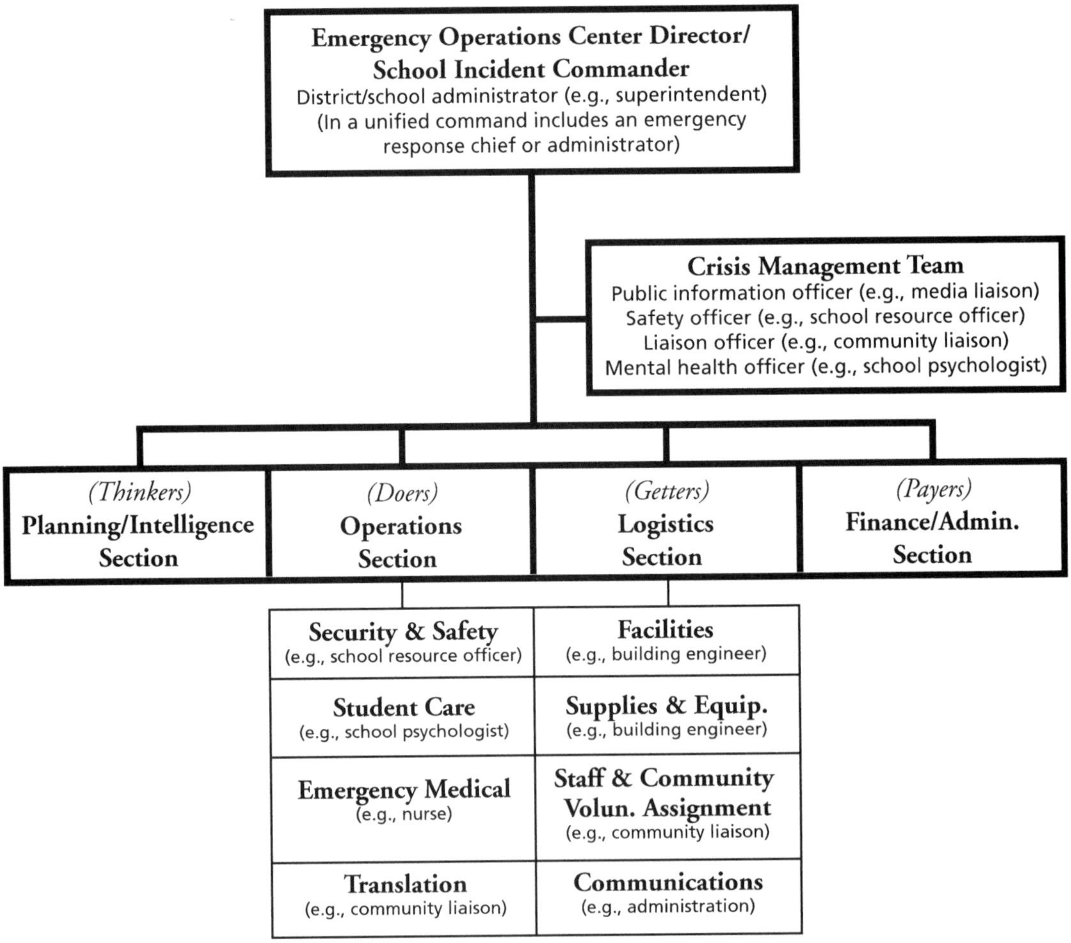

their roles on these teams. The following sections briefly review the important ICS roles and responsibilities and describe how these concepts may be applied to the school crisis team.

Incident Command

The incident commander (IC) is responsible for the initiation and continuation of all school crisis team prevention, preparedness, response, and recovery activities. A public information officer, safety officer, mental health officer, and liaison officer may also fill command roles. Because different state or community agencies will have their own crisis teams, typically the agency with the greatest interest in the crisis event type, or the one charged with legal responsibility, will take control (W. G. Green, 2002). For example, in a hostage situation, a police department's IC will typically have the greatest responsibility and in this type of crisis will have ultimate control and authority.

In schools, the IC is most often a school or district administrator. Across all levels of crisis prevention, preparedness, response, and recovery, the IC clearly delineates the objectives for the group, assigns responsibilities, and coordinates the overall response. However, when an immediate crisis response crosses multiple political boundaries or jurisdictions, with several agencies having the authority and responsibility to deal with the incident (e.g., a community disaster such as a flood), the ICS can employ a *unified command*, which involves using a collective approach, with one set of objectives developed for the entire incident (U.S. DHS, 2004). The unified command is flexible and may look different in each situation, ranging from command by a committee to use of a single IC who takes everyone's concerns into account (W. G. Green, 2002). School districts that encompass more than one jurisdiction (e.g., a district that is served by multiple police departments) should plan with all of those jurisdictions in advance to better understand how this structure would be employed in crisis situations.

The command structure also needs to have a public information officer (PIO). In some instances, such as a school-based crisis team, the role of PIO will be filled by a single IC (often the school principal). In other instances, such as a district crisis team, the role will be filled by a separate person. Regardless, the PIO works with the public, the media, and other agencies that require information about the crisis. This person will gather accurate information about the cause, size, current situation, and resources committed to the crisis (U.S. DHS, 2004).

Who fills the role of safety officer (SO) will depend on whether the team is responsible for a singular entity, such as a school, or oversees many different entities, such as a school district. A single IC may fill this role, or it may be a separate entity. The SO, who is responsible for the safety of response personnel, staff, and students, conducts ongoing assessments of hazardous environments, coordinates safety efforts among different agencies (e.g., police and fire departments), implements measures to promote crisis responder safety, and advises the command structure on all safety matters. Regardless of the use of a single IC or a unified command, there should be only one PIO and one SO (U.S. DHS, 2004).

The liaison officer is the point of contact for representatives of other government agencies, nongovernmental organizations, and private entities. Additional command staff may be necessary, depending on the incident (e.g., legal adviser, medical adviser). However, these command structure elements are not typically part of a school crisis team.

Another important ICS concept that has special relevance to crisis preparedness and response is the command post, which is the location from which all IC staff members operate to ensure a coordinated response. This post should be located in a safe area outside of the immediate crisis impact area. IC staff, regardless of the agency they represent, should all work from this single location (W. G. Green, 2002). Assuming the school administrative office is safe and not directly affected by the crisis event, this is the typical location for a school's command post. When IC staff members assemble at the command post, section chiefs for each function (described below) should be assigned. The command post must have the resources needed to organize a response, such as phones, fax machines, computers and Internet access, and confidential meeting space (see chapter 4 for further discussion of these resources).

Operations

The California Governor's Office of Emergency Services (OES, 1998) refers to this group of individuals as the "doers." Operations is responsible for actually carrying out various crisis prevention tasks, as well as for addressing immediate response and longer-term recovery needs. Examples of the operations section activities include reducing hazards, saving lives and property, establishing situational control, restoring normal operations, and addressing longer-term recovery needs (U.S. DHS, 2004). The person in charge of the operations section directs the strategic response to crises by organizing the workforce, matching supplies with needs, and managing resources. During crisis response, operations provides oversight for immediate activities such as search and rescue, reunion, medical and psychological first aid, security, and fire suppression. The active involvement of the school psychologist is particularly important here, as activities traditionally viewed as crisis intervention, or the immediate response to the psychological challenges generated by a crisis event, would fall under the control of the operations section. The student assembly and release specialist (discussed in chapter 4) also plays a critical role in reuniting students with parents. Translation, interpretation, and cultural services are essential in a crisis response and also fall under this section.

Planning and Intelligence

The planning and intelligence section consists of the "thinkers" (California Governor's OES, 1998), who collect, evaluate, and disseminate crisis information and intelligence to the IC or unified command, prepare status reports, identify and monitor crisis resources, and develop and document crisis plans, including incident objectives and strategies. During a crisis response this ICS section also identifies questions and obtains answers regarding evaluating new information; planning for future needs; and making use of recorders, logs, radios, campus maps, and buses. The section also maintains a status board to summarize what is occurring.

Within the intelligence section, one individual should serve as the school crisis evaluation leader. This team member is responsible for gathering and organizing data to examine crisis prevention, preparedness, response, and recovery efforts, and for ensuring that the school crisis plans delineate the processes used to complete the evaluation tasks. The school crisis evaluation leader is also responsible for ensuring that the goals and objectives of the school crisis plan are clearly articulated and measurable. The importance of evaluation and the role of the school crisis evaluation leader are discussed in chapter 17.

Logistics

The logistics section is responsible for obtaining all resources needed to address crises. The "getters" include personnel, equipment and supplies, and services, including transportation (California Governor's OES, 1998). When the operations section needs something, they get it from the logistics section. This section also works with the planning and intelligence section to obtain the needed resources identified by the school crisis plan.

Finance and Administration

The finance and administration section, identified as the "payers" (California Governor's OES, 1998), maintains records of all crisis prevention, preparedness, response, and recovery expenses. Though not all crisis response situations require this section, it is activated when the agency requires finance and other administrative support services (e.g., payroll, claims, and reimbursements). If only one specific aspect is needed (e.g., cost analysis), a technical specialist in the planning and intelligence section may be sufficient to fill this role (U.S. DHS, 2004). In schools, it is often the IC or administrator who is directly involved in making and approving monetary decisions. The records of expense become particularly important if federal or state funds are later allocated to crisis response and recovery.

Crisis Intervention Specialist

As one member of a multidisciplinary school crisis team, the school-based mental health professional focuses primarily on specific student care responsibilities. Typically, this team member is part of the operations section and fills the role of crisis intervention specialist (Figure 3.2 illustrates the roles and responsibilities of the operations section). The role consists of a variety of prevention, preparedness, response, and recovery responsibilities. Many chapters in this book detail the specific activities that school-based mental health professionals are involved in, including conducting psychological triage (chapter 11), reestablishing social support systems (chapter 12), providing psychological education (chapter 13), performing classroom-based crisis intervention (chapter 14), and performing individual crisis intervention (chapter 15).

An additional important role of the school-based mental health professional on the school crisis team is preparing for and attending to students with special needs. In July 2004, President Bush signed Executive Order 13347, Individuals With Disabilities in Emergency Preparedness, which emphasizes the provision of support for students with disabilities. Subsequently, the U.S. Department of Education's Emergency Response and Crisis Management Center (now known as

Figure 3.2. Elements of the ICS's operations section and their hierarchical relationships, plus examples of the school personnel that might fill the operations section roles.

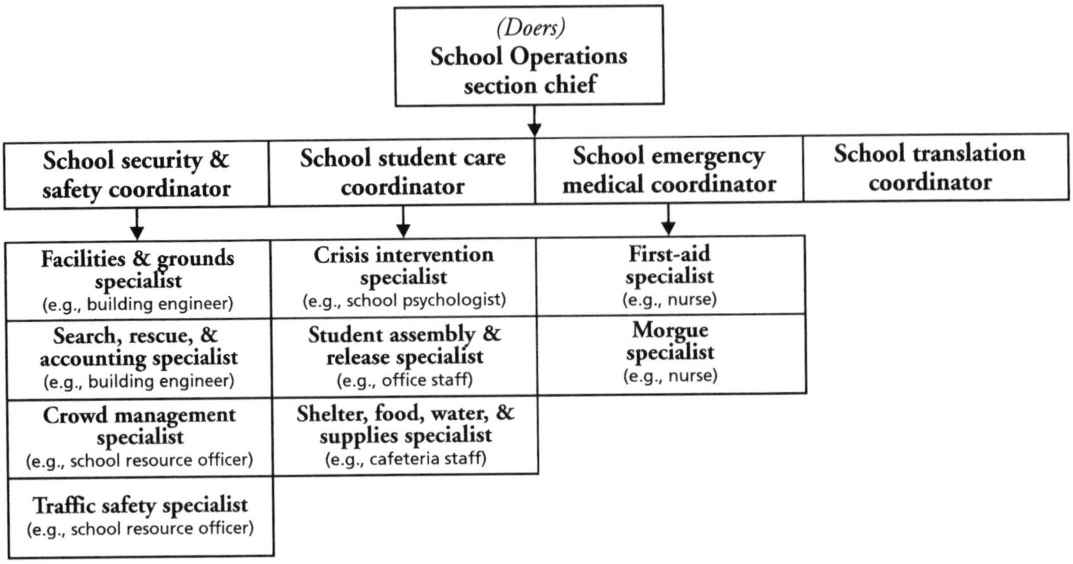

the Readiness and Emergency Management for Schools [REMS] Technical Assistance Center), released a bulletin highlighting the importance of integrating students with special needs and disabilities into emergency response and crisis management planning, across all four phases of crisis management (U.S. Department of Education, 2006b). During planning, school psychologists and special education professionals may be particularly well prepared to provide guidance on how to meet these students' physical and emotional needs.

Planning for Multiple Levels of Response

School crisis teams must be prepared for and active during all phases of a crisis. Examples of activities and responsibilities at each level of prevention, preparedness, response, and recovery for the five ICS sections are included in Table 3.1. Further discussion of these activities can be found in Brock, Jimerson, and Hart (2006) and Nickerson, Brock, and Reeves (2006).

Planning for crisis response should include the multiple levels of crisis response that different crisis circumstances will require. The four different levels of school crisis response considered within the PREPaRE model were described in chapter 1 in Table 1.3. These include minimal, building level, district level, and regional level. When district-level crisis team members are developing plans, it is important to remember that building-level crisis team members can be personally overwhelmed, not only by the number of students affected by a crisis event, but also by the emotional and physical impact of the event. Consequently, it is important for school crisis teams to have an agreement with neighboring school districts to assist in crisis response when necessary. Thus, PREPaRE recommends that the school district establish district-level and regional-level crisis teams, in addition to building-level crisis teams (Brock, Sandoval, & Lewis, 2001). The district-level team would be available to

Table 3.1. Sample Prevention, Preparedness, Response, and Recovery Responsibilities of ICS Sections

Command			
Prevention	*Preparedness*	*Response*	*Recovery*
• Collaborates with the school crisis team to establish school violence and crisis prevention priorities and delegates responsibility for the implementation of specific prevention tasks. • Informs the school community of the school's or district's violence prevention plan and provides others with information that may help prevent acts of school violence. • Facilitates the development and dissemination of safe school plans.	• Collaborates with the school crisis team to develop a comprehensive school crisis management plan and delegates responsibility for the implementation of specific preparedness tasks. • Ensures that all crisis team roles are filled, and that contact information for all team members is available. • Ensures that staff members are appropriately trained to respond to crisis events. (e.g., crisis drills and exercises). • Fosters relationships with additional emergency response resources, and maintains a listing of those resources. • Fosters relationships with the local media and develops policies for how to respond to the media. • Establishes a list of resources to ensure student and staff safety during a crisis event.	• Initiates crisis response procedures and evaluates the need for assistance from resources located outside of the school. • Provides the community with information about the school's crisis response and manages the emergency media center. • Ensures that all resources necessary for maintaining a safe school environment are available. • Facilitates communication between the school and any community-based crisis responders.	• Collaborates with the school crisis team to identify recovery priorities and delegates responsibility for the implementation of specific recovery tasks. • Provides the community with information about crisis recovery efforts and resources. • Ensures that all resources necessary to maintain a safe school environment are available. • Facilitates communication between the school and any community-based crisis responders.

Table 3.1. (continued)

Planning and Intelligence			
Prevention	*Preparedness*	*Response*	*Recovery*
• Identifies and monitors threats of violence or potentially threatening conditions. • Contributes data and information to target prevention efforts in areas of greatest need or concern. • Maintains contact with local law enforcement for reports of criminal activities (e.g., gang fights) and assesses the potential for acts of school violence. • Serves as the clearinghouse for all reports of threatening behavior. • Provides leadership to examine the effectiveness of prevention activities.	• Acquires and maintains the materials needed to gather information about crisis events quickly and efficiently. • Assesses communication options and ensures the availability of communication tools (e.g., cell phones, computers with Internet access, and two-way radios). • Maintains detailed floor plans of school buildings and grounds. • Provides leadership to examine the effectiveness of preparedness activities. • Participates in regularly scheduled meetings to continue to inform and update preparedness efforts.	• Collects facts about the incident and documents all crisis response efforts. • Provides the information that incident commanders need to assess the status of the school's response to violence and helps to identify additional response needs. • Contributes information at annual school crisis team meetings, reviews crisis team response activities, and helps identify challenges, obstacles, and lessons learned. • Provides leadership to examine the effectiveness of response activities.	• Continues to collect facts about the incident and documents all crisis recovery efforts. • Provides leadership to examine the effectiveness of recovery activities. • Provides the information that incident commanders need to assess the status of the school's recovery from the crisis and determines additional response needs.

Table 3.1. (continued)

	Operations		
Prevention	*Preparedness*	*Response*	*Recovery*
• Ensures that students and staff are provided with the training and education needed to identify and prevent potential acts of violence. • Conducts local needs assessments. • Identifies needed prevention programs. • Ensures that the appropriate guidance services are available to respond to the underlying causes of crisis events.	• Establishes student accounting procedures, student assembly and release-to-parent procedures, crowd control, and traffic management procedures. • Develops the school's capacity to provide crisis intervention services, including psychological triage and first aid. • Develops the school's capacity to meet emergency medical needs. • Ensures that the school has the ability to communicate in all languages spoken in the school community.	• Ensures that all students and staff are accounted for and evacuated to safe student assembly areas, as needed, and then releases them in a systematic manner to their parents. • Implements procedures designed to manage large crowds. • Manages traffic and ensures that emergency response vehicles have access to school grounds. • Ensures that the physical structure of school facilities and grounds are safe. • Oversees the locations where students assemble following an act of school violence and supervises parent and student reunification. • Conducts psychological triage and addresses the immediate needs of students and staff for psychological first aid. • Maintains and distributes basic need and first-aid supplies, as needed.	• Ensures that students and staff members who display signs of psychopathology are offered appropriate mental health services. • Prepares to provide the supportive services of the crisis team and psych-ological education that may be required by the anniversary of a crisis event. • Maintains communication with families of injured students and staff members. • Maintains contact with medical facilities and provides school crisis team members with medical status updates.

Table 3.1. (continued)

	Logistics		
Prevention	*Preparedness*	*Response*	*Recovery*
• Obtains crisis prevention-related materials and supplies. • Assigns staff and volunteers to specific crisis prevention activities.	• Acquires and maintains all crisis response resources, supplies, and materials. • Identifies and designates crisis response facilities (e.g., evacuation locations). • Checks to ensure that individuals have been identified to fill the various crisis response roles. • Ensures that there are reliable and redundant communication systems within and to and from school, and from all staff.	• Makes available all needed crisis response supplies and equipment. • Obtains additional resources during response efforts, as necessary. • Directs staff and volunteers to their appropriate crisis response activities. • Maintains communications to and from school, and among all school staff members.	• Continues to make available all needed crisis response supplies and equipment. • Continues to direct staff and volunteers to their appropriate crisis recovery activities. • Maintains communications to and from school, and among all school staff members.

Table 3.1. (continued)

Finance and Administration			
Prevention	*Preparedness*	*Response*	*Recovery*
• Budgets for and authorizes all crisis prevention-related expenditures.	• Budgets for and authorizes all crisis preparedness-related expenditures.	• Authorizes all crisis response-related expenditures. • Records all personnel and material costs.	• Continues to authorize all crisis response-related expenditures. • Obtains emergency financial assistance, and makes the appropriate requests for reimbursement.

Note. Source "Preventing, Preparing for, and Responding to School Violence with the National Incident Management System," by S. E. Brock, S. R. Jimerson, & S. R. Hart, 2006, in S. R. Jimerson & M. J. Furlong (Eds.), *Handbook of School Violence and School Safety: From Research to Practice* (pp. 443–458), Mahwah, NJ: Erlbaum.

help building-level teams provide support following major crises, provide consultation as needed, and coordinate and train the building-level teams.

Considerations of unique school environments are also important. For instance, in rural areas the regional team (not to mention first-responder personnel) may be hours away, and it is important to consider how to organize a response before they arrive. This should be considered in the planning stage, and may involve individuals having dual roles (e.g., a teacher may be the county's emergency medical technician and so could respond to a trauma that affects students or colleagues).

INITIATING, IMPLEMENTING, AND SUSTAINING A SCHOOL CRISIS TEAM

The school crisis team is typically initiated by district-level administration, and as discussed in chapter 2, is supported by several federal acts. The specific person responsible for team development is typically the administrator who fills the IC role. However, while such top-down development is the norm, there are examples of bottom-up efforts wherein other school staff members (e.g., school psychologists) take a team development leadership role (Brock, 2000).

The ICS provides a consistent structure for crisis teams and team member roles; however, there are many diverse contexts across schools that will need to be considered. For instance, the size and infrastructure of a given school or district may influence team composition and responsibilities. The following questions will help ICs with team organization:

1. How will district size affect crisis team ICS organization, structure, and responsibilities?
2. How will team members be selected to fill ICS functions, and how will they be replaced or given a break?
3. How will refresher training occur?
4. How will team members be trained?
5. How will community resources be used to fill ICS functions?

Initiation of school crisis teams should include consideration of potential obstacles. For instance, teams might lack the following: commitment from central administration, established policies, time and resources, and buy-in of the concept that schools are responsible for meeting crisis recovery or mental health needs. Territorial issues (e.g., "Whose job is it?"), reactive positions (e.g., "Let's wait until there is a problem"), and the myth that taking action will make the crisis worse are also potential obstacles (see discussions in Cornell & Sheras, 1998; Kline, Schonfeld, & Lichtenstein, 1995; McIntyre & Reid, 1989). The following brief discussions explore how to overcome these potential barriers.

Identifying and Establishing Policies

At the inception of the process to develop a school crisis team, the first step is to discern whether school or district policies regarding emergency and crisis management have been established. If such policies exist, these may provide the basis for further advocating the importance of related efforts. If none exist or they lack substance, then it may be necessary to first establish policies that clearly delineate the need for and commitment to establishing a school crisis team.

Securing and Sustaining the Support of Administration and Colleagues

Having the support of both central administration and local school principals is critical to establishing and sustaining crisis team activities because district-level mandates typically yield superficial crisis preparation, prevention, response, and recovery planning at the building level. For instance, developing and sustaining school crisis team activities require both time and resources, and members of an evolving crisis team should be able to allocate a portion of their time to these important responsibilities.

School-based mental health professionals and other members of an evolving crisis team can help inform and influence the attitudes of administrators so they learn to apply both a mental health and administrative perspective to a crisis and are able to strike a balance between physical and psychological safety. Ongoing communication with administrators is essential to remind them of the importance of the school crisis team's activities in fostering student safety and academic success. The following are 13 specific strategies that may be effective in securing and sustaining the support of the administration and colleagues as the crisis team members go about developing a crisis team:

1. Providing a written proposal to the school board during a working meeting, including rationale, goals, and objectives. It is important to provide this information in a context where it can be thoughtfully considered and discussed, and where questions may be asked, rather than in a public forum where there are pressures that may prohibit open discussion.
2. Using national, state, and local data to describe problems. A substantial amount of information is available online. For instance, the National Crime Victimization Survey (1992 to 2005), the School Crime Supplement to the National Crime Victimization Survey (1991 to 2005), the Youth Risk Behavior Survey (1993 to 2007), the School Survey on Crime and Safety (1999 to 2006), and the School and Staffing Survey (1993 to 2004).
3. Using effective persuasion strategies, such as crafting a clear and distinct position paper regarding the importance of school safety in student academic success.
4. Conducting annual orientations for new school board members and administration.
5. Developing a school board position statement so that an official document will be on record and can be used to orient new board members and administrators.
6. Defining the types of situations that require a crisis response, highlighting salient local considerations that necessitate activities for crisis prevention, preparedness, response, or recovery.
7. Defining the desired outcomes of crisis response and recovery so that it is clear to board members, administrators, teachers, and parents that the focus is on facilitating the health, well-being, and academic success of students.
8. Developing and annually updating documents that briefly delineate staff responsibilities relative to crisis prevention, preparedness, response, and recovery (e.g., incorporating crisis responsibilities into job descriptions).

9. Stating the district's stance on crisis preparedness through memos and other direct means of communication.
10. Embracing the philosophy that crisis prevention and preparedness is a dynamic process. An example is extending requests to teachers and others to identify contemporary concerns, engaging in simulations and readiness exercises, and then further refining crisis plans.
11. Making humanitarian arguments (e.g., most deaths are preventable).
12. Suggesting that it is the school's legal duty to intervene and pointing out that a good crisis response and intervention mitigates negative consequences on academics and contagion.
13. Stating that intervention is good public relations for the school and district.

A written proposal that describes the school crisis team should clearly delineate the crisis team's rationale, goals, and objectives and its tentative budget, and it should include any relevant supporting documentation. National, state, and local statistics can be used to describe the problem. For instance, the document might mention that nationally, suicide is the third leading cause of death among adolescents and young adults (National Adolescent Health Information Center, 2006) and that accidents are second, but many of those are thought to be disguised suicides (Brock, Sandoval, & Hart, 2006). Using local statistics often yields surprising results because the numbers are usually higher than anyone imagined. Gathering this information in a district whose administrators think they do not have a problem can generate hostility toward the person who compiles these statistics, result in blaming individuals or institutions seen as responsible, or increase fear that the situation is out of control and that nothing can be done about it. However, such information can also be the catalyst to enlist support for developing the crisis team.

Given that all school districts will at some point have to address the reality of significant crises, chapter 1's discussion of the unique school-associated consequences of crises can also be used to suggest the need for school crisis teams. Specifically, the proposal could point out that disruptive behavior at school may be the primary outcome of crisis event exposure. These unique crisis effects also include school absenteeism; school behavior problems, such as aggressive, delinquent, and criminal behavior; academic decline; and exacerbation of preexisting educational problems.

Further strengthening arguments regarding the need for school crisis teams is the impact of conditions like posttraumatic stress disorder (PTSD) on academic functioning. In a sample of 11- to 14-year-olds, it was documented that students with severe to very severe PTSD had significantly lower GPAs than students with moderate PTSD. Furthermore, following a group intervention designed to address traumatic stress consequences, reductions in PTSD symptoms were associated with improved grades (Saigh, Mroueh, & Bremner, 1997).

Finally, district administrators or board members could be encouraged to communicate with their counterparts in other districts or schools that have crisis teams. Approaches such as those discussed above can be used to encourage district administrators to establish a school crisis team that will address security and crisis prevention, preparedness, response, and recovery; school climate; mental health; and appropriate discipline.

Maintaining School Crisis Team Coherence

Strategies to maintain communication and foster coherence among crisis team members include precrisis collaboration and planning to ensure that all team members are actively involved and contributing expertise related to their specialty. Also helpful is structuring relationships to facilitate sharing and decision making, giving all team members multiple opportunities to contribute to discussions and decisions. A third strategy includes team-building activities and crisis response practice. For instance, professional development seminars, simulations, drills, and readiness exercises each provide opportunities for team members to develop skills and knowledge and also build professional relationships (refer to chapter 6 for a discussion of crisis response practice). Other approaches to maintaining coherence include accommodating diverse views and facilitating open discussions, maintaining a focus on common goals, and establishing a climate of discussing mistakes as learning opportunities. Several components to consider when establishing and sustaining a school crisis team are listed in Table 3.2. Further discussion of the importance of team coherence, and strategies to maintain it, can be found in Brock (2000) and Trump (2000).

COLLABORATION WITH CRISIS RESPONSE PARTNERS

PREPaRE emphasizes the importance of collaboration in the development of comprehensive school crisis teams. Potential collaborative partners are listed in Table 3.3. Ideally, a school crisis team involves the collaboration and cooperation of education professionals, students, parents, law enforcement, community emergency response personnel, community leaders, healthcare providers, and other professionals serving youth (Hester, 2003). Research reveals that schools and stakeholders do not always understand each other's point of view. For instance, focus groups

Table 3.2. Components to Consider When Establishing and Sustaining a School Crisis Team

- Determine what crisis teams and plans exist in the district, school, and community.
- Identify all stakeholders involved in crisis planning.
- Establish a team of qualified individuals to serve on the school crisis team.
- Secure administrative support for the school crisis team.
- Identify or develop the necessary policies to assist all school community members in a crisis.
- Develop procedures for communicating with all school community members and the media for each specific crisis event (e.g., develop the school crisis plan; see chapters 4 and 5).
- Ensure that all crisis team members and staff have appropriate training and professional development opportunities.
- Establish ongoing team meetings and select dates at the beginning of the school year to review the team infrastructure, maintain team coherence, and update the details of the school crisis plan.

Note. Primary source *Practical Information on Crisis Planning: A Guide for Schools and Communities*, U.S. Department of Education, Office of Safe and Drug-Free Schools, May, 2003. Washington, DC: Author. This document is in the public domain.

Table 3.3. Local, State, and National Collaborative Partners and Resources

Local Collaborative Partnerships

- Victims' assistance and advocates
- Community mental health and social service agencies
- University counseling centers
- Parent groups
- Businesses
- Criminal justice professionals
- Community leaders
- Private practitioners
- Police
- Fire
- Emergency medical services
- Hazardous materials crew
- Public works agencies
- Regional emergency management agencies
- Clergy
- Media
- Elected officials

State Collaborative Partnerships

- State chapter of National Organization for Victim Assistance (NOVA)
- Red Cross
- State Office of Emergency Services
- Attorney General's Office
- State National Guard
- Statewide crisis team
- State School Safety Centers

National Collaborative Partnerships

- NEAT – National Emergency Assistance Team – www.nasponline.org/resources/crisis_safety/neat.aspx
- NOVA – National Organization for Victim Assistance – www.try-nova.org
- FEMA – Federal Emergency Management Agency – www.fema.gov
- Red Cross – www.redcross.org

National Resources

- NASP (National Association of School Psychologists) – www.nasponline.org
- U.S. Department of Education – Safe and Drug-Free Schools Program – www.ed.gov/osdfs
- National School Safety Center – www.schoolsafety.us
- American Psychological Association – www.apa.org
- American Academy of Child and Adolescent Psychiatry – www.aacap.org

Table 3.3. (continued)

- American Psychiatric Association – www.psych.org
- American Association of Suicidology – www.suicidology.org
- American Academy of Experts in Traumatic Stress – www.aaets.org
- National Center for PTSD (U.S. Department of Veterans Affairs) – www.ncptsd.va.gov

conducted with students, parents, school personnel, and community agency representatives revealed that (a) parents want to be involved but do not feel welcome, (b) students want a more active role but need direction, (c) students also want to feel cared for and supported, and (d) agencies want more communication and collaboration (Leinhardt & Willert, 2002).

Despite this desire for collaboration, a national preparedness survey conducted by Graham, Shirm, Liggin, Aitken, and Dick (2006) indicated that almost half of the superintendents that responded (42.8%) had never met with local ambulance officials to discuss emergency planning. To build effective school crisis teams, it is important to engage in meaningful collaboration with others and to remember that the contributions of all stakeholders, both within the school and in the larger community, can enhance the efforts of the team. Table 3.4 offers some recommendations to facilitate collaboration when developing a school crisis team.

During the planning phase, crisis team organizers will have several unique considerations to take into account when developing teams and identifying responsibilities with collaborative community partners. First, in a large-scale crisis, experts can provide short-term consultation but should not assume the primary role in the crisis response. School staff members will be the ones that will remain with the students in the school during the longer-term crisis recovery. Second, it is important to be certain that mental health centers and other agencies have screened their personnel to ensure they are qualified. Third, controlled access to the school campus is necessary to ensure that no unauthorized individuals or groups (e.g., the media) have unlimited access to students. Fourth, regrouping with outside helpers to exchange important information before they leave the school is very important (e.g., determining which students need additional follow-up).

In the recovery and reconstruction phase, crisis team members must obtain a list of the students to whom each outside collaborative partner provided support services during immediate crisis intervention. It is also important for collaborating partners to clearly delineate what specific support services were provided to these students, and to discuss which students will need immediate ongoing support and which need a follow-up.

One important tool for the collaborations discussed here is a memorandum of understanding (MOU) with other agencies, to be prepared while in the crisis team planning stages. Establishing an MOU helps delineate in advance how non–school district agencies will collaborate with the school and will work with school personnel. Moreover, an MOU will also specify who is responsible for specific duties and responsibilities, and who should be contacted for specific needs and support (see Figure 3.3 for a sample MOU; Brock, 1999).

Table 3.4. Recommendations to Facilitate Collaboration With School and Community Stakeholders When Developing a School Crisis Team and Plan

1. Share the responsibility and work together.
2. Develop plans that focus on the involvement of school staff as opposed to outside experts.
3. Develop a long-term community commitment.
4. Create a strategic plan that includes collaboration with other stakeholders.
5. Enhance prevention planning (e.g., establish violence prevention programs).
6. Increase services and support to serve students' social, emotional, developmental, behavioral, and mental health needs, as well as academic needs.
7. Involve all stakeholders.
8. Invest in targeted teacher training and staff development about harassment, bullying, and effective classroom management. Research shows that all of these approaches lead to higher academic achievement, and research supports the link between social–emotional functioning, behavior, and academic performance.
9. Build collaborative partnerships with the community, including using existing community resources to expand and enhance school resources and hosting a series of community forums, town hall meetings, and focus groups to solicit opinions and feedback.
10. Provide opportunities for school and community stakeholders to work together prior to crisis events.
11. Structure relationships with stakeholders in a way that facilitates shared decision making in crisis planning.
12. Practice team-building activities and perform drills.
13. Embrace the value of different perspectives in achieving common goals.
14. Establish a climate of discussing mistakes to turn them into learning opportunities.

CONCLUSION

The school crisis team is an essential component of institutional efforts to develop and implement comprehensive plans to address all aspects of crisis prevention, preparedness, response, and recovery. School crisis team members must do more than simply react to immediate crisis circumstances; they must also be involved in reducing or eliminating crises, preparing for those events that cannot be prevented, and developing protocols to address the long-term (as well as immediate) consequences of school crises.

The vast array of responsibilities involved in crisis management requires that school crisis teams collaborate with professionals and agencies outside the school context. The ICS provides a standardized structure for school crisis teams and will inform efforts to collaboratively develop comprehensive crisis plans (U.S. DHS, 2004). School-based mental health professionals are likely to be most effective when they fill a very specific ICS role and are surrounded by a

Figure 3.3. Template for a memorandum of understanding to provide mutual aid in school crisis responses.

Date:

This Memorandum of Understanding addresses agreements between the ________________ County Office of Education, ____________________ County Office of Emergency Services, _________County Mental Health Services, and those school districts within ________________________ County who agreed to participate.

PURPOSE

Disasters of a large scale that occur within school districts may overwhelm the resources of that district. While this is an infrequent occurrence, it is best to be prepared for the possibility of such an occurrence by entering into mutual aid agreements with other school districts, county emergency services, and county mental health services. Such mutual aid agreements help institutions offer services to each other following major disasters. Past experience has shown that when a large-scale disaster occurs, it is difficult to coordinate services without some planning.

BACKGROUND

The origins of this Memorandum can be found in two pieces of legislation. The first is the state Emergency Services Act. This Act is designed to help mitigate the effects of natural and human-caused disasters. Among its provisions, the Act calls for disaster response partnership agreements within and between the various regions of the state. These response partnerships institutionalize the practice of "mutual aid" already employed by emergency response personnel (e.g., firefighters). Mutual aid allows regions to share emergency response resources whenever a given disaster is beyond local control.

The second origin of this agreement can be found in school safety legislation. According to this legislation, all school districts are required to have a school safety plan in place. Part of the safety plan includes disaster response procedures.

Typically, it is expected that individual schools and/or school districts will manage their own crises using their school safety plan. This Memorandum addresses those occurrences, infrequent as they may be, that tax the resources of the school district to the point where outside help is required.

An example of this type of occurrence was the school yard shooting in 1989 at Cleveland School in Stockton, California (list other local examples as appropriate). It required a crisis response that not only overwhelmed the school district's resources but also overwhelmed the County Mental Health Department. Significant coordination was required to meet the needs of the students and staff. This experience has shown the importance of crisis response planning.

AGREEMENT

1. Each individual school district has the responsibility of responding to its own crises. Additionally, it is district administration's responsibility to determine when the resources of the district are no longer adequate to deal with a situation. It is district administration's responsibility to ask for assistance when it is deemed necessary. Mutual aid support is not provided without a request from a district-level administrator.
2. If school disaster mutual aid response assistance is needed, a district-level administrator or designee will contact the Regional-Level Crisis Response Team Mutual Aid Coordinator to request assistance. The Mutual Aid Coordinator may be reached, Monday–Friday 8:00 a.m. to 5:00 p.m., through [phone number] or through the 24-hour Crisis Line at [phone number].
3. The Regional-Level Crisis Response Team Mutual Aid Coordinator will record requests for help on a call-out form developed specifically for that purpose. This documentation will indicate who is requesting help, what type of help is requested, when it is needed, where it is needed, and whether the help being requested is volunteer help or paid help.

Figure 3.3. (continued)

4. The issue of payment is raised because it is possible that an emergency situation can turn into a disaster, which will require federal assistance, at which point there may be reimbursement for costs for disaster response.
5. Following a request for mutual aid assistance, the Regional-Level Crisis Response Team Mutual Aid Coordinator will contact appropriate resources for the first response. The choice of which resources or school districts to contact may be based on geographic considerations (i.e., proximity to requesting district), but can also be based on other considerations (i.e., choosing a district that has not already been asked to provide mutual aid support).
6. School districts offering to provide mutual aid to a requesting district will provide only credentialed personnel. Mental Health Services staff responding will be either licensed clinicians or registered interns (psychiatrist, psychologist, licensed clinical social worker or professional counselor, or marriage or family counselor). Generally speaking, only staff members that have been trained in crisis response will be deployed.
7. Responding districts will provide assistance for up to 3 days. At the end of the 3 days, further agreements between individual districts, Mental Health Services, Office of Education, and Office of Emergency Services will be necessary in order to provide further assistance.
8. Unless otherwise specified, shifts of work shall be 8-hours long for the 3-day period.
9. The district requesting the help shall provide supplies for classroom activities, such as art supplies and writing materials, unless otherwise specified in the request for assistance.
10. Participating districts agree to meet annually to ensure that appropriate response procedures are still viable.

The signatures below indicate an agreement to abide by this Memorandum of Understanding for crisis response to school districts, to pledge cooperation and problem solving, and to respond appropriately for the good of the district and the county.

TERM

This Memorandum of Understanding will be in force on the date first signed below, and will be self-renewing. This Memorandum will be reviewed annually. Districts that no longer wish to participate in this Memorandum of Understanding shall notify, in writing, within 30 days, the following departments:

____
Superintendent, County Schools
____
____

____
Director, County Mental Health Services
____
____

____
Director, Office of Emergency Services
____
____

____
Superintendent, ______________
School District ______________
____

________ ______________________________________

Note. Adapted from "Memorandum of Understanding: School Crisis Response Mutual Aid," by Roger Speed, 1998, San Joaquin County Mental Health Services (in public domain), as cited in "School Crisis Intervention Mutual Aid: A County Level Response Plan," by S. E. Brock (1999) in A. S. Canter & S. A. Carroll (Eds.), *Crisis Prevention and Response: A Collection of NASP Resources* (pp. 91–94), Bethesda, MD: National Association of School Psychologists.

multidisciplinary school crisis team whose members fill each of the other ICS roles. Collaboration with community-based crisis response partners is crucial when initiating, implementing, and sustaining school crisis teams. The school crisis team is the foundation on which the school will build all school crisis prevention, preparedness, response, and recovery structures.

Chapter 4

GENERAL SCHOOL CRISIS PLANNING ISSUES

Developing a crisis plan is an essential component of preparedness, as it provides a blueprint for prevention, preparedness, response, and recovery. Sustaining the plan is equally important; it is a continuous task that should be integrated into the job descriptions of all school staff members and reviewed at least annually (Brock, Sandoval, & Lewis, 2001; Poland, 1994). Crisis plans are dynamic and should be updated regularly in response to actual crisis response experiences; current research; changing local vulnerabilities; and federal, state, and local legal requirements. Unfortunately, although over 95% of schools report having a crisis plan (Adamson & Peacock, 2007; National Center for Education Statistics [NCES], 2004), only 66% of states require that the plans be reviewed and revised periodically (School Health Policy and Programs Study [SHPPS], 2007). In addition, Trump (2003) reported that over 55% of the school-based police officers surveyed indicated their school crisis plans were not adequate, and 65% stated that their plans had not been practiced. Table 4.1 offers important questions for schools to consider when developing or reviewing their school crisis plan.

Each crisis event is unique, and even the most comprehensive school crisis plans do not cover all possible crisis events (Knox & Roberts, 2005); however, the following general considerations and guiding principles for preparing plans will better ensure crisis preparedness:

- Specify the purpose of the plan and develop a mission statement
- Provide a definition of the crises the plan will address
- Offer details on how the plan was developed and who was involved in its development
- Describe how the individual school site and larger district plans are integrated
- Specify how the school and school district will work with community-based resources.

Table 4.1. Questions for Developing and Reviewing a School Crisis Plan

- Who is primarily responsible for plan development?
- How will crisis team members be selected?
- Who is responsible for facilitating and scheduling crisis team meetings?
- To whom and how will the condensed plan be disseminated?
- To whom and how will the comprehensive plan be disseminated?
- When will the plan be reviewed and revised?
- When will staff training occur?
- What drills and exercises need to be conducted? How can these be done to minimize anxiety?
- During a crisis, how will crisis team members be identified?
- How will crises occurring outside of school hours be addressed?
- How will crisis team members stay in touch between crises?
- How will collaboration with support agencies occur?
- What specific support services will noneducational agencies provide?
- Will there be additional compensation for time spent responding to a crisis outside the contracted school day?
- How can parent organizations provide support to both staff and students?

Sustainability of the school crisis plan is also important. According to Allen and Ashbaker (2004), determining the type of training needed to ensure sustainability and deciding who to train are key considerations for ensuring that the school crisis team knowledge base does not diminish over time.

CRISIS PLANNING WITHIN A PREVENTION MODEL

PREPaRE conceptualizes school crisis planning as encompassing Caplan's (1964) three levels of prevention: primary, secondary, and tertiary (see Figure 4.1). Primary prevention includes activities designed to prevent problems and promote wellness within the school community. For example, the primary prevention of school violence includes establishing school-wide positive behavioral supports (SWPBS) and teaching violence prevention skills. Secondary prevention includes activities designed to address the challenges generated by a crisis as soon as possible so as to mitigate damage or harm. For example, in regard to students who have already manifested violent behavior, prevention activities may involve direct interventions designed to promote problem-solving skills and anger management. Secondary prevention for the victims of school violence would include preparing for and providing the immediate crisis interventions discussed in section 4 of this book. Tertiary prevention is designed to address the more significant longer-term harm generated by a school-associated crisis event. For example, tertiary prevention for the perpetrators and victims of school violence would typically require the resources and skills of professionals or agencies outside the school setting, such as mental health and child protection

Figure 4.1. Public health framework of comprehensive preventive intervention, including sample school violence interventions at each level.

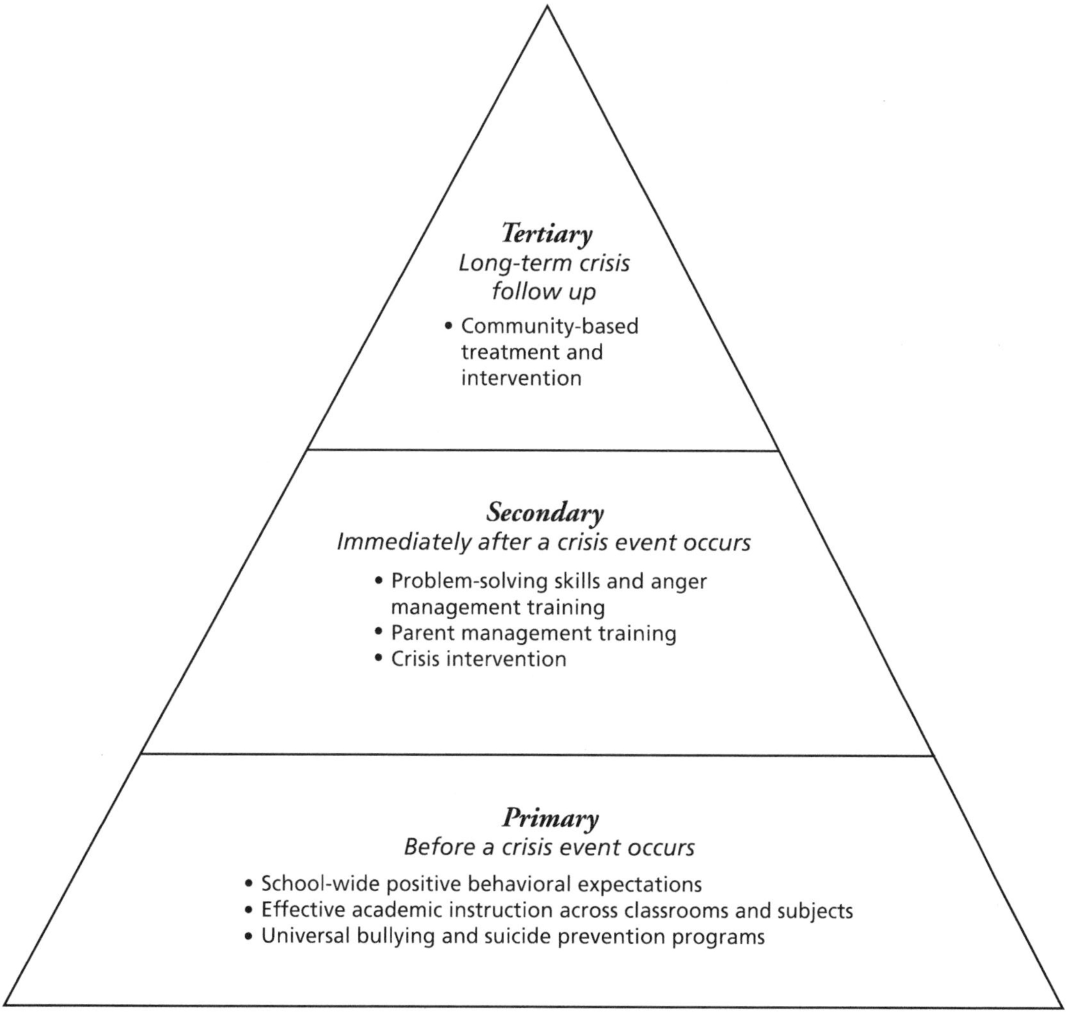

services, to give individuals the treatment and support needed for chronic or acute problems. Chapter 16 reviews this level of prevention as it relates to individuals who have the most severe levels of traumatic stress secondary to crisis event exposure.

A review of the many strategies and programs to prevent any specific type of crisis event is beyond the scope of this book. However, this important information regarding school violence prevention has been compiled in a number of other sources and is summarized in Table 4.2. The programs that show consistently positive effects are those that are cognitive–behavioral or that use behavioral instruction methods (Wilson, Gottfredson, & Najaka, 2001). In addition to considering the evidence base of each program, schools need to consider the fit between their needs and the program. Therefore, selection of a program should be guided by several factors, including (a) the needs of the school and community, identified by a needs assessment; (b) the

Table 4.2. Violence Prevention Programs and Practices

Source	*Description*
U.S. Department of Health and Human Services, Substance Abuse and Mental Health Services Administration (SAMHSA), National Mental Health Information Center, http://mentalhealth.samhsa.gov/schoolviolence/safeschools.asp	Identifies programs with evidence of their effectiveness. Includes information about programs that foster resilience, strengthen families, prevent violence, and prevent substance abuse and related problems.
U.S. Department of Education, Institute for Education Sciences, What Works Clearinghouse, http://ies.ed.gov/ncee/wwc/	Provides accessible databases and concise reports that provide educators with reviews of the effectiveness of a variety of educational interventions (e.g., programs, products, practices, and policies related to academic and other outcomes).
Center for the Study and Prevention of Violence, Safe Communities – Safe Schools Guide to Effective Program Selection: A Tool for Community Violence Prevention Efforts http://www.colorado.edu/cspv/publications/safeschools/SCSS-003.pdf	Provides information on 11 model programs that have passed the most rigorous tests of program effectiveness, 21 promising programs that met some (but not all) criteria for model programs, and 22 favorable programs, which do not meet the stringent criteria (or may be for specific populations or very expensive to run) but may still be considered. The guide also provides information about effective program planning, as well as selecting, implementing, and evaluating programs.
American Foundation for Suicide Prevention, Suicide Prevention Resource Center, Best Practices Registry (BPR) for Suicide Prevention, http://www.sprc.org/featured_resources/bpr/index.asp	Identifies, reviews, and disseminates information about best practices in suicide prevention. Includes evidence-based programs that have demonstrated positive outcomes through rigorous evaluation, expert and consensus statements that provide recommendations to guide program and policy development, and suicide prevention programs and practices (e.g., awareness materials, educational programs, and protocols) implemented in specific settings that adhere to standards.
Youth Violence: A Report of the Surgeon General, http://www.surgeongeneral.gov/library/youthviolence/chapter5/sec1.html	Identifies model and promising programs as well as those that do not work for primary, secondary, and tertiary levels of prevention.

target population (e.g., students, teachers, parents; age, race, and ethnicity); and (c) implementation resources available, such as financial resources and the staff's program knowledge and competencies (Elliott et al., 2002; Strein & Koehler, 2008). Further discussion of these levels of prevention as they relate to the prevention of school violence follows.

Primary Preventive Interventions

Increasingly, schools and districts are recognizing the importance of using universal primary prevention approaches that promote a sense of physical and psychological safety for all school community members (Gottfredson, 1997). The goal of schools is to educate students, so clearly the essential primary prevention strategy schools can use is to offer effective instruction. The more a school's students are engaged in learning, the less likely they are to experience academic and behavioral difficulties (Sutherland & Wehby, 2001).

School-wide positive behavioral supports are part of a primary prevention approach that applies behavioral principles in pursuing the goals of preventing disruptive and antisocial behavior and facilitating children's academic achievement and prosocial development (Sprague & Horner, 2006). SWPBS emphasizes creating three to five expectations for behavior that are explicitly taught, monitored, and reinforced in all school settings (e.g., classroom, cafeteria, hallway; Sugai & Horner, 2002). A primary feature of SWPBS is its use of research-validated practices and the active collection and use of data to assess student outcomes and guide decision making (Horner, Sugai, Todd, & Lewis-Palmer, 2005). Studies have found that using comprehensive approaches that include training, supervision, restructuring, and teaching of expectations and skills decrease antisocial behavior and office discipline referrals (Metzler, Biglan, Rusby, & Sprague, 2001; Sprague et al., 2001), as well as increase protective factors, such as school engagement and achievement (O'Donnell, Hawkins, Catalano, Abbott, & Day, 1998).

Another concept that has been given increased attention is social and emotional learning (SEL). SEL is a process that helps develop intrapersonal and interpersonal skills. These skills may include (a) recognizing and managing emotions, (b) caring and showing concern for others, (c) developing positive relationships, (d) making responsible decisions, and (e) handling challenging situations constructively (Collaborative for Academic, Social, and Emotional Learning, 2007; Elias et al., 1997). One program that operates from a SEL perspective is Promoting Alternative THinking Strategies (PATHS), a comprehensive prevention program that places an emphasis on teaching children to identify emotions. PATHS has been shown to reduce aggression, improve peer relationships, and result in a better classroom atmosphere (Conduct Problems Prevention Research Group, 1999; Greenberg & Kusché, 2006).

There are also universal primary prevention programs that focus on preventing bullying and suicide. For instance, the Bullying Prevention Program (Olweus, 1993) involves administering a school-wide anonymous survey to obtain information about the prevalence of bullying and victimization, the frequency of teacher intervention, the extent of parent awareness, and the locations where bullying occurs. School-wide interventions include improving supervision, particularly in less structured settings (e.g., recess, lunch, hallways), preparing teachers and other school staff members to intervene when bullying occurs, having a contact person or anonymous way for students and parents to discuss bullying situations, and having parent and teacher meetings to raise awareness of these issues.

At the class level, rules against bullying should be in place, with appropriate praise and sanctions for complying with or disobeying the rules. Olweus (1993) also recommended having class meetings where students and teachers discuss the bullying rules, sanctions, and incidents. Cooperative learning is also a part of Olweus's program. Research has found that having students work cooperatively in small groups toward a common goal enhances interpersonal liking among peers, reduces prejudice and stereotypes, and increases tolerance of individual differences (Sharan, 1980; Smith, Boulton, & Cowie, 1993).

At the individual level, when bullying occurs, bullying programs typically require school staff members to address it directly, sending the bully the message that his or her behavior is not tolerated. Discussions with the victim also occur, which involve guaranteeing that he or she will be protected from bullying. Clearly, this approach involves a great deal of follow-up. Meetings with the parents of the bully and victim are also warranted, and parent groups led by a qualified professional may also be helpful. The reader is encouraged to refer to Demaray and Malecki's (2006) detailed description of other bullying prevention and intervention programs (e.g., *The No-Bullying Program*, Bitney & Title, 2001; *Quit It*, Froschl, Sprung, & Mullin-Rindler, 1998; *Bullyproof*, Sjostrom & Stein, 1996; and *Bully Busters*, Newman, Horne, & Bartolomucci, 2000a, 2000b).

An example of a school-based suicide prevention program for adolescents is Signs of Suicide (SOS). This program combines two promising youth suicide prevention strategies: depression screening and gatekeeper programs. Students are screened for depression and risk of suicide and referred for professional help as indicated. The program also includes a video that teaches students to recognize signs of depression and suicidal thoughts in others. Students are also taught how to respond by (a) acknowledging the signs, (b) letting the person know he or she cares, and (c) telling a responsible adult. In addition, students participate in guided classroom discussions about depression and suicide. Using a randomized control group model, Aseltine and DeMartino (2004) found that the SOS program led to increased knowledge and more adaptive attitudes about depression and suicide, and significantly lowered rates of self-reported suicide attempts.

Secondary Preventive Interventions

For students who have already begun to exhibit aggressive or maladaptive behavior, secondary preventive interventions often include cognitive–behavioral group approaches, such as problem-solving skills training or anger coping therapy. In problem-solving skills training, therapists actively teach youth a five-step problem-solving process and apply the process to interpersonal scenarios through games, activities, and stories (Kazdin, 2003). The therapist models the skill, provides feedback, and manages behavior through a token economy. Similarly, in anger coping therapy, the therapist also plays an active role in modeling cognitive processes, reinforcing behavior, and providing corrective feedback (Kazdin, 1987), although the focus of this intervention is on identifying triggers to anger and developing skills to cope with the anger.

The Anger Coping Program (Lochman, Curry, Dane, & Ellis, 2001) uses a cognitive–behavioral approach designed to address the social–cognitive deficits and misperceptions of youth who display aggressive behaviors. Anger coping interventions have been shown to significantly reduce disruptive and aggressive behavior and increase prosocial behavior, when compared with minimal treatment or no treatment control groups (Lochman, Burch, Curry, & Lampron, 1984; Lochman, Lampron, Burch, & Curry, 1985) and nondirective relationship therapy (Kazdin, Bass, Siegel, & Thomas, 1989; Kazdin, Esveldt-Dawson, French, & Unis, 1987). A 3-year follow-up study found that boys who participated in the Anger Coping Program had greater problem-solving ability, higher self-esteem, and lower rates of substance abuse than their untreated peers (Lochman, 1992). It is important that these interventions be conducted by a professional with the proper training, who is attentive to the possible problems that may arise when grouping students with aggressive behavior together for an intervention (e.g., Arnold & Hughes, 1999).

Interventions that involve parents and families are also important, given their integral role in the development and maintenance of aggressive behaviors. Parent Management Training (PMT; Kazdin, 2003) teaches parents to identify, define, and observe behaviors in new ways (e.g., antecedent, behavior, consequence) and to alter behaviors using effective behavioral management (e.g., reinforcement of appropriate behavior, mild punishment such as loss of privileges or time out, negotiation, contingency contracting). PMT has been shown to reduce aggressive behavior (Kazdin, 2003; Serketich & Dumas, 1996). Schools may consider offering these trainings or becoming familiar with resources in the community that can provide such services for children at risk for violence. Some administrators have approved flexible hours for school professionals, allowing them to provide these interventions in the evening, and administrators have also found an increase in parent attendance when baby-sitting services for parents are offered. Grants, parent–teacher organization funds, and high school volunteers have been used for baby-sitting services.

Tertiary Preventive Interventions

Tertiary interventions are needed for the small percentage of students who have chronic problems with aggression. More than half of the total discipline referrals and nearly all of the serious offenses in a school are accounted for by only 6% to 9% of children (Sprague & Walker, 2000). Functional behavioral assessment (FBA) and behavior intervention plans have been proven effective (Kratochwill & McGivern, 1996), especially for externalizing behavior problems (Watson & Steege, 2003). An FBA involves gathering information about antecedents, behaviors, and consequences to determine the function of behavior (e.g., obtaining reinforcement, avoidance, or self-stimulation). Once the function of behavior is identified, a behavioral intervention plan is developed, which specifies strategies to be used, such as manipulating environmental antecedents, altering behavioral consequences, and teaching skills using behavioral principles (Zionts, Zionts, & Simpson, 2002).

Because students experiencing chronic emotional and behavioral problems have such extensive needs, it is unlikely that schools will have sufficient resources to provide for all of these needs. Therefore, outpatient therapy, day treatment, and psychiatric hospitalization should be available for youth with chronic emotional and behavioral problems to accommodate these needs (Quinn & McDougal, 1998).

Increased attention has been given to wraparound approaches that work with multiple systems (e.g., family, peers, and schools) to address the multiple needs of students who perpetrate acts of school violence. For example, multisystemic therapy (MST), designated a model program by the Center for the Study and Prevention of Violence and the surgeon general of the United States, works with the systems in a student's life, such as the family and peer group. MST empowers caregivers to serve as change agents for their children by identifying factors that interfere with caregivers' ability to provide necessary nurturance, monitoring, and discipline. The MST team uses strengths (e.g., supportive extended family, social skills of caregiver) to address these factors and support the implementation of planned interventions. MST is successful in the reduction of problem behaviors, residential placement, and re-arrest rates for students with chronic and severe behavior problems (Henggeler, Schoenwald, Rowland, & Cunningham, 2002). It also increases family cohesion, adaptability, and interaction (Bourduin et al., 1995).

PRINCIPLES OF A CRISIS PLAN

A common problem in school crisis planning is the focus on crisis response, while other team actions are ignored—that is, prevention, preparedness, and longer-term recovery (Adamson & Peacock, 2007). Adapted from Project SAVE (2001, p. 9). The 10 guiding principles that address all phases of a crisis plan follow (a summary of these principles is provided in Table 4.3).

1. *Build on what is already in place.* When establishing the prevention elements of a crisis plan it is important to identify the successful practices for promoting school safety that are already in place. A needs assessment can be conducted to identify potential risk situations and components that are missing.
2. *Involve others.* Collaboration and various viewpoints are critical to a well-developed plan. The first step in developing a comprehensive plan is to identify school staff members who are able to provide planning leadership (Adams & Kritsonis, 2006). These core team members must (a) possess foresight, or the ability to estimate the risk of crises and to plan ahead to build effective crisis teams; (b) be able to make use of data and assessments; (c) organize planning efforts; (d) help sustain the training process; (e) possess the personality characteristics to stay calm when addressing a crisis; and (f) be competent in facilitating the crisis response and recovery process. A school staff member's job title alone does not give a person these qualities, so careful selection is critical.
3. *Include comprehensive and condensed versions.* The comprehensive plan, which is used by the school- and district-level crisis teams, involves assigning specific roles, responsibilities, and procedures, integrating all areas of the ICS. It includes details for a variety of specific response protocols (e.g., lockdown, reverse evacuation, and fire drill). It is also designed to foster cooperative relationships among community partners by clearly identifying their roles and expectations (Armstrong, Massey, & Boroughs, 2006). In addition to the comprehensive plan, a condensed plan can be articulated to provide school staff with guidance on the immediate execution of specific roles and responsibilities to ensure student safety during a crisis response. It is short, easy to follow, and placed in all classroom and common areas. If

Table 4.3. Guiding Principles for Crisis Planning Development

1. *Build on what is already in place.* Existing policies, plans, and procedures should be used as the foundation for meeting any new requirements.
2. *Involve others.* Schools can gain community acceptance and support of school plans by developing the plan through an open process, with broad participation by the entire school community.
3. *Include comprehensive and condensed versions of plans.* Comprehensive plans provide detail that encompasses all activities from early prevention through longer-term crisis recovery; condensed versions provide critical guidance on the immediate execution of the plan.
4. *Focus on the local context.* School safety plans should make unique school needs, resources, and potential crises a basis for planning.
5. *Make plans user-friendly and free of jargon, with clearly defined roles and responsibilities.* Plan success depends on participants' understanding, acceptance, and involvement in their assigned roles, and all school crisis team members should have a basic understanding of the roles and responsibilities of other crisis team members.
6. *Account for the possibility that team members will be unavailable.* The plan should designate alternates to implement the plan when school crisis team members are unavailable or not in a position to perform their roles.
7. *Include training in risk assessment procedures.* Students and all school personnel need to know the risk factors and warning signs of self- and other-directed violence, and know how to report such concerns to the appropriate individuals.
8. *Provide for professional development to ensure adequate preparation and examination of effectiveness.* For plans to be effective, school staff members and other involved individuals need to be trained and provided opportunities to practice crisis roles and responsibilities.
9. *Coordinate plan elements with nonpublic schools and recognize the needs of special school populations.* Students and staff with disabilities, students with limited English, and other special student populations and schools should be addressed in all plans.
10. *Review and update plans periodically so they remain current.* Periodic review and updating of plans is necessary to ensure applicability to current conditions.

Note. From *Guidance document for school safety plans* (p. 9), by Project SAVE, 2001, Albany, NY: New York Education Department. Copyright 2001 by the New York Education Department. Adapted with permission.

judged to be appropriate, this is the plan that could be made available to the school community to help prepare them for the school crisis response.

4. *Focus on the local context.* Crisis plans must fit the individual school and district situation, needs, and available resources. Use of data-driven decision making (e.g., multihazard assessment and comprehensive needs assessment) is essential for identifying potential threats. Different threats require different crisis prevention, preparedness, response, and recovery efforts and may involve other agencies, as in the case of a school near a chemical plant.

In addition, other local people and settings must be considered. For example, nonpublic-school students who know students at a crisis-exposed public school, or students whose school is used as an evacuation shelter may be affected. Specialized evacuation plans and additional practice of the crisis procedures will be necessary for children with special needs, and substitute teachers need to be aware of the crisis plans and procedures.

5. *Make the plan user-friendly and free of jargon, with clearly defined roles and responsibilities.* The document can be successful only if each member understands the comprehensive, interdependent requirements, and is knowledgeable and prepared for his or her assigned role (Brock et al., 2001). Concern regarding this issue is highlighted by a recent survey. Adamson and Peacock (2007) reported that only two thirds of respondents felt that their school's plans outlined team members' duties and responsibilities, about 20% indicated that the plan did not outline duties, and the remaining 15% did not know if duties were outlined.
6. *Account for the possibility that team members will be unavailable.* School staff members may have duties that take them away from the building. Plans should designate an alternate for all crisis team roles (Brock et al., 2001). In particular, the incident commander must have a well-trained and clearly identified backup person who is prepared to take charge to avoid confusion (Brickman, Jones, & Groom, 2004).
7. *Include training in risk assessment procedures.* Crisis planning also includes the development of threat and suicide assessment procedures. Students and all school personnel (e.g., teaching, support, and ancillary staff) need to be taught the risk factors and warning signs of suicidal ideation and other threatening behaviors, and be empowered with knowledge of the appropriate reporting procedures. School-based mental health professionals are the most appropriate staff members to conduct these assessments. Current practice typically involves the establishment of threat assessment teams at either the district or building level (National Education Association [NEA], 2007a). More discussion of risk assessment is presented in chapter 5.
8. *Provide for professional development to ensure adequate preparation and examination of effectiveness.* A crisis plan is only as good as the school staff members who implement the plan. Staff development is necessary to advance knowledge and awareness related to the school crisis plan. This training must include crisis drills and exercises. More detail regarding the exercising of plans is offered in chapter 6, and more detail regarding the examination of crisis plan effectiveness is offered in chapter 17.
9. *Coordinate plan elements with nonpublic schools and recognize the needs of special school populations.* In addition to ensuring that general education students and campuses are prepared, crisis plans should address the needs of students and staff with disabilities, students with limited English, and other special student populations and schools.
10. *Review and update plans periodically so they remain current.* Changes in personnel, local conditions, and other factors will require periodic reviews and updating of crisis plans to ensure their applicability to current conditions.

ELEMENTS OF A CRISIS PLAN

Most crisis plans contain the elements described below, although local factors may dictate that additional elements be included in each crisis plan.

Incident Command System and Command Post Protocols

Public school crisis teams are required to be structured according to the National Incident Management System's Incident Command System (ICS; U.S. Department of Homeland Security [DHS], 2004). In fact, according to the School Health Policy and Programs Study, a majority of school crisis plans use the ICS (SHPPS, 2007). The ICS structure fosters school and district collaboration and coordination with local, state, and federal response agencies.

The incident command school staff members operate from a primary command post (typically the school office), with a secondary command post identified (typically located off school grounds). The command posts should be equipped with a variety of communication options (e.g., land lines, computers with Internet access, televisions, fax machines, photocopy machine, and any other relevant technology). Members of the planning and intelligence sections of the crisis team decide what items are needed to run the command post and the logistics members obtain the items needed. A list of additional command post equipment is provided in Table 4.4.

Student Evacuation and Assembly Protocols

In the case of an external threat, students will be evacuated to designated assembly areas inside or outside the school. These locations may also be used to shelter students from severe weather. Assembly areas were found to be in place in over 96% of schools (SHPPS, 2007).

Smaller school districts may have one common evacuation protocol. However, most school districts will have separate and somewhat unique protocols for each individual school. These protocols should include alternative shelters within walking distance of the school or accessible by bus, if transportation is available. Typical options for alternative shelters are neighboring schools, churches, or businesses. These choices may be limited, so the crisis team needs to identify the best evacuation locations in advance. Teachers must know evacuation plans, and transportation contractors and bus drivers must be part of the school and district evacuation protocol.

Students with disabilities (e.g., visual, hearing, mobility, cognitive, attention, and emotional challenges) need to be given special consideration and individual evacuation plans (U.S. Department of Education, 2006a). Provisions for staff and students with special needs are required in the crisis plans of 65% of states and 77% of districts. Although often addressed in general terms, the plans of 81% of schools address special needs students (SHPPS, 2007).

To aid evacuation, crisis response resources such as the "go-kit" or the crisis response box contain the essential supplies and information needed to conduct an orderly and rapid school crisis response (see list in Table 4.5). A crisis response cart can be used to wheel, instead of carry, items from location to location. A minimum of two go-kits is recommended, one that is stored off campus (e.g., a local police or fire station). Floor plans need to be placed within the go-kit or

Table 4.4. Command Post Equipment

Office supplies	Chairs, desks, bulletin boards, poster-making machine, computers with Internet access, fax machines, printers, copy machine, telephones, digital cameras, file folders, message pads, pens, pencils, staplers, school and district letterhead, flip charts, stamps or postage meter, poster board or status board, markers, adhesive tape, clear packing tape
Communication supplies	Media request forms, fact sheets, script for volunteers, frequently asked questions, press releases, bull horn, cell phones and chargers, TV, radio, portable speakers and microphone, confidential meeting space
Key lists	District contact numbers, list of crisis team members and assigned duties, staff and student telephone numbers, student and staff emergency cards and pictures, media directory, map of school and grounds, bell and bus schedules, list of students and their special needs (medication), list of community support agencies with phone numbers and services offered
Food and beverages	List of possible restaurants to donate or provide food
Emergency supplies	Flashlights, police radio, two-way radios, first-aid kits

Note. Primary source *School Crisis Guide: Help and Healing in a Time of Crisis*, by the National Education Association (NEA) Health Education Network, 2007a. Retrieved May 24, 2008, from http://www.neahin.org/crisisguide/before/districtelements.html.

crisis response box and also housed at an off-campus location. The floor plan should mark all windows, entrances, and exits; on and off valves for water; and ventilation, electricity, and gas systems (Brickman et al., 2004). School floor plans should be reviewed with fire, police, and other emergency response personnel prior to a crisis event.

Student Accounting and Caregiver Reunification Protocols

Procedures for immediately taking student attendance need to be developed and a protocol established for documenting those in need of medical treatment. This protocol needs to document where students have been taken for medical treatment, to aid in student–parent reunification.

Evacuation facilities can also serve as reunification sites from which parents can pick up their children (NEA, 2007a). According to the SHPPS survey (2007), family reunification procedures were required in only about half of state plans, two thirds of district plans, and three quarters of school plans. Of the elements required for a crisis plan at the state, district, and school levels, family reunification was the element least required by policy. This is concerning, as parent–child reunification is one of the most important elements of a crisis plan. As discussed in chapter 12,

Table 4.5. Elements of a "Go-Kit" or Crisis Response Box

Element	*Responsible Team Member*
Crisis Management Team phone numbers	Command Section (Critical Incident Commander)
Crisis Response Team role descriptions	Command Section (Critical Incident Commander)
Media staging area/resources	Command Section (Public Information Officer)
Media management policy	Command Section (Public Information Officer)
Community emergency resources listing	Command Section (Liaison Officer)
Emergency response personnel staging area	Command Section (Safety Officer and/or Liaison Officer)
Structural engineering resources	Command Section (Safety Officer)
Aerial photos of the campus	Planning and Intelligence Section
School community map	Planning and Intelligence Section
Campus layout (with staging areas indicated)	Planning and Intelligence Section
Blueprints of all school buildings	Planning and Intelligence Section
Crisis incident log	Planning and Intelligence Section
AM/FM battery-operated radio (batteries)	Planning and Intelligence Section
Battery-operated weather radio (batteries)	Planning and Intelligence Section
Battery-operated laptop computer (with AirPort)	Planning and Intelligence Section
Site status report forms	Planning and Intelligence Section
Damage documentation tools (e.g., cameras)	Planning and Intelligence Section
Keys for all campus facilities	Operations Section (Security & Safety Coord./F&G Sp.)
Fire alarm shutoff procedures	Operations Section (Security & Safety Coord./F&G Sp.)
Sprinkler system shutoff procedures	Operations Section (Security & Safety Coord./F&G Sp.)
Utility shutoff valves and tools	Operations Section (Security & Safety Coord./F&G Sp.)
Gas line and utility layout	Operations Section (Security & Safety Coord./F&G Sp.)
Cable television/satellite feed shutoff	Operations Section (Security & Safety Coord./F&G Sp.)
Yellow caution tape	Operations Section (Security & Safety Coord./SRA Sp.)
Search and rescue supplies and equipment	Operations Section (Security & Safety Coord./SRA Sp.)
Student photos	Operations Section (Security & Safety Coord./SRA Sp.)

Table 4.5. (continued)

Element	*Responsible Team Member*
Parent Center location	Operations Section (Security & Safety Coord./CM Sp.)
Evacuation routes and assembly procedures	Operations Section (Security & Safety Coord./SAR Sp.)
Evacuations sites	Operations Section (Security & Safety Coord./SAR Sp.)
Student disposition and release forms	Operations Section (Security & Safety Coord./SAR Sp.)
Student release procedures	Operations Section (Security & Safety Coord./SAR Sp.)
Student attendance roster	Operations Section (Security & Safety Coord./SAR sp)
Traffic management plan	Operations Section (Security & Safety Coord./TS Sp.)
Student emergency cards	Operations Section (Student Care Coord./SFW&S Sp.)
Special needs student listing (e.g., medications)	Operations Section (Student Care Coord./SFW&S Sp.)
Crisis codes established	Operations Section (Student Care Coord./CI Sp.)
Lockdown procedures	Operations Section (Student Care Coord./CI Sp.)
Crisis intervention resource listing	Operations Section (Student Care Coord./CI Sp.)
Crisis intervention procedures and resources	Operations Section (Student Care Coord./CI Sp.)
First-aid supplies list and location	Operations Section (Emergency Medical Coord.)
First-aid procedures	Operations Section (Emergency Medical Coord.)
Morgue procedures and supplies	Operations Section (Emergency Medical Coord.)
Translator listing	Operations Section (Translation Coord.)
Crisis intervention center and service rooms	Logistics Section (Facilities Coord.)
Command post and staging area signs	Logistics Section (Facilities Coord.)
Care and shelter resource list (e.g., water, food)	Logistics Section (Facilities Coord.)
Teacher roster and assignments	Logistics Section (SCVA Coord.)
Staff roster, assignments, and crisis duties	Logistics Section (SCVA Coord.)
Staff resources list and crisis duties	Logistics Section (SCVA Coord.)
List of key parent and community volunteers	Logistics Section (SCVA Coord.)
Crisis response team identification	Logistics Section (SCVA Coord.)
Communication resources listing/ locations	Logistics Section (Communications Coord.)

Table 4.5. (continued)

Element	*Responsible Team Member*
Staff phone tree (with cell phone numbers)	Logistics Section (Communication Coord.)
List designating phone lines for specific use	Logistics Section (Communications Coord.)
Office supplies	Logistics Section (Supplies & Equipment Coord.)
Flashlights (with extra batteries)	Logistics Section (Supplies & Equipment Coord.)
Emergency resource budget information	Finance Section
Emergency personnel sign-in/sign-out sheet	Finance Section
Purchase order forms	Finance Section
FEMA forms	Finance Section

Note. F&G Sp. = Facilities and grounds specialist; SRA Sp. = Search, rescue, & accounting specialist; CM Sp. = Crowd management specialist; SAR Sp. = Student assembly & release specialist; CI Sp. = Crisis intervention specialist; TS Sp. = Traffic safety specialist; SFW&S Sp. = Shelter, food, water, & supplies specialist; SCVA Coord. = Staff & community volunteer assignment coordinator. Adapted from "Preventing, Preparing for, and Responding to School Violence with the National Incident Management System" (pp. 449–450), by S. E. Brock, S. R. Jimerson, and S. Hart. In S. R. Jimerson & M. J. Furlong (Eds.), *Handbook of School Violence and School Safety,* 2006, Mahwah, NJ: Erlbaum. Copyright 2006 by Lawrence Erlbaum. Adapted with permission.

the sooner children are reunited with their families, the lower the likelihood of traumatic stress reactions.

In advance of a crisis event, parents and other caregivers need to be notified of these plans and have directions for how to get to the reunification site. In addition, to facilitate reunification, this site needs to have an accountability system for verifying the legal authority of adults picking up the students (Brickman et al., 2004; NEA, 2007a). This will typically require that copies of student emergency cards, which include information about who is authorized to pick up the child, be available. Figure 4.2 includes forms and checklists useful during student accounting and release. The forms can be used to track information on all students, including the reunification of students with parents and student sheltering and supervision.

A final reunification consideration is traffic management. Following crisis events it is not unusual for many parents to arrive at the reunification site simultaneously. Thus, procedures to facilitate traffic flow and to manage congestion must also be a part of reunification protocols.

Exercise and Crisis Drill Protocols

Schedules for crisis team meetings and practice drills or exercises should be developed at the beginning of every school year to avoid scheduling conflicts. Crisis team meetings should occur at least every other month, but monthly meetings are recommended so safety issues and current monitoring data can be discussed and proactive measures can be taken (see chapter 6 for additional information on exercising the crisis plan).

Figure 4.2. Checklists to aid the reunification of students and parents, based on an established Incident Command System structure.

Student Accounting and Release Planning Checklist

___ Ensure that the student accounting and release specialists are available, that they understand their roles, and that they are willing and able to serve.

___ Working with the student accounting and release specialist, establish a student and staff accounting procedure. This procedure should make use of current attendance rosters and must include a code for whether students and staff members are present or missing, safe and healthy, injured, or deceased.

___ Working with the crisis intervention and student release specialists, establish a protocol for informing parents and guardians that their children are missing, injured, or deceased. This protocol must involve the identification of a secure notification area.

___ Working with the student release specialist, establish a student–parent release protocol. This protocol must use the emergency cards and will require the establishment of areas for identity verification, parent waiting, and student–parent reunion. Typically the identity verification area will be in the school office. Parent waiting and reunion areas may be in the same location, but they should be separate from the areas that hold students prior to reunion (e.g., classrooms, evacuation sites). Individual parents and guardians of missing, injured, or deceased students must be given their own waiting areas.

___ Design the student–parent release protocol to recognize the importance of reuniting preschool and primary school children with their parents and guardians first.

___ Working with the crisis intervention specialist, discuss strategies for working with parents and guardians in the waiting area to ensure that they understand the procedure being followed (and the possible delays in reuniting with their children) and the importance of their reactions (upon reunification) in shaping children's traumatic stress reactions.

___ In advance of any crisis event, ensure that the student accounting and release protocol has been disseminated to parents and guardians. Dissemination options include a letter to parents from the principal, articles in a school newsletter, and placement in a student–parent handbook. Included in such documents should be information that stresses the importance of parents' reactions in shaping student perceptions of the event.

Accounting and Release Action Checklist

___ Identify yourself as the student accounting and release section leader.

___ Obtain a briefing from the incident commander, and planning and intelligence section chiefs on the situation, initial objectives, and priorities.

Figure 4.2. (continued)

___ Assemble the student accounting and release team.

___ Direct the student accounting specialist to obtain class rosters from each teacher to determine status (i.e., safe and healthy, injured, or deceased) and location (i.e., present or missing) of all students and school staff members.

___ Direct the student accounting specialist to prepare an initial student and staff information summary as soon as possible. Identify deceased, injured, or missing students or staff members to the school incident commander. Provide a copy of the information summary to the student release specialist.

___ Upon determination that students or staff members are deceased, injured, or missing, obtain the school incident commander's approval for parent or guardian notification. (Note: The coroner is the only authority who can legally declare a person dead.)

___ Work with the crisis intervention specialist and the student release specialist to ensure that the parents and guardians of missing, injured, or deceased students are removed to a secure location. This location should be separate from the parent waiting and reunion areas. Use district office or law enforcement personnel for face-to-face notification in cases of death, serious injury, or missing persons.

___ Coordinate with the school security or search and rescue unit leader to search for missing students or staff.

___ After consultation with the student accounting and student release specialists, make a recommendation for the release of students to the school incident commander. If students are released, ensure that a record is maintained showing the person to whom the student has been released, the time of departure, and other essential information.

___ After consultation with the crisis intervention specialist, recommend procedures for how the school incident commander will disseminate information about the status of students to parents or guardians. Dissemination options include the posting of lists with the names of students who are accounted for and are safe and individual notification for students who are missing, injured, or deceased.

___ Direct the student release specialist to begin to release students to parents and guardians.

___ Maintain a log noting information received and actions taken.

Releasing Students to Parents and Guardians

To expedite the release of students to their parents, a student release area should be established and procedures developed to provide for an orderly release process. The student release area should be away from the classroom; evacuation assembly; and missing, injured, or deceased notification areas.

Parents should be carefully informed of, and required to follow, release procedures. The most important tasks are to document when and to whom each student is released, and to ensure that

Figure 4.2. (continued)

parents are carefully informed about the reunification process. The original student emergency cards should be kept in the main office; copies of all emergency cards for each student should be kept in each classroom's attendance folder.

Each school should develop a release form that is consistent with the protocol they develop. A sample release form follows.

Sample Student Release Form			
Student name		Parent or caregiver name	
Student grade		Form of ID	
Authorized staff member		Release time	AM/PM
Initials		Destination	

Establish three separate parent areas. Each parent area should have crisis intervention team members available to tell parents how they can best help their child cope with the crisis event.

1. *Identity verification area.* This is where caregiver identities are verified. Here school staff will check authorization for release on the student's emergency cards (maintained in the teacher's attendance folder), and the parent or caregiver will complete duplicate copies of the release form (sample provided above), which documents their identity, destination, and time of release. Both copies of this form will then be signed by the student release specialist. The parent will keep one copy (which can be used to verify identification if necessary) and the second will be attached to the student's emergency card.

2. *Reunion area or reunion and waiting area.* After their identities have been verified, parents and caregivers wait for reunion with their children.

3. *Notification area.* This is where parents and guardians are notified that their children are missing, injured, or deceased.

Following identity verification of his or her parent or caregiver, each student will be summoned to the reunion area. Once students are physically released to a parent or caregiver, the student's name will be checked off the classroom attendance sheet by a school staff member.

SPECIAL NOTE: Younger primary-grade students should be given a priority consideration for release and reunification with their parent or guardian. Youth below the age of 7 are most likely to be traumatized by separation from parents during times of stress.

SPECIAL SITUATION: In the event that a large number of parents arrive at the same time to pick up their children and it is determined that it is the school's priority to release students to their parents or caregivers quickly, then two options are suggested.

Figure 4.2. (continued)

1. Intermediate-grade teachers may be asked to combine their classrooms with the primary-grade classroom so those teachers can help the student release specialist with reunions.

2. As parent or caregiver identities are verified, instead of calling students down one at a time, a list of parents of students from the same class who are available for reunion can be created, and students can be released in groups to parents (in the reunion or waiting area). Since parents will have a duplicate copy of their release form, they can show this form to the designated team member as they exit the reunion or waiting area with their child. Again, once students are physically released to a parent or caregiver, the student's name will be checked off the master roster by the staff.

Release of Students to Parents—Action Checklist

___ Determine the availability of supplies and the safety of areas chosen for identity verification, waiting and reunion, and notification (if applicable).

___ Set up tables and chairs, and place emergency cards and master rosters in the identity verification area. Ensure that an ample supply of release forms is available. Multiple tables, separated according to alphabetical groupings, could be set up for quicker identification of parents or caregivers. Be sure the signs identifying alphabetical groupings are elevated on an easel or wall so they can be clearly seen as parents are congregating around tables.

___ Have parents or caregivers complete the release form in duplicate; ensure that a designated school staff member has signed the form and that a destination has been indicated. Give one release form to the parent and attach the other to the emergency card. **If the name of the adult is not on the child's emergency card, the student cannot be released.**

___ If the adult's name is on the emergency card, use a walkie-talkie or messenger to summon the student to the reunion area.

___ If necessary, the incident commander should consider the need to reevaluate the optimal student–parent reunion procedure (the procedure should be adaptable to situation specific needs).

___ Check off the name and note the destination of each student on a master roster (generated from each classroom's attendance list) before releasing the student. However, if a classroom attendance list was not available and time does not allow for the creation of a roster at release, keep a copy of the student release form and develop a roster later.

Figure 4.2. (continued)

Student Release Procedures Annual Preparation

___ Maintain current classroom rosters in each classroom (as well as in the command post location).

___ Maintain an emergency card for each student in the main office and in each classroom's attendance folder that lists persons authorized to pick up student.

___ Know where to obtain tables, chairs, writing supplies, and yellow barrier tape for delineating areas for student release, waiting and reunion, and notification areas.

Note. Adapted from the crisis protocol, by the San Mateo-Foster City School District, California. Adapted with permission from the San Mateo-Foster City School District.

Communication Protocols

Communicating with school personnel is included in over 94% of school plans (SHPPS, 2007), and communication between staff and emergency personnel is a critical factor in determining immediate crisis response effectiveness. There are a variety of ways to communicate, and each has its own strengths and challenges. The crisis situation will dictate what form of communication is best, so the school crisis plan should include a variety of communication means. It is important to maintain communications (a) within buildings, (b) between buildings, and (c) between the school and community resources and agencies. Communication options include emergency channels, land-line phones, cell phones, e-mail, intercoms, walkie-talkies, reverse 911 systems, media, and written memos. Table 4.6 provides a brief summary of each of these communication options.

Media Relations Protocols

Eighty-nine percent of schools include procedures for responding to media inquiries into their school crisis plan (SHPPS, 2007). Schools or school districts that have developed positive media relations before a crisis event will find that they can be a powerful resource when disseminating important crisis information (e.g., how to obtain support services). Under best practices, having a trained public information officer is beneficial; stonewalling the media or forbidding access has been known to exacerbate a crisis, as media personnel seek alternative (and often less accurate) information sources. It is recommended that the school plan establish a media staging area adjacent to school grounds, where media personnel can give frequent (as often as hourly) updates regarding a crisis situation. Table 4.7 highlights tips for communicating and working with the media.

Table 4.6. Emergency Communication Options

1. *Emergency channel.* Many schools have an emergency channel reserved for school administration, police, and emergency personnel in the event of a crisis. The key to using an emergency channel is that all school crisis team members have access to the same channel.
2. *Land-line phones.* Assuming accessibility, these are still the most reliable communication method. Many schools have phones in every classroom so teachers are readily able to communicate with the main office. In the event of a crisis, lines can become overwhelmed due to the large volume of calls, so backup communication plans are needed. In addition, it is important to train parents and community members to not overload phone lines in the event of a crisis so that designated lines can stay open for school staff and emergency personnel use.
3. *Cell phones.* These are a powerful crisis response resource, but they have also created some challenges. Cell phones signals often become overwhelmed with the volume of calls that occur following a crisis event and will not work unless a portable cell phone tower is erected close to the site. In addition, in many areas of school buildings it may not be possible to receive a cell phone signal. Among the challenges associated with cell phones is the fact that students will use them to text message and sometimes will do so before the school has had a chance to activate their crisis team.
4. *E-mail.* If computers are accessible, e-mail can be a reliable and fast means of communicating between staff and with the school community.
5. *Intercom.* The intercom is another means of quickly communicating with students and school staff. However, caution needs to be used regarding what information is shared (i.e., avoiding excessive or unnecessary details) and how the information is presented to not unnecessarily frighten students. The intercom should not be used to share information on fatalities or horrific details, because mass hysteria can result. Some advocate the use of a code to signal when a specific plan needs to be implemented (e.g., "Mr. Moore, the superintendent is in the building," signaling a lockdown is necessary; Brock, Jimerson, et al., 2002). However, many school staff members (not to mention substitute teachers and visitors) do not remember the code, especially without routine practice. Therefore, current practice promotes being more direct, yet succinct when using the intercom to activate a crisis plan (e.g., "Teachers please lock your doors and check your e-mail for additional information").
6. *Walkie-talkies.* Although expensive, these are one of the most reliable means of communication. Playground supervisors and school resource officers should always have a walkie-talkie present that links them to the main office.
7. *Reverse 911.* Many school districts and universities have purchased a calling system called Reverse 911 that allows a recorded message to be disseminated to all phone numbers on record. This system can be very helpful because a message can be sent out to thousands of numbers within a few seconds. The caution is that phone numbers often change, and parents need to be sure to update these numbers with the school to receive the message.

Table 4.6. (continued)

8. *Written memos.* When it comes to sharing specific details and facts, dissemination of a fact sheet or letter is the most reliable with regard to the consistency of information being shared. The crisis plan needs to address who is responsible for writing and disseminating fact sheets or letters and for verifying the information through multiple and legitimate sources.

Table 4.7. Working With the Media

- Provide a media area off school grounds where media personnel can receive crisis information.
  - Notify media that they do not have access to school grounds.
  - Use security personnel, if necessary, to enforce media area boundaries and traffic flow.
- Assign only one person—the incident commander or public information officer—to communicate with members of the media and to release information regarding victims or perpetrators.
  - Withhold the names of victims or suspected perpetrators until family members have been notified and families have given permission for information to be released.
  - Verify all information before releasing it. Depending on the event, verification of crisis facts may need to be obtained from police, rescue, district administrators, school-level administrators, and/or other involved response agencies.
  - Monitor media outlets to find out about inaccurate reporting, and correct such reporting immediately.
- Work collaboratively with the media.
  - Use the media to relay important crisis information.
  - Use the media to relay information about support services.
  - Educate the media about contagion and vicarious traumatization.
- Conduct regularly scheduled press conferences.
  - Even if no new information has emerged, maintain the press conference schedule.
  - Focus on facts; do not speculate. Use a fact sheet that contains verified and approved information to be released and provide a copy of the fact sheet to members of the media when they leave.
  - Always tell the truth even if it may damage the school's or school district's reputation, then follow up with how the school or school district is addressing the problem (the problem will be worse if the media discover that the school or district lied).
  - Develop three to five key messages for the parents and community.
  - Detail the school's plan for the next day.
  - Repeat the question before giving an answer to demonstrate understanding.

Table 4.7. (continued)

  - Do not feel obligated to answer all questions. It is permissible to state: "I am sorry, I am not able to provide that information at this time," or "I do not have that information." However, avoid saying "No comment," as that may imply that the spokesperson has something to hide.
  - Ensure that the spokesperson remains calm.
  - Set and enforce clear time limits for all press conferences.
- Minimize the media exposure of students, staff, and families.
  - Use side or back entrances for students, staff, and families.
  - Provide guidelines to students and staff about communicating with the media.
  - Assign a school staff member to the victims' or perpetrators' families to help them enter and exit the school or other buildings.
- Control access to family and community meetings.
  - Deny media access to meetings.
  - Discuss the role of a parent who is also a member of the media (i.e., as a parent and not a media member) and request that specific information about the meeting not be released or used professionally.
  - Hold a short press conference after a parent or community meeting to minimize the media approaching meeting participants. Let the meeting participants know you will be doing this and what information will be released to the media.

Note. Primary source *Coping with Crisis: Lessons Learned,* by S. Poland & J. S. McCormick, 1999, Longmont, CO: Sopris West.

Visitor Sign-In Protocols

An important element of the crisis plan that has special relevance to media relations protocols is visitor sign-in procedures. These procedures can help monitor and control entrance into school buildings. The National Center for Education Statistics (NCES, 2004) reported that 97% of schools require visitors to sign in. However, such requirements are only as good as the procedures that are implemented.

CONCLUSION

This chapter introduced in general terms the concept, principles, and basic elements of a school crisis plan. In the chapter that follows, more details regarding specific crisis planning during all phases of a crisis are explored.

Chapter 5

SPECIFIC SCHOOL CRISIS PLANNING ISSUES

A one-size-fits-all approach to crisis prevention does not exist, so no two school or district plans will look exactly alike. For example, plans for preventing acts of violence (arguably a preventable crisis type) must address the complex associations between individual, family, school, and neighborhood. Because these variables differ, each school should assess its unique needs and develop comprehensive and systematic approaches to crisis prevention. Schools often use suspensions, expulsions, and a zero-tolerance approach, which refers to providing severe punishment for all types of offenses, such as possession of drugs or alcohol, fighting, or swearing) to send the message that rule breaking is not tolerated (Skiba, 2000; Skiba & Peterson, 1999). However, these strategies have been found to be ineffective, as students who have been suspended are more likely to be referred for disciplinary actions in the future (Tobin & Sugai, 1996). In addition, a disproportionate number of males and children from low-socioeconomic-status or ethnic minority backgrounds are referred for disciplinary actions, raising questions about the fairness or social justice of many disciplinary actions (Imich, 1994; Morrison & D'Incau, 1997; Skiba, Peterson, & Williams, 1997).

PREVENTION ELEMENTS OF A CRISIS PLAN

Increasing evidence suggests that most behavior problems that result in suspension and expulsion can be prevented through proactive procedures (Metzler, Biglan, Rusby, & Sprague, 2001; Sprague et al., 2001). The National Consortium of School Violence Prevention Researchers and Practitioners (2006) has advocated comprehensive and coordinated efforts to prevent school crises (e.g., school violence). Such efforts use a balanced approach that attends to physical safety; educational practices; and social, emotional, and behavioral well-being. Other aspects of the comprehensive preventive approach include securing the physical building and implementing universal, selected, and targeted preventive interventions, such as safe schools climate, positive behavior support systems, discipline codes, direct instruction, collaboration with outside agencies, and risk assessment.

Crime Prevention Through Environmental Design

One often neglected source of vulnerability for a school is its architectural design. Securing the physical building is a critical part of ensuring physical safety and preventing crises. Crime prevention through environmental design (CPTED) includes three principles important for securing a school: (a) natural surveillance, (b) natural access control, and (c) territoriality (Sprague & Walker, 2005). *Natural surveillance* refers to the ability to see and communicate what is happening in the school. A critical component of natural surveillance is providing adequate school-wide supervision. Insufficient supervision is associated with violence and bullying (Meraviglia, Becker, Rosenbluth, Sanchez, & Robertson, 2003), and increasing adult supervision on playgrounds and in hallways has resulted in fewer reported bullying incidents (Boulton, 1994; DeVoe, Peter, Noonan, Snyder, & Baum, 2005). Other possibilities for increasing surveillance include having two-way communication between the staff and front office and hiring school resource officers (Sprague & Walker).

The second principle of CPTED, *natural access control*, focuses on strategies to control who and what enters and exits the school building. Schools should have one point of entry that is blocked by a person or a lock, and all other doors to the building should be kept locked from the outside (while still allowing for unrestricted exits). Other strategies to control access include establishing a uniform visitor-screening policy and requiring employee and student identification badges. Access can also be controlled by restricting roof access and installing strategically placed surveillance cameras to deter intruders from entering the building (Sprague & Walker, 2005).

The last principle of CPTED is *territoriality*, or a reinforced sense of shared ownership so that students and staff members feel more empowered to challenge inappropriate behavior when it occurs (Schneider, Walker, & Sprague, 2000). For example, groups of students could be assigned to different areas to paint, decorate, or clean up to help ensure a sense of ownership and pride in the school (Hill & Hill, 1994). Another way to empower students and staff to challenge inappropriate behavior is to establish clear policies and an open climate so that students and others who identify a problem or potential threat feel comfortable sharing this information (National Consortium of School Violence Prevention Researchers and Practitioners, 2006; Schneider et al., 2000).

A comprehensive study of school shootings indicated that most of the perpetrators had a specific plan for the attacks and that other people were aware of that plan (Vossekuil, Fein, Reddy, Borum, & Modzeleski, 2002). Therefore procedures must be in place for communicating potential threats or issues of concern. Confidential phone lines would allow students and parents with concerns about bullying to anonymously contact school personnel (Olweus, 1993). Students and teachers could also use incident reports to document threats (Suckling & Temple, 2002). This information could be used to initiate a more formal threat assessment, which is described later in this chapter.

Safe Schools Climate

Establishing and sustaining a safe schools climate, including positive behavior supports and prevention programming, is the best protective factor for schools and one of the most effective crisis prevention strategies (Dwyer & Jimerson, 2002; Osher, Dwyer, & Jimerson, 2006). However, only 57% of principals reported that their schools include programs to promote a sense of community and social integration among students (National Center for Education Statistics [NCES], 2004). The positive behavior support and positive behavioral interventions and supports models (PBS and PBIS; http://www.pbis.org) are being used across the country to establish safe schools. The model emphasizes developing well thought out discipline codes in addition to listing positive expectations, instead of focusing on what not to do. This balance can help reinforce respect, tolerance, personal responsibility, and fairness. In addition, the positive behavior support model emphasizes the collection and analysis of data to (a) help identify critical incidents and major problems, (b) assess problem areas, including time and location of incidents in buildings and on school grounds, and (c) help provide an assessment of vulnerability (Bailey, 2006; Black, 2004).

To further establish a safe schools climate, consequences and the procedures that are followed when codes are violated need to be clearly stated and also addressed within the crisis plan. Bullying should also be defined to include physical aggression, verbal and cyber threats, name calling and rumors (emotional bullying or relational aggression), and menacing gestures. Furthermore, schools may want to consider having parents and students sign forms stating that they have read the discipline codes (Bailey, 2006).

Direct instruction to teach prosocial behaviors and prevent maladaptive behaviors are another way to help prevent crises generated by crime and violence. Consequently, they should also be an element of the comprehensive school crisis plan. Programs can include teaching bullying prevention, violence prevention, anger management, tolerance, and respect. In addition, programs must train teachers and staff (including bus drivers) how to identify bullying and early warning signs of potentially dangerous situations and how to make a confidential report of these concerns. According to one disconcerting statistic, only 35% of principals indicated they conducted such training with their staff (NCES, 2004).

Collaboration With Support Agencies

Before a crisis event, it is imperative to identify community support resources, discuss logistics of how schools and agencies will work together, and develop memorandums of understanding (MOUs) that outline the roles and responsibilities of each entity (for a discussion of MOUs see chapter 3). Some collaboration issues to consider are (a) the qualifications of agency staff, and how they are screened and trained to ensure they have the expertise to conduct crisis response work with children and adolescents; (b) the agencies' limits to confidentiality; (c) who pays for the services being offered to students and families; and (d) the specific roles, responsibilities, and boundaries for each agency and the school.

Suicide Threat Assessment

According to the 2007 Youth Risk Behavior Survey, 28.5% of youth in the United States reported feeling so sad or hopeless every day for two weeks or more in the past 12 months that they stopped doing their usual activities, 14.5% had seriously considered suicide within the past 12 months, 11.3% had made a suicide plan, 6.9% had attempted suicide, and 2% had made a suicide attempt that required medical treatment in the past 12 months (Centers for Disease Control and Prevention, 2008). The following is a brief review of steps that schools can take to prevent suicide. For more comprehensive information about risk assessment and referral procedures and documentation, readers are encouraged to consult the American Psychiatric Association (2003); Brock, Sandoval, and Hart (2006); Lieberman, Poland, and Cassel (2008); and Miller and McConaughy (2005).

All school community members should be aware of the warning signs of youth suicide—those statements or behaviors that indicate the need to refer a student for a suicide risk assessment (Poland & Lieberman, 2002). Threats, either direct (e.g., "I am going to kill myself") or indirect (e.g., "Nobody would care if I died"), should be taken seriously. These threats may be verbal or written (e.g., expressed in a class assignment, drawing, or creative writing). Some youth who are suicidal may also show a preoccupation with death and visit Internet sites about death or suicide (Miller & McConaughy, 2005). A student's having a suicide plan is also a clear warning, and an assessment of risk must obtain details about the plan, as described below. A previous suicide attempt is also a warning sign for suicide. In fact, previous attempts are the most powerful predictor of future suicidal behavior (Borges, Angst, Nock, Ruscio, & Kessler, 2008; Lewinsohn, Rohde, & Seeley, 1996). Another warning sign is making final arrangements, such as giving away prized possessions or writing good-bye notes (Lieberman et al., 2008; Miller & McConaughy, 2005). Sudden changes in behavior (e.g., withdrawing from friends, shifting from agitation to peacefulness, or mood improvement after period of depression) or habits (e.g., sleeping more or having eating problems) are also warning signs (Brock et al., 2006; Miller & McConaughy, 2005), as are symptoms of depression, especially leading to pervasive feelings of helplessness and hopelessness (Lieberman et al., 2008).

Current practice in suicide prevention involves a mental health professional conducting a thorough risk assessment interview with the student. Areas typically assessed include (a) presence of suicidal thoughts, plans, and behaviors; (b) presence of psychiatric symptoms associated with suicidality (e.g., aggression, impulsivity, hopelessness, or anxiety); (c) prior suicidal behavior; (d) current and past mental health treatment history; (e) family history; (f) current stressors; and (g) strengths and protective factors (American Psychiatric Association, 2003). During the risk assessment interview, the mental health professional should remain calm, direct, empathic, and respectful (Miller & McConaughy, 2005). It is also important for the interviewer to avoid acting shocked, arguing against suicide, minimizing the problem, leaving the child unsupervised, or promising confidentiality (Lieberman et al., 2008).

Although no rating system designating the severity of suicide risk has been agreed upon by all mental health professionals, most of them conceptualize risk on a continuum from no risk to high and imminent risk (Berman, Jobes, & Silverman, 2006; Brock et al., 2006). The determination of risk depends on several factors, such as the degree of risk (e.g., previous suicide attempt or mental health disorder), the presence of a specific plan, availability and accessibility of a method of self-harm, and presence of support (Berman et al., 2006; Miller & McConaughy, 2005).

Immediate preventive interventions for suicidal students include the following:

- Breaking confidentiality and reporting suicidal thoughts or plans to parents, school administrators, police, or a community-based mental health center, depending on circumstances.
- Notifying parents or legal guardians and asking them to come to the school immediately. If the parent is uncooperative, unavailable, or appears to place the child at greater risk, the school should escort the child to a community-based emergency mental health facility, notify the police or child protective services, or contact a mobile psychiatric response team.
- Removing access to methods.
- Teaching alternative methods of coping with feelings, other than self-harm, and providing contact information for resources (e.g., therapist, local hospitals, and suicide hotlines).
- Making appropriate referrals for other community-based services (Brock et al., 2006; Lieberman et al., 2008; Miller & McConaughy, 2005).

The results of the suicide assessment and follow-up plan should be carefully documented (Miller & McConaughy). A sample suicide risk assessment and referral protocol developed by Brock et al., which incorporates many of the ideas expressed above, is presented in Table 5.1.

Violence Threat Assessment

Although students are safer at school than away from school, and school-associated incidents of violent crimes have decreased since the early 1990s (DeVoe et al., 2005), even one act of violence in schools is cause for concern (Brock, 1999, Summer). Partly in response to high-profile school shootings, the U.S. Secret Service and U.S. Department of Education have advocated that schools use a standard approach to analyzing a variety of dangerous situations to determine the extent to which a student poses a serious threat to the safety of others (called *threat assessment*; Fein et al., 2002: Jimerson & Brock, 2004; Jimerson, Brock, Greif, & Cowan, 2004). Threat assessment rests on several principles outlined in Table 5.2. The assessment of the extent to which a student poses a threat is based on information from multiple sources and considers the facts and behaviors relevant to the student who made the threat, the situation, the setting, and the intended victim. The process requires a skeptical, inquisitive mind-set guided by 11 key questions (see Table 5.3) concerning the student's motives, capability, and risk factors.

Threat assessment should be conducted by a multidisciplinary team that may include school administrators, school resource officers, and support services staff (e.g., school psychologists, school social workers, school counselors, and deans of discipline). The major steps involved in threat assessment are shown in Figure 5.1. The process is prompted by the observation or report of a threat, defined as an expression of intent to harm someone. The threat could take the form of spoken, written, or gestured direct or indirect communication (e.g., drawing of a gun pointed to

Table 5.1. Sample Suicide Risk Assessment and Referral Protocol

1. Discuss the reasons for referral with the referring staff member and begin to establish rapport with the student suspected to be suicidal.
2. Conduct an assessment to determine the student's risk of engaging in a suicidal behavior. The risk assessment should include the following:
   a. Identify suicidal ideation.
      i. Once the student has been engaged (through a demonstration of empathy, respect, and warmth), identify suicidal intent through direct questioning (e.g., "Sometimes when people have had your experiences and feelings they have thoughts of suicide. Is this something that you're thinking about?").
      ii. If thoughts of suicide are not present, a suicide intervention is not needed, but support and assistance with the student's referring concerns will likely be required.
      iii. If thoughts of suicide are present, continue to assess the student's risk of acting upon such ideation.
   b. Assess suicide risk in the following areas.
      i. *Current suicide plan.* Directly inquire about the presence of a plan (e.g., "Do you have a plan for how you might act on your thoughts of suicide?"). The greater the planning, the greater the risk. Other specific questions to ask include "How might you do it?" "How soon are you planning on suicide?" and "How prepared are you to commit suicide?" (access to means of attempt).
      ii. *Pain.* Directly inquire about the degree to which the individual is desperate (e.g., "Does your physical or emotional pain feel unbearable?"). The more unbearable the pain, the greater the risk.
      iii. *Resources.* Directly inquire about the individual's perceptions of being alone (e.g., "Do you have any resources or reasons for living?"). The more alone, the greater the risk.
      iv. *Prior suicidal behavior.* Directly inquire about the individual's history of suicidal behavior (e.g., "Have you or anyone close to you ever attempted suicide before?"). The more frequent the prior suicidal behavior the greater the risk.
      v. *History of mental illness.* Directly inquire about the individual's mental health history (e.g., "Have you ever had mental health care?"). Depression, schizophrenias, alcohol and substance abuse, trauma, and borderline personality disorders are particular concerns.
3. Consult with fellow staff members regarding risk assessment results. A school-based suicide risk assessment should never be completed without first consulting with colleagues.
4. Consult with community mental health professionals. These are typically the individuals to whom the suicidal student would be referred.

Table 5.1. (continued)

5. Use risk assessment information and consultation guidance to develop an action plan. Action plan options are as follows:
   a. *Extreme risk.* If the student has the means of his or her threatened suicide at hand and refuses to relinquish it, follow these procedures:
      i. Call the police.
      ii. Calm the student by talking and reassuring until the police arrive.
      iii. Continue to request that the student relinquish the means of the threatened suicide and try to prevent the student from harming himself or herself. When doing so, make certain that such requests do not place anyone else in danger.
      iv. Call the parents and inform them of the actions taken.
   b. *Crisis intervention referral.* If the student's risk of harming himself or herself is judged to be moderate to high (i.e., there is a probability of the student acting on suicidal thoughts, but the threat is not immediate), follow these procedures.
      i. Determine if the student's distress is the result of parent or caregiver abuse, neglect, or exploitation. If so, contact child protective services instead of a parent or caregiver.
      ii. Meet with the student's parents (or child protective services).
      iii. Make appropriate referrals.
      iv. Determine what to do if the parent or caregiver is unable or unwilling to assist with the suicidal crisis (e.g., call the police).
   c. *Low risk.* If the student's risk of harming himself or herself is judged to be low (i.e., although the student has thoughts of suicide, the risk assessment suggests a very low probability of engaging in a suicidal behavior), follow these procedures.
      i. Determine if the student's distress is the result of parent or caregiver abuse, neglect, or exploitation. If so, contact child protective services instead of a parent or caregiver.
      ii. Meet with the student's parents (or child protective services).
      iii. Make appropriate referrals.
6. When making referrals, protect the privacy of the student and family.
7. Follow up with the hospital or clinic to ensure that the student is receiving the appropriate care.

Note. From "Suicidal Ideation and Behaviors" (pp. 231–232), by S. E. Brock, J. Sandoval, and S. R. Hart. In G. G. Bear and K. M. Minke (Eds.), *Children's Needs III: Understanding and Addressing the Developmental Needs of Children, 2006*, Bethesda, MD: National Association of School Psychologists. Copyright 2006 by the National Association of School Psychologists. Adapted with permission.

someone's head; saying "Once I get through with you, you are going to wish you had never been born"). Possessing a weapon is also presumed to be a threat unless it is clearly indicated otherwise (e.g., bringing a knife to slice food for lunch). All threats should be reported verbatim so that the team can accurately assess the severity of the threat.

After the threat is reported, the threat assessment team leader will evaluate the threat by interviewing the student and witnesses about the exact threat made, the context surrounding it,

Table 5.2. Principles of Threat Assessment

1. Recognize that targeted violence is not random or spontaneous, but the result of an understandable process.
2. Consider the individual who made the threat, the situation, the setting, and the individual who is the target.
3. Keep an investigative, skeptical mind-set.
4. Focus on facts and behaviors, not personality traits.
5. Use information from multiple sources.
6. Differentiate between *making* a threat (statement intending harm) and *posing* a threat (likelihood of causing harm).

Note. Primary source *Threat Assessment in Schools: A Guide to Managing Threatening Situations and to Creating Safe School Climates,* by R. A. Fein, F. Vossekuil, W. S. Pollack, R. Borum, W. Modzeleski, and M. Reddy, 2002, Washington, DC: U.S. Secret Service and U.S. Department of Education. This report is in the public domain.

and perceptions of the meaning of the threat. The determination is then made about the student's intention to carry out the threat by deciding whether the threat is transient or substantive. Transient threats are often rhetorical remarks or temporary expressions of anger or frustration that can usually be resolved through an apology or clarification on the scene or in the office (Cornell et al., 2005). In some cases, this should be followed up by administering a consequence or providing interventions, as needed. In contrast, a substantive threat is one that poses at least some risk that the student will carry out the threat, evidenced by the expressed intent to injure someone beyond

Table 5.3. Key Questions to Ask Regarding the Student Making the Threat

1. What are the student's motives or goals?
2. Have there been any communications of the intent to attack?
3. Does the student have inappropriate interest in weapons, violence, or other attacks?
4. Has the student exhibited attack-related behaviors, such as devising a plan, obtaining weapons, or casing sites?
5. Does the student have the capacity (i.e., time, ability, desire, and opportunity) to carry out the attack?
6. Is there evidence of hopelessness or despair?
7. Does the student have a trusting relationship with at least one adult?
8. Is violence perceived as a way to solve a problem? What are the peer influences?
9. Are the student's words consistent with his or her actions?
10. Are others concerned about this student?
11. What circumstances might trigger violence in this student?

Note. Primary source *Threat Assessment in Schools: A Guide to Managing Threatening Situations and to Creating Safe School Climates,* by R. A. Fein, F. Vossekuil, W. S. Pollack, R. Borum, W. Modzeleski, and M. Reddy, 2002, Washington, DC: U.S. Secret Service and U.S. Department of Education. This report is in the public domain.

Figure 5.1. Steps in the threat assessment process.

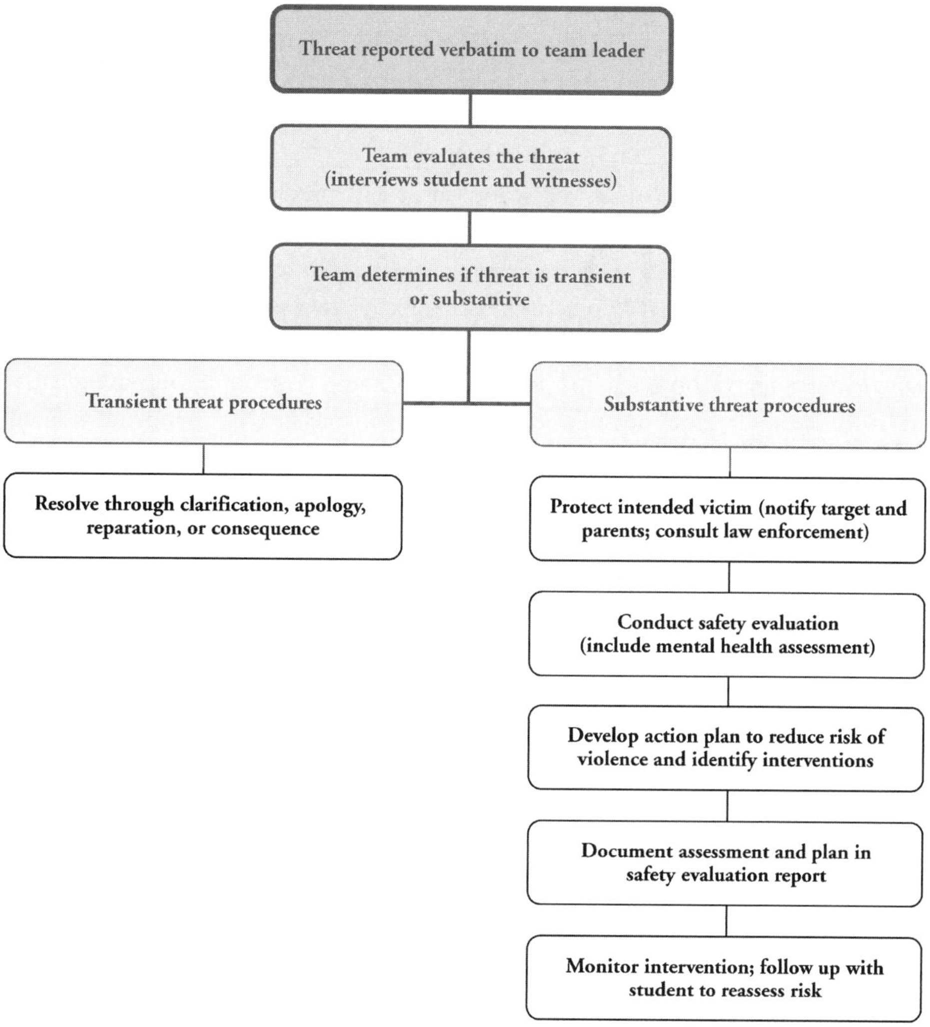

Note. Adapted from *Essential Core Knowledge Regarding Threat Assessment and Threat Management in the Schools,* by D. Cornell et al., 2005, Bethesda, MD: NASP. Copyright 2005 by the National Association of School Psychologists. Adapted with permission of the authors. See also *Guidelines for Responding to Student Threats of Violence,* by D. Cornell & P. Sheras, 2006, Longmont, CO: Sopris West.

the immediate situation. Types of information to consider also include the age of the student, the credibility of the witnesses' stories, and the discipline history of the student. Some indicators of substantive threats include a specific plan (either verbal or written), a threat that has been repeated over time, or the recruitment of an accomplice or accomplices.

A substantive threat prompts the involvement of the threat assessment team, who will conduct a safety evaluation. The school-based mental health professional conducts the mental health assessment, which includes a student interview reviewing the threat and the student's relationship with the victims. The interview may include questions about stress and situational factors; mental health symptoms; access to means to commit a violent act, including opportunity, ability, and desire; previous delinquent behavior; experiences of victimization; and coping and strengths. In addition, parents should be interviewed to ask about their knowledge of the threat, current stressors, recent behavior of the child, school functioning, peer relationships and experience of bullying, history of delinquent behavior, access to weapons, and willingness to assist in a safety plan (Cornell et al., 2005).

In the case of substantive threats, the school must take precautions to protect the intended victim by warning the student and his or her parents. It is prudent for schools to consult with law enforcement regarding the best way to protect the victim and to respond to any legal considerations. It is also essential to determine the appropriate intervention for the student who made the threat, in the form of a carefully documented and monitored safety plan. This plan may include increasing supervision (e.g., not leaving the student alone or having designated "daily check-ins" with the student), removing access to means of violence (e.g., removing weapons from the home), developing a behavioral plan, and implementing problem-solving skills training or anger coping therapy (Halikias, 2005; Cornell et al., 2005).

Threat assessment has not been subjected to rigorous empirical study, although Cornell et al. (2004) field-tested this approach in 35 schools and tracked what happened after the threat assessment procedure was implemented. They concluded that threat assessment was a safe and effective procedure, based on the fact that the threats were not carried out, and there was the same or improved behavior and relationship between the student making the threat and the intended target.

Although suicide and violence threat assessment procedures have been presented separately, there is a close relationship between other- and self-directed violence (Evans, Marte, Betts, & Silliman, 2001; Nickerson & Slater, 2008; Swahn et al., 2008). This suggests that when a student presents as being at risk for either violence toward others or suicidal behavior, it is prudent for the practitioner to conduct both a violence threat assessment *and* a suicide risk assessment (Nickerson & Slater, 2008) to ensure that the needs of the student are met in a comprehensive manner.

IMMEDIATE RESPONSE ELEMENTS OF A CRISIS PLAN

The response components of a crisis plan are critical to minimizing traumatic impact. A well-developed crisis plan and consistent practice by a school crisis team help ensure a rapid and organized response. The plan should contain the following crisis response elements: (a) instructions on activating the crisis response protocol; (b) instructions on how to contact law enforcement, response agencies, and parents; (c) de-escalation strategies to lower crisis-related dangers; (d) development of resources to respond to psychological needs; (e) instructions on communicating with staff during a crisis event; and (f) instructions on communicating with parents.

1. *Activating a crisis response protocol.* The response protocol needs to be initiated during the impact phase of a crisis. The first determination any leader must make is whether a crisis is occurring or imminent, as "without the recognition of a problem, efforts to prevent or respond to

the problem cannot be undertaken" (Cornell & Sheras, 1998, p. 297). In a crisis situation, it is easy for arguments to develop over who decides when a situation requires a response. Thus, a crisis plan should clearly specify who will initiate the response and under what circumstances, how to verify crisis facts, how law enforcement and response agencies will be notified, and how the crisis will be announced (e.g., fire alarm, public address system).

2. *Contacting law enforcement, agencies, and parents.* School staff members should be aware of the protocol for contacting law enforcement agencies (i.e., who calls 911 and under what circumstances). For example, when calling 911, do callers need to dial 9-911 or just 911? Who has the authority to contact support agencies and ask for assistance? How will parents be notified of a crisis event and directed regarding procedures to follow to reunite with their children?

3. *De-escalating the threat.* One of the best de-escalation strategies is to quickly and efficiently activate a crisis response plan. De-escalation strategies to minimize the threat are described in Table 5.4.

4. *Providing crisis intervention and responding to psychological needs.* School crisis teams need to be prepared to deliver a continuum of crisis intervention services such as that advocated within the PREPaRE model. Developing a MOU between schools and school districts and other mental health care providers can help clarify the parameters of that collaboration (see chapter 3 for a sample MOU; section 4 gives more information on the specific crisis interventions that schools should be prepared to offer).

5. *Communicating with staff.* The crisis response plan should also include procedures for conducting staff meetings, both before and after school. For example, if a student is killed in a car accident over the weekend, a staff meeting should be held both to assess how staff members are coping with the crisis event and to provide information on how staff members can support their students and each other. Substitute teachers and support staff should be included in these meetings.

6. *Communicating with parents and other key stakeholders.* During times of crisis, parents, school staff members, and school crisis team members need to be regularly informed of changes in schedules, informed about available support, and given assurances of safety and security. Thus, the crisis plan should include provisions for such communications. It may include samples of notes to be sent home to parents, press release templates, as well as phone trees and other strategies that are available in a given school community.

LONG-TERM RECOVERY ELEMENTS OF A CRISIS PLAN

With appropriate crisis response and interventions, students and school staff members will be able to return to a normal school routine. For most, this will happen relatively quickly and without formal mental health intervention. However, for some students, crisis recovery following some crisis events will be a more involved process. Thus, the crisis plan should also take longer-term recovery issues into account. Specific issues to be addressed in the crisis plan include (a) collaboration with community-based emergency response personnel, agencies, and parents; (b) instructions on how to access short-term and long-term physical and emotional support; (c) care for the caregiver (i.e., support for the needs of the crisis responder); and (d) evaluation of the crisis plan.

Table 5.4. Strategies for De-Escalating a Threat

1. Secure the physical building. Immediately secure outside doors and passageways inside the building, as stated in specified response protocol.
2. Activate triage procedures to address medical needs. Have a school nurse, if available, administer first aid until emergency response personnel arrive; if no school nurse is on-site, activate other CPR- or first-aid-trained staff.
3. Initiate traffic control measures, ensuring clear passage for response personnel.
4. Get the "go-kit" and building blueprints. Pass out supplies to crisis team members to fulfill duties.
5. Activate evacuation plans or move students to alternate shelters. Contact district transportation if buses are needed.
6. Verify students' whereabouts and take attendance. Activate attendance protocol to account for all staff and students.
7. Activate the reunification plan. Communicate with parents and caregivers via e-mail, phone chains, media, or other specified method regarding the reunification site and identification that will be required to pick up their child.
8. Activate triage procedures to address psychological needs. As soon as physical safety is ensured, assess the need for mental health interventions.
9. Screen volunteers for credentials and experience (this should have been done in advance through collaboration with support agencies); also use the parent–teacher organization for support and to help provide needs (e.g., food for staff, translation services, cultural brokers).
10. Communicate with staff, parents, media, and other stakeholders. Use a variety of communication methods to share information regarding the structure of the school day, including activities and support services available to assist with recovery.

Collaboration With Community-Based Emergency Response Personnel, Agencies, and Parents

In the event of police involvement, the school and district need to maintain regular contact with the police incident commander to receive updated, accurate, and verified information that can then be relayed to school staff members, parents, and as indicated, the media. Monitoring signs of posttraumatic stress reactions and other emotional disorders in students and staff, informing the parents and the community of new information, and highlighting services available are critical to restoring security and safety and providing support services.

Short- and Long-Term Support

The crisis plan should include provisions for short-term support, which can include restoring the physical plant and school community as soon as possible to help provide a sense of structure and routine. The plan should acknowledge that regular instruction may need to be suspended for a temporary period, but it also should emphasize the need to return to learning and routine as quickly as possible. Crisis intervention for all school community members, plus ongoing monitoring of crisis reactions, should be considered. Contingencies must provide for extra substitute teachers to help those teachers who are most affected and struggling with their own coping challenges. In addition, referral procedures should be available so that teachers can get help for students in need of extra support. The crisis plan should include a list of services provided by community-based agencies and private practitioners.

The plan should also consider issues associated with funerals or memorial services, anniversaries, and the fear of a subsequent crisis. Students, teachers, and families may need guidance and support regarding funerals and memorials. The crisis plan should establish rules regarding in-school memorials to ensure they are appropriate and helpful.

Care for the Caregiver

A caregiver is anyone (including parents and school staff) who is caring for potentially traumatized individuals. Including considerations for caregivers in the school crisis plan is critical, as 90% of school psychologists surveyed by Bolnik and Brock (2005) reported having experienced at least one physical, emotional, behavioral, cognitive, or work performance reaction to their school intervention work. More information on caring for the caregiver is presented in chapter 18.

Evaluation

Evaluating the crisis plan is necessary to improve and ensure its ongoing success in developing a safe school. In one survey that addressed crisis response evaluation, 48% of the respondents reported that evaluations occurred following a crisis, 25% reported that evaluations occurred periodically, 17% reported that evaluations occurred once a year, and 6% said evaluations took place twice a year (Adamson & Peacock, 2007). More information on examining the effectiveness of a school crisis response is presented in chapter 17.

CULTURAL CONSIDERATIONS

Annandale (2007) completed a study in which 40 sets of state crisis planning materials were reviewed for the presence of cultural considerations. Three cultural sensitivity themes emerged as the most frequently reported topics in state planning materials: (a) programs for working with students with mental and physical disabilities; (b) how to tap into community-based resources representing diverse cultural groups; and (c) cross-cultural language and communication issues. The study also reported that information related to cross-cultural sensitivity was typically embedded in the document, but cultural considerations were often not directly identified. Overall, unlike other topics such as violence, bomb threats, media, and suicide, cross-cultural issues related to diversity did not appear to be a high priority in state-suggested and mandated crisis planning materials.

Crisis planning needs to address cultural considerations, including but not limited to the diverse languages spoken within the school community. During a crisis event those students who do not speak fluent English will not understand directions being given, nor will parents understand communication after an event. To meet the school community's diverse needs, the plan will need to identify community-based resources such as translators and cultural brokers. Predicting potential needs and understanding common expressions in advance (such as different cultural groups' expressions of suffering and pain and responses to death) help the crisis team avoid over- or under-identifying students for support when their reactions are considered to be culturally acceptable.

CONCLUSION

Crisis planning can be an overwhelming task, considering all that is involved. The multidisciplinary team, following best practice guidelines covered in this chapter, should begin by setting two or three crisis goals to improve the existing school or district plan, and then implement these well, rather than try to do too much at once. Once those goals are met, then another two to three goals can be chosen, to continue working toward well-developed comprehensive plans that encompass prevention, preparedness, response, and recovery while at the same time addressing the unique needs of the school setting.

Chapter 6

EXERCISING SCHOOL CRISIS PLANS

Crisis prevention and preparedness involve not simply developing crisis teams and plans, but also practicing them so that everyone knows what to expect in the event of a crisis situation. An exercise simulates a crisis and requires team members to respond in a way that calls on them to practice their crisis team roles. The purpose of an exercise is to promote preparedness by testing plans and training teams (Federal Emergency Management Agency [FEMA], 2007b). Exercising crisis plans is valuable for a number of reasons, including those listed in Table 6.1 and discussed in this chapter.

According to the U.S. Department of Homeland Security (2007a), well-designed and well-executed school crisis exercises serve the following purposes:

- Assessing and validating policies, plans, procedures, training, equipment, and interagency agreements;
- Clarifying roles and responsibilities;
- Improving interagency coordination and communications;
- Identifying gaps in resources;
- Identifying opportunities for improvement. (p. 1)

First, these exercises identify gaps in plans (particularly with regard to preparedness, organization, training, and equipment) that need to be adjusted or replaced before they are implemented. Finding actual or potential flaws in the plan as a result of conducting these exercises provides an opportunity to correct or modify the plan. Although finding errors and modifying plans are time-consuming, this investment pays off in the long run. Crisis exercises also inform resource allocation, including training and equipment purchases, which in turn increase preparedness, affect policy or program decisions, and become the basis for future exercises (School Safety Alliances, 2004; U.S. Department of Homeland Security [DHS], 2006, 2007a, 2007b, 2007c).

Special thanks to Erica Young for her contribution to this chapter.

Table 6.1. Value of Exercising School Crisis Plans and Teams

1. Enables individual team members to practice their roles and gain experience.
2. Improves the school and district teams' capacity and effectiveness for managing crises.
3. Reveals planning gaps and difficulties with implementation.
4. Reveals gaps in resources and resource distribution.
5. Provides the opportunity to improve organizational coordination and communication.
6. Clarifies roles and responsibilities, and in doing so may prompt reassignment or retraining.
7. Assesses individual and team performance.
8. Gains school district and community acknowledgment and support for crisis planning and team development efforts.
9. Satisfies state and/or local regulatory requirements that may require evidence that the school district has conducted a formal, structured test of the crisis plan and team.

Note. Adapted from *Conducting Effective Tabletops, Drills and Exercises* (adapted from the Federal Emergency Management Agency's *IS139: Exercise Design*), by M. Taylor and C. Utzinger, 2006, U.S. Department of Education, Emergency Response and Crisis Management Training, Santa Monica, CA, September 2006.

The Virginia Department of Emergency Management's *School Crisis Management Exercise Development Guide* (2001) noted that the most practical, efficient, and cost-effective way for agencies to prepare for disasters and crises is by performing exercises. Exercises build responder proficiency and increase coordination between schools and community-based emergency response agencies. Crisis exercises are invaluable tools for putting the ideas and concepts developed by the district or school crisis team into a more realistic and dynamic context (Taylor, 2006).

According to the U.S. Department of Homeland Security (2007a): "Plans, training, equipment, and the capabilities they represent are validated through exercises" (p. 2). Training and exercises should allow the team to test and practice the key elements outlined in the school or school district's crisis plan. This practice should be built into the school calendar and reviewed on a regular basis. As discussed later in this chapter, crisis teams may implement role-play exercises, simulations, or crisis drills to foster education and understanding of procedures (Brock, Sandoval, & Lewis, 2001; Klingman, 1996; Pitcher & Poland, 1992).

This chapter begins by discussing some basic exercise considerations. It then examines the Homeland Security Exercise and Evaluation Program (HSEEP), which is designed to provide common policies and program guidance to establish a national standard for crisis plan exercises. Finally, it reviews the various types of emergency exercises that a school crisis team might consider, as well as the follow-up analytical activities to these exercises.

BASIC CONSIDERATIONS

Several considerations are important to exercising school crisis plans and teams. The PREPaRE model follows many of the U.S. DHS (2006, 2007a, 2007b, 2007c) suggested policies and procedures; however, individuals who are new to school crisis exercise planning may find many of

Table 6.2. Basic Considerations in Crisis Exercise Development

- *Assessing training needs.* The assessment include analyzing threats and hazards, selecting appropriate exercise types, assessing system capabilities, and conducting preexercise rehearsals.
- *Defining the scope.* Limits should reflect the highest priorities that can be realistically addressed in one exercise.
- *Writing a statement of purpose.* The statement should include a comprehensive preexercise notification designed to obtain support from school superintendent, staff, parents, and students. The statement should cover collaboration with participating personnel and organizations, a schedule for the exercise and planning milestones, logistics (e.g., facilities, equipment, and support), development and organization of evaluation teams, and steps to coordinate orientations and training sessions. It should also offer a concise list of exercise objectives that are simple, clear, specific, and measureable.
- *Composing a "crisis event" narrative.* A brief narrative description is used to provide background information about the emergency and will help participants approach the exercise as if it were a real situation.
- *Providing crisis event details.* Exercises can be made more real by using exercise enhancements or props (e.g., maps, actors, computers, and radios).
- *Identifying expected actions.* The main purpose of any exercise is to elicit certain thoughts and actions in participants. The exercise also can be designed to elicit one or more expected actions from one or more participants. For example, in a simulated school shooting exercise involving several students, the school nurse would be expected to (a) ascertain the urgency of the situation, (b) perform necessary first-aid procedures, (c) ask an adult or capable student to alert the administration about the situation, and (d) determine whether other students were in any immediate danger.
- *Preparing an evaluation plan and checklists.* An independent evaluator should develop an evaluation plan, which should include how exercise objectives and actions will be evaluated, monitored, and measured against plans and procedures.
- *Preparing messages and acknowledging problems.* In addition to conducting preexercise briefings, the team will plan postexercise evaluations, which include meetings and reviews, identification of the need for additional exercises and drills, and a final exercise report.

Note. From *School Crisis Management Exercise Development Guide*, by the Virginia Department of Emergency Management, July, 2001, Richmond, VA: Author. Copyright 2001 by the Virginia Department of Emergency Management. Adapted with permission. Retrieved December 4, 2008, from http://www.vaemergency.com/library/handbooks/schoolcrisisguide.pdf

the elements of the *School Crisis Management Exercise Development Guide* helpful in framing their work within the school setting (see Table 6.2; Virginia Department of Emergency Management, 2001). Although that document offers valuable information to the school-based crisis planning team, the work done by the U.S. DHS since 2001 has resulted in major technical and structural changes to methods of crisis exercise development. The PREPaRE model and other school-focused resources might make it easier for school personnel to understand and use the Department of Homeland Security's HSEEP resources.

The HSEEP is a capabilities- and performance-based exercise program that provides a standardized methodology and terminology for exercise design, development, conduct, evaluation, and improvement planning. The program constitutes a national standard for all exercises. The HSEEP helps organizations use exercises to perform objective assessments of their capabilities so that strengths and areas for improvement are identified, corrected, and shared, as appropriate, prior to a real incident. In addition, crisis plan exercises can inform and involve all school personnel, as well as the broader school community, and be directed at specific preparedness targets.

First, the plan should include a way of informing others of the exercise. Prior to the implementation of any exercise, parents, the media, and other community-based agencies should be alerted to the date, time, and purpose of the planned exercise. Letting others know about these exercises helps avoid misunderstanding (and possible panic) as to what is happening. In some cases, a lack of information has resulted in the community mistakenly believing that a real crisis was taking place. Obviously, such misunderstandings create unnecessary anxiety and negative public relations. If possible, the information that is relayed should be available in the languages represented in the community (Athey & Moody-Williams, 2003).

Second, the plan should involve all school personnel in the exercise. Well-designed training exercises should be made available to the staff members at all schools within a district. Doing so not only is cost-effective, but also helps to ensure system-wide consistency. Furthermore, involving all school personnel supports the development of multiple hierarchical crisis teams (at the school, district, and community levels).

Third, the plan should ensure collaboration with the broader school community. Selection of the type of exercise to practice should follow a careful analysis of the needs of the school system in consultation with its community and first responder partners. Challenges often arise when multiple agencies respond to a crisis, so it is important to include community participants in crisis plan exercises (Baisden & Quarantelli, 1981; Blom, 1986; Kartez & Kelley, 1988; Raphael & Meldrum, 1993). Drills and exercises should be planned and implemented to teach all involved parties the best way to respond to emergency situations in varying contexts and circumstances (Johns & Keenan, 1997).

Fourth, the plan should identify specific preparedness targets. Exercising crisis plans typically targets specific elements of the plan. A fundamental step in deciding what portion of the written plan to test would involve selecting scenarios that have relevance to the school system and its broader school community. These elements should be identified and selected before the exercise.

Fifth, the final component of the exercise process is to objectively assess whether the drill or exercise conducted to test the targeted elements has been successful. Individuals with specific backgrounds should be selected to evaluate a given crisis exercise (e.g., law enforcement personnel should be involved in the evaluation of exercises designed to address the school's response to violence).

HOMELAND SECURITY EXERCISE AND EVALUATION PROGRAM

The Homeland Security Exercise and Evaluation Program (HSEEP) was designed to provide common exercise policies and program guidance to establish a national standard for exercises (U.S. DHS, 2007a). This nationally recognized program provides standardized policy, methodology, and terminology for exercise design, development, conduct, evaluation, and plan improvement. The HSEEP reflects lessons learned and best practices from existing exercise programs, and can be modified and adapted to cover the full range of crisis events (e.g., natural disasters, terrorist attacks, or technological disasters). The five phases of crisis exercise management of the HSEEP, referred to as the exercise cycle, are summarized in Table 6.3. Though the HSEEP is offered as a national standard, to date, no systematic assessment of the application or effectiveness of the HSEEP has been published.

According to the HSEEP, establishing a foundation for designing, developing, conducting, and evaluating an exercise is critical to exercise success. This foundation creates a solid starting point from which crisis team leaders can develop and implement exercises. For schools to build such an exercise foundation, they must create a base of support, identify an exercise planning team, develop a project management timeline, and schedule planning conferences (U.S. DHS, 2007a).

According to the HSEEP, one of the most vital factors for implementing a successful exercise is skilled planning and conduct by the exercise planning team. This team is responsible for the exercise foundation, design, development, conduct, and evaluation. Table 6.4 lists the principles that should guide exercise planning teams (U.S. DHS, 2007b).

The HSEEP describes the design and development phase as building on the exercise foundation by identifying objectives, designing the scenario, creating documentation, coordinating

Table 6.3. The Crisis Exercise Cycle

1. *Foundation.* Create a base of support (i.e., get principals, administrators, and other officials on board); develop a project management timeline and establish milestones; identify an exercise planning team; schedule group planning meetings.
2. *Design and development.* Identify objectives; design the situation; create documentation; coordinate logistics; plan appropriate exercise behavior; select an evaluation method and method for improving the plan.
3. *Conduct.* Perform setup, briefings, facilitation, control, evaluation, and wrap-up activities.
4. *Evaluation.* Conduct formal postexercise evaluation to identify areas of strengths and weaknesses with regard to preparedness.
5. *Improvement planning.* Following the exercise evaluation stage, identify and assign corrective actions (based on areas of the exercise that need improvement) to responsible persons, with due dates. Track these actions through implementation, and then validate during subsequent exercises.

Note. Adapted from *Homeland Security Exercise and Evaluation Program: Vol. 1* (pp. 3–4), by U.S. Department of Homeland Security, February, 2007a, Washington, DC: Author.

Table 6.4. Exercise Planning Team Principles

- *Organized structure.* Teams are most effective when they adhere to an organized structure.
- *Project management.* Management responsibilities include ensuring the identification, development, and management of critical and supportive activities; frequent communication about project status; and use of management plans and timelines.
- *Clearly defined roles and responsibilities.* Members should be aware of their individual responsibilities as well as those of the entire team.
- *Functional area skills.* The team should ensure that a realistic and challenging scenario is chosen and that the entity running the exercise (e.g., the school) has the appropriate resources and capabilities to manage the situation.
- *Leadership.* Leadership principles include those that address mentoring, motivation, discipline, personnel, and time management.
- *Teamwork.* Members should be encouraged to strive toward group and common goals.

Note. Adapted from *Homeland Security Exercise and Evaluation Program: Vol. II* (pp. 1–2), by U.S. Department of Homeland Security, February, 2007b, Washington, DC: Author.

logistics, planning conduct, and selecting the focus for evaluation and improvement planning. Identifying crisis exercise tasks and objectives is a key element of design and development. Well-defined objectives lay the groundwork for scenario development, guide individual organizations' objective development, inform exercise evaluation criteria, and integrate various agencies' efforts toward common goals to prevent duplication of effort and to focus support on exercise priorities (U.S. DHS, 2007b).

Exercise program managers working with schools should identify a wide range of stakeholders to ensure that exercises meet as many as possible of the school's preparedness needs. Including a variety of stakeholders also helps ensure that exercises will be comprehensive, covering the full range of response disciplines, with the goal of making these exercises more realistic and applicable to crisis situations. When identifying stakeholders, crisis team leaders (e.g., incident commanders) should consider individuals, agencies, and organizations who would be involved in a crisis response, including (a) individuals with administrative responsibilities that are relevant to the exercise; (b) representatives from all first-responder disciplines to be included in exercise training sessions; (c) representatives from volunteer or nongovernmental organizations, such as the American Red Cross; and (d) representatives from the private sector. After stakeholders have been identified, program managers should create a database that includes each stakeholder's contact information, areas of expertise, and previous exercise training and experience (U.S. DHS, 2007b).

According to the HSEEP, a well-designed scenario provides a story line that makes the exercise vivid and compelling. Hazards selected for an exercise should be realistic and representative of the actual vulnerabilities found in a particular school community. Documents used during crisis exercises, which are developed in advance, should include scenario narratives, outlines of participant roles, procedures and execution of exercises, a timeline of expected actions, a reference sheet for quick questions and answers, and an exercise evaluation sheet. Exercise logistics also need to be addressed. For example, discussion-based exercises require attention to details, such as the availability of comfortable meeting rooms, refreshments, audiovisual equipment, facilitation and note-taking supplies, badges and table tents, and direction signs. Critical steps in exercise conduct include setup; briefings; management of facilitators, controllers, evaluators, players, and actors; and wrap-up and evaluation activities (U.S. DHS, 2007b).

Evaluation is a key element of any exercise. After-action discussions are often used to conduct evaluations with the exercise players; debriefings are used for facilitators, controllers, and evaluators. An after-action discussion is performed in each section of the Incident Command System (ICS) by the individuals who evaluate the exercise. This activity occurs immediately after an exercise takes place and gives crisis team members the opportunity to provide immediate feedback. After-action discussions enable evaluators to capture events while they are still fresh in team members' minds to determine their levels of satisfaction with the exercise and to identify any issues, concerns, or proposed improvements that can be made to the exercise. A debriefing, on the other hand, takes place in a more formal environment in which crisis planners, facilitators, controllers, and evaluators review and provide feedback on the exercise. Unlike the after-action discussions, debriefings may be held immediately after, or within a few days of, the exercise (U.S. DHS, 2007c).

The final phase is improvement planning. During this phase, members of the crisis team convert lessons learned from the exercise into concrete, measurable steps. The result is improved response capabilities and a plan that has been adjusted based on the review evaluation of the crisis exercise (U.S. DHS, 2007c).

The Department of Homeland Security is able to provide assistance to schools to help them implement effective exercises. For example, states receive an annual allocation of grant funds, and they are allowed to use some of these funds to strengthen their state and local prevention and intervention capabilities through crisis response exercises. More information about the Homeland Security Grant Program can be found at http://www.dhs.gov/xlibrary/assets/grants_st-local_fy07.pdf.

Independent study may be available through the Federal Emergency Management Agency's Emergency Management Institute (EMI). EMI is working to integrate the HSEEP guidance and methodology into a variety of its existing exercise training courses. More information about this initiative can be found at http://training.fema.gov/EMIWeb. In addition, many states offer exercise design, conduct, evaluation, and program management courses through state-directed training centers or in collaboration with federal agencies. For example, the California Office of Emergency Services' Readiness Program includes several exercise-related training courses for members of California's homeland security community (California Governor's Office of Emergency Services, 2007). The Department of Homeland Security also provides technical assistance to help organizations solve problems and develop creative approaches to crisis preparedness.

TYPES AND SELECTION OF SCHOOL CRISIS TEAM EXERCISES

Five types of exercises for school crisis response training and practice are summarized in Table 6.5. These include two discussion-based exercises (orientation seminars and tabletop exercises)

Table 6.5. Crisis Exercise Categories

Category	Objectives	Examples	Parties Involved
	Discussion-Based Exercises		
Orientation seminar	• Introduces new programs, policies, or plans • Reviews roles and responsibilities • Conceptualizes equipment needed for crisis response • Serves as starting point for other exercises	• Staff development trainings • Informal group discussions	• School staff • All involved agencies (e.g., police, fire, and disaster agencies)
Tabletop exercises	• Allows low-stress discussion of plans and procedures • Provides an opportunity to resolve questions of coordination and responsibility	• Written scenarios • Active shooter • Severe weather • Major power outage	• School staff • Public safety personnel
	Operations-Based Exercises		
Emergency drill	• Allows practice and perfection of emergency response • Concentrates the efforts of a single function • Provides field experience with new procedures and equipment	• Fire • Lockdown • Evacuation • Reverse evacuation • Shelter-in-place	• School staff • Students
Functional exercises	• Simulates a real emergency under high-stress conditions • Tests coordination among various functions and outside response agencies	• Public safety exercises with responding agencies • Medical emergency exercises with outside resources	• School staff • Students • Public safety personnel • Crisis response agencies
Full-scale exercises	• Tests a community's total response capability • Tests drills as close to reality as possible, using real equipment and agency personnel	• Large community emergency exercises	• All internal and external emergency management stakeholders, including students

Note. Adapted from *Homeland Security Exercise and Evaluation Program: Vol. 1* (pp. 10–12), by U.S. Department of Homeland Security, February, 2007a, Washington, DC: Author.

and three operations-based exercises (specific emergency drills, functional exercises, and full-scale exercises).

Discussion-based orientation exercises are useful in familiarizing participants with current school crisis plans, policies, and procedures. These exercises also allow school crisis team leaders the opportunity to develop new plans with the input of others who are involved. By comparison, operations-based exercises serve to validate plans, policies, and procedures; clarify roles and responsibilities; and identify gaps in resources (U.S. DHS, 2007b).

Whereas discussion-based exercises are generally used as a starting point in the progressively more complex process of exercising school crisis plans, operations-based exercises are effective for evaluating group problem-solving strategies, personnel contingencies, group message interpretations, information processing and sharing, interagency coordination, and achievement of specific objectives or goals (U.S. DHS, 2007b).

From guidance offered by the Department of Education's Readiness and Emergency Management for Schools (REMS) Technical Assistance Center (2006a), one recommendation is that school districts start with simple exercises (orientations) and work their way toward more complex exercises. Simple exercises are discussion-based, and more complex exercises are operations-based.

Orientation Seminars

This first type of exercise introduces participants to the school crisis plan and typically lasts from 1 to 2 hours (Taylor, 2006). The purpose of an orientation is to familiarize school crisis team members with crisis response roles, responsibilities, plans, procedures, and equipment. Orientations can also resolve questions about coordination and assignment of responsibilities. When these seminars include first responders, as well as school staff, such training contributes to the development of an effective comprehensive crisis response plan (U.S. Department of Education, 2006a). The elements of a typical orientation meeting are listed in Table 6.6.

Workshops are similar to seminars, but they involve more school crisis team interaction and a greater focus on producing a product. The following activities generally take place during workshops: "(a) collecting or sharing information; (b) obtaining new or different perspectives; (c) testing new ideas, processes, policies, and procedures; (d) training groups to perform coordinated activities; (e) applying problem-solving approaches to complex issues; (f) obtaining consensus; and/or (g) building teams" (U.S. DHS, 2007b, p. 30).

To be effective, workshops need to focus on a specific issue, and the desired outcome, product, or goal must be clearly defined. According to the U.S. DHS (2007b) workshop objectives might include the following:

- Identify issues that may arise when developing a collaborative plan for use by entities that have not previously worked together.
- Define new regional boundaries.
- Determine program or plan objectives.

Table 6.6. Elements of an Orientation Meeting

- Discuss a critical crisis topic or problem in a group setting.
- Introduce something new, such as policies and plans, the Incident Command System (ICS), and the Emergency Operations Center (EOC).
- Explain existing plans to new people, such as newly hired school staff members who need an explanation of the EOC, ICS, etc.).
- Introduce a cycle of exercises that prepare participants for success in more complex exercises.
- Motivate people to participate in subsequent exercises.
- Emphasize the emergency management link to school mission and community responsibility.

Note. Adapted from *Conducting Effective Tabletops, Drills and Exercises* (adapted from the Federal Emergency Management Agency's *IS139: Exercise Design*), by M. Taylor and C. Utzinger, 2006, U.S. Department of Education, Emergency Response and Crisis Management Training, Santa Monica, CA, September 2006.

- Develop an exercise scenario.
- Determine evaluation elements or performance standards. (p. 30)

Although topics and goals may vary across workshops, according to the U.S. DHS (2007b) all workshops share a number of attributes, including the following:

- They are conducted in a low-stress environment.
- They use a no-fault forum.
- Information is conveyed using a number of different instructional techniques, including lectures, multimedia presentations, panel discussions, case study discussions, expert testimony, decision support tools, or any combination thereof.
- They use facilitated, working breakout sessions.
- Goal-oriented discussions take place with an identifiable product in mind.
- There are no real-time "clock" constraints (p. 30).

Workshops generally begin with a presentation of the session's background and purpose. The agenda, including specific activities alongside expected outcomes, is also discussed at the beginning of the workshop. After the presentation, crisis team members break into groups and engage in focused discussions of specific issues. These breakout sessions are opportunities for participants to increase their interaction with issues that are relevant to their functional areas (e.g., for school psychologists to better understand their mental health crisis response roles). Ideally, breakout sessions are facilitated by someone with both subject matter knowledge and facilitation experience. Whereas one large room is sufficient for workshops, smaller rooms, such as classrooms, are most effective for breakout sessions (U.S. DHS, 2007b).

Tableto Exercises

This type of exercise helps school crisis team members identify their roles and responsibilities in different scenarios and can last from 1 to 4 hours (Taylor, 2006). Tabletop exercises analyze a crisis event in an informal, stress-reduced environment. They provide participants with an emergency scenario to analyze and increase their awareness of the roles and responsibilities of individuals who need to respond to, stabilize, and terminate the crisis, and to help others recover. Tabletop exercises are designed to prompt a constructive discussion about existing school crisis response plans as participants identify, investigate, and resolve issues (U.S. Department of Education, 2006a). Participants are encouraged to discuss issues in depth and to use slow-paced problem solving, in contrast to the rapid and spontaneous decision making that occurs under actual or simulated crisis situations. Basic components and general features of tabletop exercises are listed in Table 6.7.

There are two categories of tabletop exercises: basic and advanced. Basic exercises involve school crisis team members using their knowledge and skills to solve problems presented by the exercise leader. The problems are then discussed by the team, and the leader summarizes the resolutions. Advanced exercises involve delivery of pre-scripted messages to school crisis team members that alter the original situation. The leader introduces problems in the form of a written

Table 6.7. Components and Features of Tabletop Exercises

Components

- Low-stress discussion of coordination and policy within the school or between the school and other agencies
- Good practice environment for problem solving
- Opportunity for key agencies and stakeholders to become acquainted with one another, their interrelated roles, and their respective responsibilities
- Good preparation for a functional exercise

General Features

- Incorporate problem solving
- Allow senior officials to familiarize themselves with critical issues related to their responsibilities
- Employ conditions of a specific scenario
- Examine personnel contingencies
- Examine group message interpretation
- Allow participants to share information
- Assess interagency coordination
- Achieve limited or specific objectives
- Prepare participants for more complex exercises

Note. Adapted from *Homeland Security Exercise and Evaluation Program: Vol. II* (pp. 31–32), by U.S. Department of Homeland Security, February, 2007b, Washington, DC: Author.

message, simulated phone call, videotape, text message, etc. Exercise participants then discuss issues raised by the simulated problem, and they apply appropriate plans and procedures to resolve the presenting issues. Tabletop exercises are conducive to either a breakout or plenary format.

Emergency Drills

Drills involve the practice of a specific school crisis response procedure and, depending on the type of drill, can last from 30 minutes to 2 hours (Taylor, 2006). The goal of these emergency drills is to practice aspects of the crisis response plan and prepare teams and participants for more extensive exercises in the future. Schools typically conduct lockdown, fire, evacuation, reverse evacuation, duck-cover-hold, and shelter-in-place drills with students and staff to demonstrate the steps they should take in emergencies. The procedures as well as the responsibilities of all involved (i.e., students, teachers, staff, and emergency personnel) are addressed. These exercises may include local public safety agencies (U.S. Department of Education, 2006a). Additional descriptions of these specific types of drills are presented in Table 6.8. In addition to giving participants a chance to practice (and perfect) one aspect of the crisis plan, the emergency drill can also provide training with any new equipment, help in developing new policies or procedures, or allow practice to maintain current skills (Taylor).

Functional Exercises

Functional exercises are roundtable simulations of crisis events with realistic timelines (Taylor, 2006). These types of exercises can last from 3 to 8 hours and test one or more functions of a school's crisis response plan during an interactive, time-pressured, simulated event. Functional exercises are often conducted in a school district's emergency operations center. Participants are given directions by exercise controllers and simulators via telephones, radios, and televisions, and they must respond appropriately to the incidents as they arise. Independent evaluators candidly critique the exercise and the team's performance (U.S. Department of Education, 2006a). Functional exercises test several functions and exercise several agencies or departments without incurring the costs of a full-scale exercise. In addition, they test multiple functions of the school's or school district's crisis plan by simulating an incident in the most realistic manner possible short of moving resources to an actual site. Finally, they are highly interactive, moderately stressful, and require quick decision making (Taylor, 2006).

Roles in a functional exercise include (a) an exercise controller who manages and directs the exercise, (b) crisis team members or "players" who respond as they would in a real emergency, (c) crisis simulators or "actors" who assume external roles and deliver planned messages to the players, and (d) exercise evaluators who assess performance through observation (Taylor, 2006). The players should include the agency policy makers, as well as the crisis team coordinators and operational personnel who would direct school crisis response activities. The initiation of a functional exercise involves first gathering people where they would actually operate in an emergency and then seating players and crisis simulators in separate areas or rooms. The

Table 6.8. Emergency Drills: Types, Descriptions, and Related Crisis Events

Type of Drill	*Description*	*Related Crisis Event*
Lockdown	• Participants remain in the school building when the environment outside the school is threatening or when movement within the school building is judged to be unsafe. • Participants sit quietly in locked rooms positioned safely against a wall and away from windows and doors.	• Dangerous intruder in school building • Act of violence (e.g., stabbing, shooting, or assault) occurring somewhere in school building where the incident can be contained
Evacuation	• Participants leave an unsafe school building or facility to relocate at a predetermined setting away from the school grounds.	• Fire, bomb threat
Reverse evacuation	• Participants move from the school grounds into the school building. Reverse evacuation often leads to a lockdown or shelter-in-place procedure.	• Unsafe intruder on school grounds • Unsafe weather conditions, such as a tornado or severe storm
Duck-cover-hold	• Two procedures: ▪ Participants take cover under a nearby desk or table, making sure as much of their body as possible is under cover. Participants then cover their eyes by leaning their face against their arm. Participants hold on to the legs of the desk or table until drill or real event ceases. ▪ All participants move to the hallways of the first floor. Participants kneel on the ground and cover their face and head with both arms. Participants then drop their heads into their laps until the drill or real event ceases.	• Earthquake • Tornado • Nuclear weapon

Table 6.8. (continued)

Type of Drill	*Description*	*Related Crisis Event*
Shelter-in-place	• Participants move into a lockdown procedure, relocating to predetermined rooms on the first level of a school building that has minimal or no windows and vents. • Disaster kits are used (these contain nonperishable food, bottled water, battery-powered radio, first-aid supplies, batteries, duct tape, plastic sheeting, plastic garbage bags). • All windows and doors are sealed with duct tape and plastic sheeting. • Mechanical systems are turned off (e.g., fans, heating systems).	• Chemical, radiological, or biological weapons • Severe weather (e.g., hurricane, tornado)

Note. Adapted from *Emergency Management Institute Independent Study*, by the Federal Emergency Management Agency, March, 2003, Washington, DC: Author.

functional exercise makes use of these communication methods as a means of creating a realistic simulation to help engage the team's approach to problem solving the presented crisis scenario.

Full-Scale Exercises

The final and most elaborate, expensive, and time-consuming exercise is the full-scale exercise. These exercises are simulations of emergency situations, during which all necessary resources are actually deployed. Full-scale exercises can be as brief as a half day or can span multiple days (Taylor, 2006). The exercises evaluate the operational capabilities of school emergency management systems in a highly stressful environment that simulates actual conditions. Full-scale exercises test and evaluate most functions of the school crisis plan, including the mobilization of emergency personnel, equipment, and resources.

To design and conduct full-scale exercises, districts should collaborate with local public safety agencies. Exercise controllers (who could be school administrators or community-based disaster responders such as a fire chief) choose a scenario that is most likely to occur in the school community and involve all community stakeholders (e.g., police, fire, emergency medical response). Independent evaluators (who again could be either a school administrator or community-based disaster responder) conduct a postincident critique and develop an after-action report to identify issues that need to be corrected (U.S. Department of Education, 2006a). The goals of full-scale exercises are listed in Table 6.9.

Key points to remember about full-scale exercises are that they may require 1 to 1 ½ years to develop. Furthermore, completing a logical sequence of the orientation sessions, drills, and functional exercises prior to implementation is essential. To ensure that the full-scale exercise is not mistaken for a real crisis event, it is critical to involve media and parents on the scene of the exercise. Finally, the event to be simulated must be more than an isolated, rarely occurring event to ensure that the exercise offers some long-term value for the school system and the community (Taylor, 2006).

Selection of the Type of Exercise

To determine the types of exercises to conduct, the school crisis team should consider the types of risks or potential hazards that have a high probability of occurring in their community. In the preliminary discussions about conducting crisis exercises, the crisis team members could decide to practice some of the standard drills that school systems around the country already practice, including fire drills, lockdowns, shelter-in-place, and evacuation procedures. Districts that are vulnerable to certain natural disaster events could also conduct drills related to those potential hazards. Although predicting human-caused crises may be difficult, many naturally occurring disasters are characteristic of specific regions of the country. Among these are tornadoes, hurricanes, floods, wildfires, and earthquakes. Consideration of these potential crises will help the school crisis team in determining which drill or exercise is most appropriate.

Table 6.9. Goals of Full-Scale Crisis Exercises

1. Simulate a real event as closely as possible.
2. Evaluate the operational capability of emergency management systems in a highly stressful environment that simulates actual response conditions.
3. Coordinate the actions of several entities.
4. Test several emergency functions.
5. Activate the Incident Command System (ICS) and the Emergency Operations Center (EOC).
6. Create realistic learning exercises.
7. Use same personnel roles as the functional exercise, but now include simulated victims.

Note. Adapted from *Conducting Effective Tabletops, Drills and Exercises* (adapted from the Federal Emergency Management Agency's *IS139: Exercise Design*), by M. Taylor and C. Utzinger, 2006, U.S. Department of Education, Emergency Response and Crisis Management Training, Santa Monica, CA, September 2006.

EVALUATION AND ANALYSIS OF THE EXERCISE

Although emergency exercises promote understanding and growth, school crisis teams benefit most when postexercise evaluations are conducted after the exercise. All stakeholders, from the school district to the community emergency response agency, should participate in both the exercises and the postexercise evaluations. Follow-up evaluations attempt to capture key lessons learned from emergency response and make recommendations for improvements. Benefits include establishing a proactive management attitude, providing protection against litigation, and identifying areas for improvement (U.S. Department of Education, 2006a). Table 6.10 provides the key characteristics of postexercise evaluations.

The school crisis team must see the evaluation as an integral component of the exercise process. The team will consider when is the best time for this evaluation, which is not necessarily immediately after the exercise has concluded. In addition, it is important that a skilled facilitator

Table 6.10. Key Characteristics of Postexercise Evaluations

- Conducted immediately following the exercise.
- Include everyone who might potentially have responsibilities during crisis response.
- Engage the evaluators of the exercise.
- Have an assigned secretary to record exercise observations.
- Include a discussion of positive and negative outcomes.
- Allow time for participants to discuss their observations.
- Assess whether the exercise's goals and objectives were achieved.
- Create a postexercise evaluation report with steps for improvement.

Note. Adapted from "Emergency Exercises: An Effective Way to Validate School Safety Plans," by U.S. Department of Education REMS Technical Assistance Center, 2006a, ERCMExpress, *2*(3), 2.

Table 6.11. Steps of Postexercise Evaluation

1. Review exercise activity in terms of overall expectations.
2. Consider exercise goals and objectives. Were they specific and operationally defined?
3. Analyze completed outcomes. Did they achieve desired, expected, or unexpected results?
4. Analyze capacity to perform critical tasks. Were critical tasks achieved with existing resources?
5. Summarize exercise. Utilizing the information from items 1–4, generate a preliminary summary statement, specific to the exercise recently implemented.
6. Develop recommendations that can address the positive aspects of the current exercise and suggest specific improvements for each team member and partner participant.

Note. Adapted from "Emergency Exercises: An Effective Way to Validate School Safety Plans," by U.S. Department of Education REMS Technical Assistance Center, 2006a, ERCMExpress, *2*(3), 2–3.

run the postexercise evaluation and that the tension associated with this process must be constructive. The steps involved in a postexercise evaluation are presented in Table 6.11.

Finally, it is acknowledged that the literature pertaining to crisis management exercises and accountability measures (e.g., evacuation time, effectiveness of communication, proper distribution and use of resources) is lacking. Accountability assessment may be an important avenue for future research on the efficacy and utility of crisis exercises.

CONCLUSION

Although the overarching goal of conducting exercises is to test the viability of the school crisis plan, exercise activities may also test the capacity of the agencies that are there to support the

Table 6.12. Scenarios for Exercises and Drills

- A school bus is involved in an accident that results in multiple injuries and fatalities (also see Klingman, 1987; Toubiana, Milgram, Strich, & Edelstein, 1988).
- A student commits suicide after posting a message on the Internet and sending an e-mail message to many peers (also see Klingman, 1989).
- A flood or other local hazard occurs that kills students and family members and has a devastating impact on the community (also see Erikson, 1976).
- An airplane crashes on a school yard during recess; the pilot and passengers are killed and many children witness the crash (also see Wright, Ursano, Bartone, & Ingraham, 1990).
- A disturbed parent brings a gun to school and fires the gun toward the playground, which results in multiple injuries and fatalities (also see Armstrong, 1990; Klingman & Ben Eli, 1981).
- A group of students are kidnapped and held for ransom (also see Terr, 1981, 1983).

Note. From *Preparing for Crises in the Schools: A Manual for Building School Crisis Response Teams* (2nd ed.), p. 286, by S. E. Brock, J. Sandoval, and S. Lewis, 2001, New York: Wiley. Copyright 2000 by John Wiley & Sons. Adapted with permission.

school during a crisis. Because a critical element of crisis response is collaborative team interaction and support, the documentation and evaluation of the exercise should include a lessons learned component for all agencies involved in the simulation. Clearly, many crisis events that occur in school rely on community partners and first-responder groups to help support individuals and reduce trauma during and following a crisis. Working out these collaborative arrangements before a crisis enables all parties to know what their roles and responsibilities are before, during, and after an event takes place.

In contrast to the way fire drills are typically practiced in schools, the crisis team should insert different elements into what is often a rote repetition of the same crisis procedure. Setting up different contingencies that require in-the-moment adjustments to the core crisis response helps to create a broader capacity to handle events that may look and feel very different from the traditional practiced response. This approach to involving different contingencies could broaden the capacity of the plan and strengthen the participants' abilities to cope with the stress and difficulty of the crisis situation.

One of the goals of exercising school crisis plans is to identify problems, omissions, or duplication of efforts. Another key goal is to reinforce the importance of crisis preparedness and to demonstrate that the plan appears capable of achieving its primary objective of keeping students and staff safe and out of harm's way before, during, and after a crisis event. Exercises also enable the crisis team to comfortably promote the message that the plan is well-developed, practiced, and capable of protecting the school and its students and staff members.

Chapter 7

PREVENTING AND PREPARING FOR PSYCHOLOGICAL TRAUMA

This chapter examines how school crisis teams can prevent and prepare for the psychological trauma that individual students may experience following a school-associated crisis. Specifically, these school crisis interventions include (a) preventing crises before they occur (and thus preventing psychological trauma), (b) preparing for those crises that cannot be prevented by developing crisis intervention resources, (c) fostering student resiliency so that students are better protected from those crises that cannot be prevented, and (d) implementing emergency crisis procedures to ensure that students are safe and exposure to frightening images is minimized. This last intervention has been referred to as *immediate prevention* by Brock and Jimerson (2004).

All of the crisis interventions discussed in this chapter are intended to prevent psychological trauma and can thus be considered examples of *primary prevention* (Caplan, 1964). Because such interventions are desirable for everyone and are directed toward the entire school population, they can also be considered examples of *universally preventive interventions* (Gordon, 1983). Only to the extent that psychological trauma is not completely prevented would additional, more involved school crisis interventions (to be discussed in subsequent chapters) be considered. This consideration is important given that providing school crisis interventions when they are not truly needed may have the unintended effect of increasing student perceptions of threat, as the adult responses to crises are powerful determinants of student threat perceptions and crisis reactions (Dyregrov & Yule, 2006).

CRISIS PREVENTION

Comprehensive school crisis teams should do more than just respond to crisis events. Teams should also strive to prevent such events from occurring in the first place, and to the extent they do so, they will eliminate the possibility of individuals becoming psychological trauma victims. Examples of these activities are provided in Table 7.1, which summarizes the crisis prevention activities that address both physical and psychological safety (Reeves, Nickerson, & Jimerson, 2006a).

Table 7.1. Possible Crisis Prevention Activities

Ensure physical safety
- School building secured
- Natural surveillance of the school building
- Controlled access to school grounds
- Territoriality (a sense of school ownership among students and staff)
- Multihazard needs assessment

Ensure psychological safety
- School-wide positive behavioral supports
- Universal, targeted, and intensive academic and social–emotional interventions and supports
- School safety plan and crisis plan
- Safety education
- Identification and monitoring of potential danger and suicidal threats
- Student guidance services

PREPARATIONS FOR CRISIS INTERVENTION

Although prevention is ideal, it is not possible to prevent all crises. Thus, school crisis teams must be prepared to provide crisis intervention services to address the psychological injuries generated by crisis exposure (Allen-Heath, Ryan, Dean, & Bingham, 2007). The range of crisis intervention services that schools should be prepared to provide are presented in sections 2, 3, and 4 of this book. In addition, the PREPaRE Crisis Intervention and Recovery workshop offers an example of a crisis preparedness activity that is designed to help develop the skills needed to provide these crisis intervention or psychological first-aid services.

Although immediate crisis interventions should prove sufficient for the majority of students, a minority will manifest severe psychological injury. For these students, psychological first-aid crisis interventions will be insufficient, and they will require longer-term (typically community-based) mental health interventions. Public schools are traditionally not expected to provide these psychotherapeutic treatments; however, preparing for psychological trauma requires that, at the very least, schools have identified, and are able to make, appropriate mental health referrals. Additional information on identifying psychotherapeutic treatment options and an examination of treatments for the most severely traumatized students are presented in chapters 10 and 16, respectively.

APPROACHES TO FOSTERING STUDENT RESILIENCY

Whereas some students are more resilient and less likely to become trauma victims, others are more vulnerable to being traumatized by a crisis event. Thus, by promoting both internal and external resiliency, school crisis teams can decrease the likelihood of students becoming psychological trauma victims. Internal resiliency factors include positive coping skills, the ability to regulate emotions, self-confidence, self-esteem, a positive attitude, and an internal locus of control. External resiliency factors include a strong family and community support systems, positive peer relationships and role models, involvement in activities, and a supportive learning environment (Smith Harvey, 2007).

Fleming (2006), who conducted research on resiliency in severely abused children, found that personal relationships, a strong sense of independence, and self-reliance were among the factors that promoted resiliency. Social supports can affect both acute and long-term stress reactions (Pine & Cohen, 2002), and personal, familial, and social assets help to protect students. The Search Institute (www.search-institute.org) provides a discussion of developmental assets, with information on factors important to promoting resiliency at different stages of development. The Search Institute has surveyed more than 2 million youth across the United States and Canada since 1989 to learn about the experiences, attitudes, behaviors, and number of developmental assets youth have. Their studies have consistently revealed a strong and consistent relationship between the number of assets present in young people's lives and the degree to which they develop in positive and healthful ways (http://www.search-institute.org/research/assets). Table 7.2 lists specific examples of school-based activities that promote internal resiliency; Table 7.3 lists activities that promote external resiliency. To the extent that a school is able to promote these factors in the lives of their students, schools may be able to lower the risk for psychological injury following exposure to a crisis event.

IMMEDIATE PREVENTION: EMERGENCY PROCEDURES THAT MINIMIZE EXPOSURE

When a crisis does occur, the first priority is immediate prevention, which includes keeping students safe. To the extent that students can be kept safe following a crisis event, psychological trauma will be minimized and mental health crisis interventions will not be needed. Furthermore, the manner in which immediate crisis response team actions are taken can also be important in minimizing traumatic stress. For example, if medical triage is required, students can be shielded from viewing these medical interventions by considering the location of emergency responders in relation to crisis response procedures (e.g., student evacuation route). Minimizing student exposure to frightening crisis situations will minimize the degree of psychological trauma.

As psychological trauma can also result from media exposure, immediate prevention activities may also include limiting student exposure to media reports (in particular television viewing) of the crisis event. Consequently, immediately after a crisis event, school staff members should be given specific guidance with regard to providing students with access to crisis-related media reports in the classroom. This guidance should acknowledge that, on one hand, television and the Internet have humanized mass violence and disasters by putting faces on the victims and bereaved (Bowis, 2007). Viewing reports of crisis events can lead to an increasing awareness of world events and atrocities, and it helps people understand their part in helping others. At the same time, it must be acknowledged that viewing media reports increases crisis exposure, which can have a negative impact.

Table 7.2. Fostering Internal Resiliency at School

Promote active (or approach-oriented) coping styles. Positive coping skills can and should be taught directly by adults. Adult role modeling and guidance regarding appropriate coping strategies can lead to healthy student coping (as well as a positive school climate).

Promote student mental health. A balanced approach to supporting academic growth and meeting the social and emotional needs of students is essential. Healthy development is promoted when students know that it is appropriate to seek help and ask for support.

Teach students how to better regulate their emotions. Many programs and frameworks teach skills on managing emotions. Teaching positive skills to replace negative coping strategies can be done with universal school-wide interventions (i.e., PBS/PBIS, as discussed in chapter 4) or through student psychoeducational groups or other forms of classroom-based instruction.

Develop problem-solving skills. Direct instruction regarding problem-solving skills can help students consider the positive and negative aspects of various problem solutions.

Promote self-confidence, self-esteem, and positive attitudes. Students become more resilient when provided with situations in which they experience success both academically and socially, and in which failure is framed as a learning opportunity. Students can be taught how to reevaluate and adjust strategies that may not be working, while building on their strengths.

Promote internal locus of control. An individual with an internal locus of control believes that his or her behavior is guided by personal decisions and efforts. It is a belief that is directly related to self-confidence, self-esteem, and having the ability to regulate and control one's own emotions. Providing thought-provoking questions that allow students to reflect on how behavior is guided by personal decisions and efforts (and not just guided by external circumstances, chance, or fate) helps promote internal locus of control and personal responsibility.

Validate the importance of faith or belief systems. Faith or belief systems are important to many people and offer important supports that result in greater resiliency. Although public schools cannot promote any specific faith or belief system, they can ensure that students who already subscribe to a given religion are allowed to make use of, and have access to, their faith. In doing so, the school will help to validate its importance.

Nurture positive emotions. Staff members can be trained to demonstrate and give students the chance to practice positive emotions, such as optimism, respect, forgiveness, and empathy, while providing positive reinforcement for behaviors associated with such emotions. Training staff to praise students for successes and avoiding judgmental or harsh criticism for failure will build positive attitudes among school staff members and students and help establish a positive school climate.

Table 7.2. (continued)

Foster academic self-determination and feelings of competence. Students can be taught to direct their own course of learning by becoming involved in establishing school and classroom rules and expectations, setting realistic goals, being assertive in asking for help and resources, regularly attending school, and completing homework. Additional methods for building self-determination include teachers providing consistent and clear expectations, teaching students good study skills by developing a menu of homework and study strategies, and helping students to develop talents in activities they enjoy.

Note. Primary source *Resiliency Strategies for Parents and Educators*, by V. Smith-Harvey, November, 2007, *NASP Communiqué, 36*(3).

Table 7.3. Fostering External Resiliency at School

Support families. Schools can establish a foundation of collaboration and trust between home and school by forming positive parent–school partnerships where parents feel welcome at school, are included in decision making, and can participate by providing suggestions. In addition, parent support services such as academic curriculum nights, parent education classes, and parenting skills classes help foster the conditions that support external resiliency.
Facilitate peer relationships. Schools can foster students' sense of involvement by providing activities that engage students with their peers, such as clubs, sporting activities, leadership activities, and community service activities.
Provide access to positive adult role models. Prior collaborative relationships within the broader school community, such as with both school- and community-based organizations and agencies, can be a valuable resource for adult role models.
Ensure connections with prosocial institutions. By helping students connect with school activities or other associations, schools can provide activities that engage students and foster a sense of belonging.
Provide a caring, supportive learning environment. Schools can promote positive social connections between staff members and students, students and their peers, and home and school by modeling acceptance and tolerance through school activities and behaviors. Students can be encouraged to support their peers if the school culture includes the belief that getting help for a friend is the right thing to do (it is not "narking").
Encourage volunteerism. Students' social competence and resilience are fostered by helping others at home, in school, and in the community. Schools can create and promote a variety of opportunities for students to contribute to the well-being of others, both in school and in the broader community. Helping others fosters a sense of control and minimizes feelings of despair and helplessness.
Teach peace-building skills. Students can learn how to be appropriately assertive without being aggressive and to have self-control. Schools can teach conflict-resolution and peer-mediation skills, strategies for responding to bullies, and violence-prevention strategies.

Note. Primary source *Resiliency Strategies for Parents and Educators*, by V. Smith-Harvey, November, 2007, *NASP Communiqué, 36*(3).

CONCLUSION

The first step in addressing the mental health challenges that can be generated by school-associated crisis events is obviously to do all that is possible to prevent crises in the first place. However, recognizing that it is not possible to prevent all students from being exposed to crises, school crisis teams must ensure that they have developed the mental health resources to provide crisis intervention or psychological first-aid assistance. It is this reality that generates the need for professional development resources such as this book and the PREPaRE Crisis Intervention and Recovery workshop. Additional activities that can be undertaken before a crisis event to prevent psychological trauma include those that foster resiliency. By increasing students' resiliency, they become better protected from those crises that cannot be prevented. Finally, once a crisis has taken place, immediate prevention activities designed to ensure the safety of students and to minimize their exposure to frightening images can also help to prevent psychological trauma.

Section 2

REAFFIRM

Once a crisis event has occurred and been judged to have a potential impact on the school community, the second set of PREPaRE school crisis interventions are designed to reaffirm physical health and ensure that students (as well as parents and school staff members) perceive the school environment as secure and safe. As illustrated in Figure 1.2, these activities typically take place during crisis situations and immediately after they end, during the impact or recoil phases or during the immediate postimpact phase (Raphael & Newman, 2000; Valent, 2000). Specifically, these interventions include meeting basic physical needs, such as water, shelter, food, and clothing, and facilitating individuals' perceptions they are safe. Not only must the school community objectively be safe before any other school crisis intervention can be implemented, but school community members must also have their basic needs met and believe that the threat of danger has passed. In the words of George Everly (2003), "Needs for food, water, shelter, alleviation of pain, reunification with family members, and the provision of a sense of safety and security should all precede the utilization of psychologically-oriented crisis interventions" (p. 182).

To the extent that a school's interventions take place after a crisis event has occurred but before it has had a chance to psychologically traumatize school community members, they might be considered primary prevention. However, as the interventions are also likely to be among the first actions taken to assist acutely distressed individuals, they may be considered secondary prevention (Caplan, 1964). Furthermore, given that these crisis interventions are desirable for everyone, they can be directed toward the entire population and are thus labeled universally preventive interventions (Gordon, 1983). Depending on the crisis event, the need for these crisis interventions can last days or weeks. Although different types of interventions might occur simultaneously, mental health crisis interventions (i.e., evaluating psychological trauma and responding to individual psychological needs) are clearly secondary to ensuring physical health and perceptions of security and safety. Only after these basic needs are met do school-based mental health professionals begin to use their unique skill sets (Brown & Bobrow, 2004).

The first chapter in this section (chapter 8) reviews strategies designed to reaffirm objective physical health and safety. However, subjective perceptions of physical health and safety are at least as important as the objective situation. Consequently, chapter 9 reviews strategies designed to help ensure that school community members (in particular, students) believe they are safe and that crisis-related dangers have passed.

Chapter 8

REAFFIRM PHYSICAL HEALTH AND SAFETY

Following a school-associated crisis, the first priority is to keep students and staff members physically healthy and safe (Haskett, Scott, Nears, & Grimmett, 2008; McNally, Bryant, & Ehlers, 2003; Raphael, 2007). In some instances this response may involve implementing disaster or crisis response procedures such as evacuation or lockdown; in other cases it may involve addressing basic physical needs (e.g., providing water, food, shelter, and medications); and in still other instances a response may require reorganizing the school environment (e.g., providing a police presence on campus; Brymer et al., 2006). Regardless of the cause, when such activities are needed, they are of primary importance, and traditional mental health crisis intervention takes a back seat to ensuring physical health and safety (Everly, 2003; Joshi & Lewin, 2004; Ritchie, 2003; Ruzek et al., 2007). In the words of Brown and Bobrow (2004):

> The first step following a disaster is to ensure the safety, shelter, and sustenance of children and their caregivers. In our experience, mental health interventions are secondary. Once these basic needs are met, there is a role for mental health professionals. (p. 212)

Furthermore, before any psychological recovery and associated crisis interventions can begin, crisis-related dangers must be eliminated and physical health challenges addressed (Levy, 2008). Barenbaum, Ruchkin, and Schwab-Stone (2004) noted:

> Once traumatic events have stopped or been eliminated, the process of restoration begins. Nonpsychiatric interventions, such as provision of basic needs, food, shelter, and clothing, help provide the stability required to ascertain the numbers of youth needing specialized psychiatric care. (p. 49)

In fact, there is some evidence that crisis intervention is not effective if the crisis-related stressors are not ended first (Thabet, Vostanis, & Karim, 2005).

This is not to say that mental health is not an issue immediately following a crisis event. It is clear that negative mental health outcomes such as posttraumatic stress disorder (PTSD), depression, and phobias are more likely following crisis situations in which danger or threats are ongoing. Thus, when objective safety is quickly reaffirmed following a crisis, negative mental health outcomes can be minimized or even avoided (Hobfoll et al., 2007). However, once objective physical health and safety are restored, individual perceptions of safety present another mental health challenge. Not only must students (and staff) actually be healthy and safe, they must believe that crisis-related dangers have passed and that their health and welfare can be ensured.

This chapter focuses on reaffirming actual or objective physical health and safety. Though the recommendations that follow primarily address the needs of students, they can also be generalized to school staff members. Obviously, to the extent that staff members' needs are not met, they will be unable to fill a caregiving role.

ENSURING PHYSICAL HEALTH AND SAFETY WITHIN THE GENERAL STUDENT POPULATION

The National Child Traumatic Stress Network and the National Center for PTSD (Brymer et al., 2006) offer several practical suggestions for reaffirming physical health and safety among the general student population when a crisis has occurred. First, the school crisis team should identify officials who can address, and ideally resolve, physical safety issues that are beyond the control of crisis interveners. For example, law enforcement personnel would be brought in to address issues associated with threats and weapons. Second, the school crisis team should ensure that objects that could cause harm are removed from the school environment as soon as possible, such as broken glass or broken furniture that could cause injury. Third, the crisis team should ensure that students have a clean and safe environment in which to work and play, with adequate supervision provided at all times. For example, the school crisis team might use law enforcement or physical barriers to prevent intrusions onto school grounds by unauthorized individuals.

Finally, the team must be especially sensitive to individuals in particular subgroups who might be targets of crisis-related persecution because of their ethnic, religious, or other affiliations. For example, if an act of school violence was perpetrated by an individual with a particular group affiliation, the school crisis team should make sure students from that group are provided with extra security and are able to get safely to and from school.

ENSURING PHYSICAL HEALTH AND SAFETY WITHIN SPECIAL STUDENT POPULATIONS

Among students in special education, with disabilities, or with chronic illnesses, special actions may be needed to ensure physical health and safety. Practical suggestions for reaffirming physical health and safety among these special populations have been offered by Brymer et al. (2006) and Susan (in press).

First, ensure that adequate lighting is available and implement protective measures to minimize slipping, tripping, and falling among those with physical challenges. Second, ensure that students who lack mobility or may fall easily are placed in areas that are accessible. These areas should not require the use of stairs or be located in the lower levels of any shelter.

Third, ensure that students maintain access to mobility and sensory devices, such as wheelchairs, glasses, and hearing aids. If student volunteers are used to help transport special needs students, having that familiar and trusted individual to assist if an evacuation is required is ideal. However, the possibility that these more familiar caregivers may not be available in an emergency situation needs to be acknowledged, and alternative transport resources need to be available. For students in electric wheelchairs, reaffirming physical health would include provisions for when the chair's battery runs out of power (e.g., extra batteries or the presence of individuals strong enough to push an electric wheelchair that has run out of power).

Fourth, ensure that all self-care needs continue to be met, for example, ensure the provision of assistance with eating, dressing, and toileting. An additional power source may be necessary if a student has special healthcare needs, such as students that require suctioning.

Fifth, ensure that medications continue to be made available, for example, insulin for students with diabetes. Susan (in press) recommends that a 72-hour supply of such medications be on hand, and that a list containing the names of students and their medications and dosages be readily accessible.

Finally, ensure that students with pervasive developmental disorders (e.g., autistic disorder) avoid unfamiliar and overstimulating environments. They may benefit from social stories (or scripts) that describe crisis response procedures. For those with sensory issues (e.g., hypersensitivity to sounds), caregivers must be mindful of the sounds, such as fire alarms, that may trigger strong emotional reactions. Students with cognitive delays may not understand the threat presented by the crisis event; therefore, if school personnel are able to clearly communicate that the student is physically safe, the danger of psychological trauma will be minimized. However, students with cognitive delays may be unable to communicate their physical needs, which may increase their psychological vulnerability.

RESPONDING TO ACUTE NEEDS

Reaffirming physical health and safety includes attending to the medical and safety needs of both general and special education students (as well as school staff members). For example, if an individual displays signs of shock or has other medical needs, or appears to present a risk of harm to self or others, emergency medical assistance should be immediately obtained. Until help arrives, the school crisis team member should stay with the affected individual, remain calm, and do his or her best to ensure physical health and safety (Ruzek et al., 2007).

Responding to acute needs also involves helping to calm and orient those individuals who present as emotionally overwhelmed and extremely disoriented. Indications that an individual is

Table 8.1. Signs of Emotionally Overwhelmed Students

- Appear glassy eyed and vacant, disoriented, or incapacitated by worry.
- Do not respond to questions or commands.
- Demonstrate extreme emotional reactions (e.g., uncontrolled crying or hyperventilation), uncontrolled physical reactions (e.g., shaking or trembling), or frantic searching behaviors.
- Engage in dangerous or risky activities.

Note. From *Psychological First Aid: Field Operations Guide* (2nd ed.), p. 49, by M. Brymer et al., 2006, Los Angeles: NCTSN. Copyright 2006 by National Child Traumatic Stress Network and National Center for PTSD. Adapted with permission.

overwhelmed are presented in Table 8.1; some basic recommendations for taking care of individuals who are so affected by the crisis that they are unable to perform basic tasks (e.g., eating or decision-making) are presented in Table 8.2. A more detailed discussion of how to orient emotionally overwhelmed crisis survivors, including those who present as extremely distraught, is presented by Brymer et al. (2006, pp. 50–53) and in chapter 15 of this book.

Table 8.2. The Initial Response to Emotionally Overwhelmed Students

- If a primary caregiver is available, and is capable of supporting the student, help them be reunited immediately. Give the caregiver information (provided below) that will help her calm the child.
- If a primary caregiver is physically unavailable or not capable of supporting the student, consider doing the following:
  - Address any immediate concerns that are the focus of the student's distress.
  - Provide the student with a safe, calm, and private environment where he or she can calm down.
  - Remain calm, quiet, and available to the student, but do not force conversation (doing so may contribute to cognitive or emotional overload).
  - Remain nearby; let the student know you are available to help, if needed, by engaging with other nonthreatening tasks in the vicinity; for example, engage in small talk, talk to other students, or complete paperwork.
  - Once the student has regained some emotional control, let him or her know you are available to discuss crisis-related challenges or problems.
  - Provide factual information that helps orient the student to the current situation and what has been done and is being done to address the crisis.

Note. From *Psychological First Aid: Field Operations Guide* (2nd ed.), p. 50, by M. Brymer et al., 2006, Los Angeles: NCTSN. Copyright 2006 by National Child Traumatic Stress Network and National Center for PTSD. Adapted with permission.

ENSURING PHYSICAL COMFORT

Following crisis events, making the school environment more physically comfortable will help to ensure that basic needs are being met and will soothe students' anxiety (Brymer et al., 2006). If possible, school crisis team members should consider things like room temperature, lighting, and air quality. Brymer et al. also suggested that giving younger children toys such as soft teddy bears can not only help to soothe and comfort, but also be used to reinforce physical health care priorities. This can be done, for example, by sharing with students that on hot, humid days, their teddy bear needs to drink plenty of water.

PROVIDING ACCURATE REASSURANCES

Finally, school crisis team members and other caregivers must avoid making promises they cannot keep (Brymer et al., 2006). Specifically, they should not reassure individuals that they are completely safe and that crisis-related dangers have completely passed if they are not certain this is in fact the case. However, caregivers should recognize that in situations in which the dangers have not passed, individuals who are able to reestablish or maintain a relative sense of safety have a significantly lower risk of negative mental health outcomes than those who are not able to do so (Hobfoll et al., 2007). Therefore, crisis team members should do everything possible to ensure physical health and safety, without giving false reassurances, while conveying to the school community that dangers are being addressed.

Another approach is to provide students and the school community with strategies to cope with ongoing stressors. For example, in a situation involving aggressive violence in which the perpetrator of the act is still at large, the magnitude of law enforcement activity can be shared (e.g., patrols have been dramatically increased), and adaptive behaviors that help to ensure safety can be reinforced (e.g., review stranger-danger rules). In addition, crisis interveners should not promise to provide students with goods or services (e.g., food, water, or blankets) unless they are certain that these materials are available (Brymer et al., 2006). If a specific time line for the availability of such goods or services is known, the crisis team can announce when these will be available.

CONCLUSION

Although restoring actual safety is essential, school crisis teams should be aware that subjective perceptions can be as important as objective physical health, if not more important. Chapter 9 presents ways of addressing student perceptions of security and safety.

Chapter 9

ENSURE PERCEPTIONS OF SAFETY AND SECURITY

It is not enough for school community members to actually be safe following a crisis. For psychological recovery to begin, individuals must *believe* they are safe (Charuvastra & Cloitre, 2008). Simply put, those individuals who have had their psychological sense of safety reaffirmed (and as a result, do not exaggerate crisis-related risks) have a lower risk for negative mental health outcomes. Believing that one is safe can affect both the biology and psychology of traumatic stress. For example, according to Ruzek et al. (2007), "Promotion of a psychological sense of safety can reduce biological aspects of post-traumatic stress reactions, and can positively affect cognitive processes that inhibit recovery, including a belief that 'the world is completely dangerous' and exaggeration of future risk" (p. 22). Conversely, individuals who believe that crisis-related dangers have not passed or who exaggerate crisis-related risks are at greater risk for negative mental health outcomes (Bryant, Salmon, Sinclair, & Davidson, 2007; Hobfoll et al., 2007).

This chapter begins with an examination of how students' psychological safety depends on how adults react to and behave in a crisis. It then presents steps to promote a subjective sense of safety, which may include minimizing exposure to crisis scenes and images, reuniting or locating significant others, providing factual information about the crisis event, and returning to a school environment that makes school safety concrete and visible. Although this chapter primarily addresses the needs of students, many of the recommendations that follow can also be generalized to school staff members. Obviously, to the extent that staff perceptions of psychological safety are not realized, they will be unable to fill a caregiving role.

THE EFFECT OF ADULT REACTIONS AND BEHAVIORS

Adult reactions are important in bringing about not only objective physical health and safety, but also perceived safety and security, especially for young children (Dyregrov & Yule, 2006; Eksi et al., 2007). Young children often look to their adult caregivers for guidance regarding how stressful or threatening a given event is. If adults behave as if an event is highly traumatic (regardless of its objective threat), younger children will likely respond accordingly. A study by B. L. Green et al. (1991) reported that maternal posttraumatic stress disorder (PTSD) symptoms actually predicted child PTSD 2 years after a dam collapse and flood. Nader and Pynoos (1993) supported this observation when they reported that "there is a commonality in the level of anxiety among children and the adults in their environment" (p. 17).

More recent research data also support the observation that adult reactions predict child reactions. Landolt, Vollrath, Timm, Gnehm, and Sennhauser (2005) found that the severity of the father's PTSD was an especially important predictor of the child's PTSD 12 months following a traffic accident. In interpreting this finding and addressing why fathers are important to the posttraumatic adjustment of their children, Landolt et al. stated: "One may speculate that children react more strongly to their fathers' symptoms because this is less common for them. In Western society, fathers are expected to be strong and to handle difficult situations without displaying excessive emotions" (p. 1281). In other words, these data can be interpreted as suggesting that children look to adults to gauge the seriousness of a threatening situation. If they see what are judged to be excessive reactions among their caregivers, they are more likely to view the event as a traumatic stressor and in turn more likely to become psychological trauma victims. Ostrowski, Christopher, & Delahanty (2007) also found caregiver reactions to be predictive of PTSD among their children. Specifically, they found that boys' PTSD symptoms 6 weeks following a traumatic injury, and both boys' and girls' PTSD symptoms 7 months following the same injury, were predicted by maternal posttraumatic stress symptoms.

The associations between adult and child traumatic stress represent casual, rather than causal, connections; however it is nevertheless prudent to recommend that the behavior of caregiving adults be carefully monitored following exposure to a crisis event. These data and their interpretations suggest that if school staff members are able to implement emergency procedures in a calm and controlled manner, then students are likely to view the circumstances as more controllable and thus less threatening. This point reinforces the discussion in chapter 1, that school crisis teams must accurately assess the nature of a crisis event and its potential to generate traumatic stress. If school staff members are observed to behave as if a crisis event is highly traumatic, students (especially younger students) are likely to react accordingly (i.e., to believe that they are not safe). In contrast, if adults assess the traumatic nature of a crisis event and then follow established plans to provide appropriate support services to those likely affected by the event, this response will most effectively address the needs of students and staff and avoid exacerbating the situation.

MINIMIZING CRISIS EXPOSURE

Consistent with the guidance offered in chapter 7, minimizing exposure to the crisis event itself, its immediate aftermath (including the suffering of others), and subsequent media coverage may also foster a sense of psychological safety (Brymer et al., 2006; Ruzek et al., 2007). This may involve directing ambulatory students away from the crisis site and ensuring that they are not allowed to view medical triage activities. In other words, individuals who are shielded from potentially upsetting crisis-related scenes and images will typically find it easier to reestablish a sense of psychological safety compared with those who are directly exposed to such images.

Fostering a sense of psychological safety and security can also include minimizing the crisis exposure that might be generated by media coverage of the crisis event. If survivors have access to media coverage (e.g., television or radio broadcasts), excessive viewing of that coverage can be upsetting. This is especially true for children and adolescents (Brymer et al., 2006). Parents are encouraged to (a) monitor their children's exposure to such media and discuss their concerns or questions, (b) let their children know that they are monitoring the situation and will provide them with updates, (c) be careful about what is said around their children, (d) discuss and clarify things that might be upsetting for their children, and (e) be mindful of the student's developmental level and language abilities when providing access to media reports. Data that support these recommendations come from research conducted following the Oklahoma City bombing and the World Trade Center disaster in 2001.

Pfefferbaum et al. (1999) reported that TV exposure correlated significantly with posttraumatic symptoms at 7 weeks following the 1995 Oklahoma City bombing. In a later study, Pfefferbaum et al. (2001) reported that television exposure following a bombing disaster accounted for a slightly greater percentage of posttraumatic stress symptom variance (5.8%) than did physical or emotional exposure (3.2% and 5.3%, respectively). Among children surveyed who did not have physical or emotional exposure to the bombing (i.e., did not hear or feel the blast and did not know anyone injured or killed), self-reports of the amount of television exposure were significantly related to posttraumatic stress symptoms (accounting for 6% of the total posttraumatic stress symptom variance).

Pfefferbaum et al. (2001) also cautioned that the identified relationships were not necessarily indicative of direct causal effects, with regard to the association between adult and child traumatic stress reactions. Higher levels of disaster-related television viewing may be a sign of distress (and not a cause of such distress). Regardless of the nature of this relationship, the authors concluded that "disaster-related television viewing by children should be monitored," and children's caregivers "should be available to address their emotional reactions, to answer questions, and to correct misperceptions" (p. 209). In addition, Gurwitch, Sitterle, Yound, and Pfefferbaum (2002) suggested that following the bombing, children who were not physically or emotionally proximal to the bombing, but who reported having extensive TV viewing of the event, also reported a higher number of traumatic stress symptoms than did other children who reported lower amounts of such viewing. These findings suggest that either being directly exposed or being simply a passive observer of a traumatic event, even by viewing it on TV, may place students at risk for traumatic stress reactions.

In research conducted following the World Trade Center disaster, Hoven et al. (2004) reported that, among children, media exposure was related to separation anxiety disorder symptoms. Similarly, Saylor, Cowart, Lipovsky, Jackson, and Finch (2003) reported that among elementary school students, those who saw media images of death or injury and who saw reports on the Internet (versus TV or print media) had more PTSD symptoms. In addition, these researchers found that it did not matter if the images children were exposed to were considered to be "positive" (e.g., a presidential address or heroic helping) or "negative" (e.g., distressed individuals, death or dying, or the attack itself). From their data, Saylor et al. reported: "It appears that greater amounts of exposure, both positive and negative, correspond with more PTSD symptoms" (p. 1636).

Blanchard et al. (2004) reported that among college students, hours of TV watched following the World Trade Center attacks were in some cases a predictor of traumatic stress. Among adults, Ahern et al. (2002) reported that frequent viewing of people falling or jumping from the towers was strongly related to PTSD. This relationship was increased among respondents who were directly affected by the events of 9/11. In addition, the authors reported that the relationship between PTSD and viewing of traumatic TV images, among those only directly involved or affected by the attacks, had not been previously documented. The Ahern et al. study concluded that clinicians should recommend that people directly affected by a disaster reduce their exposure of disaster coverage. In a more recent analysis, Ahern, Galea, Resnick, and Vlahov (2004) found that respondents who reported having viewed TV images of the attacks more frequently had a higher prevalence of probable PTSD. Respondents who viewed the most TV had a 66% greater likelihood of having probable PTSD than those who viewed the least TV.

Again, it is important to reiterate the limitations of correlational studies, that is, that the associations between TV viewing and traumatic stress represent casual correlations not causal connections. Researchers remain uncertain about whether respondents who had more psychological symptoms watched more TV because of these symptoms or if watching TV contributed to these symptoms. In addition, there is reason to question whether people with PTSD recalled seeing more TV in retrospect because they felt more affected by the events or whether their preexisting anxiety made them more likely to watch TV. However, as Quallich (2005) suggested, given that avoidance of trauma reminders is a core PTSD symptom, individuals with this disorder should be unlikely to watch a lot of TV. Doing so would be inconsistent with their avoidance symptoms and supports a causal connection between TV viewing and PTSD.

Nevertheless, even without definitive causal connections between TV viewing and traumatic stress, it seems prudent to recommend that the television viewing habits of children (especially younger children) be carefully monitored following crises (Otto et al., 2007). Given the data interpretations described above, it is suggested that media viewing of crisis events may be sufficient to produce symptoms of traumatic stress among children and should be minimized.

REUNITING OR LOCATING PRIMARY CAREGIVERS AND SIGNIFICANT OTHERS

For younger students, separation from families can be particularly stressful during times of crisis (see chapters 4 and 12). For example, it has been reported that, among preschool earthquake survivors, separation from parents and siblings during an evacuation was sufficient to generate symptoms of PTSD (Azarian & Skriptcheko-Gregorian, 1998b). This finding is not surprising given that parents and other caregivers play an important role in promoting children's perceptions of safety and security. Failure to reunite students with primary caregivers may increase the students' perceptions of the crisis situation as dangerous and threatening. This in turn would increase the probability of traumatic stress reactions.

Given these observations, reconnecting students with their primary caregivers and significant others should be given a high priority following a crisis event (Brymer et al., 2006), with special priority being given to reuniting the youngest students with parents (Brock, Sandoval, & Lewis, 2001). If reunification of students with caregivers will be delayed, students should at least be informed about the location and status of significant others (ideally allowing separated children to communicate with primary caregivers in some way). Of course it would be important to avoid making promises that cannot be kept.

If the status of primary caregivers or significant others is not clear, it is important to reassure children that they are physically safe and to ensure the provision of what Brymer et al. (2006) referred to as a "child-friendly space" (p. 31). Important elements of such an environment include provision of (a) a quiet waiting room that is removed from crisis-related activities, (b) caregivers who are experienced in caring for children and who are able to constantly supervise children, and (c) developmentally appropriate games and activities that can help to pass time. Brymer et al. also suggested that it may be appropriate to ask older children and adolescents to mentor younger children, while at the same time giving these older children and adolescents developmentally appropriate opportunities to connect with their peers.

Finally, before students are reunited with their primary caregivers, parents should be reminded of how important their initial reactions will be to shaping their child's threat perceptions (see chapter 13). They need to be told "to be careful about what they say in front of their children, and to clarify things that might be upsetting for them" (Brymer et al., 2006, p. 32).

PROVIDING CRISIS FACTS AND ADAPTIVE INTERPRETATIONS

Psychological education and intervention activities (discussed in chapters 13, 14, and 15) may also be helpful in fostering perceptions of safety and security. Specifically, students may feel safer if they are helped to gain cognitive mastery over the event (i.e., understand the reality of the danger). For example, following one school shooting there was a persistent rumor that only one of two gunmen had been accounted for. In reality, the lone gunman had committed suicide. Interventions that dispelled this rumor were important to helping students understand that the danger had passed. This knowledge helped students believe that they were in fact safe (Brock et al., 2001).

Given that students (in particular younger students) can be confused by a crisis event and have incorrect beliefs about it (Allen, Dlugokinski, Cohen, & Walker, 1999), providing factual information may help students realize they are safe and secure. This is especially critical, given that children's beliefs about a stressor can be more frightening than reality (Armstrong, 1990; Blom, Etkind, & Carr, 1991), and that excessively negative appraisals about a crisis are significant contributors to traumatic stress (Hobfoll et al., 2007). Bryant et al. (2007) concluded that "[t]he current data suggest that early interventions that aim to enhance adaptive interpretations, particularly addressing perceptions of ongoing threat or vulnerability, may be effective in reducing subsequent PTSD reactions in children" (p. 2506). In other words, it is sometimes possible to foster perceptions of safety and security by providing individuals with information about (a) the current crisis status and what is being done by the school and community to address the situation, (b) how they can ensure their own personal safety, and (c) services available to students and their families that address crisis-related challenges (Ruzek et al., 2007). For example, Brymer et al. (2006) suggested that the following take place:

> Ask [students] if they have any questions about what is going to happen, and give simple accurate information about what they can expect.... Be sure to ask about concerns regarding current danger and safety.... Try to connect [students] with information that addresses these concerns. If you do not have specific information, do not guess or invent information in order to provide reassurance. Instead, develop a plan with the [student] for ways you and he/she can gather the needed information. (p. 29)

Of course, crisis interveners must not reassure students that they are safe unless they have factual information that this is the case. In such an instance, the school crisis team should focus on providing students with the knowledge and skills needed to address ongoing threats (e.g., reviewing lockdown procedures in situations that present an ongoing threat of violence). Providing such information may help students perceive the threat as relatively more controllable and therefore potentially less traumatic. Furthermore, before proceeding with these activities, the intervention team should ensure that the students are emotionally stabilized and are able to process crisis facts and make adaptive interpretations (see Tables 8.1 and 8.2). Finally, the kinds of factual information that may help ensure students' perceptions of security and safety include (a) what students can do to ensure their physical safety, (b) what others are doing to ensure that students are safe, (c) the current status of the crisis event (e.g., whether the danger has passed or is still present), and (d) resources that can be accessed to better ensure safety (see Table 9.1).

RETURNING STUDENTS TO A SAFE SCHOOL ENVIRONMENT

Returning students and staff to a school environment, especially one that ensures that steps taken to ensure safety are not only effective but also concrete and visible, can also help foster perceptions of security and safety. Doing so may also help dismantle any classically conditioned associations

Table 9.1. Information to Ensure Students' Perceptions of Security and Safety

- Tell students what they can do to ensure their physical safety.
- Inform them about what others are doing to ensure the students' safety.
- Report on the current status of the crisis event (e.g., whether the danger has passed or is still present).
- Provide resources that can be accessed to better ensure safety (e.g., a law enforcement presence on school grounds).

between dangerous crisis-related stimuli and harmless school-related images, people, and things (Ruzek et al., 2007). For example, having a strong police presence on campus following acts of violence might be helpful. In addition, the routines and presence of friends, teachers, and other professionals at school offer natural supports that will support healthy adjustment (see chapter 12).

PROVIDING OPPORTUNITIES TO TAKE ACTION

Finally, feelings of helplessness or dependency are a defining feature of traumatic stress. These feelings may be reduced by encouraging school community members to participate in getting supplies needed for comfort. For example, assuming it is safe to do so and students are able, teachers might send them to the cafeteria or the office to get needed supplies, rather than asking an adult to bring supplies to the classroom.

CONCLUSION

In response to crisis events, reaffirming physical health and ensuring perceptions of safety and security can be considered primary and universally provided crisis interventions. However, as the impact phase of a crisis comes to an end, the recoil phase begins, and the school environment begins to stabilize, other school crisis interventions (described in chapters 12 through 16) will become appropriate actions. However, before beginning any school-based mental health intervention, assessment of individual psychological trauma must take place. Section 3 (chapters 10 and 11) will examine this important crisis intervention prerequisite.

Section 3

EVALUATE

After physical health and safety have been reaffirmed, the next set of school crisis interventions are strategies designed to evaluate the psychological impact of a crisis event. A commonly used term for the evaluation of psychological trauma following large-scale disasters is *psychological triage*, which is defined by the National Institute of Mental Health (2001) as follows:

> The process of evaluating and sorting victims by immediacy of treatment needed and directing them to immediate or delayed treatment. The goal of triage is to do the greatest good for the greatest number of victims. (p. 27)

Though secondary to ensuring actual and perceived physical health and safety, as illustrated in Figure 1.2, these interventions may begin to take place as soon as the immediate threat of a crisis ends, during the recoil or immediate postimpact phases. However, some evaluation activities may take place months or even years after the crisis event, that is, during the recovery/reconstruction phase (Raphael & Newman, 2000; Valent, 2000). For example, although it is rare, in some instances crisis reactions can have a delayed onset. In addition, crisis anniversaries (e.g., the 1-year anniversary of the crisis event) and other similar crises often renew crisis reactions and may require some assessment of the need for crisis intervention assistance.

As these interventions aim to identify psychological trauma victims as soon as possible so that they can be provided needed crisis intervention, they would be considered a form of secondary prevention (Caplan, 1964). This level of school crisis intervention is initially directed toward the entire population, as school crisis interveners attempt to identify subgroups of students who have an above-average risk for being psychologically traumatized. Thus, at least initially, they can be labeled *universally preventive interventions* (Gordon, 1983). As these subgroups are identified, attention is directed toward individuals who are judged to have above-average risk for being psychological trauma victims. This is done by detecting those students who demonstrate warning signs or symptoms of psychological trauma or who are judged to have a predisposition for being traumatized. Thus, they can also be considered *selected* and *indicated* preventive interventions (Gordon).

The first chapter in this section (chapter 10) reviews the rationale for, and conceptual foundations of, psychological triage. This includes a careful review of the risk factors that increase the odds of an individual becoming a psychological trauma victim and the warning signs of traumatic stress. The second chapter in this section (chapter 11) reviews the practical issues critical to the evaluation of psychological trauma. When considering this topic, it is important to acknowledge that this evaluation is not a discrete intervention or event; rather, it is a process. The evaluation begins by identifying risk for psychological trauma and directing the attention of crisis intervention accordingly. Next, as crisis intervention services are provided and contact made with students and their caregivers, warning signs of traumatic stress are observed by and reported to crisis intervention team members. From this information, treatment decisions are further refined to address the individual student needs. Finally, as the crisis event enters the postimpact and recovery/reconstruction phases, decisions are made regarding which students will need longer-term community-based mental health interventions and appropriate referrals based on data gathered as a part of initial responses to psychological needs (or crisis interventions).

Chapter 10

RATIONALE AND ASSESSMENT VARIABLES FOR EVALUATING PSYCHOLOGICAL TRAUMA

This chapter provides background information important to the identification and subsequent treatment of psychological trauma victims. It examines why the evaluation of psychological trauma must be a prerequisite to crisis intervention services. It then discusses the empirical basis regarding the risk factors for, and warning signs of, psychological trauma. Knowledge of these variables is essential to the practice of psychological triage (chapter 11), and valuable when providing psychological education to caregivers (chapter 13).

RATIONALE FOR ASSESSING PSYCHOLOGICAL TRAUMA

There are several important reasons for making the evaluation of psychological trauma a primary crisis intervention. They include the facts that (a) the consequences of crisis exposure are idiosyncratic, and (b) some crisis interventions have the potential to cause harm.

Idiosyncratic Consequences of Crisis Exposure

The evaluation of psychological trauma is made necessary by the fact that not all individuals will be equally affected by crisis exposure, and recovery from crisis exposure is the norm (Brymer et al., 2006; McNally, Bryant, & Ehlers, 2003). As a result, different individuals will require different interventions (Berkowitz, 2003; Kilic, Özgüven, & Sayil, 2003; Lonigan, Phillips, & Richey, 2003). Though some crisis survivors will need intensive intervention, others will need very little (if any) assistance (Vijayakumar, Kannan, Ganesh Kumar, & Devarajan, 2006). It is clear that when it comes to crisis intervention, "one size does not fit all" (National Institute of Mental Health [NIMH], 2001; Ritchie, 2003, p. 46). In addition, at this time, there is no evidence that any one global crisis intervention will prevent subsequent psychopathology (Litz, Gray, Bryant, & Adler, 2002). Therefore, from the evaluation of psychological trauma, school crisis interventions need to be tailored to address specific individual crisis intervention needs.

Although virtually anyone with sufficient trauma exposure will display some initial crisis reactions, according to the National Institute of Mental Health, a "sensible working principle in the immediate post incident phase is to expect normal recovery. The presumption of clinically significant disorders in the early post-incident phase is inappropriate, except for individuals with preexisting conditions" (NIMH, 2001, p. 6). Because recovery from crisis exposure is the norm, crisis intervention assistance should only be offered in response to a demonstrated need (Everly, 1999). Therefore, school crisis interveners should take their lead from students, school staff, and other caregivers, providing assistance according to need rather than universally providing all students with the same intervention. In the words of McNally et al. (2003): "Not everyone exposed to trauma either needs or wants professional help" (p. 73).

Idiosyncratic Consequences of Crisis Intervention

The need to identify and assist individuals who require immediate crisis intervention support is readily apparent; however, less obvious is the need to identify those who may *not* require assistance and allow them to manage the crisis independently. This is important, because providing highly directive crisis intervention assistance to students who do not need it may cause harm. For example, if crisis intervention takes place in a group setting, there is a potential for contamination effects. Students (and especially staff members) who are distressed can have a negative impact on otherwise unaffected students (Berkowitz, 2003; Everly, 1999). Thus, without a careful evaluation of psychological trauma risk, some crisis interventions may actually increase the crisis exposure of some students.

Furthermore, providing crisis intervention assistance to individuals who do not need it may unintentionally and inaccurately communicate that they are not capable of coping with the crisis independently. As a consequence, they may fail to recognize sources of internal and external resiliency that are operating in their lives (such as those discussed in chapter 7). Reports have shown that self-perceptions of one's ability to cope and to control the recovery process are important to successfully adjusting to traumatic circumstances (Frazier, Tashiro, Berman, Steger, & Long, 2004; Norris, Byrne, Diaz, & Kaniasty, 2002); therefore, it is essential to avoid giving the impression that crisis-exposed individuals are not capable problem solvers. Finally, providing highly directive crisis intervention support when it is not needed may not only generate self-fulfilling prophecies, but may also unnecessarily stigmatize individuals.

ASSESSMENT VARIABLES

As discussed in chapter 1, the evaluation of psychological trauma begins with an examination of crisis event variables and consideration of the fact that not all crisis events are equally devastating. Relative event predictability, consequences, duration, and intensity interact with the crisis type and increase the likelihood that some events will be more devastating than others (see Figure 1.1).

However, whereas such knowledge will generate a basic estimate of *how many* school community members might be expected to become psychological trauma victims, it will not inform school-based mental health professionals about *which* school community members are most likely to have been traumatized by a given event. Such individual trauma assessments, which are critical to the determination of individual crisis intervention needs, require evaluation of risk factors and warning signs.

As illustrated in Figure 10.1, crisis event variables interact with risk factors (i.e., crisis exposure, personal vulnerabilities, and threat perceptions) and in turn generate the warning signs of psychological traumatization, that is, initial and durable crisis reactions. Although many initial crisis reactions are not to be overly pathologized (and can be considered common reactions), if these reactions persist over time, they may in fact be symptoms of mental illness, such as posttraumatic stress disorder (PTSD). Furthermore, some initial reactions are so severe that they require immediate mental health treatment referrals and are predictive of subsequent psychopathology. The discussion that follows explores the empirical basis for the risk factors and warning signs that should serve as the basis for making school crisis intervention treatment decisions.

Risk Factors

Risk factors are those variables that predict psychological trauma. Arguably, the most powerful objective risk factor is physical proximity to the crisis event. However, emotional proximity is also a significant predictor, and, in addition, personal vulnerabilities have been shown to make some individuals more likely to experience traumatic stress. Besides these more objective risk factors, the individual's subjective impressions of the crisis event (which as illustrated in Figure 10.1 are influenced by exposure and personal vulnerabilities) are central in determining risk for traumatic stress.

Crisis Exposure: Physical Proximity

Physical proximity refers to where individuals were when the crisis occurred or how close they were to the traumatic event. The closer they were physically (i.e., the more direct their exposure in terms of seeing or hearing the event), the greater the risk of psychological trauma. Conversely, the more physically distant they were, the lower the risk of psychological injury (Bradburn, 1991; Gil & Caspi, 2006; Groome & Soureti, 2004; Keppel-Benson, Ollendick, & Benson, 2002; Lawyer et al., 2006; Lonigan, Shannon, Finch, Daughtery, & Taylor, 1991; Pynoos et al., 1987; Pynoos et al., 1993; Udwin, Boyle, Yule, Bolton, & O'Ryan, 2000).

The highest risk for psychological trauma should be assigned to those individuals who required medical or surgical attention and those who had crisis exposures that were particularly intense and of long duration (NIMH, 2001). For example, Kolaitis et al. (2003) reported that, following the 1999 Athens earthquake, children who sustained injuries and those whose homes were damaged were most likely to have higher posttraumatic stress scores. Not surprisingly, more severe injuries are associated with a greater probability of experiencing significant traumatic stress among young adults and children (Haden, Scarpa, Jones, & Ollendick, 2007). In addition, following the World Trade Center attacks, Hoven et al. (2004) reported that direct exposure was related to separation anxiety disorder symptoms among children. Finally, Eksi et al. (2007) reported that children and adolescents who witnessed death following an earthquake were more likely to develop PTSD than those without such exposure.

Results of a phone survey conducted by Galea et al. (2002) 5 to 7 weeks following the 9/11 attacks further illustrate the importance of physical proximity in determining traumatic stress. Specifically, those adults who lived closest to ground zero (i.e., residents who lived south of Canal

Figure 10.1. Factors that should be considered when evaluating psychological trauma.

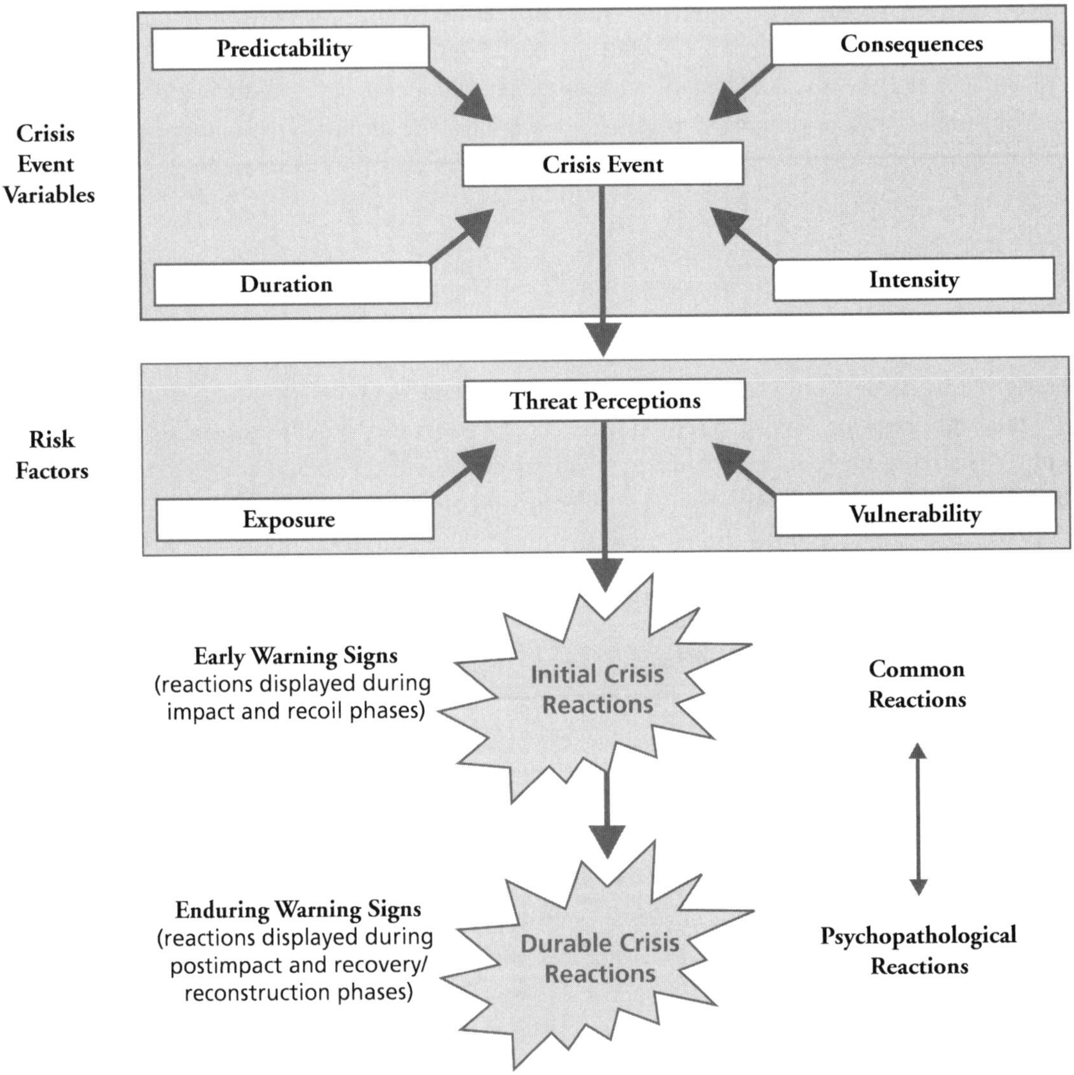

Note. Crisis event variables are those general factors that generate the potential for a given event to be psychologically traumatic. *Risk factors* are the unique individual variables that increase the odds that a given event will generate individual psychological injury. *Warning signs* are those factors that, when present, signal that an individual may have actually become a psychological trauma victim.

Street) were more likely to report PTSD symptoms than those who were more distant from the World Trade Center (i.e., residents who lived between 110th Street and Canal Street). Although only 6.8% of the latter group reported PTSD symptoms, 20% of those who lived near ground zero reported these symptoms. In addition, regardless of residence, directly witnessing the attacks on the World Trade Center also had a significant effect. Among those who did not witness the event, only 5.5% reported PTSD symptoms. In contrast, among those who had witnessed the attacks, 10.4% had these symptoms.

Another earlier study by Pynoos et al. (1987) also demonstrated the dominant influence of exposure to a crisis event in predicting the development of posttraumatic stress reactions among school children. This study assessed the self-reports of children's (ages 5 to 13 years) stress reactions following a sniper attack on a school playground that left one student and one passerby killed, and 13 others wounded. As illustrated in Figure 10.2, a strong relationship between physical proximity and PTSD symptoms was demonstrated using the PTSD Reaction Index.

From these studies it is suggested that physical proximity should be considered when making all initial treatment decisions in crisis intervention. More specifically, all individuals directly involved in or exposed to a crisis event should be given a high priority for crisis intervention assistance. Conversely, those who were more physically distant from a crisis event should typically be given a lower priority. However, physical proximity is not the only factor that needs to be considered (Marshall et al., 2007). For example, Pynoos et al. (1987) reported that a significant number of students (18%) who were physically removed from the crisis event (i.e., they were off track, or on vacation, at the time of the shooting) were significantly affected by the shooting, that is, they demonstrated moderate to severe PTSD symptoms (see Figure 10.3). Among the other

Figure 10.2. Relationship between physical proximity to a crisis event and traumatic stress reactions.

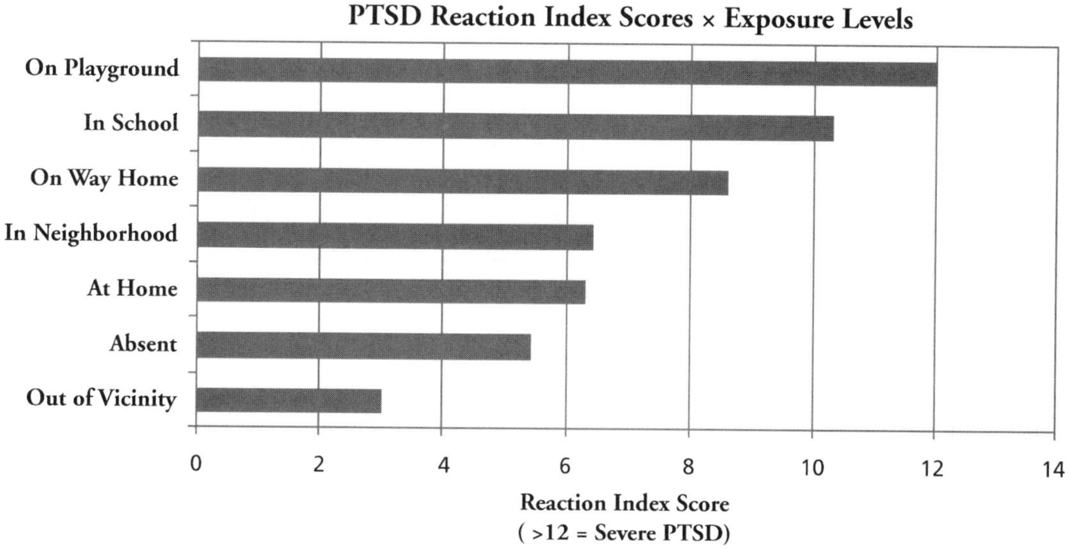

Note. From "Life Threat and Posttraumatic Stress in School-Age Children," by R. S. Pynoos et al., 1987, *Archives of General Psychiatry, 44,* p. 1059. Copyright 1987 by the American Medical Association. Reprinted with permission.

Figure 10.3. Relationship between crisis event exposure categories and severity of traumatic stress reactions.

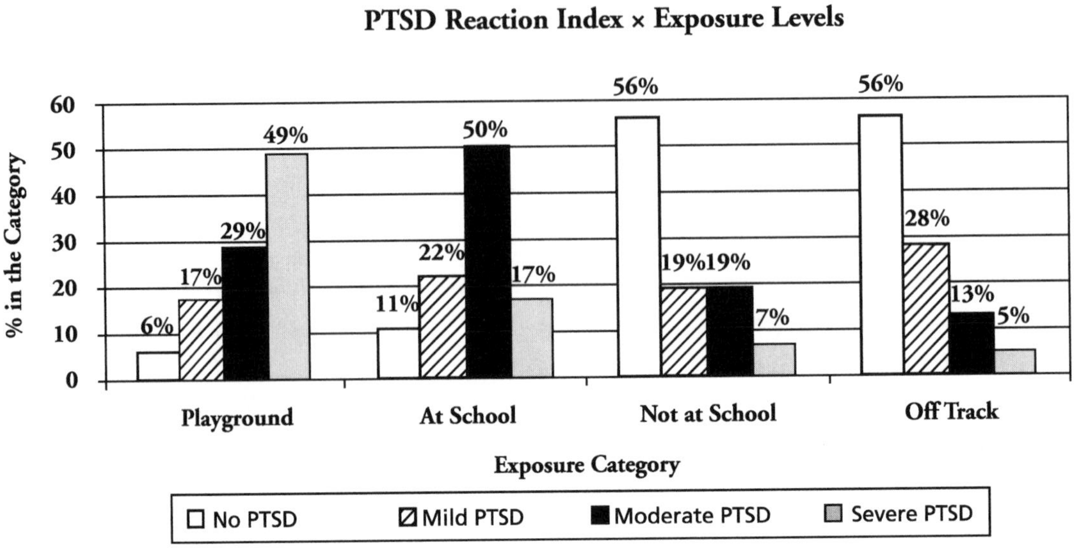

Note. According to Pynoos et al. (1987), "Using PTSD Reaction Index categories (<7 = no PTSD; 7 to 9 = mild; 10 to 12 = moderate; >12 = severe), ... a χ^2 analysis indicated significant differences in the proportion in these categories across the four exposure levels ($\chi^2 = 61.5$, df = 9, p = <.001)" (p. 1059). It is significant to note that even among the group of students who were the most physically removed from the shooting (Off Track), 18% demonstrated moderate to severe PTSD. From "Life Threat and Posttraumatic Stress in School-Age Children," by R. S. Pynoos et al., 1987, *Archives of General Psychiatry, 44,* p. 1059. Copyright 1987 by the American Medical Association. Reprinted with permission

variables that might explain such traumatization is emotional proximity or the relationships students may have had with crisis victims.

Crisis Exposure: Emotional Proximity

After physical proximity, emotional proximity is the next most powerful predictor of crisis reactions. Knowing someone who was a crisis victim is associated with negative mental health outcomes. In particular, it would appear that those who are bereaved are an especially high risk group (Eksi et al., 2007; NIMH, 2001). For example, 17.8% of Manhattan Island residents who had a friend or relative killed on 9/11, reported symptoms of depression 5 to 8 weeks after the attack (vs. 8.7% who did not suffer such a loss; Galea et al., 2002). Similarly, following the 1999 Athens earthquake, youth who demonstrated more significant traumatic stress included those whose relatives were injured (Kolaitis et al., 2003).

Figure 10.4, which provides data from a report on the effects of the World Trade Center attack on New York City Public School students, reveals the power of emotional proximity (Applied Research and Consulting et al., 2002). As illustrated in the figure, the closer the relationship students had with 9/11 victims, the more likely they were to demonstrate PTSD, Furthermore, a dramatic increase in PTSD was noted among those who had a parent or sibling killed in the attacks. It documents the need to make those who are bereaved an especially high

Figure 10.4. Relationship between traumatic stress and the closeness of relationships with crisis victims.

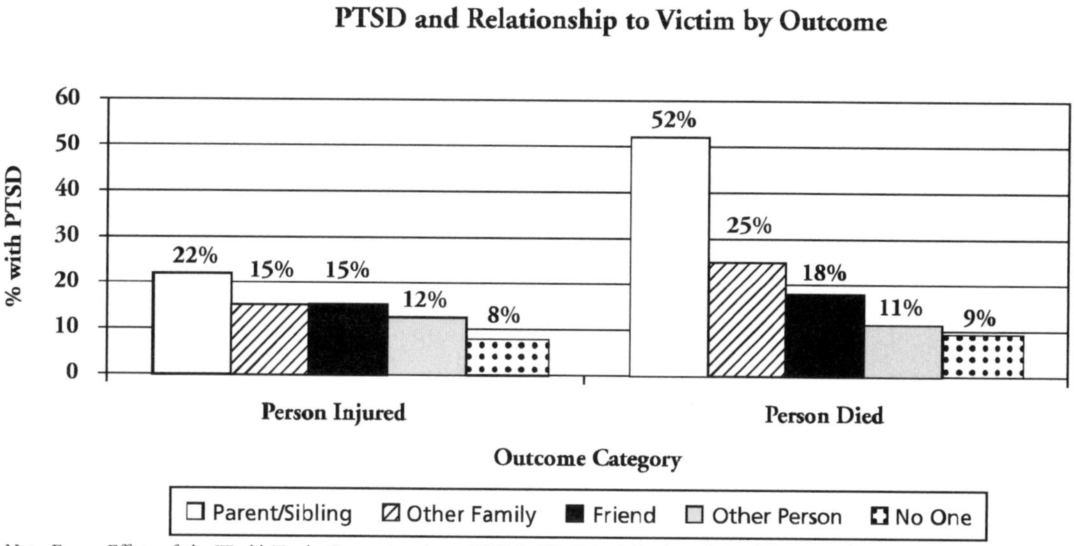

Note. From *Effects of the World Trade Center Attack on NYC Public School Students: Initial Report to the New York City Board of Education* (p. 34), by Applied Research and Consulting, Columbia University Mailman School of Public Health, & New York Psychiatric Institute, 2002. Copyright 2002 by the New York City Board of Education. Reprinted with permission.

priority for crisis intervention services, as they have a particularly high risk of developing PTSD. Similarly, Eksi et al. (2006) found that following an earthquake, depression was more likely among children who had lost a family member.

Emotional proximity also includes knowing someone who knew crisis victims and who had media exposure. For example, a study of sixth graders who lived within 100 miles of Oklahoma City at the time of the 1999 bombing found that media exposure and having a friend who knew someone killed or injured were both predictors of traumatic stress, even for those who had no direct physical exposure and didn't personally know any victims (Pfefferbaum et al., 2000).

Personal Vulnerability Factors

Physical proximity addresses where students were at the time of a crisis, and emotional proximity addresses whether students knew someone involved in a crisis, but personal vulnerabilities essentially address *who the student is* at the time of the crisis. This set of variables includes the so-called personal baggage that everyone carries and influences how they respond to life circumstances. These variables can also be considered risk factors that increase the probability of psychological trauma and, as such, should result in increased vigilance for warning signs of traumatic stress. Although crisis exposure variables are specific to the crisis situation, personal vulnerabilities are general risk factors that are applicable to all situations (not just the crisis event). There are two types of personal vulnerability variables that the evaluator of psychological trauma risk will need to consider: internal and external. Internal variables are those factors that operate within the individual, and external variables are those environmental factors that surround the individual.

Personal Vulnerability: Internal Factors

As shown in Table 10.1 a number of internal vulnerability factors can increase a student's risk for becoming a psychological trauma victim. Specifically, these risk factors are (a) the use of avoidance coping, (b) the presence of precrisis psychiatric challenges, (c) poor ability to regulate emotions, (d) low developmental levels and/or poor problem-solving ability, and (e) the presence of a trauma history.

The first vulnerability factor has its origins in the children's coping literature, which makes distinctions between active (or approach) and avoidance coping strategies (Ayers, Sandler, West, & Roosa, 1996; Ebata & Moos, 1994). Active coping strategies are direct and deliberate actions aimed at solving crisis problems. Avoidance coping, on the other hand, is thoughts and actions that attempt to focus away from a stressful situation (e.g., to stop thinking about or dealing with the stressor; Sandler, Wolchik, MacKinnon, Ayers, & Roosa, 1997). This latter type of coping behavior is consistently associated with a greater incidence of mental health concerns.

However, in extremely high-stress situations, some initial avoidance coping may be adaptive. One example is the case of an individual who is held up at gunpoint in the parking lot of a local shopping center. After giving the robber his wallet, he calmly gets into his car and drives home. However, at the moment he walks in the door, he breaks down, cries, and begins to feel distressed. In this instance, avoidance coping can be seen as having bought the individual time to get to a place where it was physically and emotionally safe to confront the frightening reality of being robbed at gunpoint.

Nevertheless, it is clear that individuals who continue to employ avoidance coping as a longer-term problem-solving strategy are more likely to have a poorer mental health outcome (Gil & Caspi, 2006; Krause, Kaltman, Goodman, & Dutton, 2008). Consistent with this observation, Silver, Holman, McIntosh, Poulin, and Gil-Rivas (2002), in their nationwide longitudinal study of psychological responses to 9/11, made the point that several coping strategies, particularly those involving denial or disengagement from coping, related to higher levels of distress 6 months after the event. In contrast, active coping strategies, such as accepting the event, are associated with less long-term stress. Similarly, Stallard and Smith (2007) found that children's cognitive coping style was a significant predictor of posttraumatic stress 8 months following a traffic accident.

Finally, it has been documented that both state (i.e., situation-specific) and trait (i.e., typical) avoidance coping are associated with an increased risk for PTSD (Dempsey, Overstreet, & Moely, 2000; Gil & Caspi, 2006) and indicate a greater need for crisis intervention support (Gil, 2005).

Table 10.1. Internal Vulnerability Factors

1. Avoidance coping
2. Preexisting mental illness
3. Poor emotional regulation
4. Low developmental level
5. Psychological trauma history

Regarding how such coping may affect traumatic stress, Dempsey et al. speculated that the use of avoidance coping strategies may impede children's ability to understand and integrate crises or prevent the habituation to recurrent trauma-related thoughts.

Another internal vulnerability factor is the individual's baseline mental health. Generally speaking, mentally healthy individuals are better able to cope with crisis events than are those with preexisting mental illness. Thus, having a preexisting mental illness would be considered a risk factor that increases vulnerability to traumatic stressors. For example, Breslau (1998) reported that preexisting major depression and anxiety disorders increase the risk of PTSD. Similarly, Gil-Rivas, Holman, and Silver (2004) reported that a history of mental health disorders was associated with increased reports of high levels of 9/11-related acute trauma symptomatology (which in turn placed individuals at greater risk for higher levels of longer-term symptomatology).

A third internal vulnerability factor is poor regulation of emotion. Typically, individuals with easy temperaments are less prone to emotional reactions subsequent to crisis exposure. Conversely, individuals who are known to have a negative temperament, become easily upset, and have difficulty calming down appear to be more vulnerable to psychological trauma and thus should be given a higher priority for crisis intervention treatment (McNally et al., 2003).

A fourth internal vulnerability factor is having a low developmental level or poor problem-solving skills. Once an event is judged threatening, and all other factors are held constant, the lower the developmental level of the crisis survivor, the greater the psychological trauma (Applied Research and Consulting et al., 2002; Caffo & Belaise, 2003; Hoven et al., 2004; King, King, Foy, & Gudanowski, 1996; Schwarz & Kowalski, 1991; Silva et al., 2000; Singer, Flannery, Guo, Miller, & Leibbrandt, 2004). This greater vulnerability of younger children is likely due to several factors: a relative lack of coping experience and skills; perception, understanding, and memory of the event; susceptibility to parental distress (Caffo & Belaise, 2003); a smaller social support network; and less well developed emotional regulation (Lonigan et al., 2003). In addition to chronological age, relative cognitive ability is related to risk for PTSD among people exposed to trauma. For example, Silva et al. (2000) reported that higher IQ was associated with lower severity of PTSD symptoms following exposure to traumatic stressors (i.e., experiencing war, witnessing violence, or being sexually abused).

Although lower developmental level is generally a risk factor for psychological trauma, an important exception needs to be noted. In some cases, high developmental level may cause a child's understanding of an event to seem more threatening, and low development may be protective. Consistent with this possible exception, Stallard and Salter (2003) stated: "Children of this age [7 to 11 years] may not, however, have the necessary knowledge or level of cognitive development to understand the degree of threat or potential implications posed by the trauma" (p. 451). Groome and Soureti (2004) further reported that following the 1999 Athens earthquake in the district closest to the earthquake, younger children had higher scores on measures of PTSD and anxiety. Conversely, in the district farthest away from the earthquake, older children had the highest scores on these measures. In interpreting these results, it was suggested that while the younger children who were closer to the earthquake had more symptoms because of fewer coping strategies (among other factors), older children who were more distant from the earthquake had more symptoms because of a greater understanding of the event.

A fifth internal vulnerability factor is having a history of prior traumatization (Bremner, Southwick, Johnson, Yehuda, & Charney, 1993; Breslau, 1998; Brewin, Andrews, & Valentine, 2000; Hoven et al., 2004; Imanaka, Morinobu, Toki, & Yamawaki, 2006; Möhlen, Parzer, Resch, & Brunner, 2005; Nader, Pynoos, Fairbanks, & Frederick, 1990; Nemeroff, 2004; Nemeroff et al., 2006; Olff, Langeland, & Gersons, 2005). According to Yehuda and Hyman (2005), "it may be that the real consequence of terrorism in children is to create a basis for risk for psychopathology in response to subsequent trauma exposure" (p. 1777). Though there is some suggestion in the literature that having coped with previous stressful events in an adaptive way might help people cope with future traumas, this appears to be true only when the exposure to current crises is low. "When exposure is high, the 'protective' value of having coped with previous life stressors seems to disappear" (Lecic-Tosevski, Gavrlovic, Knezevic, & Priebe, 2003, p. 547).

Children who have experienced repeated traumatic stressors, especially child abuse and neglect, are more likely to develop traumatic stress reactions, disassociate, and display mood swings than single-incident trauma survivors (Terr, 1991; Widom, 1999). In explaining how trauma history serves as a risk factor for traumatic stress, Olff et al. (2005) suggested that these experiences can adversely affect the development of coping skills and that they promote a heightened automatic response to stress.

Research conducted by Galea et al. (2002) highlights the importance of assessing trauma history. In a phone survey of Manhattan Island residents, conducted several weeks after the World Trade Center attacks, it was found that among individuals who had no prior trauma history, only 4.2% reported symptoms of traumatic stress. On the other hand, among those individuals with two or more significantly stressful events in their personal histories, 18.5% reported PTSD symptoms. In addition, among those with no trauma history, only 5.6% reported symptoms of depression, while among those with two or more stressful events, 24.1% reported such symptoms. When it comes to identifying traumatic stress, it is especially important to identify individuals who have experienced prior crises that are similar in nature to the current crisis event. Supporting this observation, Nader et al. (1990) reported that a school shooting was more traumatic for those youth who had previously been the victims of violent acts such as child abuse.

Personal Vulnerability: External Factors

There are two external vulnerability factors: (a) family resources and (b) extrafamilial social resources (see Table 10.2). The one word that best summarizes these risk factors is "aloneness." In other words, these are variables that, when present, at the very least result in trauma-exposed individuals viewing themselves as being all alone in coping with the stressor. Results of two meta-analyses have clearly documented that the absence of such external support systems is a powerful predictor of traumatic stress reactions (Brewin et al., 2000; Ozer, Best, Lipsey, & Weiss, 2003). From data such as those reviewed in this section, the reestablishment of naturally occurring social support systems is suggested to be a primary and critical school crisis intervention (see discussion in chapter 12).

The first vulnerability factor is the physical absence of familial support. When such support systems are absent or depleted, trauma-exposed students are at greater risk for traumatic stress reactions (Yorbik, Akbiyik, Kirmizigul, & Söhmen, 2004). For example, among Cambodian refugee youth, not being able to reunite and live with a nuclear family member after being forced

Table 10.2. External Vulnerability Factors

1. Lack of family resources and support
    a. Physical absence of family resources
    b. Psychological absence of family resources
    c. Parental traumatic stress
    d. Ineffective and uncaring parenting
    e. Poverty
2. Lack of extrafamilial social resources
    a. Social isolation
    b. Lack of perceived social support

to leave their country (following the massive trauma inflicted by the Pol Pot regime) was predictive of maladaptive adjustment. Kinzie, Sack, Angell, Manson, and Rath (1986), who studied these youth concluded "having reestablished some contact with family members in this setting [the United States] mitigated some of the symptoms of the severe trauma, while being alone or in a foster family exacerbated the disorder" (p. 375).

In some circumstances, family resources may be physically present but practically (or psychologically) unavailable to provide support to trauma exposed youth. When this support system is psychologically absent or depleted, youth are more alone and thus at greater risk for traumatic stress reactions and maladaptive coping (Barenbaum, Ruchkin, & Schwab-Stone, 2004). To the degree a student's family is dysfunctional, trauma-exposed youth will have increased difficulty adapting to stressors and may look to other less prosocial resources, such as substance abuse, to cope (Hilarski, 2004). Furthermore, maternal and paternal mental health appear to be important determinants of how well children cope with traumatic events (Kilic et al., 2003; Qouta, Punamäki, & El Sarraj, 2005).

Parental traumatic stress (e.g., PTSD) may also make family support resources practically (or psychologically) unavailable to traumatized youth and thus increase both actual and perceived aloneness. For example, it has been suggested that when a young person is living in an environment in which caregivers are significantly distressed, caregivers may be less likely to independently recognize their children's need for mental health support and intervention (Brown & Bobrow, 2004). However, it would appear that parental traumatic stress does more then simply render family resources unavailable to youth. As discussed in chapter 9, adult reactions to traumatic events may in fact be a cause of traumatic stress. When a primary caregiver suffers from traumatic stress, not only does it deprive the child of an important coping resource, but it also may increase the child's perceptions of the crisis event threat (as children often look to adult reactions to gage the danger presented by a given crisis event). If significant adults (e.g., parents) behave as if an event is very dangerous, then children are likely to respond accordingly (Qouta, Punamäki, & El Sarraj, 2003; Shaw, 2003).

While necessary, the physical and psychological presence of a family is not sufficient when it comes to preventing aloneness and fostering recovery from traumatic event exposure. For example, it has been well established that the nature and quality of the parent–child relationship is an important source of resiliency, and specific parenting characteristics that have been associated with resiliency include warmth, structure, and high expectations (Doll & Lyon, 1998). Further, the degree of family support predicts children's long-term emotional response to stressful events (Shaw, 2003), and according to Qouta et al. (2005): "It is well accepted that supportive and wise parents enhance children's mental health and favorable cognitive-emotional development, in general ..., and in traumatized families in particular" (p. 150). Thus, it is important to consider the quality of the parent–child relationship when evaluating risk for traumatic stress, and to consider youth to be at greater risk if they come from homes where they are exposed to ineffective and uncaring parenting.

Economic status is another familial resource that can affect the individual's traumatic stress reactions. Specifically, poverty is a risk factor that has been suggested to increase the risk of psychological trauma (Brymer et al., 2006). Students who come from impoverished backgrounds are more likely to have experienced prior traumatic events and trauma-related psychopathology, such as PTSD (Buka, Stichick, Birdthistle, & Earls, 2001; Seedat, Nyamai, Njenga, Vythilingum, & Stein, 2004).These families are often less able to access resources needed to mitigate crisis-generated problems (Brymer et al., 2006).

In addition to the absence of family resources, the actual or perceived absence of extrafamilial social relationships is also important and has been associated with vulnerability to traumatic stress. Individuals who must face a crisis without supportive and nurturing friends or relatives have been found to suffer more from PTSD than those with such resources (McNally et al., 2003). As discussed in chapter 7, close peer friendships, access to positive adult models outside of the family, and strong connections to prosocial organizations or institutions are protective, as are positive school experiences (academic or nonacademic). Individuals who have social supports can be expected to show lower levels of distress following a crisis. For example, a study of World Trade Center survivors by Galea et al. (2002) indicated that 10.2% and 15.5% of individuals with low levels of social support reported having symptoms of PTSD and depression, respectively, whereas only 4.4% and 5.6% of individuals with high levels of such support reported having symptoms of these disorders. Thus, it is essential that the evaluation of psychological trauma risk systematically examine the social supports available to students in the recovery environment as well as students' history of using these supports under stressful circumstances (Litz et al., 2002).

Not only is actual or perceived social support important, but so are perceptions of such support. For example, according to Norris et al. (2002), "With few exceptions, disaster survivors who subsequently believe that they are cared for by others, and that help will be available if needed, fare better psychologically than disaster survivors who believe they are unloved and alone" (¶ 3). Furthermore, according to McNally et al. (2003), "perceived lack of social support is strongly linked to heightened risk for PTSD" (p. 67).

Threat Perceptions

The next assessment variable, and the final risk factor considered when assessing trauma risk, is threat perceptions. These subjective impressions are arguably the most important risk factor

(Weaver & Clum, 1995), and the subjective experience of the individual is an important predictor of psychological trauma (Ehlers & Clark, 2000; Giannopoulou et al., 2006; Gil & Caspi, 2006; King, King, Fairbank, Keane, & Adams, 1998; Kutz & Dekel, 2006; Laubmeier & Sakowski, 2004; Shaw, 2003; Tatum, Vollmer, & Shore, 1986; Warda & Bryant, 1998). Simply put, traumatized individuals will have perceived the event as extremely negative. Viewing a crisis event as highly threatening, and having catastrophic views about oneself immediately after being exposed to a crisis, predicts traumatic stress reactions (Ehlers, Mayou, & Bryant, 1998). For example, Groome and Soureti (2004) reported that among children exposed to an earthquake, subjective reports of believing that their lives were in danger were associated with greater amounts of anxiety.

Adult reactions appear to be important influences on children's threat perceptions, especially among younger children. As discussed in chapter 9 and earlier in this chapter, parental traumatic stress reactions are considered to increase a child's vulnerability to traumatic stress. Events that were not initially perceived as threatening may become more threatening if children observe adults behaving in a way that suggests the event was dangerous or traumatic (Shaw, 2003). B. L. Green et al. (1991) found that following a dam failure, among children ages 2 to 7 years, traumatic stress symptoms were more influenced by parental reactions (i.e., severity of parental PTSD) than by the children's direct disaster exposure. For example, in the instance of a child who has fallen from a swing, if the child looks at the parent's face and sees a look of panic, he or she will respond to the parent's distress by crying. This is a common example of how children look to adults to gauge the degree to which a given situation is threatening.

Warning Signs

The final evaluation variable, warning signs, are the reactions of an individual during a crisis event. As illustrated in Figure 10.1, warning signs require crisis event exposure and are a consequence of youth's subjective views of the threat presented by the crisis event (which are influenced by crisis exposure and personal vulnerabilities). Warning signs include emotional, cognitive, physical, and interpersonal or behavioral reactions to crises. These reactions and their consequences are among the specific targets of crisis intervention efforts.

Although the risk factors discussed earlier in this chapter are variables that simply increase the odds of psychological trauma, warning signs (or crisis reactions) are variables that may also indicate that psychological trauma has in fact occurred. As such, they are important indicators of crisis intervention treatment priorities and needs. Especially when combined with risk factors, the presence and durability of warning signs may signal that an individual has become a psychological trauma victim and requires highly directive crisis intervention assistance and possibly longer-term mental health treatment.

As illustrated in Figure 10.1, early warning signs are those initial crisis reactions (typically displayed during the impact and recoil phases of a crisis event) that are not necessarily indicative of psychopathology. On the other hand, enduring warning signs are those more durable crisis reactions (typically displayed during the postimpact and recovery/reconstruction phases) that are more likely to reflect an underlying psychopathology.

Table 10.3. Common Initial Crisis Reactions

Emotional		*Cognitive*	
Shock	Depression or sadness	Impaired concentration	Decreased self-esteem
Anger	Grief	Impaired decision-making ability	Decreased self-efficacy
Despair	Irritability	Memory impairment	Self-blame
Emotional numbing	Hypersensitivity	Disbelief	Intrusive thoughts or memories[b]
Terror/fear	Helplessness	Confusion	Worry
Guilt	Hopelessness	Distortion	Nightmares
Phobias	Loss of pleasure from activities		
	Dissociation[a]		
Physical		*Interpersonal/Behavioral*	
Fatigue	Impaired immune response	Alienation	Avoidance of reminders
Insomnia	Headaches	Social withdrawal/isolation	Crying easily
Sleep disturbance	Gastrointestinal problems	Increased relationship conflict	Change in eating patterns
Hyperarousal	Decreased appetite	Vocational impairment	Tantrums
Somatic complaints	Decreased libido	Refusal to go to school	Regression in behavior
	Startle response	School impairment	Risk taking
			Aggression

Note. [a]Examples include perceptual experience, such as "dreamlike," "tunnel vision," "spacey," or on "automatic pilot." [b]Reenactment play among children. Sources *Psychosocial Issues for Children and Adolescents in Disasters,* by A. H. Speier, 20000; and *Disaster Mental Health Services,* by B. H. Young, J. D. Ford, J. I. Ruzek, M. Friedman, and F. D. Gusman, 1998.

Chapter 1 defined the crisis state and suggested that responding to associated crisis reactions was a primary reason for crisis intervention. This chapter provides greater detail regarding the manifestations of the crisis state. This discussion includes an examination of the distinction between common (early warning signs) and potentially psychopathological (enduring warning signs) crisis reactions. Although some reactions are expected following crisis exposure, there is no one normal or expected crisis reaction or set of reactions. Different individuals will have different reactions to the same event. Thus, this section also examines factors contributing to individual differences in crisis reactions, including developmental level and culture.

Early Warning Signs

Especially in the immediate aftermath of traumatic event exposure, some crisis reactions are to be expected. In fact, it has been suggested that some anxiety is normal and part of the healthy response to situations that require increased vigilance (Hobfoll et al., 2007). Thus, at least initially, crisis responders should avoid classifying initial crisis reactions as mental illness (see Table 10.3; Brymer et al., 2006; NIMH, 2001; Ruzek et al., 2007). In most cases, these are normal reactions to unusual circumstances and will subside within a few weeks if students have the support of family, teachers, and friends. The classification of crisis reactions as being an indication of psychopathology should not begin until a week or more after the crisis event has ended (McNally et al., 2003). However, when these common crisis reactions are especially acute or are combined with certain specific risk factors, they should be carefully monitored. For example, if the crisis event caused a physical injury or the death of a family member, or if the individual had a preexisting psychological problem or exposure to the crisis event was particularly intense or of long duration, the individual may require follow-up mental health crisis intervention (NIMH, 2001).

Although it is important to avoid overly pathologizing initial crisis reactions, it is also important to acknowledge that some students (typically a minority of those exposed to a crisis event) will demonstrate more severe reactions that may signal the need for referral to a community-based mental health professional. Reactions include those that interfere with necessary activities such as sleeping, eating, drinking, decision making, and other essential life tasks. Not only do these functional impairments in and of themselves threaten physical health and welfare, but they also may predict anxiety disorders (Hobfoll et al., 2007).

Additional research has also shown that individuals who were acutely distressed during a crisis event (e.g., had extreme negative emotional reactions or demonstrated acute panic and dissociative states) were more likely to develop PTSD than those who remained calm and in control of their emotions (Bernat, Ronfeldt, Calhoun, & Arias, 1998; Lawyer et al., 2006; Martin & Marchand, 2003; McFarlane & Yehuda, 1996). Similarly, Vaiva et al. (2003) reported that among individuals hospitalized after a motor vehicle accident, those who had "fright" reactions (operationalized as "having, at least momentarily, a complete absence of affect, or lack of thought, or loss of words, or being spaced out, or all of these symptoms") had a 17 times greater risk of meeting PTSD diagnostic criteria (p. 397). In addition, Frommberger et al. (1998), who also studied motor vehicle accident victims, reported that individuals who developed PTSD demonstrated more symptoms of depression, anxiety, and PTSD a few days after the accident than individuals who did not develop such mental illness. Finally, among individuals who were hospitalized for blunt or penetrating trauma and were considered victims of community violence, the severity of acute traumatic stress symptoms, measured 5 days after the traumatic event, was the single most powerful predictor of PTSD a year later (Denson, Marshall, Schell, & Jaycox, 2007). These findings suggest that school-based mental health professionals responsible for evaluating psychological trauma should strive to identify those students who were observed or reported to be acutely distressed during the crisis event.

Another group of initial crisis reactions that has been suggested to be predictive of traumatic stress includes increased arousal (e.g., exaggerated startle responses, hypervigilance, irritability, and sleep disturbance). These reactions have been found to differentiate individuals who developed PTSD from those who did not develop this disorder. In contrast, persistent reexperiencing (e.g., distressing and intrusive memories) was suggested to be less worrisome in the days after a crisis event and considered to be part of normal reappraisal (McFarlane & Yehuda, 1996).

In addition to crisis reactions, maladaptive coping strategies—that is, counterproductive behaviors designed to manage or cope with crisis experiences and reactions—that present a risk of harm to self or others sometimes emerge as a consequence of exposure to crisis events (American Red Cross, 1991; Azarian & Skriptchenko-Gregorian, 1998b; Berman, Kurtines, Silverman, & Serafini, 1996; de Wilde & Kienhorst, 1998; McNally et al., 2003). For example, the presence of the following maladaptive behaviors would signal the need for an immediate referral to a community-based mental health professional: (a) extreme substance abuse or self-medication, (b) suicidal or homicidal thinking, (c) extreme inappropriate anger toward and abuse of others, and (d) the taking of excessive precautions (e.g., only sleeping with a weapon nearby). All caregivers should be aware of the potential for such maladaptive coping behaviors and to recognize that they signal the need for referral to a community-based mental health professional.

Table 10.4 lists the initial crisis reactions discussed in this section that may signal the need for referral to a community-based mental health professional. As discussed in chapter 1 and listed in Table 1.5, these reactions may reach the point at which they meet the criteria for one or more diagnoses under the *Diagnostic and Statistical Manual of Mental Disorders* (DSM-IV-TR; American Psychiatric Association, 2000).

Enduring Warning Signs

Even for less worrisome initial crisis reactions such as persistent reexperiencing, if they endure (i.e., they do not remit or they worsen after a week or more) they may have developed into mental illness. Although initial crisis reactions might be adaptive or protective, prolonged states of emotional distress may lead to a variety of mental health challenges (Harvey & Bryant, 1998; Shalev & Freedman, 2005).

Acute stress disorder and posttraumatic stress disorder (PTSD) are the two most common diagnoses associated with traumatic event exposure. Diagnostic criteria for these disorders are provided in Tables 10.5 and 10.6. Although treating students and staff who develop these serious and potentially debilitating psychiatric conditions is not typically a part of the school crisis intervention response (this is typically a part of the community-based mental health response to disaster), it is important for school-based mental health professionals to be able to recognize them and make appropriate referrals. (For further discussion of PTSD and the identification, assessment, and treatment of this disorder in the school setting, see Nickerson, Reeves, Brock, and Jimerson, 2009).

Developmental Variations

Crisis reactions are to a significant extent dependent upon the child's level of development (Joshi & Lewin, 2004). The importance of recognizing the effects of developmental status on crisis reactions is emphasized by the results of several studies of PTSD symptoms among children (Carrion, Weems, Ray, & Reiss, 2002; Scheeringa, Wright, Hunt, & Zeanah, 2006; Yorbik et al., 2004). Collectively these studies suggest that developmental differences in children's expression of symptoms, and difficulty verbalizing how a crisis event is affecting them, can significantly underestimate the number of preschool youth who have PTSD. For example, Carrion et al. (2002) concluded that PTSD diagnostic criteria may not be appropriate for

Table 10.4. Warning Signs of Psychopathology and Indicators of the Need for Immediate Mental Health Crisis Intervention

Peritraumatic dissociation[a]
- Derealization (e.g., feeling as if in a dream world)
- Depersonalization (e.g., feeling as if your body is not really yours)
- Reduced awareness of surroundings (e.g., being in a daze)
- Emotional numbness/detachment (e.g., feeling emotionally detached/estranged; lack typical range of emotional reactions; reduced interest in previously important/enjoyed activities; feeling as if there is no future career, marriage, children, or normal life span)
- Amnesia (i.e., failure to remember significant crisis event experiences)

Intense peritraumatic emotional reactions[b]
- Fear (e.g., of dying)
- Helplessness
- Horror

Intense peritraumatic hyperarousal[c]
- Panic attacks
- Hypervigilance and exaggerated startle reactions (e.g., unusually alert and easily startled)
- Difficulty falling or staying asleep (sometimes a result of the re-experiencing symptom of disturbing dreams)

Significant depression[d]
- Feelings of hopelessness and worthlessness
- Loss of interest in most activities
- Early awakening
- Persistent fatigue
- Virtually complete lack of motivation

Psychotic symptoms[e]
- Delusions
- Hallucinations
- Bizarre thoughts or images
- Catatonia

Maladaptive coping[f]
- Extreme substance abuse or self-medication
- Suicidal or homicidal thinking, extreme inappropriate anger toward or abuse of others, or the taking of excessive precautions (e.g., only sleeping with a light on or with a weapon nearby)

Note. Sources [a]Bernat, Ronfeldt, Calhoun, & Arias, (1998); Ehlers, Mayou, & Bryant (1998); Grieger, Fullerton, & Ursano (2003); Koopman, Catherine, & David (1994); Lawyer et al. (2006); Tichenor, Marmar, Weiss, Metzler, & Ronfeldt (1996); Weiss, Marmar, Metzler, & Ronfeldt (1995). [b]Bernat et al., (1998); Brewin, Andrews, & Rose (2000); Lawyer et al. (2006); Simeon, Greenberg, Knutelska, Schmeidler, & Hollander (2003); Viaiva et al (2003). [c]Galea et al. (2002); Galea et al. (2003); Lawyer et al. (2006); McFarlane & Yehuda (1996); Tucker, Pfefferbaum, Nixon, & Dickson, (2000). [d]Frommberger et al. (1998). [e]Gracie et al. (2007); Kaštelan et al. (2007). [f]Azarian & Skriptchenko-Gregorian (1998b); Berman, Kurtines, Silverman, & Serafini (1996); de Wilde & Kienhorst (1998); Matsakis (1994); McNally et al. (2003).

Table 10.5. DSM-IV-TR Diagnostic Criteria for 308.3 Acute Stress Disorder

A. The person has been exposed to a traumatic event in which both of the following were present:
  (1) the person experienced, witnessed, or was confronted with an event or events that involved actual or threatened death or serious injury, or a threat to the physical integrity of self or others
  (2) the person's response involved intense fear, helplessness, or horror

B. Either while experiencing or after experiencing the distressing event, the individual has three (or more) of the following dissociative symptoms:
  (1) a subjective sense of numbing, detachment, or absence of emotional responsiveness
  (2) a reduction in awareness of his or her surroundings (e.g., "being in a daze")
  (3) derealization
  (4) depersonalization
  (5) dissociative amnesia (i.e., inability to recall an important aspect of the trauma)

C. The traumatic event is persistently reexperienced in at least one of the following ways: recurrent images, thoughts, dreams, illusions, flashback episodes, or a sense of reliving the experience; or distress on exposure to reminders of the traumatic event.

D. Marked avoidance of stimuli that arouse recollections of the trauma (e.g., thoughts, feelings, conversations, activities, places, people).

E. Marked symptoms of anxiety or increased arousal (e.g., difficulty sleeping, irritability, poor concentration, hypervigilance, exaggerated startle response, motor restlessness).

F. The disturbance causes clinically significant distress or impairment in social, occupational, or other important areas of functioning or impairs the individual's ability to pursue some necessary task, such as obtaining necessary assistance or mobilizing personal resources by telling family members about the traumatic experience.

G. The disturbance lasts for a minimum of 2 days and a maximum of 4 weeks and occurs within 4 weeks of the traumatic event.

H. The disturbance is not due to the direct physiological effects of a substance (e.g., a drug of abuse, a medication) or a general medical condition, is not better accounted for by Brief Psychotic Disorder, and is not merely an exacerbation of a preexisting Axis I or Axis II disorder.

Note. Reprinted with permission from the *Diagnostic and Statistical Manual of Mental Disorders*, Fourth Edition, Text Revision (pp. 471–472). (Copyright 2000) American Psychiatric Association.

children and that, among children, the failure to meet all of the PTSD diagnostic criteria may "not indicate a lack of posttraumatic stress problems, but may be due to developmental differences in symptom expression" (p. 172). As a result, rather than seeking a threshold of symptoms, Carrion et al. suggested that a more precise diagnosis of pediatric PTSD would involve assessment of symptom intensity and the extent to which crisis reactions cause functional impairment. Similar conclusions were reached by Yorbik et al. (2004), who studied a sample of children ages 2 to 16 years who had presented with symptoms of PTSD following an earthquake. They concluded that

Table 10.6. DSM-IV-TR Diagnostic Criteria for 309.81 Posttraumatic Stress Disorder

A. The person has been exposed to a traumatic event in which both of the following were present:
   (1) the person experienced, witnessed, or was confronted with an event or events that involved actual or threatened death or serious injury, or a threat to the physical integrity of self or others.
   (2) the person's response involved intense fear, helplessness, or horror. **Note:** In children, this may be expressed instead by disorganized or agitated behavior.

B. The traumatic event is persistently reexperienced in one (or more) of the following ways:
   (1) recurrent and intrusive distressing recollections of the event, including images, thoughts, or perceptions. **Note:** In young children, repetitive play may occur in which themes or aspects of the trauma are expressed.
   (2) recurrent distressing dreams of the event. **Note:** In children, there may be frightening dreams without recognizable content.
   (3) acting or feeling as if the traumatic event were recurring (includes a sense of reliving the experience, illusions, hallucinations, and dissociative flashback episodes, including those that occur on awakening or when intoxicated). **Note:** In young children, trauma-specific reenactment may occur.
   (4) intense psychological distress at exposure to internal or external cues that symbolize or resemble an aspect of the traumatic event.
   (5) physiological reactivity on exposure to internal or external cues that symbolize or resemble an aspect of the traumatic event.

C. Persistent avoidance of stimuli associated with the trauma and numbing of general responsiveness (not present before the trauma), as indicated by three (or more) of the following:
   (1) efforts to avoid thoughts, feelings, or conversations associated with the trauma
   (2) efforts to avoid activities, places, or people that arouse recollections of the trauma
   (3) inability to recall an important aspect of the trauma
   (4) markedly diminished interest in participation in significant activities
   (5) feeling of detachment or estrangement from others
   (6) restricted range of affect (e.g., unable to have loving feelings)
   (7) sense of foreshortened future (e.g., does not expect to have a career, marriage, children, or a normal life span)

D. Persistent symptoms of increased arousal (not present before the trauma), as indicated by two (or more) of the following:
   (1) difficulty falling or staying asleep
   (2) irritability or outbursts of anger
   (3) difficulty concentrating
   (4) hypervigilance
   (5) exaggerated startle response

Table 10.6. (continued)

E. Duration of the disturbance (symptoms B, C, and D) is more than 1 month.

F. The disturbance causes clinically significant distress or impairment in social, occupational, or other important areas of functioning.

Specify if:

Acute: if duration of symptoms is less than 3 months

Chronic: if duration of symptoms is 3 months or more

Specify if:

With Delayed Onset: if onset of symptoms is at least 6 months after the stressor

Note. Reprinted with permission from the *Diagnostic and Statistical Manual of Mental Disorders*, Fourth Edition, Text Revision (p. 468). (Copyright 2000) American Psychiatric Association.

current diagnostic criteria are not sufficient for PTSD diagnosis among preschool children and that newly developed fears and regressive behaviors should be added to the diagnostic criteria for this age group.

Given these observations, a critical component of crisis intervention is understanding how students' developmental level influences their crisis reactions (and directs specific crisis interventions; Feeny, Foa, Treadwell, & March, 2004). The following are some of the unique features of crisis reactions at different developmental levels, based on several sources' (American Psychiatric Association, 2000; Berkowitz, 2003; Cook-Cottone, 2004; Dulmus, 2003; Joshi & Lewin, 2004; NIMH, 2001; Yorbik et al., 2004).

In general, the crisis reactions of *preschool youth* are not as clearly connected to the crisis event as is typically observed among older children. For example, in this age group, reexperiencing the trauma might be expressed as generalized nightmares. Crisis reactions also tend to be expressed nonverbally and may include clinginess, tantrums, crying and screaming more readily and often, trembling, and frightened facial expressions. The temporary loss of recently achieved developmental milestones might be observed (e.g., loss of bowel or bladder control, bedwetting, thumb sucking, fear of the dark, or fear of parental separation). Finally, the preschool child may reexperience the crisis event through trauma-related play (that does not relieve accompanying anxiety), which may be compulsive and repetitive.

Reactions among *younger school-age youth* tend to be more directly connected to the crisis event and event-specific fears may be displayed. However, to a significant degree the crisis reactions of young school-age children continue to be expressed behaviorally (e.g., behavioral regression, clinging and anxious attachment behaviors, refusal to go to school, irritability, or anxiety). Diminished emotional regulation (e.g., irrational fears) and increased behavior problems (e.g., outbursts of anger and fighting with peers) may be observed. In addition, feelings associated with traumatic stress reactions are often expressed in terms of concrete physical symptoms (e.g., stomachaches and headaches). Older children may continue to reexperience the trauma through play, but such play will be more complex and elaborate (when compared with that of preschoolers), and often includes writing, drawing, and pretending. Repetitive verbal descriptions of the event (without appropriate affect) may also be observed. Given these reactions it is not surprising that problems paying attention and poor schoolwork may also be noted.

As *adolescents* begin to develop abstract reasoning abilities, crisis reactions become more and more like those manifested by adults. A sense of a foreshortened future may be reported. This age group is more prone to using oppositional and aggressive behaviors as coping strategies as they strive to regain a sense of control. Other maladaptive coping behaviors reported in this age group include school avoidance, self-injurious behaviors, suicidal ideation, revenge fantasies, and substance abuse. Again, given these reactions it is not surprising that older school-age youth and adolescents may have particular difficulty concentrating or be moodier (which may cause learning problems).

Cultural Variations

Other important determinants of crisis reactions in general, and grief in particular, are family and cultural and religious beliefs. For example, in the dominant African American culture, coping is often viewed as an act of will that is controlled by the individual, and failure to cope is associated with weakness. In the dominant Asian American culture, feelings and problems are often not expressed so as to avoid losing respect. In both instances, crises can cause feelings of shame, which can affect crisis reactions (Sullivan, Harris, Collado, & Chen, 2006). Culture also influences the types of events that appear to be threatening in the first place and affects how individuals assign meaning to a threat. Culture also influences how individuals or communities express traumatic reactions, and how the traumatized individuals or communities view and judge their own responses (Tramonte, 1999).

Klingman (1986) highlighted the importance of cultural awareness. In describing the interventions conducted by crisis workers as they notified parents of their child's death in a school bus accident, he stated that cultural awareness among crisis interveners:

> proved valuable in that they were prepared for various culturally based manifestations of traumatic grief reactions, and thus refrained from requesting the use of sedatives in cases in which the parents' reactions to a death notification on the surface seemed extreme but were in line with their cultural norms. (p. 55)

All providers of crisis intervention should inform themselves about cultural norms with the assistance of community cultural leaders who best understand local customs. (For further discussion of this topic see Sandoval and Lewis, 2002.)

CONCLUSION

The development of psychological trauma is the result of a complex interaction between the nature of the crisis event (some events are more frightening than others), the survivor's unique crisis exposure (physical and emotional proximity), crisis threat perceptions, preexisting personal vulnerabilities, and crisis reactions. In other words, psychological trauma is a consequence of what happened (i.e., the nature of the crisis event), where crisis victims were and who they knew at the time of the crisis (i.e., crisis exposure), how they viewed the event (i.e., threat perceptions), who they were and the environment that supported them at the time of the crisis (i.e., personal vulnerabilities), and how they reacted to the crisis (i.e., crisis reactions). Though these factors can provide guidance regarding who may be in need of crisis intervention services, the interactions among these variables are very complex and not yet completely understood. Crisis interveners therefore need to be attentive to the crisis intervention literature for future guidance regarding the specific variables (and variable combinations) that best predict traumatic stress reactions.

Chapter 11

A MODEL FOR THE PRACTICE OF PSYCHOLOGICAL TRIAGE

Psychological triage necessarily involves multiple methods and sources and is a dynamic process, not an event (Saltzman, Pynoos, Layne, Steinberg, & Aisenberg, 2001). The PREPaRE triage model reviewed in this chapter describes the evaluation of psychological trauma as occurring at three different levels—that is, primary, secondary, and tertiary. These levels are summarized in Table 11.1.

Primary assessment of psychological trauma establishes initial crisis intervention treatment priorities and makes initial decisions about what form of crisis intervention (if any) school community members need. It is based on known risk factors for psychological trauma. These variables include known crisis facts and precrisis individual characteristics. When available, the initial crisis reactions of individuals may also provide a basis for primary evaluation treatment decisions.

Secondary assessment of psychological trauma takes place as the initial immediate crisis interventions are provided. This level goes beyond the known crisis facts and individual characteristics (or risk factors) and initial crisis reactions (or early warning signs) and examines individual threat perceptions and more durable crisis reactions, both reactions observed by crisis interveners and those observed by other caregivers. This level of triage reevaluates and refines crisis intervention treatment priorities and needs. As the magnitude of individual crisis reactions is recognized, this level of triage begins to identify who may require community-based mental health treatment referrals.

Finally, the *tertiary assessment* of psychological trauma takes place during the concluding stages of the crisis intervention. This level continues to evaluate known crisis facts, individual characteristics, and threat perceptions (or risk factors) and continues to monitor student crisis reactions (or enduring warning signs). This level of triage identifies those individuals for whom school-based crisis intervention is by itself insufficient. Its primary goals are (a) the identification of those individuals who appear to require community-based mental health treatment and (b) the making of appropriate referrals.

Table 11.1. Levels of Psychological Triage

Triage Level	*Timing*	*Variables Considered*	*Goals*
Primary	Before immediate crisis interventions are provided	Selected risk factors (crisis exposure, vulnerabilities) and warning signs (initial crisis reactions) for psychological trauma	1. Establish initial treatment priorities 2. Make initial decisions about individual crisis intervention needs
Secondary	During the provision of crisis interventions	Risk factors and warning signs for psychological trauma	1. Refine treatment priorities 2. Match crisis intervention to individual needs 3. Begin to consider psychotherapeutic treatment referrals
Tertiary	As the crisis intervention response concludes	Risk factors and warning signs for psychological trauma	1. Identify individuals who require ongoing psychotherapeutic treatment

Before the different levels of psychological triage are presented in detail, several prefacing comments are in order. First, there is currently no research regarding the effectiveness of any specific approach to psychological triage. Though clearly based on an understanding of the available empirical literature, the practical model presented in this chapter is currently pending empirical validation. Dependent measures of particular interest would be low rates of false positives and false negatives when it comes to the identification of psychological trauma victims.

Another important preface to this discussion of the practice of triage is that this process requires preparation. As suggested in section 1 of this book, for school crisis interventions to be effective, including the assessment of psychological trauma, they must take place within the context of a broader school crisis response team. In addition, before conducting any triage of psychological trauma victims, school crisis interveners must have previously identified the school- and community-based mental health resources that crisis intervention will require. In-service staff development training (such as participation in a PREPaRE workshop) might be one way to develop school-based resources; additional community-based resources might include community mental health centers, university counseling or psychology training programs, and private mental health practitioners. For example, Brock, Sandoval, and Lewis (2001) recommended the use of a Private Practitioner Referral Questionnaire to identify the community-based mental health resources that severely traumatized students will require (see Figure 11.1). The questionnaire is used to identify community-based mental health resources and to survey local professionals regarding a variety of psychotherapy issues.

In addition to identifying mental health resources, school crisis teams should identify other community-based support resources that might be required to address some crisis problems.

Figure 11.1. The Private Practitioner Referral Questionnaire, which identifies community-based mental health resources.

Private Practitioner Referral Questionnaire

Thank you for providing us with information that will help us to make more appropriate referrals to you and your colleagues. Please complete as much of the questionnaire as is possible and return it in the attached, self-addressed envelope.

Name ______________________ Title ______________________
Office Location ______________________ License(s) ______________________
Phone Number(s) ______________________ License Number(s) ______________________

Training and Experience

1. What degrees do you hold? ______________________
2. What schools did you attend? ______________________
3. How long have you been in practice? ______________________
4. What other types of special training do you have? ______________________

Financial Questions

5. What type of insurance do you accept? ______________________
6. What payment options do you offer? ______________________
7. Would you consider a therapeutic fee adjustment? YES / NO
8. Do you offer a sliding fee schedule? YES / NO
9. What are your current fees? (Attach fee schedule if available.) ______________________

Logistics

10. Are you currently taking new referrals? YES / NO
    If no, when will you do so? ______________________
11. What are your work hours? ______________________
12. Do you work evenings? YES / NO
13. Do you work Saturdays? YES / NO
14. Do you have a waiting list? YES / NO
    If yes, how long is the typical wait before the first session? ______________________

Therapeutic Issues

15. With which of the following populations do you feel you are best trained to work? (Circle all that apply that you.)

    Children *Adults* *Adolescents* *Families*

16. Which of the following issues and/or areas do you consider to be your specialties? (Circle all that apply.)

substance abuse	*child abuse*	*grief processing*
eating disorders	*crisis therapy*	*attention deficit disorders*
anger issues	*suicide prevention*	*suicidal ideation*
empowerment issues	*codependency*	*crisis intervention*
creative divorce	*divorce mediation*	*transitional issues*
decision making	*family communication*	*self-esteem/self-concept*
depression	*behavior analysis*	*conduct disorders*

Others? (please list) ______________________

Figure 11.1. (continued)

17. Which of the following therapeutic techniques do you employ? (Circle all that apply.)

behavior modification	*bio-feedback*	*Hypnosis*
EMDR	*client-centered*	*cognitive-behavioral*
RET	*relaxation*	*sand tray*
play therapy	*stress inoculation training*	*cognitive therapy*
creative therapies	*psychoanalysis*	*supportive group therapy*

Others? (Please list.) ______________________________

18. What special programs or services do you offer? ______________________________
19. Do you conduct group therapy? YES / NO
20. Are you bilingual? YES / NO
    If yes what language(s) do you speak? ______________________________
21. Are the services of an interpreter available to you? YES / NO
    If yes, what language(s) do your interpreters speak? ______________________________
22. Do you have expertise working with specific ethnic/cultural groups? YES/NO
    If yes, specify the group(s). ______________________________
23. When making a referral to you, what information would you find most helpful? ____________
    ____
24. What type of arrangements do you make with your clients for assistance during your non-work hours when they are experiencing a crisis? ______________________________
25. On average, how many times per month will you see the typical client? ____________
26. How long are your sessions? ______________________________
27. Please list any other information that may help us make more appropriate referrals to you.
    ____
    ____
    ____
    ____
    ____
    ____
    ____
    ____
    ____
    ____
    ____
    ____
    ____
    ____
    ____
    ____
    ____
    ____
    ____
    ____
    ____

Note. From *Preparing for Crises in the Schools* (pp. 131–132), by S. E. Brock, J. Sandoval, & S. Lewis, 2001, New York: Wiley. Copyright 2001 by John Wiley & Sons. Reprinted with permission.

Examples of these resources include American Red Cross chapters, Victim Witness programs, the Federal Emergency Management Agency (FEMA), and the State Office of Emergency Services (OES).

Finally, other important evaluation of psychological trauma preparedness activities, which will be discussed in detail later in this chapter, include obtaining and developing psychological trauma screening tools and developing crisis intervention referral forms.

PRIMARY EVALUATION OF PSYCHOLOGICAL TRAUMA

Given that the first priority of all school crisis team members is to reaffirm physical health and perceptions of safety and security, initial evaluation of psychological trauma may take place during or immediately after a crisis event. For example, as a school-based mental health professional helps to ensure that students are physically safe, he or she can be making note of those students who are demonstrating acute distress. However, regardless of exactly when the evaluation activities begin, for the reasons discussed in chapter 10 (i.e., not all individuals will be equally affected by the crisis event, and some crisis interventions have the potential to cause harm), evaluation should be conducted before individuals are offered school crisis intervention.

According to Litz, Gray, Bryant, and Adler (2002), these initial evaluations are "not intended for diagnostic purposes but rather to flag those individuals who may require special attention because they are statistically more likely to develop problems as time progresses" (p. 129). Consistent with this observation, primary evaluation is designed to identify those individuals at-risk for psychological trauma and most likely to be in need of a crisis intervention response. It requires knowledge of the crisis facts (i.e., physical and emotional proximity to the crisis event) and familiarity with the population (i.e., knowledge of personal vulnerabilities) affected by the crisis event. When available, information regarding the initial crisis reactions displayed by individuals during the crisis event should also be a part of primary evaluation.

Adapted from a document originally developed by Brock et al. (2001), the Primary Risk Screening form (provided in Figure 11.2) is designed to facilitate this level of triage. Considering the risk factors for psychological trauma discussed in chapter 10, this form attempts to quantify risk of psychological traumatization using variables known to be correlated with psychological trauma. A Total Primary Risk Screening Rating score can be used to rank order individuals in terms of their crisis intervention treatment priority (with higher scores indicating greater treatment priorities). It should be cautioned that this tool, though considered to be empirically informed (i.e., it quantifies variables known to be correlated with traumatic stress), is not norm-referenced nor empirically validated. Thus, clinical judgment should guide its use.

During crisis intervention, it is recommended that this form be completed by crisis intervention team members whenever their attention is directed toward a given student (or staff member). For example, as a crisis intervention team member directly observes a given student or consults with a teacher about a student, he or she would complete this form. Then the crisis intervention team member would ensure that the operations section chief or crisis intervention specialist is given a copy of the form to track individuals and assign crisis intervention treatment priorities.

Figure 11.2. Primary Risk Screening form to be completed for all individuals from the population affected by a crisis.

Primary Risk Screening

Student ______________________ M ___ F ___ Date ______________

Referred by ______________________ Teacher/Counselor ______________

Dominant Language ______________________ Screener ______________

A. Crisis Exposure

1. Physical Proximity

10	8	6	4	2	0
Crisis victim; physically injured	Crisis victim; physically threatened	Crisis witness	In the vicinity of the crisis	Absent by chance from the site of the crisis event	Out of the vicinity of the crisis event

Describe crisis event exposure: ______________________

____

____

____

2. Duration of Exposure

5	4	3	2	1	0
Weeks	Days	Hours	Minutes	Seconds	None

3. Emotional Proximity

5	4	3	2	1	0
Parent(s) or sibling(s)	Other family member(s)	Best and/or only friend(s)	Good friend(s)	Friend(s) or acquaintance(s)	Did not know victim(s)

Elaborate on relationship(s) with crisis victim(s): ______________________

____

B. Personal Vulnerabilities

	Yes	*No*	*Elaborate*
Known/suspected mental illness			
Avoidance coping style			
Developmental immaturity			
Previous trauma or loss			
Poor self-regulation of emotion			
Lack of family resources			
Lack of social resources			
Total			

C. Immediate Crisis Reactions

5	3	1	0
Acutely distressed	Moderately distressed	Mildly distressed	Remained calm

Primary Risk Screening Rating

Primary Risk Screening Category	*Rating*
Physical proximity to the crisis event	
Duration of exposure to the crisis event	
Emotional proximity or relationship(s) with crisis victims(s)	
Preexisting personal vulnerabilities	
Immediate crisis reactions	
Total	

Note. From *Preparing for Crises in the Schools* (pp. 138–139), by S. E. Brock, J. Sandoval, and S. Lewis, 2001, New York: Wiley. Copyright 2001 by John Wiley & Sons. Adapted with permission.

In the use of this form, the greatest intervention priorities would be those individuals who (a) were most intimately involved in the crisis event, (b) had or have the closest relationships with crisis victims, (c) have the most personal vulnerabilities, and (d) displayed acute stress reactions during the crisis event. Conversely, those who were relatively removed from the crisis event, who had or have no relationship with the crisis victims, have no personal vulnerabilities, and remained calm during the crisis event would be the lowest intervention priorities. The former groups of individuals would be seen as soon as practical (if not immediately), whereas the provision of crisis intervention for the latter group could be delayed (or not provided at all) until after the needs of the highest treatment priorities have been addressed.

Along with determining crisis intervention priorities, the primary evaluation of psychological trauma guides the selection and provision of specific types of crisis interventions. These crisis interventions will be discussed in greater detail in section 4 of this book. For now it is sufficient to note that evaluation data can be used to qualitatively classify individuals as being at low, moderate, or high risk for psychological trauma. With this information, crisis interveners can make decisions about specific crisis intervention treatments. Figure 11.3, the Psychological Trauma Risk Checklist, provides a form that can be used to begin estimating these risk levels (it can also be used as a part of the secondary evaluation of psychological trauma). In addition to reaffirming physical health and perceptions of safety and security, the other "universal" interventions described in chapters 12 and 13 may be appropriate for the individual in the low-risk category. The "selected" interventions described in chapters 13, 14, and 15, may be appropriate for the individual in the moderate to high risk categories. Finally, the "indicated" interventions described in chapter 16, would only be considered for the individual in the high-risk category.

SECONDARY EVALUATION OF PSYCHOLOGICAL TRAUMA

In the days following a crisis event, initial crisis interventions are provided based on the primary evaluation of psychological trauma. It is as these initial interventions are offered that the secondary evaluation of psychological trauma begins. This level of triage involves ongoing careful monitoring of individual crisis reactions and adjustment. It is designed to identify those who are demonstrating not only early warning signs, but also enduring warning signs (i.e., more durable crisis reactions) of psychological trauma.

When considering the crisis reactions demonstrated immediately following a crisis event, the classification of these reactions as indicating mental illness should not typically begin until a week or more after the crisis event has ended (Litz et al., 2002). Thus, the secondary evaluation of psychological trauma should initially avoid labeling common crisis reactions as symptoms of psychopathology. However, it will be important for crisis interveners to be vigilant for the more extreme and durable crisis reactions and coping behaviors (typically displayed by a minority of crisis survivors) that may be psychopathological and signal the need for community-based mental health assistance. When initial reactions are extreme or present a danger to self or others, and do not lessen over time, community-based mental health assistance will typically be indicated.

Figure 11.3. Psychological Trauma Risk Checklist, for determining levels of risk for psychological trauma.

Psychological Trauma Risk Checklist		
Low Risk	*Moderate Risk*	*High Risk*
Physical proximity	*Physical proximity*	*Physical proximity*
☐ Out of vicinity of crisis site	☐ Present on crisis site	☐ Crisis victim or eye witness
Emotional proximity	*Emotional proximity*	*Emotional proximity*
☐ Did not know victim(s)	☐ Friend of victim(s) ☐ Acquaintance of victim(s)	☐ Relative of victim(s) ☐ Best friend of victim(s)
Internal vulnerabilities	*Internal vulnerabilites*	*Internal vulnerabilites*
☐ Active coping style ☐ Mentally healthy ☐ Good self-regulation of emotion ☐ High developmental level ☐ No trauma history	☐ No clear coping style ☐ Questions exist about precrisis mental health ☐ Some difficulties with self-regulation of emotion ☐ At times appears immature ☐ Trauma history	☐ Avoidance coping style ☐ Preexisting mental illness ☐ Poor self-regulation of emotion ☐ Low developmental level ☐ Significant trauma history
External vulnerabilities	*External vulnerabilities*	*External vulnerabilities*
☐ Living with intact nuclear family members ☐ Good parent–child relationship ☐ Good family functioning ☐ No parental traumatic stress ☐ Good social resources	☐ Living with some nuclear family members ☐ Parent–child relationship at times stressed ☐ Family functioning at times challenged ☐ Some parental traumatic stress ☐ Social resources/relations at times challenged	☐ Not living with any nuclear family members ☐ Poor parent–child relationship ☐ Poor family functioning ☐ Significant parental traumatic stress ☐ Poor or absent social resources
Immediate reactions during the crisis	*Immediate reactions during the crisis*	*Immediate reactions during the crisis*
☐ Remained calm during the crisis event	☐ Displayed mild to moderate distress during the crisis event	☐ Displayed acute distress (e.g., fright, panic, dissociation) during the crisis event
Current/ongoing reactions & coping	*Current/ongoning reactions & coping*	*Current/ongoning reactions & coping*
☐ Only a few common crisis reactions displayed ☐ Coping is adaptive (i.e., it allows/facilitates daily functioning at precrisis levels)	☐ Many common crisis reactions displayed ☐ Coping is tentative (e.g., the individual is unsure about how to cope with the crisis)	☐ Mental health referral indicators displayed (e.g., acute dissociation, hyperarousal, depression, psychosis) ☐ Coping is absent or maladaptive (e.g., suicidal/homicidal ideation, substance abuse)
Total:	Total:	Total:

Note. The checklist is used to classify psychological trauma risk factors and warning signs into low, moderate, and high risk categories. From "Best Practices for School Psychologists as Members of Crisis Teams: The PREPaRE Model" (p. 785), by S. E. Brock and J. Davis. In A. Thomas and J. Grimes (Eds.), *Best Practices in School Psychology V*, 2008, Bethesda, MD: National Association of School Psychologists. Copyright 2008 by the National Association of School Psychologists. Reprinted with permission.

Two primary methods of evaluating psychological trauma are recommended as crisis interventions begin to be offered. The first is to obtain or develop and make use of crisis intervention referral procedures and forms. The second is to obtain or develop and make use of crisis reaction screening tools.

Crisis Intervention Referral Procedures and Forms

Given that the primary evaluation of psychological trauma will likely be unable to independently identify all psychological trauma victims, the use of a crisis intervention referral mechanism is essential. One possible vehicle for making these referrals involves the development of crisis intervention referral forms. The essential elements of such a document, which help to further document the presence of both psychological trauma risk factors and warning signs, include identifying information plus questions about crisis exposure (physical and emotional proximity), personal vulnerabilities, initial and durable crisis reactions, and the presence of maladaptive or dangerous coping behaviors (especially those that involve any degree of lethality). Adapted from a form developed by Brock et al. (2001), a sample school crisis intervention referral form is provided in Figure 11.4.

Psychological Trauma Screening Tools

As crisis interveners begin to have contact with students, their teachers, and other caregivers, they will have the opportunity to directly assess psychological trauma. One approach is to administer traumatic stress screening measures to school community members, which can be done in both individual and group (or classroom) settings. From reviews of the literature provided by Ohan, Myers, and Collett (2002) and Strand, Sarmiento, and Pasquale (2005), Table 11.2 lists some of the available tools. *The use of these measures should not take the place of good clinical skills and judgment.* These measures are not sufficient when it comes to making any mental health diagnoses. However, they are helpful in further identifying individuals who may require additional and more direct and intensive crisis interventions, and who may need to be evaluated for community-based mental health psychotherapeutic treatment. The following discussion provides a review of these measures.

The Trauma Symptom Checklist for Children (TSCC; Briere, 1996) is a norm-referenced, commercially available, 54-item self-report measure designed to assess both posttraumatic stress disorder (PTSD) and trauma-related psychological symptomatology (a 44-item version is also available that does not include items related to possible sexual abuse). Developed for youth ages 8 to 16 years, it is a paper-and-pencil questionnaire that can be administered individually or in a group setting such as a classroom. Administration time is approximately 15 to 20 minutes. Strand et al. (2005) reported that this measure is "exceptionally well-evaluated" (p. 65). Boyle (2003) reported that "the TSCC is a very useful, if somewhat limited, measure for the psychometric assessment of traumatic symptoms in children and adolescents" (¶ 10). Finally, Viswesvaran (2003) reported that "the TSCC is a short and useful instrument to assess trauma symptoms in children" (¶ 12).

Figure 11.4. Sample of a crisis intervention referral form.

School Crisis Intervention Referral Form

Date ____________________ Parent ____________________
Student ____________________ Address ____________________
Birth Date ____________________ Phone H ____________________
Teacher ____________________ W ____________________
Grade ____________________ Primary Language
Student ____________________
Parent(s) ____________________

REASON FOR REFERRAL TO THE CRISIS INTERVENTION TEAM

Physical closeness to the crisis ____________________

Duration of crisis exposure ____________________

Relationship(s) with crisis victims ____________________

Immediate reactions to the crisis ____________________

Did the youth view the crisis as threatening? YES NO
(Elaborate) ____________________

Has the youth experienced a similar event in the past? YES NO
(If YES, elaborate) ____________________

Has the youth experienced any other traumas within the past year? YES NO
(If YES, elaborate) ____________________

Does the youth have an emotional disturbance (e.g., ADHD, depression)? YES NO
(If YES, elaborate) ____________________

Is the youth developmentally immature? YES NO
(If YES, elaborate) ____________________

Figure 11.4. (continued)

Crisis Reaction Checklist[1]

(Check all that you believe apply to the youth you are referring for crisis intervention)

GENERAL FEELINGS GENERATED BY THE CRISIS

__Fear __Helplessness __Horror

GENERAL BEHAVIORS GENERATED BY THE CRISIS

__Disorganized __Agitated

SPECIFIC FEELINGS AND BEHAVIORS GENERATED BY THE CRISIS

Reactions That Suggest Feeling Unconnected With Emotions, Activities, and/or Others

__Has lost interest in previously enjoyed activities.
__Reports feeling separated, detached, or estranged from others.
__Reports feeling separated or detached from own body.
__No longer shows previous range of emotions.
__Reports feeling guilty about having survived or about not having been more severely affected by the event.
__Reports feeling that life is unreal and/or like a dream.

Reactions That Suggest a Reexperiencing of the Crisis

__Reports constant and unwanted memories, thoughts, images, and/or perceptions (e.g., smells) of the event.
__Exhibits repetitive play that may be symbolic of the event (among preschoolers such play may simply have frightening themes and may not necessarily be symbolic of the event).
__Reports having frightening dreams or nightmares.
__Reports having dreams about the event.
__Reports feeling as if the event were reoccurring.
__Displays intense emotional distress when exposed to crisis reminders.
__Displays physiological reactivity (e.g., rapid heart rate, sweating, headaches) when exposed to crisis reminders.

Reactions That Suggest an Avoidance of Crisis Reminders

__Avoids talking about the crisis.
__Avoids situations/locations that are associated with the crisis.
__Avoids crisis reminders.
__Does not remember important elements of the event.
__Does not expect to grow up, get married, go to college, etc.

Reactions That Suggest an Increased Level of Physical Arousal

__Has difficulty falling asleep.
__Awakens in the middle of the night and cannot get back to sleep.
__Displays an exaggerated startle response.
__Appears to have difficulty concentrating.
__Has difficulty completing tasks.
__Displays increased irritability.
__Displays increased aggressiveness.
__Appears to be hypervigilant.
__Reports physical problems such as stomach- and headaches.
__Appears to be depressed.

---

[1] Adapted from the *Diagnostic Criteria for Posttraumatic and Acute Stress Disorders* (American Psychiatric Association, 2000), and from Schäfer et al. (2004) and Young et al. (1998).

Note. From *Preparing for Crises in the Schools* (pp. 152–154), by S. E. Brock, J. Sandoval, and S. Lewis, 2001, New York: Wiley.

Table 11.2. Traumatic Stress Screening Tools

Measure	*Author*	*Age Group*	*Admin. Time*	*Availability*
Trauma Symptom Checklist for Children	Briere (1996)	7–16 yrs.	15–20 min.	http://www3.parinc.com
Children's PTSD Symptom Scale	Foa (2002), Foa et al. (2001)	8–15 yrs.	10 min.	foa@mail.med.upenn.edu
Parent Report of Posttraumatic Symptoms	Greenwald & Rubin (1999)	Grds. 4–8	5 min.	http://www.childtrauma.com/ax.html#m
Child Report of Posttraumatic Symptoms	Greenwald & Rubin (1999)	Grds. 4–8	5 min.	http://www.childtrauma.com/ax.html#m
Child's Reactions to Traumatic Events Scale	Jones et al. (2002)	8–12 yrs.	5 min.	rtjones@vt.edu
UCLA PTSD Reaction Index for DSM-IV (Child, Adolescent, and Parent)	Pynoos et al. (1998) Steinberg et al. (n.d.)	7 yrs–adult	20 min.	Asteinberg@mednet.ucla.edu
Children's PTSD Inventory	Saigh (2004), Saigh et al. (2000)	6–18 yrs.	5–20 min.	http://www.HarcourtAssessment.com
Pediatric Emotional Distress Scale	Saylor (2002), Saylor et al. (1999)	2–10 yrs.	5–10 min.	http://www.mentalhealth.org/publications/allpubs/SMA95-3022/default.asp

The Children's PTSD Symptoms Scale (CPSS; Foa, 2002; Foa, Johnson, Feeny, & Treadwell, 2001) is a criterion-referenced, 26-item self-report measure designed to assess PTSD and general distress. Developed for youth ages 8 to 18 years, it assesses the frequency of PTSD symptoms within the past month as well as functional impairment. It can be administered individually or in a group setting such as a classroom. Scores can be calculated for each of the DSM IV-TR symptom clusters (American Psychiatric Association, 2000). Administration time is approximately 10 minutes. The completed protocol takes approximately 5 minutes to score. Strand et al. (2005) reported that "preliminary studies reveal strong psychometric properties" (p. 65).

The Parent Report of Posttraumatic Stress (PROPS) and the Child Report of Posttraumatic Stress (CROPS; Greenwald & Rubin, 1999), respectively, are 24- and 32-item self- and parent-report questionnaires/interviews designed to assess a broad range of PTSD symptoms. Developed for youth ages 6 to 18 years, this measure can be administered through an interview or by paper and pencil. Administration time is 5 minutes, and a completed protocol takes approximately 1 minute to score. Strand et al. (2005) reported this measure to have good reliability but noted that further validity studies are warranted (p. 68).

The Child's Reactions to Traumatic Events Scale-Revised (CRTES-R; Jones, Fletcher, & Ribbe, 2002) is a criterion-referenced, 23-item self-report questionnaire designed to assess psychological responses to stressful events. Developed for youth ages 8 to 12 years, this measure can be administered through an interview or paper and pencil. Administration time is 10 minutes, and a completed protocol takes approximately 5 minutes to score. Ohan et al. (2002) reported that "preliminary psychometric properties have been examined," and though there are limited data on this measure "it shows promise as a potential tool for assessing posttraumatic reactions in youth" (p. 1409). This measure has been translated into Spanish.

The UCLA PTSD Reaction Index for DSM-IV (Child, Adolescent, and Parent; Pynoos, Rodrigues, Steinberg, Stuber, & Frederick, 1998) is a 20- to 22-item self-report measure designed to screen for the presence of a traumatic event and the frequency of PTSD symptoms. Developed for children ages 7 to 12 years, adolescents ages 13 years and older, and their parents, it can be administered in an interview or group setting (e.g., classroom). Its three sections assess for DSM-IV-TR diagnostic criteria (i.e., reexperiencing, avoidance, and emotional numbing; increased arousal symptoms; crisis event exposure; and immediate crisis reactions). Administration time is approximately 20 minutes. A particular strength of this measure is that training regarding its use is available on the Internet at http://www.nctsnet.org/nctsn_assets/video/ptsdproducer_files/Default.htm. Although the psychometric properties of this measure are still under study, its predecessor (upon which this measure is based) had strong psychometric properties (Strand et al., 2005). As a result, it is discussed in this chapter. Furthermore, recent research has begun to supply the data needed to suggest that this measure is valid and reliable (Ellis, Lhewa, Charney, & Cabral, 2006). This measure has been translated into Spanish.

The Children's PTSD Inventory (CPTSD-I; Saigh, 2004; Saigh et al., 2000) is a norm-referenced, commercially available, 50-item structured interview designed to establish the presence of PTSD symptoms. Unlike most of the other measures discussed in this section, it cannot be administered in a group setting. Thus, it is best reserved for use with those individual students for whom concern regarding psychological trauma is great. Developed for youth ages 6 to 18 years, this measure assesses PTSD symptoms, trauma history, and current functioning. Its five sections correspond to the DSM-IV-TR symptom clusters (i.e., crisis event exposure and reactions; reexperiencing, avoidance, and emotional numbing; increased arousal symptoms; and acute distress or impairment). Administration time depends on trauma history. Youth without a history of traumatic event exposure can be assessed in 5 minutes; among those with such a history, the interview will require 15 to 20 minutes. The completed protocol takes approximately 10 minutes to score. Strand et al. (2005) reported this measure to have "strong psychometric results" (p. 58), and Christopher (2007) reported that the CPTSD-I "can be a practical assessment instrument if used by skillful, knowledgeable, and experienced clinicians" (¶ 10). Finally, Doll and Osborn (2007) reported that "the inventory's reliability and validity are promising. ... Early indications are that the Children's PTSD Inventory will be a very strong diagnostic tool" (¶ 8). It is available in Spanish.

The Pediatric Emotional Distress Scale (PEDS; Saylor, 2002; Saylor, Swenson, Reynolds, & Taylor, 1999) is a 21-item paper-and-pencil parent-report scale designed to detect elevated levels of symptoms and behavior following traumatic event exposure. Developed for children ages 2 to 10 years, it includes behaviors suggested to be associated with traumatic event exposure. Average administration time is 7 minutes, and the completed protocol takes 4 minutes to score. Regarding its psychometric properties, Strand et al. (2005) reported that "it is among the most robust of the one-page symptom checklists" (p. 69). This measure is provided in Figure 11.5.

The Psychological Trauma Risk Checklist (a primary evaluation tool shown in Figure 11.3) is an additional informal screening tool that parallels the risk factors and warning signs of psychological trauma discussed in chapter 10. In addition, Figure 11.6 presents an informal, semistructured interview form (Secondary Screening of Risk Interview) that can be used during individual crisis intervention and will help to collect data important to the secondary evaluation of psychological trauma.

TERTIARY ASSESSMENT OF PSYCHOLOGICAL TRAUMA

The tertiary assessment of psychological trauma takes place during the concluding stages of the school-based crisis intervention (in some cases weeks after acute traumatic stressors have terminated). This level continues to evaluate known crisis facts and individual characteristics (or risk factors) and to monitor individual crisis reactions (or warning signs), and it is designed to identify that minority of individuals for whom the immediate school-based crisis intervention response is by itself insufficient. It has as its primary goals (a) the identification of those students who appear to require community-based mental health treatment and (b) the making of appropriate referrals. Critical to this final level of psychological triage is the ability to track those individuals who have been evaluated for psychological trauma and provided one or more school-based crisis interventions.

Especially following mass disasters, it is essential to have a tool for tracking the large numbers of school community members who are potential psychological trauma victims. Figure 11.7 provides a sample Psychological Triage Summary Sheet, originally developed by Brock et al.

Figure 11.5. Sample of a traumatic stress screening tool.

Pediatric Emotional Distress Scale (PEDS)

If you have a child between the ages of 2 and 10: Please circle one number for each item to describe how often your child has shown each behavior IN THE LAST MONTH.

Gender of child to be rated (M/F) ______ Child's birth date: (M/D/Y)________________

	Almost Never	Sometimes	Often	Very Often
1. Acts whiny	1	2	3	4
2. Wants things right away	1	2	3	4
3. Refuses to sleep alone	1	2	3	4
4. Has trouble going to bed/falling asleep	1	2	3	4
5. Has bad dreams	1	2	3	4
6. Seems fearful without good reason	1	2	3	4
7. Seems worried	1	2	3	4
8. Cries without good reason	1	2	3	4
9. Seems sad and withdrawn	1	2	3	4
10. Clings to adults/doesn't want to be alone	1	2	3	4
11. Seems "hyperactive"	1	2	3	4
12. Has temper tantrums	1	2	3	4
13. Gets frustrated too easily	1	2	3	4
14. Complains about aches and pains	1	2	3	4
15. Acts younger than used to for age (i.e., bedwetting, baby talk, thumb sucking)	1	2	3	4
16. Seems to be easily startled	1	2	3	4
17. Acts aggressively	1	2	3	4
18. Creates games, stories, or pictures about ____________________	1	2	3	4
19. Brings up____________________________in conversation	1	2	3	4
20. Avoids talking about ______________________even when asked	1	2	3	4
21. Seems fearful of things that are reminders of ________________	1	2	3	4

For items 18 to 21, if your child has had a major trauma or stress in the last year, please describe it on the line provided (e.g., has a loved one in the war, illness, death or loss, accident, natural disaster). Then rate their behavior with regard to the trauma/stress. (Further describe trauma/stress.) ____________________

____
____
____
____
____
____

Note. This measure has three scales: Anxious/Withdrawn (items 6, 7, 8, 9, 14, 15, 16), Acting Out (items 1, 2, 12, 13, 17), and Fearful (items 3, 4, 5, 6, 10). A total scale clinical cutoff score of 28 or greater is suggested as indicating the need for further evaluation of traumatic stress. The other clinical cutoff scores are Anxious/Withdrawn, ⩾10; Acting Out, ⩾14; and Fearful, ⩾9. From *Pediatric Emotional Distress Scale*, by C. F. Saylor, 2002. Reprinted with permission.

Figure 11.6. Sample of a secondary screening interview form.

Secondary Screening of Risk Interview

Outline

Student Name: ______________________ Teacher: ______________________

Crisis Intervener: ______________________ Date: ______________________

What were the youth's crisis exposure, perceptions, and reactions?

1. What do you remember about the crisis? *[Note aspects of the crisis the youth does not remember.]* ______________________

2. How close were you to the crisis? *[Note physical proximity to the crisis.]* ______________________

3. How long were you exposed to the crisis? *[Note duration of the crisis exposure.]* ______________________

4. How threatening was the crisis for you? Did you feel as if you could have been killed or injured? *[Note any aspects of the event that were perceived as involving actual or threatened death or serious injury, or a threat to physical integrity of self.]* ______________________

5. How did you react when the crisis occurred? *[Note any reports of acute distress (e.g., panic and/or dissociation).]* ______________________

6. How well do(did) you know the crisis victim(s)? *[Note if the victim was a crisis fatality, how important the victim(s) were to the interviewee, and if they were an immediate family member.]* ______________________

Does the youth report reexperiencing the crisis?

7. Do you constantly think about the crisis? *[Note recurrent/intrusive memories (e.g., images, thoughts, smells) that the interviewee finds distressing and wishes could be stopped.]* ______________________

8. Do you have bad dreams? YES NO
   8a. If YES, ask for description of dreams. ______________________

   8b. If YES, ask how frequently they occur? ______________________

9. Do you ever feel as if the event were happening again? *[Note reports of illusions, hallucinations, and flashbacks.]* ______________________

10. What does it feel like when [What do you think it would feel like if] you return to the scene of the crisis? *[Note reports of intense psychological distress.]* ______________________

11. What does it feel like when someone or something reminds you of the crisis? *[Note reports of psychological distress.]* ______________________

12. How do you physically respond when someone or something reminds you of the crisis? *[Note reports of physiological reactivity.]* ______________________

Figure 11.6. (continued)

Does the youth avoid people, situations, and/or things that are considered crisis reminders?

13. Do you find yourself trying to avoid thinking, feeling, and/or talking about the crisis? ______

14. Do you try to avoid activities, places, people, or situations that remind you of the crisis? ______

Does the youth report feeling unconnected with emotions, activities, and/or others since the crisis?

15. Are there activities that were important to you before the crisis that are no longer of interest? ______

16. Since the crisis, have you found yourself feeling different or separated from other people? *[Note feelings of detachment and/or estrangement. Note a reduction in awareness of environment (i.e., in a daze).]* ______

17. What emotions have you been able to feel since the crisis? *[Note a restricted range of affect. Note feelings of numbing, detachment, or a lack of an emotional response.]* ______

18. Do you think your life will be different now? In what way? ______

19. Are you feeling any different about your future since the crisis? *[Note feelings of a foreshortened future.]* ______

Does the youth report an increased level of arousal since the crisis?

20. Are you having sleeping difficulties? *[Note difficulties falling or staying asleep.]* ______

21. Since the crisis, have you found that you have had difficulty controlling your temper? *[Note any reports of irritability or angry outbursts.]* ______

22. Have you had difficulty concentrating on your school work? ______

23. Do you feel that you are/have been "hypervigilant" since the crisis? ______

24. Do you experience an exaggerated startle response since the crisis? ______

Figure 11.6. (continued)

Does the youth report feeling guilty about having survived and/or not having been more severely affected by the crisis?

25. Do you feel guilty about what happened? ______

26. Do you think you could have done something to prevent the crisis? ______

27. Do you want to "get even" or seek revenge? ______

Does the youth report more physical illnesses, aches, and/or pains since the crisis?

28. Have you felt sick since the crisis? *[Note any reports of headaches, stomachaches, bowel or bladder problems, etc.]* ______

Does the youth report any self-destructive thoughts and/or dangerous impulsive behaviors?

29. Do you find yourself acting impulsively since the crisis? ______

30. Have you engaged in any behaviors that might harm you since the crisis? ______

31. Either prior to or since the crisis, have you had thoughts of suicide/homicide? YES NO
[If YES continue with question 32, if NO skip to question 33. If YES make an ***immediate*** *crisis intervention referral.]*

32. How often have you had these suicidal/homicidal thoughts? ______

32a. Do you have a plan? YES NO
[IF YES continue with question 32a, if NO skip to question 32b.]

32a-i. How would you commit suicide/homicide? ______

32a-ii. Do you have the means to carry out your plan? ______

32a-iii. When would you commit suicide/homicide? ______

32b. Have you ever previously attempted suicide/homicide? ______

32c. Is there anyone or anything that could keep you from killing (self or other)? ______

Does the youth report crisis reactions to have an effect on their daily functioning?

33. Have you had difficulty completing your school work since the crisis? ______

Figure 11.6. (continued)

34. What will you do when you leave school today?__________

35. Will you be in school tomorrow?__________

36. Have you had difficulty taking care of yourself since the event?__________

37. Have you had difficulty relating with your friends since the crisis?__________

Does the youth acknowledge the presence of any resources that could help him or her cope with the crisis?

38. How do you think the crisis will affect your family and friends?__________

39. Is there anyone in your family that you can talk to about the crisis?__________

40. Is there anyone outside of your family that you can talk to about the crisis?__________

41. Would you like to talk again, or perhaps join a group of students to discuss the crisis?__________

42. What type of coping strategies have you used in the past? Which ones have worked well and which ones did not help you as much?__________

43. Are you currently involved in any activities that you enjoy?__________

44. When you have free time, what do you enjoy doing?__________

45. What strategies do you think you will use or can use to help you cope with this crisis?__________

Summary *[Is response in proportion to degree of exposure? Is the student over- or underreacting to the crisis?]*

Note. For use by a school-based crisis intervener to help identify crisis reactions. In addition to investigating symptoms of acute distress, the interview also explores recollections of the crisis event and experience, investigates suicidal or homicidal ideation, and examines whether the crisis reactions are affecting daily functioning. The interview also explores the availability of resources that might prove helpful in adaptive coping with the crisis circumstances. Sources: Los Angeles Unified School District (1994), the American Psychiatric Association (2000), and Brock, Sandoval, and Lewis (2001).

(2001). This form helps document the names of all students who were brought to the attention of school-based crisis interveners following an event. In addition to listing crisis intervention treatment priorities, this form also allows crisis interveners to quickly view the general psychological trauma risk factors, identify individuals responsible for crisis intervention services, and document each individual's current crisis intervention status. Finally, it also documents any parental contacts that have been made.

Generally speaking, this level of triage is focused on individuals with severe or potentially dangerous crisis reactions and those whose reactions do not lessen with the passage of time. Typically, their crisis intervention needs are beyond what the school can provide, and community-based mental health resources are often required. Conversely, this level of triage can rule out, as being in need of intervention, trauma-exposed individuals who do not manifest symptoms after approximately 2 months. According to the National Institute of Mental Health, these individuals "generally do not require follow-up" (NIMH, 2001, p. 9). Consistent with this

Figure 11.7. Psychological Triage Summary Sheet, to assist in the documentation of psychological triage decisions (also for use in conjunction with the Primary Risk Screening Form in Figure 11.2).

Psychological Triage Summary Sheet

(Confidential, for School Crisis Team use only)

Date	Name	Teacher	Risk Rating[1]	Risk Category[2]	Crisis Intervener	Parental Contact[3]	Status[4]
	1.						
	2.						
	3.						
	4.						
	5.						
	6.						
	7.						
	8.						
	9.						
	10.						
	11.						
	12.						
	13.						
	14.						
	15.						
	16.						
	17.						
	18.						
	19.						
	20.						

[1] Record initial risk screening rating from the Primary Risk Screening form.

[2] Record the risk category(ies) that is (are) likely to have caused psychological trauma. *Category Codes: V = victim; I = directly involved; W = witness; F = familiarity with victim(s); MI = preexisting mental illness; DIm = developmental immaturity; TH = trauma history; R = lack of resources; Em = severe emotional reactions; PT = perceived threat.*

[3] Record information regarding parental contact. *Parental Contact Codes: SM = attended school meeting; HV = home visit; Ph = phone contact.*

[4] Record information regarding the current need for crisis intervention services and support. *Status Codes: A = active (currently being seen); W/C = watch and consult (not currently being seen); F? = needs follow-up; I/A = inactive (not being seen and no follow-up is judged to be needed); PT = community-based psychotherapeutic treatment referral (immediate crisis intervention not sufficient).*

Note. From *Preparing for Crises in the Schools* (p. 140), by S. E. Brock, J. Sandoval, and S. Lewis, 2001, New York: Wiley. Copyright 2001 by John Wiley & Sons. Adapted with permission.

Figure 11.8. Relationship between the evaluation of psychological trauma and the specific crisis interventions suggested by obtained data.

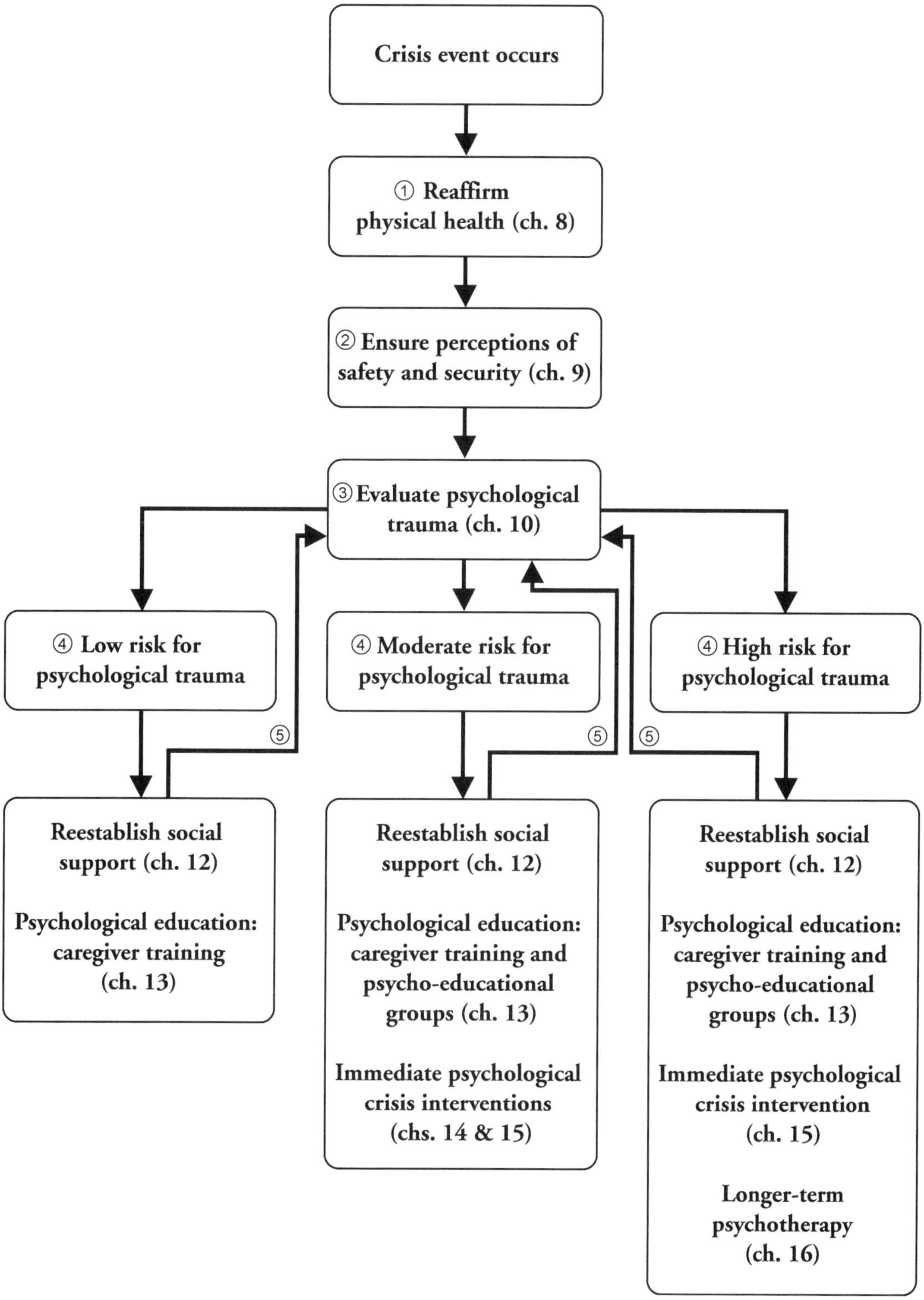

conclusion, a recent review of the literature found that delayed onset PTSD, in the absence of any previous symptoms, is rare (Andrews, Brewin, Philpott, & Stewart 2007).

CONCLUSION

Before moving on to the specific school-based crisis interventions discussed in the chapters that follow, it is important to relate the evaluation of psychological trauma to the provision of these interventions. To that end, Figure 11.8 illustrates the relationship between the crisis event, the evaluation of psychological trauma, assessed trauma risk levels, and specific school-based crisis interventions. As the figure illustrates, after a crisis event occurs the first steps are to (1) reaffirm physical health (i.e., make sure school community members actually are safe) and (2) ensure perceptions of safety and security (i.e., make sure school community members believe they are safe). As soon as possible, but necessarily before providing crisis intervention, the next step is to (3) evaluate psychological trauma risk. Using primary risk assessments, (4) the crisis intervention team makes initial crisis intervention treatment decisions. As initial crisis interventions are provided, (5) the degree of psychological injury is reevaluated and (4) more informed crisis intervention treatment decisions are made.

Section 4

PROVIDE INTERVENTIONS AND RESPOND

The next set of school crisis interventions are strategies designed to provide interventions and respond to the psychological needs indicated by the evaluation of psychological trauma. Although secondary to reaffirming actual and perceived physical health and safety, interventions may begin to take place as soon as the immediate threat of a crisis ends, during what Valent called the *recoil* phase and Raphael and Newman called the *postimpact* phase. However, as illustrated in Figure 1.2, some interventions may take place months or years after the crisis event, that is, during the recovery and reconstruction phase (Raphael & Newman, 2000; Valent, 2000). In rare instances, severe crisis reactions can have a delayed onset. In addition, crisis anniversaries (e.g., the 1-year anniversary of the crisis event or the birthday of a crisis victim) often renew crisis reactions and may require some crisis intervention assistance.

The interventions described in this section strive to respond as soon as possible to individuals who have been affected by a crisis. Thus, they would be considered a form of secondary prevention (Caplan, 1964). These interventions are directed toward individuals within the school community who are judged to have at least some risk for being psychological trauma victims and include the approaches designed to respond to higher-risk individuals who have signs or symptoms of psychological trauma or who are judged to have a predisposition for being traumatized. As illustrated in Figure S4.1, PREPaRE conceptualizes school crisis interventions as including Gordon's (1983) three different levels of intervention: "universal," "selected," and "indicated" crisis interventions. Universal interventions (or Tier 1) are those provided to all individuals who are judged to have any risk of psychological trauma. Selected interventions (or Tier 2) are those provided to individuals who are judged to be moderately to severely traumatized. Indicated interventions (Tier 3) are those provided to individuals who are judged to be severely traumatized. School-based crisis interveners should strive to employ the least restrictive level of crisis intervention (Tier 1) so as not to interfere with natural recovery mechanisms.

Figure S4.1. Levels of school crisis interventions, from least (Tier 1) to most (Tier 3) restrictive.

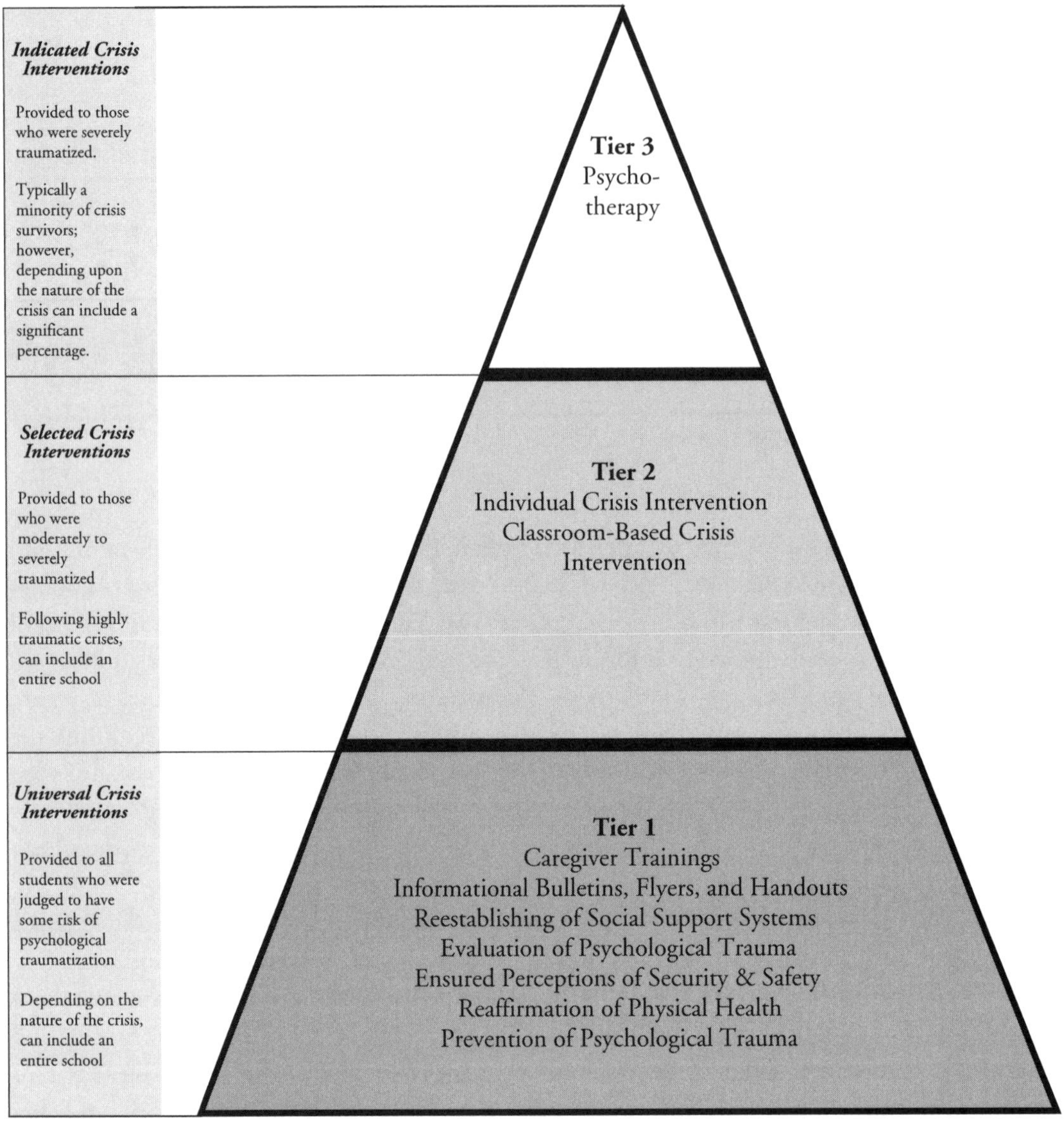
Indicated Crisis Interventions
Provided to those who were severely traumatized.
Typically a minority of crisis survivors; however, depending upon the nature of the crisis can include a significant percentage.
Tier 3
Psycho-therapy
Selected Crisis Interventions
Provided to those who were moderately to severely traumatized
Following highly traumatic crises, can include an entire school
Tier 2
Individual Crisis Intervention
Classroom-Based Crisis Intervention
Universal Crisis Interventions
Provided to all students who were judged to have some risk of psychological traumatization
Depending on the nature of the crisis, can include an entire school
Tier 1
Caregiver Trainings
Informational Bulletins, Flyers, and Handouts
Reestablishing of Social Support Systems
Evaluation of Psychological Trauma
Ensured Perceptions of Security & Safety
Reaffirmation of Physical Health
Prevention of Psychological Trauma

Note. From "Best Practices for School Psychologists as Members of Crisis Teams: The PREPaRE Model" (p. 1495), by S. E. Brock, A. B. Nickerson, M. A. Reeves, and S. R. Jimerson. In A. Thomas and J. Grimes (Eds.), *Best Practices in School Psychology V*, 2008, Bethesda, MD: National Association of School Psychologists. Copyright 2008 by the National Association of School Psychologists. Reprinted with permission.

The previously discussed prevention of psychological trauma (chapter 7), reaffirmation of physical health, (chapter 8), ensuring of perceptions of safety and security (chapter 9), and evaluation of psychological trauma risk all fall into the universal intervention category. Assuming that the school crisis team has reason to believe that all school community members have been exposed to a given crisis event, it would be appropriate to provide these interventions on a universal (or school-wide) basis. This section adds three interventions to the universal intervention category: reestablishing support systems (chapter 12); disseminating informational bulletins, flyers, and handouts; and providing caregiver training (chapter 13). In addition, this section also examines three crisis interventions that might be considered selected interventions: psychoeducational groups (chapter 13), and classroom-based and individual crisis intervention (chapters 14 and 15, respectively). Finally, this section concludes with a review of those indicated crisis interventions offered to individuals who appear to have been severely traumatized (chapter 16).

The reestablishment of naturally occurring social support systems (chapter 12) might be considered the primary crisis intervention. For many (and in some cases most) students exposed to a school-associated crisis event, these resources (which include parents, other caregivers, and peers) will be sufficient in promoting adaptive coping. However, for others, simply reconnecting them with their support systems may not be enough. Thus, chapter 13 discusses psychological education. This crisis intervention includes both (a) providing caregivers with direction on how to best foster coping among their children (caregiver training) and (b) giving students direct instruction on how to cope with the crisis event (psychoeducational groups).

Chapters 14 and 15 offer discussions of more directive crisis intervention techniques. These classroom-based and individual crisis intervention approaches are the strategies that a school-based mental health professional might use when directly intervening with traumatized students. Finally, chapter 16 reviews the community-based psychotherapeutic treatment options that highly traumatized students will need. Typically offered to a minority of individuals exposed to a school-associated crisis event, the mental health interventions discussed in chapter 16 may not be offered in the school setting and often require community-based mental health resources.

Especially during the early phases of a crisis intervention, assessing psychological trauma risk continues to be an important intervention element. As the crisis event enters the postimpact and the recovery and reconstruction phases, more informed decisions are made regarding which individuals will need which crisis interventions based on data gathered as a part of initial responses to psychological needs.

Chapter 12

REESTABLISH SOCIAL SUPPORT SYSTEMS

Reestablishing social support systems is one of the oldest and arguably the most powerful of crisis interventions, and there is evidence that the use of this intervention reduces the risk for traumatic stress (Charuvastra & Cloitre, 2008; Haden, Scarpa, Jones, & Ollendick, 2007; Weems et al., 2007). Long before school crisis interventions became part of the professional literature, students, families, and teachers found ways to cope with adversity, which often involved making use of naturally occurring social support systems. This chapter defines social support and reviews relevant theory and research about its importance in fostering recovery following potentially traumatic events. It also presents practical suggestions for how to reestablish social support after a crisis, reviews limitations or barriers to establishing social support, and examines cultural considerations important to reestablishing support systems.

SOCIAL SUPPORT: DEFINITION AND IMPORTANCE

Caplan (1974) defined social support as important interpersonal relationships that affect an individual's psychological and social functioning and lead to greater resiliency in the face of adversity. Similarly, Cobb (1976) described social support as information from others indicating that one is loved, cared for, valued, and belongs. More recently, social support has been defined as "an individual's perception that he or she is loved or cared for, esteemed, and valued by people in his or her social network, which enhances personal functioning, assists in coping adequately with stressors, and may buffer him or her from adverse outcomes" (Demaray, Malecki, Davidson, Hodgson, & Rebus, 2005, p. 691; Malecki & Demaray, 2002). In exploring the concept of social support, mental health care professionals have made distinctions between (a) social embeddedness, which refers to the structural components of support (size of network, level of activity, and closeness); (b) received support; and (c) perceived support, or one's sense of belonging and belief that support is available (Norris, Friedman, et al., 2002).

Despite differences in definitions, it is generally agreed that social support is important to positive adjustment. Two primary theoretical frameworks attempt to explain how social support influences adjustment: the main effect hypothesis, and the stress-buffering model. The *main effect hypothesis* asserts that all people, regardless of the amount of stress they experience, benefit from social support (S. Cohen, Gottlieb, & Underwood, 2001; S. Cohen & Wills, 1985). According to this hypothesis, accessible social support provides individuals with ongoing opportunities to experience positive, stable, and socially rewarding interactions with others in their community (S. Cohen & Wills, 1985; Joseph, 1999). Indeed, research reveals that social support has a positive impact on an individual's mental health (S. Cohen et al., 2001). For example, higher quantities of, and fewer disruptions to, social support in early childhood are associated with fewer internalizing and externalizing behaviors over time (Appleyard, Egeland, & Sroufe, 2007).

The other theoretical framework is the *stress-buffering model*, which asserts that social support may serve as a buffer that protects individuals in stressful situations (S. Cohen & Wills, 1985). According to this model, social support may influence psychological and adjustment outcomes by (a) preventing an individual from responding in a way that would exacerbate a typical stressful event, or (b) reducing the number of physiological responses experienced during the situation, thereby preventing the onset of maladjusted outcomes (S. Cohen & Wills, 1985; Frey & Rothlisberger, 1996; House, 1981).

Social support comes from multiple sources. Cauce, Felner, and Primavera (1982) identified three major sources of potential support for children: family; formal support (e.g., teachers, therapists); and informal support (e.g., friends, other adults). In House's (1981) description (more recently used by Malecki and Demaray, 2003a), sources of social support include parents, teachers, classmates, and close friends. Not only does developmental level affect how youth react to crisis events, but it also influences who will be the most important social support providers. Specifically, younger children will rely primarily on family members such as parents and grandparents for social support (Frey & Rothlisberger, 1996; Furman & Buhrmester, 1992), whereas adolescents will have begun to rely more on friends, extended family members, and romantic partners for support (Furman & Buhrmester, 1992; Levitt, Guacci-Franco, & Levitt, 1993; Levitt et al., 2005; Nickerson & Nagle, 2005). Teacher support has been reported to decline as a child grows older. It has been suggested that the ability to connect with several teachers might not be as realistic in secondary school, compared with the elementary school environment, when children typically have one teacher (Furman & Buhrmester, 1992). Contemporary initiatives in middle schools and high schools to develop small learning communities are an example of efforts to build social support within the secondary school context, and positive outcomes have resulted among students and teachers (Cotton, 2001; Oxley, 2001, 2004; Raywid, 1996).

Perceived social support has been linked to positive outcomes for children facing many different life circumstances, such as those classified as at risk or disadvantaged (Cauce et al., 1982; VanTassel-Baska, Olszewski-Kubilius, & Kulieke, 1994) and those with a history of sexual abuse (Tremblay, Hebert, & Piche, 1999). In addition, lack of support from adults and peers is a risk factor for victimization (Brock, Nickerson, O'Malley, & Chang, 2006; Duncan, 2004; Hazler & Carney, 2000). For example, victims of bullying and school violence report lower levels of perceived support from teachers and peers than do nonvictims (Furlong, Chung, Bates, &

Morrison, 1995; Rigby, 2000). Rigby and Slee (1999) also found that perceived low social support was related to suicidal ideation.

In light of the potent influence of social support, it is not surprising that an individual's recovery from trauma is aided by the availability of those supports (Litz, Gray, Bryant, & Adler, 2002). Low levels of social support following trauma has been found to be a strong predictor of posttraumatic stress disorder (PTSD), whereas higher levels are associated with a lower likelihood of developing this disorder (Ozer, Best, Lipsey, & Weiss, 2003). Furthermore, lower levels of support are related to more severe traumatic stress symptoms in children exposed to chronic violence (Jones, 2007), and social support serves as a strong moderator for acute and long-term mental health problems in children exposed to trauma (Caffo & Belaise, 2003).

In addition to actual social support, perceptions of such support from friends and family have been found to mediate the relationship between child maltreatment and the development of a variety of positive outcomes, such as trust, autonomy, and intimacy (Pepin & Banyard, 2006). The importance of encouraging students to make use of their social support systems has been revealed following a natural disaster. Specifically, the levels of depression among third, fourth, and fifth graders were lower among those students who had sought out social support relative to those who did not seek such support (Jeney-Gammon, Daugherty, Finch, Belter, & Foster, 1993).

REESTABLISHMENT OF SOCIAL SUPPORT AFTER A CRISIS

Given expectations for recovery following exposure to a crisis event (National Institute of Mental Health [NIMH], 2001), reestablishing and empowering natural social support systems should be a primary intervention for school crises (Brock & Jimerson, 2004; Litz et al., 2002; Norris, Byrne, Diaz, & Kaniasty, 2002; Shalev, Tuval-Mashiach, & Hadar, 2004). Both children and parents are likely to identify family members as the greatest source of support in times of crisis (Horowitz, McKay, & Marshall, 2005), and often is the only crisis intervention that is required (Barenbaum, Ruchkin, & Schwab-Stone, 2004). Generally, with appropriate support from these naturally occurring resources, the vast majority of children demonstrate positive adjustment over time (Gist & Lubin, 1999). Therefore, all other school crisis interventions should complement the assets of naturally occurring social support systems, and be prepared to pick up where they leave off. As noted by Berkowitz (2003) and addressed in chapter 10, providing highly directive crisis intervention assistance when it is not required may unintentionally and inaccurately communicate to families and other support systems that they are inadequate when it comes to aiding students' adaptive coping.

A variety of specific techniques might serve to reestablish naturally occurring social support systems (see Table 12.1). These include (a) reuniting students with their parents and other caregivers, friends, teachers, and classmates, and (b) returning students to familiar school environments and routines. Facilitating the development of connections with individuals, agencies, and other community-based organizations is also important. Finally, specific techniques for reestablishing natural social support systems should include empowering parents and other caregivers with crisis recovery information that will help them realize their caregiving potential.

Table 12.1. Activities That Schools May Consider to Help Foster Social Support

- Reunite students with their caregivers, friends, teachers, and classmates
- Return students to familiar school environments and routines
- Empower caregivers with crisis recovery information
- Make get well or condolence cards for the victims and victims' families
- Provide caregiver training (see chapter13)
- Structure classroom discussions focusing on tolerance and caring for each other
- Support communications between students and families and the community agencies and organizations

Reuniting Students With Primary Caregivers

Children should be reunited with their primary caregivers and families as soon as possible (Pitcher & Poland, 1992). It is especially important to make this reunification a priority for younger preschool and primary grade students (Brock & Jimerson, 2004). Separation of children from parents during crises can have long-term effects (Wilson, Raphael, Meldrum, Bedosky, & Sigman, 2000), and fewer symptoms of PTSD have been observed among children living with their families compared with those separated from their families (Yorbik, Akbiyik, Kirmizigul, & Söhmen, 2004). Therefore, the focus should be on reuniting children with their primary caregivers as soon as possible following a crisis.

To reunite children and families efficiently, schools must have plans and policies in place so that these familiar practices can be implemented during crises (Joshi & Lewin, 2004). As discussed in chapter 4, schools must keep accurate and updated emergency records to know how to contact parents and guardians in the event of an emergency. These records should also include a number of people who can be contacted in a crisis situation and a list of names of caregivers authorized to pick up the student in the event that a parent or guardian cannot be reached.

For example, the Montgomery County Public Schools (n.d.) plan emphasizes informing caregivers not to go to the school during crises. This allows the school to assess the situation and activate the appropriate crisis response procedures and is important because the process and sites for reunification may vary depending on the nature of the crisis. In the case of a hazardous chemical release, the students would be evacuated, and parents coming to the school would be placed in danger and unable to reunite with their children. Schools should have several means of notifying parents of emergencies, such as an automated emergency communication system (e.g., *Connect*-ED, http://www.blackboardconnect.com/default.asp?z=20080603135825), e-mail, the school Internet site, local media, reverse 911, and phone trees.

When an event affects the community outside the school, it is also important to have a plan for reunifying staff and teachers with their own children and family members after their crisis response duties are completed. Teachers and other school personnel are often torn between wanting to help their own students while at the same time ensuring the safety and security of their own loved ones. This becomes especially challenging if the crisis response requires them to stay beyond normal contract hours.

As discussed in chapter 4, implementing an orderly and efficient process for reunification of students and caregivers is important. This process includes posting signs to direct parents through the process and having team members to receive and direct parents when they arrive at the reunification area. Some team members are available to direct parents, others escort students to meet their parents, and still others are posted at check-in tables arranged alphabetically or by grade to verify that the individual is authorized to pick up the student (Montgomery County Public Schools, n.d.). When reuniting students with their caregivers, it is critical that there be someone who can explain linguistic distinctions and who is accepted by families from diverse cultural backgrounds to facilitate communication (Barenbaum et al., 2004).

In some crisis situations (e.g., natural disasters), children may be separated from their parents, which places them at greater risk of injury. For example, during and after hurricanes Katrina and Rita, more than 5,000 children were separated from their families. In the efforts to quickly get people to safety, many families were separated and ended up in different locations as they moved from their homes to the evacuation centers and elsewhere. These situations called for large-scale planning and coordination. After Hurricane Katrina, the National Center for Missing and Exploited Children (NCMEC) activated the Katrina Missing Persons Hotline and handled 32,716 calls (Broughton, Allen, Hannemann, & Petrikin, 2006).

Reuniting Students With Peers and Teachers

Peers and teachers are also important providers of social support for students. With the onset of early adolescence, peers become an even greater source of support (J. P. Allen & Land, 1999). For instance, although fourth graders were much more likely to report turning to a parent than a peer when feeling upset, eighth graders were twice as likely to report turning to a peer rather than a parent (Nickerson & Nagle, 2005). Teachers can also be important providers of social support for many students (Johnson, 2000; Klingman, 2001; Vernberg, La Greca, Silverman, & Prinstein, 1996). Supportive relationships with teachers are important predictors of the psychological well-being of students who have been traumatized (Barenbaum et al., 2004). Therefore, in the hours, days, and weeks following a crisis, making provisions for students to access these supports is important. For instance, after a crisis event, some schools open their doors for staff and students to congregate during nonschool hours to give them opportunities to provide support to each other. Providing activities that focus students' attention away from the negative emotions caused by a trauma may also be helpful (Prinstein, La Greca, Vernberg, & Silverman, 1996). Opportunities for peer interaction should be structured and well supervised (e.g., through recreational activities, focused art activities) to promote supportive peer relationships (Swick, Dechant, & Jellinek, 2002). This is important given findings that middle school girls in an urban area reported that they did not trust peers, and boys said they relied on membership in gangs for support (Horowitz, McKay, & Marshall, 2005). Adults can take an active role in ensuring that the support offered by peers will be helpful and productive, as opposed to compounding the problem.

Returning Students to Familiar Environments and Routines

Restoring structured education by returning students to familiar environments and routines following crises helps in terms of establishing stability and continuity (Barenbaum et al., 2004). The school setting provides predictable routines, as well as consistent rules for behavior, which help promote a sense that school is a safe and predictable place (Barenbaum et al., 2004; Cole et al., 2005; Demaree, 1994). The tasks and responsibilities assigned to students within the school environment can also help them cope and avoid isolation (Barenbaum et al., 2004). Therefore, getting the school ready to be occupied after a crisis event (e.g., natural disaster or school shooting) and identifying alternate locations for schooling, such as a neighboring school or community center, should be a top priority.

A return to community routines and natural environments is important to recovery, as evidenced by the fact that reduced community disruption is associated with less traumatic stress (Brymer et al., 2006). Crisis situations are less traumatic when disruptions to family life are minimized (Kolaitis et al., 2003), as the highest risk of psychopathology comes when there is family displacement or disruption (Caffo & Belaise, 2003). In addition to physically returning children to homes, schools, and communities, and thereby reconnecting children with the traditions, culture, and spiritual practices that were part of their lives prior to the crisis, can be helpful in reaffirming hope for the future (Barenbaum et al., 2004). Parents often want to minimize expectations placed on children after they have been through a traumatic event; however, routine, structure, and familiarity is essential in helping children know that they will recover and life will go on.

Having a sense of community, characterized by cohesion, participation, and safety, can be helpful in building resilience (Joshi & Lewin, 2004). For example, survivors of the Columbine High School shooting reported that it was helpful to feel that there was a large network of community support. Concrete indicators of this support included people wearing ribbons to represent the school and memorials in the form of posters, cards, and flowers (Hawkins, McIntosh, Silver, & Holman, 2004). Even though survivors grieve in different ways and may not all agree on outward ways of expressing grief, community solidarity can greatly support the grieving process.

Tangible forms of support from extended family and community members can also be very helpful for parents who need to focus on being physically and emotionally available for their children (Swick et al., 2002). After a school shooting, parents reported that child care, prepared meals, and necessary supplies were helpful in relieving normal household responsibilities (Hawkins et al., 2004). In some situations, it may be helpful for a member of the extended family to move in, or move closer, to provide additional support (Swick et al., 2002).

In summary, mobilizing powerful, inclusive, and long-lasting community support within indigenous networks should be the primary objective of crisis intervention and policy (Norris, Bryne, et al., 2002).

Empowering Caregivers With Knowledge

The goal of reestablishing natural social supports presumes that caregivers are willing and able to provide the support needed for children to recover from their crisis exposure. Given the importance of social supports in aiding recovery from psychological trauma, caregivers must be given the knowledge they need to realize the potential of that social support. As discussed further in chapter 13, psychoeducation with caregivers is focused on anticipated reactions to traumatic events, signs of potential problems that deserve further attention, and ways parents can respond appropriately to their children.

It is generally agreed that caregivers should respond by listening and understanding when children and adolescents need to express their fear, anger, and distress about what has happened (Barenbaum et al., 2004; Grosse, 2001; Heath & Sheen, 2005). In addition, in the weeks following a crisis, caregivers should spend increased amounts of time with their children, offering a calm influence (Pitcher & Poland, 1992). Maintaining clear, consistent, and developmentally appropriate limits for behavior is also important in promoting a sense of safety and predictability (Cole et al., 2005; Swick et al., 2002). In terms of specific behaviors that are helpful, adolescent survivors from the Columbine High School shooting reported that spending time talking with and being hugged by others was helpful (Hawkins et al., 2004).

LIMITATIONS OR BARRIERS TO SOCIAL SUPPORT

Although naturally occurring social support systems are very powerful, they do have their limitations. The most obvious and devastating problem is when the crisis results in the death or loss of the child's source of social support (Norris, Friedman, et al., 2002). As discussed in chapter 10, children who have a family member or close friend die are at especially high risk for PTSD (NIMH, 2001). For children, the death of a parent is especially traumatic. Following 9/11, 52% of students in the New York City public schools who lost a parent had PTSD (Applied Research and Consulting et al., 2002).

Caregivers may be in need of financial, emotional, and other assistance (Swick et al., 2002), which underscores the importance of developing collaborative relationships with community support agencies. Caregivers who survive a crisis event may have been traumatized, which may limit their capacity to provide the support needed for the child (Norris, Friedman, et al., 2002). For example, exposure to life-threatening conditions or chronic exposure to a crisis event may inhibit the caregiver's capacity to provide necessary forms of support, such as sharing experiences or being sensitive and encouraging (Qouta, Punamäki, & El Sarraj, 2005; Yap & Devilly, 2004). In such cases, parents' own psychological distress and psychopathology may make them unable to render needed support and nurturance to their child; therefore, in order to help the child, the parent must be helped first.

Reestablishing social support is sometimes limited when that support is not perceived as helpful. Pepin and Banyard (2006) found that although perceived social support from friends and family was highly related to positive developmental outcomes, the same relationship was not found for received support. Given the importance of perceptions of support, caregivers should avoid providing support that will be judged as unhelpful. For example, from a qualitative study of survivors of a school shooting, adolescent survivors reported that the following types of support were not helpful: (a) requests from parents to talk about things, with parents then quickly becoming angry; (b) parents' attempts to overprotect or smother (e.g., screening calls, offering unwelcomed gestures); (c) efforts to get students to talk about the incident, particularly in structured counseling settings (Hawkins et al., 2004).

Naturally occurring social support systems may also be insufficient to meet the needs of some children and adolescents after a crisis, particularly those with preexisting mental health challenges. This is not to suggest that such supports are irrelevant for these high-risk students; in fact, social supports may be especially important for individuals with such challenges. For example, in a national study of adolescents following 9/11, Gil-Rivas, Holman, and Silver (2004) found that adolescents with a history of mental health difficulties needed greater parental support to help them use adaptive coping strategies and to regulate their emotional responses. However, these children and adolescents may have also needed additional supports, such as psychological treatment.

CULTURAL CONSIDERATIONS

Several cultural considerations are relevant to reestablishing social support after a crisis. For instance, racial and ethnic differences have been found in students' perceptions of the necessity and importance of social support (Cauce et al., 1982; Demaray & Malecki, 2002). Different cultural groups have different values, beliefs, and preferences for accessing social support, which should be acknowledged and respected by schools seeking to support students and families after a crisis.

Although African Americans have faced ongoing challenges with political, economic, and cultural oppression in the United States, Black adolescents have reported perceiving a greater degree of total social support available to them than their White or Hispanic peers report (Cauce et al., 1982). Therefore, the source of social support may differ for different groups. For example, African American children and parents living in urban areas also indicated a clear preference for turning to family members for social support, as opposed to relying on professionals, who are often viewed with distrust (Horowitz et al., 2005). Jones (2007) found that formal kinship support, spirituality, and an Afrocentric perspective were protective factors for African American children exposed to chronic violence. The church and religious community are also important sources of social support for African Americans (Kim & McKenry, 1998). In addition, use of collaborative religious coping, which views the self and God as working together to solve problems, is related to resilience among African Americans (Molock, Puri, Matlin, & Barksdale, 2006). Together, this research suggests that school-based mental health professionals seeking to help African American students cope with crises should be particularly aware of the formal kinship support, which may embody values of harmony, interconnectedness, authenticity, and balance, and aware of the importance of the Black church.

There is also evidence to suggest that the social supports needed by Asian Americans differ. Asian American children and adults have reported perceiving less social support than White children (Demaray & Malecki, 2002; Liang & Bogat, 1994; Wellisch et al., 1999). Within Asian American families, members have highly interdependent roles within a cohesive, patriarchal structure (Harrison, Wilson, Pine, Chan, & Briel, 1990), and there is a belief that needs should be met within the family (Herrick & Brown, 1998; Wellisch et al., 1999). In addition, Asian culture values self-discipline, which may lend itself more to self-directed coping (e.g., try harder, control thoughts; Liang & Bogat, 1994) as opposed to eliciting support from friends, which may lead to feelings of indebtedness or obligation (Wellisch et al., 1999). Interestingly, a comparative study of Anglo American and Chinese college students found that although social support played a stress-buffering role for Anglo Americans, it did not for Chinese students. In fact, social support had negative stress-buffering effects for Chinese students with an external locus of control (Liang & Bogat, 1994). School-based mental health professionals working with Asian Americans should be cognizant of the strong value for self-discipline and for having needs met within the family. They should also respect the patriarchal structure present in many Asian American families. Consequently, school crisis interveners need to understand that some of these students, when urged to rely on outside support, may perceive the provision of support as a sign of vulnerability (Liang & Bogat, 1994) and as possibly creating a sense of obligation (Wellisch et al., 1990).

The Hispanic culture is characterized by a strong sense of family, such as family obligations, frequent contact, and family support (Harrison et al., 1990; Zayas, Lester, Cabassa, & Fortuna, 2005). Hispanic families generally provide high levels of emotional support; however, instrumental or informational support may be lacking if parents do not have such resources available (Valle & Bensussen, 1985). Research has also found that despite Hispanic students' reported attempts to receive support from parents and teachers (Morrison, Laughlin, Miguel, San Smith, & Widaman, 1997; Wintre, Hicks, McVey, & Fox, 1988), they reported less social support from teachers than do White students (Demaray & Malecki, 2003). Clearly, Hispanic and Latino students will seek support from families; however, students who are acculturated may also seek support from close friends.

Native Americans reported less frequent total social support and social support from a variety of sources (e.g., parents, teachers, classmates, and close friends), compared with children and adolescents from other ethnic groups (Demaray & Malecki, 2003). Native American students rated overall total social support or social support provided by a particular source as less important as compared to other students of differing ethnic status (Demaray & Malecki). Native Americans are at risk for a variety of negative outcomes; however, extensive outreach with formal establishments (e.g., health clinics, social welfare programs) and with less formal unconventional institutions (e.g., outdoor places where youth congregate, community events, and neighborhood volunteers), have been found helpful in reducing these risks (May, Serna, Hurt, & DeBruyn, 2005).

CONCLUSION

Social support is linked with a variety of positive outcomes, including help in recovery from trauma. Therefore, reestablishing and empowering social support systems should be a primary intervention for school and community crises. Reuniting students with primary caregivers, peers, and teachers, as well as returning students to familiar environments and routines, is essential following crisis exposure. The reestablishment of social supports should be guided by knowledge of the limitations of these supports and important cultural considerations.

Chapter 13

PSYCHOLOGICAL EDUCATION

Treatment aimed at providing social support without fostering a sense of empowerment may actually impede the natural recovery process, in part by defeating a survivor's sense of self-efficacy (Howard & Goelitz, 2004). In some instances, school-based crisis intervention may need to do more than simply link students to their family, teachers, and friends; it may need to explicitly teach school community members what they can do to take care of themselves and others, and in so doing, better enable them to mitigate traumatic stress reactions (Phipps & Byrne, 2003). Consistent with this observation, PREPaRE includes psychological education (or psychoeducation) as another crisis intervention strategy.

During the recoil and postimpact phases of a crisis, the primary goal of psychological education is to provide students and their parents and other caregivers with knowledge that assists them in understanding, preparing for, and responding to the crisis situation and to the resulting crisis-generated problems and initial crisis reactions. During the recovery and reconstruction phase, these activities can help predict and prepare the school community for anniversary reactions.

Psychoeducation attempts to give crisis survivors increased control over the recovery process, promote social support, and teach approach-oriented coping strategies wherein the individual takes a direct and action-oriented approach to addressing crisis challenges (Hobfoll et al., 2007; Phoenix, 2007; Ruzek et al., 2007). These factors are related to a reduced risk of posttraumatic stress (Charuvastra & Cloitre, 2008; Frazier, Steward, & Mortensen, 2004; Stallard & Smith, 2007). They also can reduce the stigma associated with mental health interventions, capitalize on personal strengths, and increase individuals' sense of self-worth. Psychological education can also be beneficial in providing early connections to mental health resources (Howard & Goelitz, 2004; Lukens & McFarlane, 2004). An advantage of these activities includes their ability to present individuals with a range of interventions.

Research conducted by Allen, Dlugokinski, Cohen, and Walker (1999) supports the need for psychological education following crisis exposure. They studied more than 6,000 elementary school children in Oklahoma City following the bombing of the Murrah Federal Building. These researchers found that younger children needed to be provided with crisis facts because they were the least likely to understand what was going on, were the most likely to be confused, and had the highest number of facts wrong. In addition, this same study highlighted the need to provide students (particularly younger children) with adaptive coping strategies, as this group was most likely to use avoidance as a coping mechanism, which as a long-term coping strategy is associated with negative mental health outcomes. (Stallard & Smith, 2007).

Additional reports offer further support for the use of psychological education as a crisis intervention strategy (Lukens & McFarlane, 2004; Phoenix, 2007). According to Brown and Bobrow (2004), "Emerging studies of school-based psychoeducational programs for children exposed to trauma have found improvements in participants' knowledge of trauma and attitudes to risk-taking behavior" (p. 212). Furthermore, the clinical observations of Howard and Goelitz (2004) as they provided psychological education to individuals proximal to, and affected by, the World Trade Center disaster suggested that this intervention has merit. Specifically, they observed that recipients of psychological education were clearly relieved when they learned that their reactions to the crisis event were typical responses to unusual circumstances. In addition, Howard and Goelitz observed that "psychoeducation allows the natural recovery process to unfold without over helping the approximately 75% of the population that does not require formalized mental health care" (p. 8).

Although psychological education is a promising crisis intervention, it has limitations. Specifically, psychological education by itself does not reduce crisis symptoms, in particular more severe and long-term crisis reactions. Especially in high-risk groups (i.e., acute trauma victims), it is critical that this intervention be paired with other mental health interventions that directly address crisis reactions (Howard & Goelitz, 2004). Furthermore, although it has been documented to be an effective element of tertiary prevention (Amstadter, McCart, & Ruggiero, 2007; Lukens & McFarlane, 2004; Oflaz, Hatipoğlu, & Aydin, 2008), research is limited regarding its use as an immediate and brief secondary intervention.

This chapter offers three examples of psychological education: informational documents, caregiver trainings, and student psychoeducational groups. The first two examples are primarily designed to help school staff and family members achieve their caregiving potential. Doing so may require school-based crisis interveners to teach caregivers how to best foster adaptive coping among the children in their care. Caregiver trainings can be conducted in a 45-minute session, although more time should be set aside if a significant number of questions are anticipated. The third example is a more direct crisis intervention approach designed to provide the students themselves with knowledge that will teach them coping techniques. Approximately 60 minutes should be devoted to student psychoeducational groups. These groups are typically provided immediately after a crisis event (within hours to days after the event). For example, if a student dies in an accident after school, these groups may take place the morning after the accident. Because psychological education is considered routine practice in a school setting, parental consent is typically not required, although it is a good idea to inform parents that such lessons will be provided.

INFORMATIONAL DOCUMENTS

The first psychological education strategy involves the dissemination of informational documents. Typically, these materials are designed to help students, parents, and other caregivers understand the crisis event and its potential effects, and to identify a range of resources available to help manage crisis-generated problems (Litz, Gray, Bryant, & Adler, 2002). They can parallel, complement, or supplement the information provided through other psychological educational approaches (e.g., caregiver trainings or student psychoeducational groups).

In the school setting (especially at the elementary level), these documents are primarily aimed at giving caregivers the information they need to help students cope with a crisis. However, at the secondary level it may also be appropriate to provide these documents to students themselves. These documents can be made available through the school or the mass media.

When families within a given school community speak languages other than English, these materials need to be translated. When done well, such translations can be time-consuming, so to the extent possible, they should be translated in advance of crises. Figure 13.1 illustrates the process that Brock, Navarro, and Terán (2008) employed when translating an English document to Spanish for use following the 2007 southern California wildfires. As indicated in the figure, the original English document was submitted for translation (to busy school psychologists) on October 25, and the final Spanish version was not available until October 31. The English and Spanish versions of these documents are provided in Figure 13.2, which can be found at the end of this chapter.

This process used a procedure similar to Brislin's (1970) back-translation method. It began by having a native Spanish speaker translate the original English document into Spanish (i.e., Jimerson, Brock, & Cowan, 2003). The document was then retranslated into English by a second native Spanish speaker who did not know the wording of the original English version. Next, one of the original English-version authors reviewed the retranslated English version and (making use of the track changes function) indicated a number of copyedits and wording changes. Finally, the native Spanish speakers collaborated to make the indicated changes to the Spanish translation and produced a final translation of the handout.

A rich sample of informational documents relevant to psychological education following crisis events is available at the National Association of School Psychologists website (www.nasponline.org). Table 13.1 also provides a menu of such documents, including translated psychoeducational materials.

Although distribution of psychoeducational documents is possibly sufficient in addressing the needs of individuals with limited trauma exposure or lower risk of psychological trauma, this crisis intervention strategy has its limitations. Specifically, it has been documented that among acute trauma victims (i.e., those treated in a hospital emergency room following a traumatic injury), self-help informational booklets that address psychological trauma appear by themselves to be insufficient. More sophisticated interventions, with direct therapeutic contact, are required for those with more direct or severe trauma exposure and psychological injury (Scholes, Turpin, & Mason, 2007).

Figure 13.1. Steps in the process of translating a psychological education informational handout from English into Spanish.

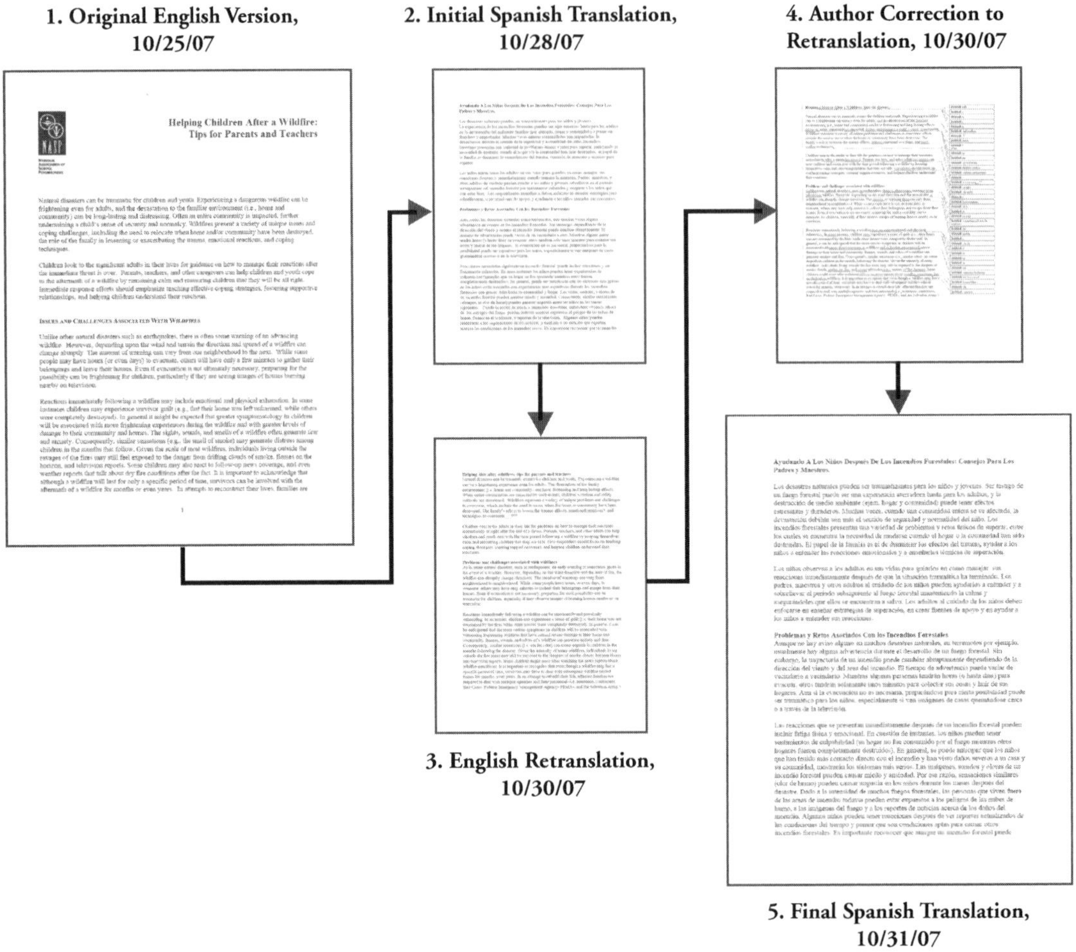

Note. From *The English to Spanish Translation of Psychoeducational materials for use During School Crisis Intervention,* by S. E. Brock, L. Navarro, & E. Teran, March, 2008. Reprinted with permission of the authors.

CAREGIVER TRAINING

In some instances school-based crisis interveners need to provide parents, teachers, and other caregivers with more active and direct training. The importance of caregiver training is highlighted by Berkowitz (2003), who states: "Parental attention and support are among the factors that may be most amenable to early intervention efforts as well as most salient in prevention of poor outcomes for children" (p. 297).

A PREPaRE caregiver training is similar to the student psychoeducational group that will be discussed later in this chapter. The primary difference is that the caregiver training is oriented

Table 13.1. Informational Documents Providing Guidance on Responding to Children's Crisis Reactions

1. A National Tragedy: Helping Children Cope (handout from the National Association of School Psychologists)
   - http://www.nasponline.org/resources/crisis_safety/terror_general.aspx
2. Children and Violence (a *Health & Outreach* Web page of the National Institute of Mental Health)
   - http://www.nimh.nih.gov/health/topics/child-and-adolescent-mental-health/children-and-violence.shtml
3. Coping With Traumatic Events
   - http://www.samhsa.gov/trauma/index.aspx
4. Finding Comfort in Books: Publishers Recommend Books for Children Dealing With Crisis and Tragedy
   - http://www.scbwi.org/news%5Finfo/Children%5FCrisis.pdf
5. Helping Children Cope With Disaster
   - http://www.fema.gov/rebuild/recover/cope_child.shtm
6. Helping Children Cope With Fear and Anxiety
   - http://mentalhealth.samhsa.gov/publications/allpubs/CA-BKMARKR02/default.asp
7. Helping Children Cope With Loss
   - http://www.nmha.org/index.cfm?objectid=C7DF9628-1372-4D20-C884BF860DEF0A67
8. Helping Children Cope With Natural Disasters
   - http://www.nccic.acf.hhs.gov/poptopics/disasters.html
9. Helping Young Children Cope With Trauma
   - http://www.redcross.org/services/disaster/keepsafe/childtrauma.html
10. *Psychological First Aid: Field Operations Guide* (the U.S. Department of Veterans Affairs manual includes handouts for crisis survivors)
    - http://www.ncptsd.va.gov/ncmain/ncdocs/manuals/nc_manual_psyfirstaid.html
11. Tips for Helping Students Recovering From Traumatic Events
    - http://www.ed.gov/parents/academic/help/recovering/part_pg9.html
12. Tips for Survivors of a Traumatic Event: What to Expect in Your Personal, Family, Work, and Financial Life
    - http://www.samhsa.gov/MentalHealth/Tips%20for%20Survivors-What%20to%20Expect_LOW_RES.pdf
13. Tips for Talking to Children in Trauma: Interventions at Home for Preschoolers to Adolescents
    - http://mentalhealth.samhsa.gov/publications/allpubs/NMH02-0138/default.asp

Table 13.1. (continued)

14. Tips for Talking to Children After a Disaster: A Guide for Parents and Teachers
    - http://mentalhealth.samhsa.gov/publications/allpubs/ken-01-0093/default.asp
15. Helping Children With Special Needs: Tips for School Personnel and Parents
    - http://www.nasponline.org/resources/crisis_safety/specpop_general.aspx
16. NASP Crisis Resources in Spanish and Other Languages
    - http://www.nasponline.org/resources/crisis_safety/index.aspx

toward taking care of others (versus taking care of oneself). Whereas the student psychoeducational group is primarily concerned with teaching students about self-care, and secondarily concerned with teaching them to care for others, the opposite is true of the caregiver training.

Caregiver Training Goals

PREPaRE caregiver training has four goals (see Table 13.2). The first goal is to ensure that caregivers have the facts about the crisis. Achieving this goal will give caregivers the knowledge they need to help children understand the crisis event and dispel crisis rumors (which are often more frightening than the crisis facts; Howard & Goelitz, 2004).

The second goal of caregiver training is to ensure that common crisis reactions are identified and normalized. Achieving this goal will prepare caregivers for reactions they might see in their children as well as those they themselves might experience. When discussing these common initial reactions, caregivers should be informed that natural recovery from crisis reactions is the norm (Brown & Bobrow, 2004; Howard & Goelitz, 2004). Because crisis survivors often fear they are "going crazy," caregivers should be advised to help dispel these beliefs and recognize that most

Table 13.2. Caregiver Training Goals and Subgoals

Following caregiver training, caregivers will have knowledge of the following:

1. Crisis facts.
2. Common crisis reactions.
3. Psychopathological crisis reactions and coping behaviors.
    - Caregivers know how to make referrals for both school- and community-based mental health crisis intervention assistance.
    - Caregivers who themselves appear to be having difficulty coping with crisis reactions are identified and offered additional assistance.
4. Strategies for responding to and managing crisis reactions.
    - Caregivers understand that their own crisis reactions will influence their children's crisis reactions.

initial crisis reactions are common responses to abnormal situations (Howard & Goelitz, 2004). The discussion of crisis reactions in chapter 10 should provide school-based crisis interveners with the guidance needed to facilitate this discussion among groups of caregivers.

Although the training should stress the normality of crisis reactions and the likelihood of natural recovery following crisis exposure, it is also important to inform caregivers that more severe psychological injury is possible. The third goal of caregiver training is to ensure that caregivers can recognize psychopathological crisis reactions and coping strategies, and that they know how to make referrals for professional mental health crisis intervention (Berkowitz, 2003). Briefly, the following behaviors and symptoms signal the need for an immediate crisis intervention referral: dissociation, intense emotional reactions, and significant panic or arousal (Lawyer et al., 2006), as well as any dangerous immediate coping behaviors, such as suicidal or homicidal ideation (see chapter 10). Reactions that have not begun to dissipate after a week or more may also indicate significant psychological injury (American Psychiatric Association, 2000). In addition, the direct contact provided by this form of crisis intervention gives school-based crisis interveners an opportunity to identify those parents, teachers, or other caregivers who may not be able to support the children under their care (Howard & Goelitz, 2004).

The fourth goal of caregiver training is to ensure that specific strategies for managing crisis reactions are identified and explicitly taught. Achieving this goal will give caregivers tools that they can use to help their children cope with crisis reactions and problems. Caregiver training can help promote healthy forms of coping by identifying a range of available resources (Brown & Bobrow, 2004; Howard & Goelitz, 2004) and by promoting active or approach-oriented coping strategies (Litz et al., 2002). Related to this goal, it is also important to ensure that specific helpful caregiver reactions to children's traumatic stress are identified (i.e., calm, controlled, and empathetic reactions). Caregivers also often need to be specifically instructed on how best to respond to their children; this includes educating them about how their own crisis reactions can shape their children's perceptions of the crisis event (Brymer et al., 2006). As discussed in chapter 10, parental reactions to crises are a predictor of a young child's traumatic stress reactions (Scheeringa & Zeanah, 2001).

Caregiver Training Elements

PREPaRE caregiver trainings typically last less than 1 hour and consists of four specific elements or steps (see Table 13.3). Ideally initiated by at least one crisis intervention team member who is familiar to the group, the first step ("Introduce") lasts about 5 minutes and involves orienting

Table 13.3. Steps in a PREPaRE Caregiver Training

Time: less than 1 hour

1. *Introduce* caregivers to the training (5 minutes).
2. *Provide* crisis facts (10 minutes).
3. *Prepare* caregivers for the reactions that may follow crisis exposure (15 minutes).
4. *Review* techniques for responding to children's crisis reactions (15 minutes).

caregivers to the training session. This includes ensuring that participants understand the goals, process, and elements of the training. If the leader or leaders of the training session are not familiar to the group, then a school staff member who is known to the group (e.g., the school principal) should introduce the crisis intervention team members to participants.

The second step in a caregiver training ("Provide") lasts about 10 minutes and involves ensuring caregivers have the crisis facts that will allow them to help children understand the crisis event. If the crisis was particularly complicated or it is anticipated that caregivers themselves will have a significant number of questions about the event, then additional time should be allocated to this step. When providing these facts, it is important that the leader advise caregivers about the possibility of information transmission of PTSD (Baranowsky, Young, Johnson-Douglas, Williams-Keeler, & McCarrey, 1998; Kassai & Motta, 2006). The training leader should suggest that caregivers let the students' questions guide the information that is given, and should advise caregivers to be careful about giving crisis details that have not been requested. In particular, they should avoid giving young children information they would not likely learn about on their own or that would unnecessarily frighten them.

The third step ("Prepare") lasts about 15 minutes and involves giving caregivers information about the common initial crisis reactions seen among both children and caregivers themselves. The goal of this part of the training is to prepare caregivers for common crisis reactions and to normalize them. Also important to this part of the training is the identification of psychopathological crisis reactions. The discussion of crisis reactions in chapter 10 and Tables 10.3 and 10.4 should help the school-based crisis intervener in accomplishing the goals of this step of the training.

The fourth and final step ("Review") lasts about 15 minutes and involves examining techniques for responding to children's crisis reactions. Specific strategies might include (a) direct instruction regarding stress management and relaxation techniques, (b) bibliotherapy (or making use of stories and books that help children think about and understand the crisis event), (c) identification of existing supports (e.g., parents, friends, teachers, and school psychologists and counselors), and (d) identification of adaptive coping strategies and redirection away from maladaptive strategies (e.g., exercise instead of alcohol abuse). Specific helpful responses to children exposed to a crisis event should also be reviewed. The need to be empathetic and the importance of adult reactions in shaping children's threat perceptions should be emphasized. It is also important to provide caregivers with information regarding how to make referrals for individuals who may require further school- and community-based mental health crisis intervention assistance. Informational documents that may prove useful during this step are listed in Table 13.1. In particular, "Information on Coping," in the *Psychological First Aid Field Operations Guide* (Brymer et al., 2006, pp. 77–89), is an especially helpful resource in training caregivers.

When instructing caregivers about responding to children's crisis reactions, interveners need to be aware of the ways in which youth from diverse cultural groups may attribute meaning to the crisis event. They should suggest caregiver responses that are respectful of individual beliefs and customs. For example, many individuals from diverse cultures rely on extended family, including "church families," to help them cope. Encouraging caregivers to think about unique sources of support that the children they are caring for rely on can help ensure that the intervention is more sensitive to individual diversity.

STUDENT PSYCHOEDUCATIONAL GROUPS

For some groups of students, and following some crisis situations, simply giving caregivers information designed to help them realize their caregiving potential (i.e., caregiver training) will be insufficient. Consequently, school-based crisis interveners will need to provide more direct student crisis interventions.

The PREPaRE student psychoeducational group is similar to the caregiver training. The primary difference is that the student psychoeducational group is oriented toward taking care of oneself (versus taking care of others). Whereas the caregiver training is primarily concerned with taking care of others, and secondarily concerned with helping others, the opposite is true of the student group. These sessions are primarily concerned with helping students acquire knowledge that will help them take care of themselves, and secondarily concerned with teaching students about how best to care for their peers.

Student Psychoeducational Group Goals

PREPaRE student psychoeducational groups have four goals (see Table 13.4). The first goal of these groups is to ensure that students are in possession of crisis facts, and that crisis-related rumors, which are often more frightening than facts, are dispelled (Brock, Sandoval, & Lewis, 2001). Achieving this goal will help to ensure that students have a reality-based understanding of the crisis event (Howard & Goelitz, 2004).

The second goal of student psychoeducational groups is to identify and normalize common crisis reactions. Achieving this goal will prepare students for reactions that they might see in themselves as well as those that their peers might experience. As is the case during caregiver training, when school-based crisis interveners are discussing these common reactions, they should inform students that recovery from their crisis reactions is the norm (Brown & Bobrow, 2004; Howard & Goelitz, 2004). Because crisis survivors often fear they are "going crazy," crisis interveners should strive to dispel these beliefs and help students to recognize that most initial crisis reactions are common reactions to abnormal situations (Howard & Goelitz, 2004). The

Table 13.4. Student Psychoeducational Group Goals and Subgoals

Following student psychoeducational groups, students will have knowledge about the following:

1. Crisis facts (rumors are dispelled).
2. Common crisis reactions.
3. Psychopathological crisis reactions and coping strategies.
    - Students know how to make referrals (primarily for themselves, but also for their peers) for both school- and community-based mental health crisis intervention assistance.
    - Through observation of the group process, students who appear to be having difficulty coping with crisis reactions are identified and provided additional crisis intervention assistance.
4. Strategies for managing their own stress reactions.

importance of normalizing crisis reactions is emphasized by McNally, Bryant, and Ehlers (2003), who cite studies suggesting that the belief one is losing one's mind (vs. experiencing a temporary and expected response to a traumatic event) may increase risk for PTSD. Specifically, they state:

> For example, appraisal of intrusive thoughts as meaning that one is about to lose one's mind ... may foster attempts to suppress intrusive thoughts, which in turn may lead to a paradoxical increase in their frequency.... excessively negative appraisals of the trauma and its consequences motivate trauma survivors to engage in behaviors that maintain the problems. (p. 53)

As in caregiver training, while the leader should stress the normality of crisis reactions and identify recovery as the norm following crisis exposure, it will also be important to help students identify the signs of more severe psychological injury. Thus, the third goal of a student psychoeducational group is to ensure that students are able to recognize psychopathological crisis reactions and coping strategies, and that they know how to make self-referrals for school- and community-based mental health crisis intervention assistance. The importance of providing referral information is emphasized by reports that two thirds of New York City public school students with PTSD subsequent to 9/11 did not seek any treatment (Applied Research and Consulting et al., 2002). In addition, the direct contact with students that this form of crisis intervention provides also gives school-based crisis interveners an opportunity to identify students who may need more intensive interventions; that is, it is an example of secondary triage (Howard & Goelitz, 2004).

The fourth and final goal of a student psychoeducational group is to ensure that specific strategies for managing crisis reactions are identified or explicitly taught. Achieving this goal provides students with tools they can use to adaptively respond to their own crisis reactions and crisis-generated problems. Specifically, student psychoeducational groups are designed to help promote healthy forms of coping and include the identification of a range of support resources (Brown & Bobrow, 2004; Howard & Goelitz, 2004). When successful, students emerge having developed their own plan for coping with crisis reactions.

Student Psychoeducational Group Elements

Student psychoeducational groups typically last about 1 hour and consist of five specific elements or steps (see Table 13.5). Ideally initiated by a school-based crisis team member who is familiar to the students, the first step in the student psychoeducational group ("Introduce") lasts about 5 minutes and involves orienting students to the lesson. This will involve ensuring that students understand the goals, process, and elements of the session. If the leader of the session is not familiar to the students, then it is recommended that a school staff member who is known to the students (e.g., a classroom teacher) introduce the leader to the students. Group rules can either be identified or, as is the case in many classrooms that already have established group discussion procedures, reinforced.

The second step ("Answer") lasts about 20 minutes and involves addressing questions students have about the crisis event. The recommended strategy is a question-and-answer format.

Table 13.5. Steps in a PREPaRE Student Psychoeducational Group

Time: about 1 hour
1. *Introduce* students to the lesson (5 minutes).
2. *Answer* questions and dispel rumors (20 minutes).
3. *Prepare* students for the reactions that may follow crisis exposure (15 minutes).
4. *Teach* students how to manage crisis reactions (15 minutes).
5. *Close* by ensuring that students have a crisis reaction management plan (5 minutes).

Because these details can be overwhelming, the leader or leaders should anticipate that students may have difficulty understanding a given fact the first time it is presented. Thus, the school-based crisis interveners need to be prepared to repeat crisis facts (Brock et al., 2001). When completing this step, leaders should keep in mind that young children may have had particular difficulty understanding the traumatic event and are much more susceptible to distortions. For example, following a school-yard shooting that involved a lone gunman attacking a primary school playground and then killing himself, there was a persistent rumor that there were two gunmen (a rumor fueled by the fact the gunman had shot at the playground from two separate locations; Brock et al., 2001). In this instance, acquiring cognitive mastery over what had happened (i.e., knowing the crisis facts) resulted in the event becoming much less threatening.

However, this observation does not mean that the group leader should give students all crisis facts. The possibility that traumatic stress can be generated by learning about a traumatic event must be kept in mind. In some cases, even though an individual was not personally exposed to a crisis or witnessed the event, being told about an incident or event that constituted a direct threat to the life or well-being of someone else may be sufficiently traumatic to result in PTSD (American Psychiatric Association, 2000). Examples include being told about the death of a relative whose body was mutilated by shrapnel, or learning about the fate of a classmate who was shot by a sniper. Thus, it is recommended that leaders of a student psychoeducational group let student questions guide the information that is given, and that unasked-for details be avoided (Servaty-Seib, Peterson, & Spang, 2003). In particular, it would be important to avoid giving students information that they would not necessarily know about (e.g., details about cause of death) that would unnecessarily frighten them.

The third step in the student psychoeducational group ("Prepare") lasts about 15 minutes and involves helping students anticipate the reactions that follow exposure to a crisis event. The first goal of this step involves identifying how crisis events affect people. This crisis intervention strives to prepare students for what to expect from themselves, their classmates, and even their caregivers (e.g., teachers and parents). In addition, this stage focuses on normalizing most initial crisis reactions. The leader should explicitly acknowledge that, with time, most reactions will become less intense and that recovery is the norm. However, it is also important to acknowledge that if the reactions do not lessen with time (or are to intense to manage independently), then a referral for crisis intervention assistance will be needed. The group leader should identify those crisis reactions that signal the need for immediate crisis intervention assistance (e.g., suicidal or homicidal ideation). Finally, it is most important to explain how students can obtain crisis intervention assistance both for themselves and others. With an understanding of how they are being affected and what some potential future concerns might be, students will be ready for instruction on how to cope with the crisis event.

The fourth step in the student psychoeducational group ("Teach") lasts about 15 minutes and involves reviewing techniques for responding to crisis reactions. The primary goal is to help students identify strategies that will help them (and those they care about) manage crisis reactions and problems. Specific strategies to achieve this goal include (a) teaching stress management and relaxation techniques, (b) identifying existing supports (e.g., parents, friends, teachers, and school psychologists and counselors) and referral procedures, and (c) identifying adaptive coping strategies and redirecting students away from maladaptive strategies (e.g., exercise instead of alcohol abuse). Table 13.1 provides resources that might prove helpful when providing this instruction; "Information on Coping," offered in the *Psychological First Aid Field Operations Guide* (Brymer et al., 2006, pp. 77–89) is an especially helpful resource. In addition, Table 13.6 provides a list of stress management resources, and Table 13.7 provides adaptive coping strategies. Finally, to summarize the student psychoeducational group's focus on individuals' strengths, it is important to compliment the problem-solving skills of students and to be positive about their ability to cope.

Again, when it comes to providing instruction on coping, a special note about cultural diversity is needed. Specifically, crisis interveners need to be aware of the ways students from diverse cultural groups may attribute meaning to the crisis event and suggest coping strategies that are respectful of individual beliefs and customs. Students from diverse cultures may use specific and relatively unique activities to help them cope. Encouraging students to think about their unique sources of support can help ensure that the intervention is more sensitive to individual diversity.

Table 13.6. Stress Management Resources

1. Managing Stress and Recovering From Trauma
   - http://www.ncptsd.va.gov/pfa/Tips_for_Relaxation.pdf http://www.imt.net/~randolfi/StressLinks.html
2. Stress Management and Emotional Wellness
   - http://www.optimalhealthconcepts.com/Stress
3. Oklahoma State University Stress Management Library
   - http://www.pp.okstate.edu/ehs/links/stress.htm
4. Stress Virtual Library
   - http://www.dialogical.net/stress/managestress.html
5. Stress Management: How to Reduce, Prevent, and Cope With Stress
   - http://www.helpguide.org/mental/stress_management_relief_coping.htm
6. Stress Management Tips for Parents of College Students in the Aftermath of the Virginia Tech Shootings (stress management tips from the American Psychological Association's Help Center.com)
   - http://apahelpcenter.org/articles/article.php?id=153

Table 13.7. Adaptive Coping Strategies for Dealing With Traumatic Stress Reactions

1. Talk with others who have been through the same crisis experience.
2. Participate in local, state, and national associations or groups that aim to prevent future crises.
3. Obtain training that will help prevent and mitigate future crisis events.
4. Incorporate physical exercise into your routine.
5. Get normal amounts of rest and sleep.
6. Avoid alcohol and drugs.
7. Maintain normal routines and comfortable rituals.
8. Eat well-balanced and regular meals.
9. Surround yourself with support (e.g., partners, pals, and pets).
10. Pursue your passions (don't feel guilty about finding pleasure in life).
11. Practice stress-management techniques (e.g., meditation, progressive muscle relaxation, or guided imagery).
12. Embrace your spirituality or belief systems.

Note. Source *School Crisis Intervention Workshop, School Crisis Intervention Workshop,* by S. E. Brock, S. R. Jimerson, R. Lieberman, R. Zatlin, and L. Huff.

The fifth and final step in a student psychoeducational group ("Close") can be as short as 5 minutes and involves ensuring that students have a plan for managing their own crisis reactions. For example, it can involve an assignment (which could be given as homework) that asks students to write a list of specific activities they feel they can engage in to cope with the crisis event. This could be an assignment that, like other schoolwork products, could be used by the instructor to gauge whether a lesson has been understood. The completed assignment can also be used as an additional measure of psychological trauma (i.e., secondary triage). The content of individual student self-care plans may suggest which students are in need of additional crisis intervention support. Finally, in concluding the session, the leader should again make sure that all students know how to obtain crisis intervention assistance.

CONCLUSION

Psychological education is a promising approach to addressing initial traumatic stress. It respects the fact that most individuals exposed to a given traumatic stressor will find, either within themselves or within their immediate caregiving environment, the resources needed to cope with crises. It also helps to ensure that students and caregivers are empowered with the knowledge to better ensure adaptive coping. Psychological educational approaches also establish contact between crisis intervention team members and the crisis survivors and caregiving community without the stigma often associated with both school- and community-based mental health interventions. Not only does this contact increase access to mental health resources, but it also gives crisis interveners the opportunity to evaluate how students and their caregivers are coping with a stressful event.

Figure 13.2. The original English document and the final Spanish translation of the informational documents that address the natural disaster of wildfires.

NASP

Helping Children After a Wildfire: Tips for Parents and Teachers

Natural disasters can be traumatic for children and youth. Experiencing a dangerous wildfire can be frightening even for adults, and the devastation to the familiar environment (i.e., home and community) can be long-lasting and distressing. Often an entire community is impacted, further undermining a child's sense of security and normalcy. Wildfires present a variety of unique issues and coping challenges, including the need to relocate when home and/or community have been destroyed, the role of the family in lessening or exacerbating the trauma, emotional reactions, and coping techniques.

Children look to the significant adults in their lives for guidance on how to manage their reactions after the immediate threat is over. Parents, teachers, and other caregivers can help children and youth cope in the aftermath of a wildfire by remaining calm and reassuring children that they will be all right. Immediate response efforts should emphasize teaching effective coping strategies, fostering supportive relationships, and helping children understand their reactions.

Issues and Challenges Associated With Wildfires

Unlike other natural disasters such as earthquakes, there is often some warning of an advancing wildfire. However, depending upon the wind and terrain the direction and spread of a wildfire can change abruptly. The amount of warning can vary from one neighborhood to the next. While some people may have hours (or even days) to evacuate, others will have only a few minutes to gather their belongings and leave their homes. Even if evacuation is not ultimately necessary, preparing for the possibility can be frightening for children, particularly if they are seeing images of homes burning nearby on television.

Reactions immediately following a wildfire may include emotional and physical exhaustion. In some instances children may experience survivor guilt (e.g., that their home was left unharmed, while others were completely destroyed). In general it might be expected that greater symptomatology in children will be associated with more frightening experiences during the wildfire and with greater levels of damage to their community and homes. The sights, sounds, and smells of a wildfire often generate fear and anxiety. Consequently, similar sensations (e.g., the smell of smoke) may generate distress among children in the months that follow. Given the scale of most wildfires, individuals living outside the ravages of the fires may still feel exposed to the danger from drifting clouds of smoke, flames on the horizon, and television reports. Some children may also react to follow-up news coverage, and even weather reports that talk about dry fire conditions after the fact. It is important to acknowledge that although a wildfire will last for only a specific period of time, survivors can be involved with the aftermath of a wildfire for months or even years. In attempts to reconstruct their lives, families are often required to deal with multiple people and agencies (e.g., insurance adjustors, contractors, the Red Cross, the Federal Emergency Management Agency (FEMA), and the Salvation Army).

Possible Reactions of Children and Youth to Wildfires

Most children will be able to cope over time with the help of parents and other caring adults. However, some children may be at risk of more extreme reactions. The severity of children's reactions will depend on their specific risk factors. These include exposure to the wildfire, personal injury or loss of a loved one, relocation from their home or community, level of parental support, the level of physical destruction, and preexisting risks, such as a previous traumatic experience or mental illness. Symptoms may differ depending on age but can include:

- **Preschoolers**—thumb sucking, bedwetting, clinging to parents, sleep disturbances, loss of appetite, fear of the dark, regression in behavior, and withdrawal from friends and routines.
- **Elementary School Children**—irritability, aggressiveness, clinginess, nightmares, school avoidance, poor concentration, and withdrawal from activities and friends.
- **Adolescents**—sleeping and eating disturbances, agitation, increase in conflicts, physical complaints, delinquent behavior, and poor concentration.

A small minority of children may be at risk of posttraumatic stress disorder (PTSD). Symptoms can include those listed above, exhibited over an extended period of time. Other symptoms may include reexperiencing the wildfire during play and/or dreams; anticipating or feeling that a wildfire is happening again; avoiding reminders of the wildfire; general numbness to emotional topics; and increased arousal symptoms such as inability to concentrate and startle reactions. Although extremely rare, some adolescents may also be at increased risk of suicide if they suffer from serious mental health problems like PTSD or depression. Students who exhibit these symptoms should be referred for appropriate mental health evaluation and intervention.

Immediately Following a Wildfire: Information for Teachers and Parents

Remain calm and reassuring. Children take their cues from adults, especially young children. Acknowledge the loss or destruction, but emphasize the community's efforts to cleanup and rebuild. To the extent it is possible to do so, assure them that family and friends will take care of them and that life will return to normal.

Acknowledge and normalize their feelings. Allow children to discuss their feelings and concerns, and address any questions they may have regarding the event. Listen and empathize. An empathetic listener is very important. Let them know that their reactions are normal and expected.

Encourage children to talk about wildfire-related events. Children need an opportunity to discuss their experiences in a safe, accepting environment. Provide activities that enable children to discuss their experiences. This may include a range of methods (both verbal and nonverbal) and incorporate varying projects (e.g., drawing, stories, audio and video recording). Seek the help of the school psychologist, counselor, or social worker if you need help with ideas or managing the conversation Promote positive coping and problem-solving skills. Activities should teach children how to apply problem-solving skills to wildfire-related stressors. Encourage children to develop realistic and positive methods of coping that increase their ability to manage their anxiety and to identify which strategies fit with each situation.

Emphasize children's resiliency. Focus on their competencies. Help children identify what they have done in the past that helped them cope when they were frightened or upset. Bring their attention to other communities that have experienced wildfires and recovered.

Strengthen children's friendship and peer support. Children with strong emotional support from others are better able to cope with adversity. Children's relationships with peers can provide suggestions for how to cope and can help decrease isolation. In many wildfire situations, friendships may be disrupted because of family relocations. In some cases, parents may be less available to provide support to their children because of their own distress and feelings of being overwhelmed. Activities such as asking children to work cooperatively in small groups can help children strengthen supportive relationships with their peers.

Take care of your own needs. Take time for yourself and try to deal with your own reactions to the situation as fully as possible. You will be better able to help your children if you are coping well. If you are anxious or upset, your children are more likely to feel the same way. Talk to other adults such as family, friends, faith leaders, or counselors. It is important not to dwell on your fears or anxiety by yourself. Sharing feelings with others often makes people feel more connected and secure. Take care of your physical health. Make time, however small, to do things you enjoy. **Avoid using drugs or alcohol to feel better.**

Immediately Following a Wildfire: Specific Information for Schools

Allow time for staff to discuss their feelings and share their experiences. A wildfire may result in the temporary closure of a school. Upon return to school, it is important to allow time for a group discussion (in a safe and caring context) for staff to discuss their feelings and share their experiences. It is essential that teachers and staff be given permission to take care of themselves in order to ensure that they will be able to help their students. Handouts regarding possible trauma reactions among children and other relevant information can be valuable resources for caring adults (e.g., some handouts are available at www.nasponline.org). School personnel (including your school crisis team members) should also have the opportunity to receive support from a trained mental health professional. Providing crisis intervention is emotionally draining and caregivers will need an opportunity to process their crisis response. This could include teachers and other school staff if they have been serving as crisis caregivers for students.

Provide time for students to discuss the wildfire. Depending on the situation, teachers may be able to guide this discussion in class, or students can meet with the school psychologist or other mental health professional for a group crisis intervention. Classroom discussions help children to understand the wildfire. They also encourage students to develop effective means of coping, discover that their classmates share similar questions, and develop peer support networks. Teachers should not be expected to conduct such discussions if children are severely impacted or if they themselves are distressed.

Identify children and youth who are high risk and plan interventions. Risk factors are outlined in the above section on children's reactions. Interventions may include classroom discussions, individual counseling, small group counseling, or family therapy. From classroom discussions, and by maintaining close contact with teachers and parents, the school crisis response team can help determine which students need counseling services. A mechanism also needs to be in place for self-referral and parent-referral of students.

Secure additional mental health support. Although many caregivers are often willing to provide support during the immediate aftermath of a wildfire, long-term services may be lacking. School mental health professionals can help provide and coordinate mental health services, but it is important to connect with community resources as well in order to provide such long-term assistance. Ideally these relationships would be established in advance.

Helping Children Adjust to Relocation After a Wildfire

The frequent need to relocate after a wildfire creates unique coping challenges. It may contribute to the social, environmental, and psychological stress experienced by children and their families. Children will be most impacted by the reactions of their parents and other family members, the duration of the relocation, their natural coping style and emotional reactivity, and their ability to stay connected with friends and other familiar people and activities. To the extent possible parents and other caregivers should:

- Provide opportunities for children to see friends.
- Bring personal items that the child values when staying in temporary housing.
- Establish some daily routines so that the child is able to have a sense of what to expect (including returning to school as soon as possible).
- Provide opportunities for children to share their ideas and listen carefully to their concerns or fears.
- Be sensitive to the disruption that relocation may have and be responsive to the needs of the child.
- Consider the developmental level and unique experiences of each child; it is important to remember that as children vary, so will their responses to the disruption of relocation.

In addition, school personnel should:

- Try to determine the status of every child in the school. Make sure that each child absent from school is contacted by school personnel and a record is kept.
- Determine the unique needs of every child whose home might have been destroyed or sustained damage following the wildfire. Help connect these children to supportive resources.
- Find out the phone numbers and addresses of every student that had to relocate. In this way classmates may be able to write notes or make phone calls.
- Help to provide accurate information and address inaccurate rumors or myths.
- Provide opportunities for children to discuss the event and how they are coping in the aftermath. It takes time for children to understand and adjust following a wildfire.
- Understand that it is perfectly normal for children to discuss the event over and over again.
- Use the creative arts (e.g., drama, art, band, chorus, photography) to help children express their emotions.
- Bring in agencies into the school that can help families deal with needs related to housing, finances, and insurance. Help children get any necessary medical and emotional assistance.
- Increase staffing for before and after school care. If possible, extend the service for additional hours and even on weekends.
- Utilize the information about the wildfire in related subject areas. Science, math, history, and language arts are especially relevant.
- Use drama, art, music, and photography to help children express their emotions.
- Develop an advisory committee of students to report back to school staff about what resources and changes in routines will help them cope in the aftermath.
- Most of all, listen to all the students. If you listen closely enough they will be able to tell you what they need.

Internet Resources

American Red Cross Wildfire Resources
http://www.redcross.org/services/disaster/keepsafe/readywildfire.html
http://www.redcross.org/news/ds/fires/wfire_pop/practice/firesafety.html
Discovery Channel School Wildfire Lesson Plans for Teachers
http://pictures.discovery.com/dppages/wildfire/teacher/teacher.html
Federal Emergency Management Agency Wildfire Resources
http://www.fema.gov/pdf/hazards/wfie.pdfhttp://www.fema.gov/rrr/talkdiz/wildfire.shtm

Adapted from:

Lazarus, P. J., & Jimerson, S. R., Brock, S. E. (2002). Natural disasters. In S. E. Brock, P. J. Lazarus, & S. R. Jimerson (Eds.), *Best practices in school crisis prevention and intervention* (pp. 435–450). Bethesda, MD: National Association of School Psychologists.

Lazarus, P. J., & Jimerson, S. R., Brock, S. E. (2003). *Helping children after natural disasters: Information for parents and teachers.* Bethesda, MD: National Association of School Psychologists. Available online www.nasponline.org.

Developed by:
Shane R. Jimerson, University of California, Santa Barbara
Stephen E. Brock, California State University, Sacramento
Katerine C. Cowan, National Association of School Psychologists

For further information on helping children cope with crises, visit www.nasponline.org.

Ayudando A Los Niños Después De Los Incendios Forestales: Consejos Para Los Padres y Maestros

Los desastres naturales pueden ser traumatizantes para los niños y jóvenes. Ser testigo de un fuego forestal puede ser una experiencia aterradora hasta para los adultos, y la destrucción de medio ambiente (ejem. hogar y comunidad) puede tener efectos estresantes y duraderos. Muchas veces, cuando una comunidad entera se ve afectada, la devastación debilita aún más el sentido de seguridad y normalidad del niño. Los incendios forestales presentan una variedad de problemas y retos únicos de superar, entre los cuales se encuentra la necesidad de mudarse cuando el hogar o la comunidad han sido destruidas. El papel de la familia es el de disminuir los efectos del trauma, ayudar a los niños a entender las reacciones emocionales y a enseñarles técnicas de superación.

Los niños observan a los adultos en sus vidas para guiarlos en como manejar sus reacciones inmediatamente después de que la situación traumática ha terminado. Los padres, maestros y otros adultos al cuidado de los niños pueden ayudarlos a entender y a sobrellevar el periodo subsiguiente al fuego forestal manteniendo la calma y asegurándoles que ellos se encuentran a salvo. Los adultos al cuidado de los niños deben enfocarse en enseñar estrategias de superación, en crear fuentes de apoyo y en ayudar a los niños a entender sus reacciones.

Problemas y Retos Asociados Con los Incendios Forestales

Aunque no hay aviso alguno en muchos desastres naturales, en terremotos por ejemplo, usualmente hay alguna advertencia durante el desarrollo de un fuego forestal. Sin embargo, la trayectoria de un incendio puede cambiar abruptamente dependiendo de la dirección del viento y del area del incendio. El tiempo de advertencia puede variar de vecindario a vecindario. Mientras algunas personas tendrán horas (o hasta días) para evacuar, otros tendrán solamente unos minutos para colectar sus cosas y huir de sus hogares. Aún si la evacuación no es necesaria, preparándose para cierta posibilidad puede ser traumático para los niños, especialmente si ven imágenes de casas quemándose cerca o a través de la televisión.

Las reacciones que se presentan inmediatamente después de un incendio forestal pueden incluir fatiga física y emocional. En cuestión de instantes, los niños pueden tener sentimientos de culpabilidad (su hogar no fue consumido por el fuego mientras otros hogares fueron completamente destruidos). En general, se puede anticipar que los niños que han tenido más contacto directo con el incendio y han visto daños severos a su casa y su comunidad, mostrarán los síntomas más serios. Las imágenes, sonidos y olores de un incendio forestal pueden causar miedo y ansiedad. Por esa razón, sensaciones similares (olor de humo) pueden causar angustia en los niños durante los meses después del desastre. Dado a la intensidad de muchos fuegos forestales, las personas que viven fuera de las areas de incendio todavía pueden estar expuestos a los peligros de las nubes de humo, a las imágenes del fuego y a los reportes de noticias acerca de los daños del incendio. Algunos niños pueden tener reacciones después de ver reportes actualizados de las condiciones del tiempo y pensar que son condiciones aptas para causar otros incendios forestales. Es importante reconocer que aunque un incendio forestal puede durar un período específico de tiempo, los sobrevivientes tendrán que encargarse de arreglar los asuntos relacionados con el fuego por los próximos meses o años. En el intento de reconstruir sus vidas, las familias afectadas tendrán que encargarse de hacer trámites con varias personas y agencias (Agencias de seguro, contratistas, la Cruz Roja, la Agencia Federal Encargada de Emergencias (FEMA), y el Ejército de Salvación.)

Posibles Reacciones de Los Niños y Jóvenes Después de Los Incendios Forestales

La mayoría de los niños logran superarse del incendio forestal con la ayuda de sus padres y otros adultos al cuidado de los niños. Sin embargo, algunos niños pueden estar en riesgo de tener reacciones extremas. La severidad de las reacciones de los niños dependerá de factores específicos. Estos factores incluyen estar expuestos al incendio, tener daño personal o pérdida de un ser querido, mudarse de su hogar o comunidad, el nivel de apoyo de los padres, el nivel de la destrucción física, y de riesgos pre-existentes al incendio, tales como previas experiencias traumáticas o enfermedades mentales. Los síntomas pueden ser diferentes y pueden depender según la edad del niño. Estos síntomas pueden incluir:

- **Niños de edad pre-escolar** - chuparse el dedo pulgar, orinarse en la cama, apegarse extremadamente a los padres, tener problemas para dormir, pérdida del apetito, miedo a la oscuridad, regresión en comportamientos y pérdida de interés en amigos y rutinas diarias.
- **Niños de escuela primaria** – irritabilidad, agresión, apegarse extremadamente a los padres, pesadillas, evitar ir a la escuela, poca concentración y pérdida de interés en amigos y actividades favoritas.
- **Adolescentes** – problemas de dormir y de apetito, ansiedad, incremento en conflictos, quejarse de dolores físicos, comportamiento delincuente y poca concentración.

Una pequeña minoría de niños puede estar en riesgo de desarrollar un desorden de estrés post-traumático (PTSD.) Se pueden presentar los síntomas mencionados en la sección previa y estos pueden estar presentes por un periódo de por lo menos un mes. Otros síntomas pueden incluir imitar la experiencia del incendio forestal a través de juegos o durante el sueño, creer o sentir que el incendio esta ocurriendo de nuevo, evitar recordar el incendio forestal, tratar de evitar cualquier tema de sentido emocional y tener un nivel elevado de síntomas de nervios, tales como inhabilidad para poder concentrarse y reacciones de susto. En pocos raros casos, algunos adolescentes pueden estar a riesgo del suicidio si ellos ya sufrían de una enfermedad mental como PTSD o depresión. Los estudiantes que muestren estos síntomas deben de ser referidos para poder hacer una evaluación mental y recibir las intervenciones apropiadas.

Después de un Incendio Forestal: Información Para Padres y Maestros

Permanezca Calmado. Especialmente si se encuentra entre niños, ellos van a decidir la gravedad de un evento basándose en las reacciones de los adultos. Aunque los adultos deberían de reconocer las pérdidas y la destrucción, el enfoque debería estar en los esfuerzos de limpieza y reconstrucción de la comunidad. Si es posible, hable con los niños para asegurarles que sus familiares y amigos se encargarán de cuidarlos y que sus vidas regresaran a la normalidad.

Reconozca y normalice los sentimientos de los Niños. Permita que los niños hablen acerca de sus sentimientos y preocupaciones y hagan preguntas acerca del evento. Escuche y muestre que entiende sus sentimientos. Escuchar con empatía es muy importante. Ofrezca actividades que le permitan a los niños compartir sus experiencias. Estas actividades pueden incluir dibujar, contar historias, y crear grabaciones de video y audio. Consulte con un psicólogo escolar, consejero o trabajador social si necesita ideas o ayuda en como manejar estas conversaciones con los niños.

Promueva capacidades de superación positivas y habilidades para resolver Problemas. Enséñele a los niños a superar el estrés relacionado con el incendio forestal. Ayúdelos a como manejar su ansiedad.

Enfatice las cualidades de los Niños. Enfóquese en sus habilidades. Ayúdelos a identificar las cosas o técnicas que han usado en el pasado y que les han ayudado a sentirse mejor cuando han sentido miedo o tenido preocupaciones. Hable acerca de otras comunidades que hayan pasado por la misma experiencia y que han logrado recuperarse del incendio forestal.

Fomente las Amistades y el Apoyo de los Niños. Los niños que cuentan con un buen apoyo emocional logran superarse de la adversidad. Las amistades con otros compañeros pueden ayudar a disminuir el sentimiento de sentirse sólo o aislado. Los incendios forestales pueden interrumpir las amistades cuando las familias se mudan a otro lugar. En algunos casos, los padres pueden estar menos disponibles para proveer el apoyo a los niños debido a que tienen sus propias preocupaciones que atender. Actividades tales como invitar a los niños a trabajar cooperativamente en grupos pequeños puede reforzar el apoyo de sus compañeros y las relaciones de amistades.

Hacerse cargo de uno Mismo. Tome tiempo para usted mismo y trate de sobreponerse de sus propias reacciones. Usted podrá ayudar mejor a los niños cuando supere sus propias reacciones del incendio forestal. Si usted se siente nervioso, probablemente los niños se sentirán de la misma manera. Hable con otros adultos como sus familiares y amigos, líderes religiosos o consejeros. Es importante que no permita angustiarse con pensamientos de miedos y ansiedad. Compartir sus sentimientos con otros crea relaciones de amistad más estrechas y hace que la persona se sienta aún más segura. Cuide su salud física. Disponga de tiempo para hacer las cosas que a usted le gusta hacer. ***Evite el uso de las drogas o el alcohol para sentirse mejor.***

Ayudando a los Niños a Adaptarse Cuando se Mudan por Causa de un Fuego Forestal.

Tener que mudarse después de un incendio forestal puede presentar ciertos obstáculos en el proceso de recuperación. Esto puede añadir innecesario estrés social, psicológico y del medio ambiente a las experiencias de los niños y sus familias. La reacción de los padres y otros miembros familiares, la duración de la mudanza temporal, las reacciones emocionales, las habilidades de recuperación y de mantener una relación estrecha con amigos y familiares, son algunos de los factores que más impacto tendrá en los niños. Los padres y otros adultos deberían de:

- Ofrecer oportunidades para que los niños tengan contacto con sus amigos.
- Permitir que el niño lleve consigo sus artículos de más valor sentimental a la nueva casa o albergue.
- Establecer rutinas diarias para que los niños tengan la sensación de tener control de lo que va a pasar y de lo que se espera de ellos (regresar a la escuela lo más pronto posible).
- Ofrecer oportunidades para que los niños compartan sus ideas y escuchar cuidadosamente sus temores y preocupaciones.
- Ser sensible a las interrupciones causadas por las mudanzas y responder a la necesidades de los niños.
- Considerar el nivel de desarrollo y las experiencias únicas de cada niño. Es importante recordar que cada niño tiene reacciones diferentes cuando se enfrentan al estrés de mudanzas y de evacuaciones.

Recursos de Información en el Internet

Guía de Consejería de Crisis para Niños y Familias en Casos de Desastres
http://www.crid.or.cr/crid/CD_comunitario/pdf/spa/doc14509/doc14509-contenido.pdf
U.S. Department of Homeland Security
http://www.listo.gov/ninos/parents/index.html
Tensión Relacionada al Incendio Forestal: Consejos Para Hablar con sus Niños
http://www.sbcphd.org/documents/press/ZacaFireTalktoKidsSPANISH.pdf

Información obtenida de:

Lazarus, P. J., & Jimerson, S. R., Brock, S. E. (2002). Natural disasters. In S. E. Brock, P. J. Lazarus, & S. R. Jimerson (Eds.), *Best practices in school crisis prevention and intervention* (pp. 435–450). Bethesda, MD: National Association of School Psychologists.

Lazarus, P. J., & Jimerson, S. R., Brock, S. E. (2003). *Helping children after natural disasters: Information for parents and teachers.* Bethesda, MD: National Association of School Psychologists. Disponible en www.nasponline.org.

Escrito por:
Shane R. Jimerson, Universidad de California, Santa Barbara
Stephen E. Brock, Universidad Estatal de California, Sacramento
Katherine C. Cowan, Asociación Nacional de Psicólogos Escolares

Traducido por;
LLecenia Navarro, Universidad Estatal de California, Sacramento
Evelyn Terán, Universidad Estatal de California, Sacramento
Marcela Muñoz, Universidad Estatal de San Diego

Para obtener mas información acerca de como ayudar a los niños a superar una crisis, visite www.nasponline.org.

Note. Only information relevant to Spanish-speaking caregivers was included in the Spanish translation. From *Helping Children After a Wildfire: Tips for Parents and Teachers* and *Ayudando A Los Niños Después De Los Incendios Forestales: Consejos Para Los Padres y Maestros* (L Navarro, E. Terán, and M. Muñoz, Trans.), by S. R. Jimerson, S. E. Brock, and K. Cowan, 2003, Bethesda, MD: National Association of School Psychologists. Copyright 2003 by the National Association of School Psychologists. Reprinted with permission.

Chapter 14

CLASSROOM-BASED CRISIS INTERVENTION

This chapter begins to examine the immediate psychological crisis interventions that more traumatized students require. As a rule, these interventions are active and direct attempts on the part of the crisis intervener to facilitate adaptive coping and directly respond to symptoms of traumatic stress. The immediate psychological crisis interventions discussed in this chapter and the next (i.e., classroom-based and individual, respectively) aim at reestablishing immediate coping (or the ability to address basic day-to-day challenges) and not necessarily crisis resolution. These interventions are provided by crisis interveners and are designed to help students independently cope with crisis-generated problems (if the psychological injury was not severe), or from which they can access more intensive services, referred to in this book as psychotherapeutic treatment (if the psychological injury was severe). The more intensive interventions (chapter 16) are often not a part of the school crisis intervention response and typically require collaboration with community-based mental health professionals.

Before proceeding with this discussion of immediate psychological crisis interventions, it is important to emphasize that these interventions (which can also be referred to as psychological first-aid) are not a substitute for psychotherapeutic interventions. More involved interventions are required to address the more severe consequences of trauma exposure, such as posttraumatic stress disorder (PTSD; Bisson, McFarlane, & Rose, 2000; Lewis, 2003; Stallard & Salter, 2003). It is also important to reiterate that when it comes to crisis intervention, "one size fits all" solutions can be counterproductive if interventions are provided to individuals who do not truly need them. For example, they may waste valuable crisis intervention resources, pathologize normal crisis reactions, increase crisis exposure, generate negative self-fulfilling prophecies, or reduce an individual's sense of self-efficacy (Berkowitz, 2003).

In addition, when considering working with the psychologically traumatized and emotionally labile students who require these psychological interventions, crisis interveners should acknowledge the small but real possibility that crisis reactions and coping behaviors may place crisis team members in potentially dangerous situations. Given this possibility, the intervention must also consider how to respond to the student who is, for example, homicidal or suicidal. When confronted with such a situation, crisis team members should understand that they are not expected to place themselves in danger. Rather they should collaborate with law enforcement and other first responders to address these situations.

The immediate psychological crisis intervention explored in this chapter is similar to interventions sometimes identified as *debriefing* (Mitchell & Everly, 1996) and *group crisis intervention* (M. A. Young, 1998). However, as will be discussed below, there are important modifications to these approaches in the PREPaRE classroom-based crisis intervention (CCI) session that address both developmental issues and recent empirical investigations.

As an intervention designed to prevent or treat PTSD, these interventions are controversial. However, the PREPaRE CCI is considered to be a form of immediate psychological first-aid and is not designed to prevent or treat the more psychopathological consequences of traumatic event exposure such as PTSD. In fact, as will be discussed below, it is not recommended that students who are judged to be at highest risk for psychopathological reactions (e.g., acute or physically injured trauma victims) be included in a CCI session. A PREPaRE CCI recognizes (a) that school-associated crisis events can simultaneously affect a significant percentage of a student body (and group crisis intervention approaches are thus sometimes necessary), and (b) that students (particularly younger students) may require concrete examples of the commonality of their crisis experiences and reactions to help them understand that what they are going through is not necessarily abnormal.

CLASSROOM-BASED CRISIS INTERVENTION INDICATIONS AND CONTRA-INDICATIONS

Psychological debriefings have been the subject of several empirical investigations. Although some have suggested the available data do not support the continued use of psychological debriefing following crisis exposure (Bisson, Jenkins, Alexander, & Bannister, 1997; Conlon, Fahy, & Conroy, 1999; Devilly & Annab, 2008; Devilly & Varker, 2008; Litz, Gray, Bryant, & Adler, 2002; Mayou, Ehlers, & Hobbs, 2000; van Emmerik, Kamphuis, Hulsbosch, & Emmelkamp, 2002), others have stated that it has a role in crisis intervention (Campfield & Hills, 2001; Chemtob, Thomas, Law, & Cremniter, 1997; Jacobs, Horne-Moyer, & Jones, 2004; Richards, 2001).

All of the studies above, both questioning and supporting classroom-based intervention, involved adults and older adolescents; *none* focused on children. Recently, however, Stallard et al. (2006) conducted what is believed to be the first randomized controlled trial of early psychological debriefing among young people. In that study, youth ages 7 to 18 years who had been treated at a hospital following a road traffic accident were randomly assigned to individual debriefing (n = 82) or control (n = 76) conditions. First, all study participants were assessed by a clinician for PTSD. Then approximately 4 weeks after their accidents, participants in the individual debriefing group engaged in a detailed reconstruction of their accident. Next, they were helped to identify their thoughts and to discuss their emotional reactions. Information about common thoughts and feelings was then provided to help normalize crisis reactions. Finally, written information was provided on how to cope with common problems. Participants in the control group were asked a series of neutral, non-accident-related questions.

Approximately 8 months after their accidents, Stallard et al. (2006) reevaluated 70 debriefing group youth and 62 control group youth, and it was found that children in both groups showed significant reductions on all measures of traumatic stress. While the debriefing condition could not be suggested to be more effective than the control, it was not suggested to cause harm (as was reported to be the case in previous adult accident survivor studies, that is, Hobbs, Mayou, Harrison, & Warlock, 1996; Mayou et al., 2000). Furthermore, the study authors acknowledged that the control group's contact with a researcher during the initial assessment "may have provided a framework in which the child's symptoms could be acknowledged, validated and normalized" (p. 132). Finally, the authors acknowledged that because the debriefings were not offered in a group setting (each participant had a unique trauma experience), the process of normalization was significantly different from what would have occurred in a group debriefing. In addition, it was not offered as an immediate crisis intervention. Rather, it was offered 4 weeks after the traumatic event.

Given the Stallard et al. (2006) findings, further research on the efficacy of CCI with school-age youth is clearly in order. However, because there are no data suggesting that these techniques have caused harm, and because there are data suggesting it to be effective in some situations, the authors of PREPaRE argue that it is premature to rule out this school crisis intervention. Instead, it is recommended that CCI be considered an option for reestablishing the immediate coping of groups of students who have been secondarily or vicariously exposed to a common crisis event (Brock & Jimerson, 2004). However, some conclusions regarding the indications and contra-indications of CCI can be drawn from an examination of the literature. To ensure that this intervention is helpful and does not cause harm, the factors described next should be attended to by crisis intervention teams considering the use of CCI.

Indications

As summarized in Table 14.1, indications for the use of CCI appear to include its use with individuals who were exposed to a crisis event but were not acute trauma victims (Jacobs et al., 2004). Studies that indicate CCI to have some potential have in common its use with trauma-exposed individuals who were not physically injured (which differentiates them from studies suggesting that such approaches have either no or negative effects). For example, Campfield and Hills (2001) found that among robbery survivors who were neither physically injured nor threatened with a gun, an immediate debriefing (offered less than 10 hours after the crisis) resulted in a more rapid reduction of traumatic stress than did delayed debriefing (offered more than 48 hours after the crisis).

Another indication for the use of CCI is its use as part of a comprehensive crisis intervention program (such as PREPaRE). Common among studies that indicate CCI to have some potential is its use as part of a comprehensive crisis intervention program. For example, among bank employees who were survivors of armed robberies (but not injured, shot at, or taken hostage), a combination of precrisis education, debriefing, and individual support was associated with lower rates of psychological trauma than was debriefing as a stand-alone intervention (Richards, 2001). Furthermore, among adults who experienced property damage as a result of a natural disaster

Table 14.1. Indications and Contra-Indications of Classroom-Based Crisis Intervention

Indications
1. Participants who are secondary or vicarious crisis survivors.
2. Offered as a part of a comprehensive crisis intervention program.
3. Offered as a more involved (i.e., longer) crisis intervention.
4. Used in a group setting with individuals exposed to a common crisis event.

Contra-indications
1. Participants who are primary or acute crisis survivors.
2. Offered as a stand-alone crisis intervention.
3. Offered as a brief crisis intervention.
4. Used as an individual crisis intervention.
5. Employed with individuals who have been exposed to different crisis events.
6. If the group is historically hurtful, divisive, or not supportive.
7. If the crisis event generates polarized needs or is politicized.
8. Whenever witness credibility is a concern.

(Hurricane Iniki), approximately 3 hours of sharing and subsequent normalization of crisis experiences and reactions, when combined with 2 hours of psychological education offered several months after the crisis event, appeared to reduce the impact of the crisis event (Chemtob et al., 1997).

A third indication for the use of CCI is its use as a more involved (i.e., of longer duration) crisis intervention. Common to the studies that reported positive outcomes following a group crisis intervention was a longer group session time. For example, the average duration of the group interventions in the Campfield and Hills (2001), Chemtob et al. (1997), and Richards (2001) studies, which suggested positive outcomes following participation, was over 2 hours. Conversely, the average duration of the debriefing interventions in the Bisson et al. (1997), Devilly and Varker (2008), and Mayou et al. (2000) studies, which suggested negative outcomes following participation, was less than 1 hour.

A final indication for CCI use is in group settings with individuals exposed to a common stressor. Two of three studies reviewed reported positive outcomes following a group crisis intervention when it was offered to groups who had experienced a common stressor (Campfield & Hills, 2001; Richards, 2001). In two of three studies that reported negative outcomes, the debriefing was offered only to individuals or couples (Bisson et al., 1997; Mayou et al., 2000), so there was no opportunity for crisis survivors to realize the possible benefits of not feeling alone in their crisis experiences or reactions.

Contra-Indications

As summarized in Table 14.1, contra-indications for the use of CCI include its use with individuals who were acute trauma victims (Jacobs et al., 2004). Common among all studies in which debriefing had negative outcomes was the inclusion of participants who had physical injuries or who could be considered to be acute trauma victims. For example, among adults and older adolescents who were hospitalized following a severe burn or a traffic accident, individual debriefings were suggested to cause harm when offered soon after the injury (Bisson et al., 1997) or when offered to those who were most psychologically traumatized (Mayou et al., 2000; Sijbrandij, Olff, Reitsma, Carlier, & Gersons, 2006).

The second and third contra-indications for the use of CCI are when it is offered as a stand-alone intervention or as a brief crisis intervention. In such instances it is possible that the intervention does not allow adequate emotional processing, and may instead increase arousal and anxiety levels (which is predictive of traumatic stress; Ruzek et al., 2007). Common among studies in which debriefing was shown to have negative outcomes was its use as a one-off intervention, with no additional crisis intervention offered (Devilly & Varker, 2008; Mayou et al., 2000). For example, Bisson et al. (1997) reported that following a single or "one-off" 45-minute individual or couple debriefing, acute burn victims were more likely to have developed PTSD at a 13-month follow-up than the control group that received no psychological intervention (26% vs. 9%). From these data, Bisson et al. concluded that the data "seriously question the wisdom of advocating one-off interventions posttrauma." (p. 78).

The fourth and fifth contra-indications for the use of CCI would be its use individually (not as a group intervention) and its use with individuals exposed to different crisis events. As was mentioned above, in such situations there is no opportunity for crisis survivors to realize the hypothesized benefits of understanding that they are not alone in their crisis experiences and reactions. This need is suggested by the PREPaRE authors to be especially important among younger children who lack abstract reasoning abilities. These students will require concrete examples of the commonality (and thus the normality) of their crisis experiences and initial crisis reactions.

Additional contra-indications suggested by Johnson (1993, 2000) include CCI's use with groups that are historically hurtful, divisive, or not supportive, and whenever the crisis event generates polarized needs or is politicized. Obviously, such circumstances would make group work counterproductive.

Finally, any group approach to crisis intervention, including student psychoeducational groups, is contraindicated when a crime has been committed and potential group members are witnesses to the crime. The importance of this CCI contraindication is highlighted by research suggesting that crisis memory of participants in a debriefing group can be affected by listening to the accounts of group members who give incorrect information. Specifically, Devilly, Varker, Hansen, and Gist (2007) found that when a researcher deliberately provided misinformation to a debriefing group, group participants were more likely to report seeing events that did not in fact take place, compared with those who were not debriefed.

CLASSROOM-BASED CRISIS INTERVENTION GOALS

The primary goal of a PREPaRE CCI is to reestablish immediate coping ability (see Table 14.2). Although CCI does not purport to resolve crisis-generated challenges, it does strive to place students in a position from which these problems can be addressed (either independently, if the psychological injury is not severe, or with school- or community-based crisis intervention

Table 14.2. Classroom-Based Crisis Intervention Goal and Subgoals

Following classroom-based crisis intervention sessions, the following goals will have been achieved:

1. Students have an improved ability to immediately cope with the crisis event and crisis-generated problems.
   a. Crisis facts are understood and rumors are dispelled.
   b. Crisis experiences are understood and crisis reactions are normalized.
   c. Students feel more connected to their peers by virtue of common experiences and reactions.
   d. Psychopathological crisis reactions and maladaptive coping strategies are identified, students know how to make self-referrals for school-based crisis intervention assistance, and secondary triage has been conducted.
   e. Students have strategies for managing stress reactions and crisis-generated problems.

assistance if the injury is severe). To achieve this end, the CCI session has several subgoals. Similar to the student psychoeducational groups discussed in chapter 13, the CCI's first subgoal is to help students understand the crisis event and to dispel crisis-related rumors. These rumors are many times more frightening than the objective crisis facts (Blom, Etkind, & Carr, 1991) and may generate ongoing appraisals of continuing threat or danger (e.g., the school shooting survivors who incorrectly believed that there were two shooters, not just one; Armstrong, 1990). Obviously these misperceptions will increase threat perceptions, will interfere with recovery, and may be consistent with certain cognitive models of the development of traumatic stress (Ehlers & Clark, 2000).

The second subgoal of a PREPaRE CCI session (again similar to the student psychoeducational group) is to ensure that common crisis experiences and reactions are identified and normalized. However, unlike the student psychoeducational groups, CCI gives students an opportunity to share individual crisis experiences and reactions (i.e. their story). Because the CCI session is designed for groups of students who are homogeneous in terms of crisis exposure and reactions, and because it is contraindicated for the more acutely traumatized, this addition provides students with concrete examples of common mild to moderate crisis experiences and reactions. Again, making these experiences and reactions concrete is important, because without concrete examples of their shared crisis experiences and reactions, many students (particularly younger children) will find it challenging to understand that their own experiences and reactions are common. As with the student psychoeducational groups, CCI can also help reinforce student perceptions that recovery is the norm and expected.

The third subgoal of a PREPaRE CCI session is also aided by the group's homogeneity in terms of crisis exposure and reactions. In hearing that their peers share similar crisis stories and reactions, students are helped to feel less alone and more connected to their classmates. In other words, the well-constructed CCI group will guarantee that students hear their peers relating common experiences and reactions. It is suggested that students' realization that they are not alone in addressing the crisis—that they are facing the crisis situation with others—will help them reestablish immediate coping. In other words, it will help give students the emotional strength needed to address the traumatic event and its consequences.

As is the case in a student psychoeducational group, while the normality of crisis reactions should be stressed and recovery identified as the norm, the CCI should also help students to identify the signs of more severe psychological injury. Thus, the fourth subgoal of a PREPaRE CCI session is to ensure that students are able to recognize psychopathological crisis reactions and coping strategies, and that they know when it is necessary to refer themselves for assistance through both school- and community-based mental health crisis intervention. The importance of providing information about self-referral is emphasized by reports that, following 9/11, two thirds of New York City public school students who exhibited PTSD symptoms did not seek any treatment (Applied Research and Consulting et al., 2002).

In addition, the direct contact with students that this form of crisis intervention provides gives school-based mental health professionals an opportunity to identify those who are in need of more intensive interventions (i.e., it is an example of secondary triage; Howard & Goelitz, 2004). In other words, by holding CCI sessions, crisis intervention teams have a better understanding of which students may need more intense crisis intervention assistance. CCI also has the practical advantage of allowing crisis interveners to evaluate larger groups of students at one time.

The fifth and final goal of a PREPaRE CCI session is to ensure that specific strategies for managing crisis reactions are identified or explicitly taught. As is the case during student psychoeducational groups, students receive adaptive coping strategies they can use to respond to their own crisis reactions or crisis-generated problems. Specifically, CCI sessions are designed to help promote healthy forms of coping and include the identification of a range of support resources (Brown & Bobrow, 2004; Howard & Goelitz, 2004). When successful, students emerge from the CCI session having developed their own plan for coping with crisis reactions. (A helpful resource that can be used to guide this element of CCI is "Information on Coping," offered in the *Psychological First Aid Field Operations Guide* (Brymer et al., 2006, pp. 77–89).

GENERAL CONSIDERATIONS FOR CLASSROOM-BASED CRISIS INTERVENTION

Before proceeding to a detailed discussion of the specific elements of a CCI session, discussion of some general considerations is required (Brock, 1998).

Who Should Participate

As its name implies, classroom-based crisis intervention sessions are often naturally occurring classroom groupings. CCI participants should be homogeneous in terms of developmental level and degree of crisis exposure, experiences, and impact (Berkowitz, 2003; Brock, 1998; Mitchell & Everly, 1996; Weinberg, 1990; Wollman, 1993). Having homogeneous groups will help to ensure that participants hear other group members sharing common experiences and reactions. It is possible that if the group is heterogeneous in terms of crisis exposure, experiences, and impact, CCI participation may be harmful. For example, participation may be traumatic if the session introduces information that students may otherwise not have had to confront (e.g., the crisis experiences and reactions of other more directly affected students; Berkowitz, 2003; Everly, 2003).

An especially important and sensitive issue when constructing CCI groups is that of cultural diversity. Crisis interveners need to keep in mind that students from different cultural groups may attribute different meanings to the crisis event (e.g., may explain the event as an unavoidable accident, or an act of God or of a spirit force), and may have different beliefs or customs regarding their response to the event, such as how to show respect for the deceased. Though such diversity is very enriching to the general school environment, crisis interveners need to consider how CCI sessions might interact with students' culturally unique coping styles.

It is strongly recommended that participation in a CCI session be voluntary (Jacob & Feinberg, 2002; McNally, Bryant, & Ehlers, 2003). As mentioned in chapter 10, some avoidance coping can initially have an adaptive function, giving individuals the time needed to mobilize their internal and external resources to cope with crisis-generated challenges. Requiring CCI participation may force some students to confront the crisis event before they are ready to do so. However, careful monitoring of children who opt out of CCI participation ensures that avoidance coping does not become a long-term or primary coping strategy.

Optimal CCI Group Size

The optimal size of a CCI session is 8 to 30 students. Large groups are not recommended (Mitchell & Everly, 1996) because they may inhibit sharing and the expression of reactions (Brock, 1998).

Where to Offer CCI Sessions

Whenever possible, the CCI session should be offered within a natural environment such as a classroom. Doing so helps to make more concrete the premise that crisis reactions are common (and not necessarily pathological), avoids unnecessary labeling of students as patients, provides reassuring structure and routine, and fosters group processes (Brock, 1998; Klingman, 1987). In addition, recognizing the importance of reaffirming physical health and safety, crisis interveners should ensure that the CCI room has access to food, water, tissues, and restrooms.

When to Offer CCI Sessions

For adult emergency response personnel, such as firefighters, Mitchell and Everly (1996) have recommended providing debriefings 72 hours after the crisis event has ended. However, for children it has been recommended that psychological debriefings not be offered right away and that offering them a week or more after the crisis event may be most appropriate (Stallard & Salter, 2003). Besides avoiding the risk of offering CCI too soon, before students are ready to process the crisis event, the wait also allows the crisis intervention team to evaluate psychological trauma and organize homogeneous groups.

From anecdotal observations and practical considerations it is suggested that school crisis intervention teams not begin to offer CCI until, at the very least, it is judged that students believe that crisis-related dangers have passed (a prerequisite to psychological interventions; Charuvastra & Cloitre, 2008). This also allows for fact verification and crisis intervention team preparation, ensures that sufficient time is available to offer this intervention, and allows for the screening necessary to ensure group homogeneity.

Given the findings reviewed above that suggest that brief sessions may have negative effects, it is strongly recommended that accommodations be made to ensure that the entire process, which can last 3 or more hours, can be completed. If this cannot be accomplished, and only limited time is available, then a student psychoeducational group may be the more appropriate crisis intervention.

CCI Providers

CCI is a team effort with at least a 1:10 ratio of crisis intervention team members to students (Brock, 1998; Weinberg, 1990). Ideally, at least one team member should be familiar to the group. The fact that familiar adults are present and active in problem-solving efforts can be reassuring and offers hope that crisis problems can be addressed. When crisis intervention team members are familiar to CCI participants and are nonjudgmental and supportive, student willingness to share is promoted (Kneisel & Richards, 1988). This assists in the identification of students who are manifesting severe crisis reactions.

The CCI crisis intervention team leader should be a school-based mental health professional trained in group processes (Brock, 1998). The other team members, or cofacilitators, should monitor individual student reactions and be available to assist students who need individual attention, such as those who are acutely distressed or who leave the CCI session.

The Role of the Teacher

Especially when conducted with naturally occurring classroom groups, CCI sessions should actively involve classroom teachers. As younger children often look to caregivers when determining how stressful a crisis event is, the presence of a teacher who is viewed as being in control and active in solving crisis-generated problems may reduce threat perceptions (and thereby reduce psychological traumatization). On the other hand, classroom teachers also may have been significantly traumatized by a school-associated crisis event, and thus unable to fill a caregiving role and participate in the CCI session. Though it may be appropriate for teachers to shed a tear or two in front of their students, it would be counterproductive if they were to lose emotional control.

Decisions About Follow-Up

Given the research described above, which was interpreted as suggesting that single-session crisis interventions are insufficient, it is important that follow-up crisis intervention services be available to all CCI participants. Although CCI and other forms of psychological first-aid may be sufficient in addressing minor injuries, more involved interventions will be required for students who have been more significantly traumatized.

Parental Permission

According to Everly, Lating, and Mitchell (2005), group crisis intervention sessions "should be voluntary, accompanied by some form of relevant informed consent when intervention goes beyond simple information or educational briefings" (p. 238). For school crisis intervention, this means that obtaining some sort of parental consent to participate in a CCI session is required (Litz et al., 2002). Obtaining such permission also makes use of parents' expertise regarding the readiness of their children to participate in a CCI session and further ensures that only students who are ready for such a crisis intervention experience participate. This is an issue that should be reviewed with a school district's legal counsel; however, use of a passive consent form may be sufficient. Table 14.3 provides a template for such a consent form.

Limits of Confidentiality

For any school-based mental health professional it will be important to ensure that student rights to the confidentiality of information shared in the CCI session are respected (Brymer et al., 2006). Thus, some discussion of confidentiality should take place as the CCI session begins. However, as is the case for any intervention provided by school- and community-based mental health professionals, there are limits to such confidentiality, and these limits should be acknowledged. These limits include situations in which the student requests that information be shared, there is any indication of danger to participants or others, or there is a legal obligation to share otherwise confidential information (Jacob & Feinberg, 2002).

CLASSROOM-BASED CRISIS INTERVENTION ELEMENTS

Before beginning CCI, the crisis intervention team should verify that all group members are appropriate participants and that the appropriate permissions have been obtained. As summarized in Table 14.4, the six steps of the PREPaRE CCI begin with (a) introducing students to the session, (b) providing students with crisis facts and dispelling crisis rumors, (c) sharing personal crisis stories, and (d) identifying common crisis reactions. The last two elements involve (e) empowering students with information about self-care and caregiving and (f) closing, with an emphasis on beginning the process of looking toward the future and placing the crisis in the past.

Introduce the Session

The first step, which lasts about 10 to 15 minutes, includes the identification of the CCI crisis intervention team leader and cofacilitators, and explanation of the purpose, sequence, and rules of the session (including discussion of confidentiality). Students are told that they are not allowed to leave the room without permission. However, they are also told that active participation is

Table 14.3. Passive Consent Form Template for Classroom Crisis Intervention

Date

Dear Parent,

As you know, our school community has experienced a traumatic event [AS INDICATED OFFER APPROPRIATE CRISIS FACTS]. Currently, our school crisis intervention team is engaged in a number of different activities designed to help our students understand and cope with this tragedy [AS INDICATED SUMMARIZE THE CRISIS INTERVENTION BEING OFFERED]. One such activity is known as Classroom-Based Crisis Intervention. Using this approach our school psychologist [LIST THE OTHER MEMBERS OF THE CRISIS INTERVENTION TEAM TO BE INVOLVED] will be available to meet with a group of students who have had similar crisis experiences. During this meeting we will answer student questions about the event, allow them to share their experiences and reactions to the crisis, and help them to find ways to cope with the event in a healthy manner. This letter is designed to inform you that we feel your child may benefit from such a session and one will be offered on [STATE THE DATE AND TIME OF THE CCI]. As always, if you have any questions about this group activity, please feel free to contact one of us.

If for any reason you DO NOT want your child to participate in this Classroom-Based Crisis Intervention session (including if you don't feel your child is ready to share his or her crisis experiences and reactions), please complete the form below and return it to the [SCHOOL NAME] Office by [DATE].

Sincerely,

______________________	______________________
Name	Name
Principal	School Psychologist

______ I DO NOT want my child to participate in a Classroom-Based Crisis Intervention at this time.

Parent Name (Print) ______________________

Student Name (Print) ______________________

Parent Signature ______________________

Date ____________

voluntary, and students who do not want to be in the room during discussion should be given an alternative activity that is neutral and does not press for any exploration of crisis experiences or reactions. In addition, it will be important to state that verbal or physical violence or abuse will not be tolerated. As appropriate, students may participate in the creation of the specific CCI

Table 14.4. Steps in a PREPaRE Classroom-Based Crisis Intervention

Time: about 4 hours

1. Introduce students to the session (10 to 15 minutes).
2. Provide crisis facts and dispel rumors (30 minutes).
3. Share crisis stories (30 to 60 minutes).
4. Identify crisis reactions (30 minutes).
5. Empower students (60 minutes).
6. Closing (30 minutes).

session rules; and doing so may help engender the sense that they are capable problem solvers. The following statement can be used to begin this step of CCI:

> I'm sorry this happened to your (our) school. When bad things like this happen, it is often helpful to talk about it. So, we are going to spend some time today talking. From our discussion we will have a better understanding of what happened, how it has affected us, and what we can do to help ourselves and each other. (Brock, Sandoval, & Lewis, 2001, p. 188)

Provide Crisis Facts and Dispel Rumors

This step lasts approximately 30 minutes and is virtually identical to "answer questions and dispel rumors" in the student psychoeducational group. As in the psychoeducational group, the recommended strategy in a CCI is a question-and-answer format (Servaty-Seib, Peterson, & Spang, 2003). The following statement in Brock et al. (2001) can be used to begin this step of CCI:

> We have experienced an event that was so unusual we might find it hard to understand. I would like to share with you what we know about this tragedy. Feel free to ask questions. It's important that you understand what happened. (p. 188)

To avoid frightening students by giving them unnecessary details about the event, crisis interveners should let student questions guide the information that is given. Doing so helps to avoid giving students information they do not already have and that would unnecessarily frighten them. School crisis interveners should be sure to provide only factual information; if questions are asked that cannot be answered, they can offer to investigate the issue further but should not offer any speculation.

Especially when working with younger children it is important to be prepared to repeat crisis facts (Lord, 1990). Because the crisis event will likely be novel and crisis details overwhelming, crisis intervention team members should anticipate that students will have difficulty understanding these facts. In addition, because younger children are susceptible to distortions about the crisis event, this CCI element is designed to identify crisis-related rumors and to explicitly correct these misperceptions.

Finally, it is important to keep participants' developmental level in mind when providing crisis facts. While children ages 7 to 11 years may be most concerned with basic factual information, adolescents may inquire about more abstract crisis issues (e.g., the potential danger or threat, the role of fate, the impulse for revenge; Stallard & Slater, 2003).

Share Crisis Stories

The sharing of crisis experiences can last 30 to 60 minutes depending on the size of the group. *Once this part of the session begins, it is important not to allow students to leave the group setting until after the "Empowerment" step has concluded.* While everyone should be given a chance to share their story, no one should be required to do so. A statement that can be used to begin this step of CCI is the following:

> We have all just shared a common experience. To illustrate this I would like to give as many of you as possible the chance to share some basic information about your experiences. You don't need to provide excessive detail about what happened, but do give enough so that we can gain a basic understanding of your crisis story. Who would like to start?

As this prompt suggests, it is not recommended that students provide detailed descriptions of their crisis experiences. Rather, it is hoped that students will provide just enough information so that the commonality of the group's crisis experiences can be made concrete. If a student does begin to provide excessive detail, then the crisis interveners will need to determine if the information being presented has the potential to unnecessarily increase the anxiety levels of the other CCI participants. If the detail is judged to have the potential to do so, then it may be necessary to carefully and gently tell the student that a basic understanding of their story has been obtained and that it is time to give other students the chance to share.

During this CCI step, the crisis intervention team needs to ensure that no mistakes have been made in group construction. If an acutely traumatized student has mistakenly been included in the group and begins to share especially traumatic crisis experiences, the team should quickly validate the experiences and prevent the student from sharing excessive detail, as doing so may be traumatic to the other students. The CCI team should then consider the necessity of gently removing the acute trauma victim from the group and providing him or her with a more appropriate individualized crisis intervention. The removal of a student from the classroom may cause some anxiety among the remaining students and should be dealt with directly.

Finally, at this step the crisis intervention team needs to consider the most appropriate way of leading a trauma discussion among young children. For example, Stallard and Salter (2003) suggested that younger children may be more able to provide verbal accounts of a crisis if they talk while drawing a picture of the event. Use of art also provides a natural opportunity to break up the CCI session, which can be especially important for younger students who will have difficulty remaining seated for long periods of time (Brock, 1998). When employing such art materials, it is important to keep in mind Morgan and White's (2003) guidelines for use of art in crisis intervention. These guidelines include (a) giving children a choice about using art or talking about what was created when sharing their crisis stories, (b) making use of dry materials (e.g., crayons and pencils versus finger paint), and (c) crisis interveners not offering students detailed interpretations of the art.

Identify Crisis Reactions

This CCI step lasts approximately 30 minutes and can involve either teaching common reactions (perhaps the most appropriate approach for younger students) or asking individual students to share how the crisis event is affecting them. For example, the following statement in Brock et al. (2001) can be used to begin this step of CCI:

> Following an event, such as the one we've just experienced, it is not unusual for people to feel and behave differently for a while. Some common reactions are (identify common reactions). These are normal reactions to an abnormal situation. (p. 189)

Regardless of the approach used (i.e., direct instruction or individual sharing or both), student reactions must be framed so they can be viewed as common (Brock, 1998). This can be reinforced by asking those who have experienced specific reactions to raise their hands. For example, if a student shares that he or she is having nightmares about a crisis event, the CCI team leader should validate this reaction as normal and state: "Bad dreams and other sleep difficulties are very common following a crisis event." The team leader should then ask how many other students have experienced a similar reaction and do so in a way that guarantees several other participants will respond in the affirmative. For example, the leader might state: "By a show of hands, how many of you are also having bad dreams, problems getting to sleep or staying asleep, or any other sleep-related difficulties?" Using an approach such as this will help make concrete for students the fact that they are experiencing common reactions.

While emphasizing that most initial crisis reactions are common, CCI team members should keep in mind that many of these reactions are unsettling, and it is not uncommon for students to fear that they are going crazy. Group sharing and crisis intervention team anticipation of crisis reactions helps normalize these frightening symptoms. The CCI team should also let students know that recovery is the norm and that with time, for most people, reactions will dissipate. However, students should also be told what to do if they feel that they are unable to manage their reactions. This is a natural time to ensure that students are aware of self-referral procedures for obtaining one-on-one crisis intervention. As this step ends, asking future-oriented questions may help students to predict experiences they will have and coping skills they may need. For example, students can be asked: "What do you think will happen next?" "Will your friends and family continue to be affected?" or "What concerns you?"

During this step some emotional release should be anticipated and can provide data important to secondary triage. Crisis team members can be very helpful here, as they can monitor individual student reactions, evaluate the severity of distress, and counsel and gently remove an acutely distressed student that may have mistakenly been included in the group. These students will require more individualized crisis intervention. In addition, if allowed to stay in the group, the acutely distressed student may become the group's focus. It is important to acknowledge that the removal of a distressed student from the classroom may cause anxiety that needs to be addressed.

Empower Participants

Having gained an understanding of how they are being affected and what some potential future concerns might be, students are ready to move on to a discussion of how to cope with the event. This empowerment step may last up to 60 minutes, and during this time the focus shifts from symptom sharing to symptom solving. The primary goal is to help students begin to participate in activities that help them regain a sense of control. Important to the attainment of this goal is the identification of coping strategies. A statement that can be used to begin this step of CCI is: "Crises can make us feel helpless. I would like to see us take action or make plans to help us now and in the future" (Brock et al., 2001, p. 189).

The importance of this step is emphasized by the observation that when students believe they are in control of the forces that dictate their experiences, they are more resistant to stress (Luthar, 1991), and the CCI team may begin this step by identifying previously developed coping strategies. They should reinforce those that are adaptive and explicitly offer alternatives when maladaptive strategies are proposed. During this step facilitators might review basic stress management techniques (e.g., getting needed sleep, food, exercise, and talking to friends and family). Alternatively, they might encourage students to work together on developing strategies to gradually desensitize each other to trauma-related fears. As indicated, it is appropriate to become very directive and tell students exactly what they need to do to cope.

This step can conclude with a review of students' newly identified or reestablished coping skills and should compliment their ability to address crisis problems. Once students have moved beyond the identification of crisis experiences and reactions and have been empowered with coping strategies, it would be appropriate at this point to break from the session, if necessary, and allow students to leave the group setting (Brock, 1998).

Close the Session

This last CCI step may last up to 30 minutes and focuses on beginning to place the crisis event in the past and moving forward. For example, a statement that can be used to begin this step is "What can we do to help place this event behind us and move on with our lives?" (Brock et al., 2001, p. 189). This step may include developing memorials, preparing to attend or participating in funerals, writing get well cards and letters to victims, and if the class has experienced the death of a classmate or teacher, discussing what to do with the deceased's desk and belongings.

In concluding CCI, the crisis intervention team should answer any remaining questions and remind students that they have shared a common experience and are displaying common reactions to abnormal circumstances. They should acknowledge that, for some students, it might be some time before they are truly able to place the event in their past and move on with their lives. However, at the same time they should strive to be positive about the future and remind students that, although memories will remain, with time, crisis reactions will typically lesson. The importance of doing so is highlighted by Hobfoll et al. (2007), who suggested that instilling a sense of hope among trauma survivors is essential to obtaining a positive outcome. Similarly, Ruzek et al. (2007) stated:

> Those who maintain optimism (because they can hope for their future), positive expectancy, a feeling of confidence that life and self are predictable, or other hopeful beliefs (e.g., in God, that there is a high probability that things will work out as well as can reasonably be expected) [are likely to have] more favorable outcomes after experiencing mass trauma. (p. 23)

Finally, the crisis intervention team should reassure students that additional crisis intervention services are available and reiterate self-referral procedures.

CLASSROOM-BASED CRISIS INTERVENTION FOLLOW-UP ACTIVITIES

Following the CCI session, all parents and caregivers need to be informed about how they can help students cope. Psychological education recommendations, which should be provided to the families of all CCI participants, include (a) listen to and spend time with your child, (b) offer, but do not force, discussion about the trauma, (c) reassure your child that he or she is safe, (d) offer assistance with everyday tasks and chores, (e) respect your child's privacy, and (f) do not take anger or other reactions personally (Mitchell & Everly, 1996).

After the CCI session has ended, at least one, but preferably all, of the CCI team members should remain with group participants. At the very least, one team member should be available to students throughout the remainder of the school day, to allow students additional opportunities to seek support and to have questions answered. This also gives crisis interveners additional opportunities to assess how individual students are coping (that is, to conduct secondary psychological triage).

Finally, as soon as possible after CCI has concluded, the session should be debriefed by the operations section chief and/or the crisis intervention specialist. This review of the CCI session typically occurs at the end of the school day and serves two important purposes. First, it facilitates secondary psychological triage and helps in making decisions regarding who will need additional crisis intervention assistance. Second, crisis interveners should focus on their own reactions and coping, given the research findings, that such work has an effect on school crisis team members (Bolnik & Brock, 2005). In particular, special attention needs to be directed toward the classroom teacher. If needed, crisis intervention services should be made available to the teacher and other CCI team members.

CONCLUSION

Some school-associated crisis events can simultaneously affect large numbers of students, and given schools' limited resources, this may require group approaches to crisis intervention. If students are not suspected to have significant psychological injuries, then simply reconnecting them to their caregivers or providing psychological education, or both, may be sufficient. However, if the injury is judged to be more severe (but not acute), then CCI might be indicated. In addition, by allowing for the provision of crisis intervention assistance to groups (often naturally occurring classroom groupings), the carefully constructed CCI group also has the advantage of making concrete the normality of crisis experiences and reactions. Students who are allowed to share basic elements of their crisis stories and brief descriptions of how they have been affected by the crisis event will come to realize that they are not alone in their experiences and reactions. This should, in turn, help to give them the emotional strength needed to adaptively cope with crisis-generated problems. In addition, this group approach, and its sharing of crisis stories and reactions, can be a powerful triage tool that helps to ensure that no student with significant psychological injury slips through the cracks of a school-based crisis intervention.

Chapter 15

INDIVIDUAL CRISIS INTERVENTION

Most crisis-exposed students (and staff members) will experience brief and manageable initial crisis reactions; some will display more acute or durable responses (or both) that overwhelm their coping abilities and may also be predictive of later psychopathology. Although the empirical literature on meeting the immediate needs of these more traumatized students is limited, the elements of individual crisis intervention (ICI) described in this chapter have been recommended as the most appropriate immediate response to these more severely affected students (Brymer et al., 2006; Hobfoll et al., 2007; Ruzek et al., 2007).

This form of immediate psychological crisis intervention is not psychotherapy, nor is it a substitute for psychotherapy, and it does not have crisis resolution as its goal. Rather, it aims to place crisis-exposed students in a position from which they can independently cope with crisis-generated problems (if the psychological injury was not severe), or from which they can access psychotherapeutic treatment (if the psychological injury was severe). Chapter 16 discusses the treatment options that should be made available to that minority of students who appear to have developed some sort of psychopathology secondary to their crisis event exposure. These more intense services are often not a part of the school crisis intervention response and typically require collaboration with, and referral to, community-based mental health professionals.

Regardless of training or level of expertise, ICI is a first step in the helping process. Whether this intervention is provided by a school psychologist or a classroom teacher, all caregivers are equal here and, with sufficient training, can be appropriate ICI providers. The difference is that, whereas the crisis intervener who is a school-based mental health professional may maintain involvement long after the immediate ICI response has ended, the classroom teacher, for example, will find his or her responsibilities concluded at the end of the ICI response (when a student is referred to a community-based mental health professional).

INDIVIDUAL CRISIS INTERVENTION GOALS

The immediate ICI discussed in this chapter employs a basic problem-solving model and is adapted from the psychological first-aid techniques originally identified by Slaikeu (1990) and more recently by Brymer et al. (2006) and Ruzek et al. (2007). As summarized in Table 15.1, its primary goal is to help crisis-exposed individuals reestablish their immediate coping or problem solving skills. Subgoals include (a) providing physical and emotional support, which includes ensuring the individual's physical and psychological safety and containing emotional distress; (b) identifying crisis-generated problems; (c) supporting adaptive coping; and (d) assessing the individual's psychological trauma risk and linking him or her to the appropriate helping resources. Each of these goals has been identified as important to immediate individual crisis intervention (Litz, Gray, Bryant, & Adler, 2002; Phipps & Byrne, 2003; Wilson, Raphael, Meldrum, Bedosky, & Sigman, 2000).

Reestablishing Immediate Coping

Sometimes the individual in crisis is like the deer frozen in the headlights of an oncoming car. He or she is quite literally immobilized (or overwhelmed) by apparently unsolvable crisis-generated problems. In this instance the school crisis intervener's primary task is to help the individual take some steps (no matter how small) towards coping with crisis generated problems (Brock, Sandoval, & Lewis, 2001). The following ICI subgoals are important to reaching the primary goal of reestablishing immediate coping.

Providing Physical and Emotional Support

In some situations, such as a hurricane or other natural disaster, individuals' failure to immediately cope with their altered conditions may place them in situations that threaten their physical safety (e.g., not recognizing that they need to stay out of the sun and maintain hydration on hot and humid days). Thus, an important subgoal of immediate ICI is to provide the physical support needed to ensure that individuals are physically safe. In addition, before psychological recovery from traumatic event exposure can begin, students must not only be safe, but must believe that crisis-related dangers have passed (see chapters 8 and 9). Although physical support and safety can be considered ICI priorities, the provision of emotional support is also essential

Table 15.1. Individual Crisis Intervention Goal and Subgoals

Primary Goal:

1. Reestablish immediate coping.

   Subgoals:

   a. Provide physical and emotional support (ensure physical and psychological safety and begin to contain distress).
   b. Identify crisis-generated problems and support adaptive coping
   c. Assess trauma risk and link to helping resources.

because it helps to contain the emotional distress (e.g., panic) that will interfere with adaptive coping and problem solving (Ruzek et al., 2007).

Identifying Problems and Supporting Adaptive Coping

With physical safety ensured and emotional distress contained, crisis-exposed individuals will be able to begin the problem-solving process. ICI subgoals include identifying the problems generated by the crisis event, supporting adaptive coping, and beginning the problem-solving process. A successful ICI intervention may not resolve all crisis-generated problems, but from such crisis intervention it should be clear that the individual is moving in the right direction, toward addressing the crisis-generated problems.

Assessing Trauma Risk and Linking Student to Resources

Finally, like other crisis interventions that involve direct contact with crisis-exposed individuals (i.e., student psychoeducational groups and classroom-based crisis intervention), ICI can be considered an important part of the secondary psychological triage discussed in chapter 11. A subgoal of ICI is to assess the individual's risk for psychological injury and then link the student (or staff member) with the appropriate helping resources. If the psychological injury is minor—that is, coping challenges are not overwhelming the individual and adaptive coping strategies have been identified—then simply reconnecting the individual with natural support systems (and providing some caregiver training as needed) may be all that is required. In contrast, if the psychological injury is severe—that is, coping challenges are overwhelming the individual and adaptive coping strategies cannot be identified—then the individual may need to be referred for more intense, often community-based psychotherapeutic support (see chapter 16).

GENERAL CONSIDERATIONS FOR INDIVIDUAL CRISIS INTERVENTION

Before proceeding to a detailed discussion of the specific elements of an ICI, this section discusses some general considerations.

Who Should Be Offered ICI

Any individual who appears to be having immediate coping challenges would be an appropriate target of this basic problem-solving strategy. In particular, this is the initial crisis intervention that should be considered for individuals who are acute trauma victims (e.g., those who were physically injured). On the other hand, among persons who are less severely traumatized, less directive crisis interventions should be considered (e.g., reestablishing support systems and psychological education).

As with classroom-based crisis intervention, unless the individual's situation is judged to present danger to self or others, he or she should be given a choice regarding whether or not to participate in ICI (Jacob & Feinberg, 2002). At least initially, some avoidance coping can have an adaptive function; that is, it gives individuals the time needed to mobilize the internal and external resources required to cope with crisis-generated challenges. Requiring ICI participation may force some individuals to confront the crisis event before they are ready to do so (see chapter 10). That said, it would be important to carefully monitor and support individuals who opt out of ICI so as to ensure that avoidance coping has not become a longer-term (or primary) coping strategy.

Where ICI Should Be Offered

ICI is designed to be used anywhere crisis-exposed individuals are found (e.g., on the playground, in a classroom). However, crisis team members providing this type of intervention must keep in mind the need to reaffirm physical health and safety and the perception of safety. Thus, it is important to ensure that ICI settings have access to food, water, tissues, and restrooms, and to otherwise convey a sense of physical safety.

When to Offer ICI

ICI can be offered as soon as the individual appears ready to begin identifying crisis-generated problems and problem solving; that is, as soon as he or she is emotionally stable. For example, individuals who do not respond to questions, or who are crying, hyperventilating, or shaking uncontrollably, are not ready to begin problem solving. Rather, they will first need to be emotionally stabilized (Brymer et al., 2006).

ICI Providers

School-based mental health professionals will have had prior training that makes them especially well suited to providing ICI. However, with the appropriate psychological education and training, any caregiver who is able to convey a sense of calmness and control in crisis situations could become an appropriate ICI provider. The presence of familiar caregiving adults who are filling crisis intervention roles helps students to reestablish the belief that they are safe, and in turn helps to contain their distress (Ruzek et al., 2007).

When Follow-Up Is Needed

Follow-up crisis intervention services should be available to all ICI participants. While such first aid may be sufficient in addressing minor injuries, more involved interventions (such as those discussed in chapter 16) will be required for individuals who have been more significantly traumatized.

Parental Permission

It is always preferable to obtain parental permission before providing any crisis intervention assistance (Ruzek et al., 2007). However, ICI is not a planned psychotherapeutic treatment, so providing immediate assistance to an acutely distressed student is appropriate even without parental consent (Jacob & Feinberg, 2002). Of course, it is critical to contact the student's parents or caregivers as soon as possible, especially in the case of acute distress. Such contact has several goals: (a) to inform them of their child's status and possible need for additional support, (b) to evaluate their status and determine their ability to provide such support, and (c) to provide the appropriate psychological education regarding how to best address their child's needs.

Limits of Confidentiality

For any school- or community-based mental health professional it will be important to respect individual rights to the confidentiality of information shared in the ICI session (Brymer et al., 2006). However, as is the case for any intervention provided by mental health professionals, there are limits to such confidentiality. These limits should be acknowledged as ICI is initiated. The limits include situations in which the individual requests that information be shared, there is any indication of danger to the crisis survivor or others, or there is a legal obligation to share otherwise confidential information (Jacob & Feinberg, 2002).

INDIVIDUAL CRISIS INTERVENTION ELEMENTS

In the PREPaRE model, ICI consists of five primary elements: (a) establishing psychological contact, (b) verifying emotional readiness to identify and address crisis-generated problems, (c) identifying and prioritizing crisis problems, (d) beginning to address crisis problems, and (e) evaluating attainment of ICI goals. Each of these elements is discussed in detail in the sections that follow and summarized in Table 15.2. However, potential crisis interveners should first attend to the guidelines for the delivery of immediate crisis intervention (or "psychological first aid") offered by Brymer et al. (2006) and presented in Table 15.3.

Establishing Psychological Contact

The first ICI step involves making psychological contact with the person in crisis. Establishing rapport with the individual who has been exposed to a crisis event is not necessarily difficult. Individuals in crisis are often very open to someone who is willing and able to help. When beginning ICI, it is important for the crisis intervener to introduce him- or herself (even if you are a familiar face), to discuss issues associated with confidentiality, and to inquire about any unmet basic needs. As discussed in chapters 8 and 9, crisis survivors need to feel safe and have their basic needs met before they can begin the process of recovery. Brymer et al. (2006) suggested that the crisis intervener begin ICI by saying something like the following: "Hi Lisa, I'm ___________ and I'm here to try to help you and your classmates in dealing with the current situation. Is there anything you need right now? I can get you some water and juice, and we have a few blankets and toys in those boxes."

Empathy, respect, and warmth are the vehicles used to make psychological contact. Empathy involves listening to what the individual is saying and trying to understand the individual's crisis story and to identify how he or she feels. To show understanding, the intervener then restates both facts and feelings in his or her own words. Empathy is different from sympathy, which would involve feeling what the person in crisis is feeling. Thus, even if the intervener has not had the same experience, he or she can understand the individual's situation. From such empathy,

Table 15.2. Elements of Individual Crisis Intervention

1. Establish psychological contact.
   a. Introduction:
      i. Identify self.
      ii. Inquire about and address basic needs as indicated.
   b. Empathy:
      i. Identify crisis facts.
      ii. Identify crisis-related feelings.
   c. Respect:
      i. Pause to listen.
      ii. Do not dominate the conversation.
      iii. Do not try to smooth things over.
   d. Warmth:
      i. Ensure that verbal communication is congruent with nonverbal behaviors.
      ii. Consider the use of and provide physical contact, as indicated.
2. Verify emotional readiness to begin problem identification and problem solving.
   a. If not, stabilize the student.
   b. If the student is ready, begin the problem-solving process.
3. Identify and prioritize crisis-generated problems. Identify the most immediate concerns.
   a. Inquire about what happened.
      i. Understand the crisis story.
   b. Inquire about the problems generated by the crisis event.
   c. Rank order crisis-generated problems.
4. Address crisis-generated problems. Encourage the crisis survivor to be as responsible for coping with crisis-generated challenges as is possible.
   a. Ask about coping attempts already made.
      i. Validate adaptive coping strategies already identified by the crisis survivor.
   b. Facilitate exploration of additional coping strategies.
      i. As indicated, encourage the crisis survivor to identify his or her own adaptive coping strategies.
   c. Propose alternative coping strategies.
      i. As indicated, do not hesitate to explicitly direct the crisis survivor toward adaptive coping strategies.
         - If lethality is low *and* student is capable of action, then take a facilitative stance (i.e., the crisis survivor initiates and is responsible for coping actions).
         - If lethality is high *or* student is not capable of acting, then take a directive stance (i.e., the crisis intervener initiates and is responsible for coping actions).

Table 15.2. (continued)

5. Evaluate and conclude the ICI session. Ensure that the individual is moving toward adaptive crisis resolution.
   a. Secure identifying information.
      i. Identify and ensure connection with primary natural social support systems (e.g., parents, teachers).
   b. Agree on a time for recontact and follow-up.
   c. Assess if immediate coping has been restored.
      i. Physical and emotional support has been obtained, and any lethality has been reduced.
      ii. Crisis problems have been identified and adaptive coping has been initiated.
      iii. From assessed trauma risk level, the student is linked to appropriate helping resources.
         - If these goals have not been obtained, then restart the ICI process.
         - If these goals have been obtained, compliment the student on his or her problem-solving skills, convey the expectation that they will cope well with the trauma, and conclude the immediate psychological crisis intervention.

crisis survivors realize they are being understood. Important active listening skills used during this part of an ICI intervention are paraphrasing, summarizing, and checking perceptions.

Respect is communicated by pausing to listen and (at least initially) avoiding dominating the conversation or trying to smooth things over. In other words, instead of offering lectures or immediately offering explanations or solutions, the crisis intervener offers to talk about and listen to the person's perceptions of the crisis event. It is also important to avoid being judgmental and instead to communicate a willingness to enter into a problem-solving relationship with the person in crisis.

Finally, warmth is critical to making psychological contact with crisis-exposed individuals. Warmth is expressed by nonverbal behaviors such as gestures, posture, tone of voice, touch, and facial expressions. Congruence between what the crisis intervener says and what his or her nonverbal behaviors communicate is essential. When working with younger children it will be important to get down to the child's eye level, use a calm reassuring voice, and be as nonthreatening as possible (Ruzek et al., 2007).

Physical contact or touch can be helpful in establishing warmth, as it can have a calming effect. However, it must be used carefully. Some individuals may be very comfortable with a caring crisis intervener placing a reassuring arm around their shoulder, but others may not be comfortable with such touch and it might actually serve as a reminder of the crisis event (e.g., in instances in which the crisis survivor was the target of child abuse). In addition, consistent with guidance offered by Brymer et al. (2006), the intervener should listen for and validate any response that suggests that the type of contact is appropriate with regard to the child's cultural and

Table 15.3. Delivery of an Individual Crisis Intervention

Professional Behavior

- Operate only within the framework of an authorized school crisis intervention team response.
- Model healthy responses; be calm, courteous, organized, and helpful.
- Be visible and available.
- Maintain confidentiality as appropriate.
- Remain within the scope of your expertise and your designated role.
- Make appropriate referrals when additional expertise is needed or requested by the student and/or the student's caregiver(s).
- Be knowledgeable and sensitive to issues of culture and diversity.
- Pay attention to your own emotional and physical reactions, and practice self-care.

Guidelines for Delivering Psychological Crisis Intervention

- Politely observe first; do not intrude. Then ask simple, respectful questions of the student and/or his caregiver(s) to determine how you may help.
- Make contact by providing practical assistance (food, water, blankets).
- Initiate contact only after you have observed the situation, and the student or his or her caregiver has determined that contact is not likely to be intrusive or disruptive.
- Be prepared to have students either avoid you or overwhelm you with contact.
- Speak calmly; be patient, responsive, and sensitive.
- Speak slowly, in simple, concrete terms; do not use acronyms or jargon.
- If a student wants to talk, be prepared to listen. While listening, focus on hearing what he or she wants to tell you and on how you can help.
- Acknowledge the positive features of what the student has done to keep safe.
- Give information that directly addresses the student's immediate goals and clarify answers repeatedly as needed.
- Give information that is accurate and age-appropriate for the student.
- When communicating through a translator or interpreter, look at and talk to the student or caregivers you are addressing, not at the translator or interpreter.
- Remember that the goal of crisis intervention is to reduce distress, assist with current needs, and promote adaptive functioning, not to elicit details of traumatic experiences and losses.

Some Behaviors to Avoid

- Do not make assumptions about what the student is experiencing or what he or she has been through.
- Do not assume that everyone exposed to a disaster will be traumatized.
- Do not pathologize; keep in mind that acute reactions are understandable and expectable given what students exposed to a disaster have experienced. Do not label reactions as symptoms or speak in terms of diagnoses, conditions, pathologies, or disorders.

Table 15.3. (continued)

- Do not talk down to or patronize the student, or focus on his or her helplessness, weakness, mistakes, or disability. Focus instead on what the student has done that is effective or may have contributed to helping others in need, both during the disaster and in the present setting.
- Do not assume that all students want to talk or need to talk to you. Remember that being physically present in a supportive and calm way helps affected students feel safer and more able to cope.
- Do not "debrief" by pressing for details of what happened.
- Do not speculate or offer possibly inaccurate information. If you cannot answer a student's question, do your best to learn the facts.

Interventions With Children and Adolescents

- For young children, sit or crouch at the child's eye level.
- Help school-age children verbalize their feelings, concerns, and questions; provide simple labels for common emotional reactions (for example, mad, sad, scared, worried). Using extreme words like "terrified" or "horrified" to describe a child's reactions may increase their distress.
- Listen carefully and check in with the child to make sure you understand him or her.
- Be aware that the child may show developmental regression in behavior and use of language.
- Match your language to the child's developmental level. Because younger children typically have less understanding of abstract concepts like "death," use direct and simple language as much as possible.
- Reinforce these techniques with the child's parents or caregivers to help them provide appropriate emotional support to their child.

Note. From *Psychological First Aid: Field Operations Guide* (2nd ed.), p. 7–10, by M. Brymer et al., 2006, Los Angeles: NCTSN. Copyright 2006 by National Child Traumatic Stress Network and National Center for PTSD. Adapted with permission.

social norms. For example, cultural norms and values influence how close to stand to someone, how much eye contact to make, or how acceptable it is to offer therapeutic touch. According to Brymer et al., "You should look for clues to a survivor's need for 'personal space,' and seek guidance about cultural norms from community cultural leaders who best understand local customs" (p. 23).

Verifying Emotional Readiness to Begin Problem Identification and Solving

Once psychological contact is made, crisis-exposed individuals will typically feel understood, accepted, and supported. As a result, the intensity of their emotional distress will have been reduced and their energy redirected toward problem-identification and problem-solving activities. However, before beginning those activities, it will be important to ensure the crisis survivor is emotionally ready to do this work. Brymer et al. (2006) identified the signs of individuals who may be emotionally overwhelmed and thus not able to immediately begin this problem-solving process (see chapter 8, Table 8.2). Briefly, these are individuals who appear immobilized by crisis problems, are unresponsive, are demonstrating extreme emotional or physical reactions (or both), or are engaging in behaviors that present some degree of risk for physical harm. These intense immediate crisis reactions are particularly worrisome because they represent significant coping challenges, and if allowed to continue unchecked they may develop into psychopathology (Hobfoll et al., 2007).

Options for stabilizing emotionally overwhelmed individuals include first reestablishing contact with the student's primary caregivers, and then giving them the caregiver information (summarized in Table 8.3) that will help them to calm their child (after informing them about the importance of controlling their emotions in order to contain the youth's emotional distress). If primary caregivers are physically or emotionally unavailable, then the school crisis intervener will need to take action to promote emotional stabilization. In addition to Brymer et al.'s (2006) suggestions for stabilizing the emotionally overwhelmed crisis survivor, others are offered in Table 15.4. If none of these interventions prove sufficient in stabilizing acute emotional distress, the ICI process should be concluded, and an immediate referral to a community-based medical or mental health professional is indicated.

Identifying and Prioritizing Crisis Problems

Once psychological contact with the crisis survivor has been established and emotional stability ensured, the next step is to identify and prioritize the problems generated by the crisis event. Once the individual is able to begin the problem-solving process, the crisis intervener asks the individual if he or she is ready to tell his or her crisis story. During this step the crisis intervener should be prepared for the possibility of an emotional release. Information about the individual's crisis experience and associated problems can be elicited by asking questions such as those provided in Table 15.5. However, when engaging in this type of questioning it is important to keep in mind the following caution offered by Brymer et al. (2006): "In clarifying disaster-related traumatic experiences, avoid asking for in-depth descriptions that may provoke additional distress. Follow the survivor's lead in discussing what happened. Don't press survivors to disclose details of any trauma or loss" (p. 58).

Once the intervener understands the crisis survivor's experience, the next step is to explore the range of problems generated by the crisis. Often these are presented as a jumble of needs, and it is important for the crisis intervener to help the crisis survivor prioritize problems in terms of what needs to be addressed right away, such as issues dealing with physical health, and problems that can be addressed later (Brymer et al., 2006). When listening to crisis problems, it is especially important to be attentive to, and inquire about, available personal and social resources that can assist in crisis resolution: the fewer the resources, the greater the concern. Finally, it is also important to inquire about the possible presence of any degree of lethality (i.e., any chance that the student may be at risk for hurting him- or herself or someone else).

Table 15.4. Suggestions for Stabilizing the Emotionally Overwhelmed Student

1. Ask the student to listen and look at you.
2. Find out if the student knows who and where he or she is, and what is happening.
3. Ask the student to describe the surrounding environment.
4. Identify where the student and crisis intervener are currently located.
5. Consider employing "grounding" techniques. Foster grounding by stating the following:
   After a frightening experience, you can sometimes find yourself overwhelmed with emotions or unable to stop thinking about or imagining what happened. You can use a method called 'grounding' to feel less overwhelmed. Grounding works by turning your attention from your thoughts back to the outside world. Here's what you do:
   - Sit in a comfortable position with your legs and arms uncrossed.
   - Breathe in and out slowly and deeply.
   - Look around you and name five nondistressing objects that you can see. For example, you could say, "I see the floor, I see a shoe, I see a table, I see a chair, I see a person."
   - Breathe in and out slowly and deeply.
   - Next, name five nondistressing sounds you can hear. For example: "I hear a woman talking, I hear myself breathing, I hear a door close, I hear someone typing, I hear a cell phone ringing."
   - Breathe in and out slowly and deeply.
   - Next, name five nondistressing things you can feel. For example: "I can feel this wooden armrest with my hands, I can feel my toes inside my shoes, I can feel my back pressing against my chair, I can feel the blanket in my hands, I can feel my lips pressed together."
   - Breathe in and out slowly and deeply.

   You might have children name colors that they see around them. For example, say to the child, "Can you name five colors that you can see from where you are sitting? Can you see something blue? Something yellow? Something green?" (pp. 51–52)

Note. From *Psychological First Aid: Field Operations Guide* (2nd ed.), p. 51–52, by M. Brymer et al., 2006, Los Angeles: NCTSN. Copyright 2006 by National Child Traumatic Stress Network and National Center for PTSD. Adapted with permission.

Addressing Crisis-Generated Problems

The primary goal of this ICI step is to make certain that the crisis survivor has identified adaptive coping strategies and has made some movement in the direction of adaptive problem solving. When addressing crisis problems it is important to allow individuals to do as much as they can by themselves. To the extent that crisis survivors are capable of solving crisis problems independently, crisis interveners should allow them to do so. However, the intervener should not hesitate to be highly directive when it comes to addressing crisis-generated problems and taking some kind of action.

Table 15.5. Possible Questions to Ask When Identifying Crisis Problems

1. To determine the nature and severity of the student's crisis experience, introduce your questions:
   - I know that you've been through a lot of difficult things. May I ask you some questions about what you have been through?
     a. Where were you during the crisis?
     b. Did you get hurt?
     c. Did you see anyone get hurt?
     d. How afraid were you?
2. To help identify problems generated by the death of a family member or close friend ask:
   - Did someone close to you get hurt or die as a result of the crisis event?
   - Who got hurt or died?
3. To help identify problems generated by the immediate postdisaster circumstances and ongoing threat ask:
   - Do you need any information to help you better understand what has happened?
   - Do you need information about how to keep you and your family safe?
   - Do you need information about what is being done to protect your classmates and community?
4. To help identify problems generated by being separated from, or concerned about, the safety of loved ones ask:
   - Are you worried about anyone close to you right now?
   - Do you know where they are?
   - Is there anyone especially important, like a family member or friend, who is missing?
5. To help identify problems generated by physical illness or the need for medication ask:
   - Do you have any medical or mental health conditions that need attention?
   - Do you need any medications that you don't have?
   - Do you need to have a prescription filled?
   - Can you get in touch with your doctor?
6. To help identify problems generated by losses incurred as a result of the disaster (for example, home, school, personal property, or pets) ask:
   - Was your home destroyed or badly damaged?
   - Did you lose other important personal property?
   - Did a pet die or get lost?
   - Was your school or neighborhood destroyed or badly damaged?
7. To help identify problems generated by extreme feelings of guilt or shame state:
   - It sounds as if you are being really hard on yourself about what happened.
   - It seems that you feel you could have done more.

Table 15.5. (continued)

8. To help identify if prior losses or crisis experiences are generating problems state or ask:
   - Sometimes events like this can remind people of previous bad times.
   - Have you ever been in a disaster before?
   - Has some other bad thing happened to you in the past?
   - Have you ever had someone close to you die?
9. To help identify whether any specific activities are being (or will be) disrupted by the crisis event ask:
   - Were any special events (birthday, graduation, beginning of the school year, vacation) coming up that were disrupted by the crisis?
10. To help identify any other problems that might have been generated by the crisis event ask open-ended questions such as:
    - Is there anything else we have not talked about that is important for me to know?

Note. Crisis interveners will need to exercise caution when asking these questions. Different students in different situations will be more or less able to participate in this problem-identification activity. From *Psychological First Aid: Field Operations Guide* (2nd ed.), p. 57–62, by M. Brymer et al., 2006, Los Angeles: NCTSN. Copyright 2006 by National Child Traumatic Stress Network and National Center for PTSD. Adapted with permission.

As the crisis intervener addresses crisis-generated problems, he or she should begin by asking the crisis survivor about the coping attempts they have already made. If the attempts are adaptive and judged to have the potential to be effective, then all that may be required is to validate and reinforce the positive direction the individual is taking in regard to coping.

If the individual is having difficulty generating his or her own adaptive coping ideas, then the crisis intervener should next facilitate discussion of strategies. Examples of solutions the crisis intervener may propose in response to crisis-related coping challenges include trying a new behavior, redefining the problem, obtaining outside (third-party) assistance, and making specific environmental changes. If the crisis problem is stress, then the crisis solution might be stress reduction. On the other hand, among adults, if the crisis problem is financial, then the crisis solution might involve contacting the Federal Emergency Management Agency or other disaster resources. Similarly, among adults, if the crisis problem is legal, then the crisis solution might involve obtaining a lawyer or contacting a victim assistance or witness program.

Again, however, to the extent that the crisis survivor is unable to generate adaptive solutions to crisis problems on their own, the crisis intervener should not hesitate to be highly directive. From these interventions it is hoped that a plan will be developed that addresses crisis problems (both immediate and later needs).

When it comes to taking action, if lethality is low and the individual is capable of acting on his or her own behalf, then the crisis intervener can be *facilitative* (i.e., we will talk, but you will act on your own). The contract for action is between the crisis intervener and crisis survivor and ranges from active listening to giving advice. Although it is important to be as nondirective as possible (to reinforce the crisis survivor's sense that he or she is a capable problem solver), if lethality is high or the individual is not capable of acting on his or her own behalf, then the crisis

Table 15.6. Possible Questions to Ask When Assessing Problem-Solving Resources

1. To help identify thoughts about causing harm to oneself or other people state or ask:
   - Sometimes situations like these can be very overwhelming.
   - Have you had any thoughts about suicide? (For children in the primary grades use the words "harming yourself" instead of suicide.)
   - Have you had any thoughts about harming someone else?
2. To help assess the availability of social support systems ask:
   - Are there family members, friends, or community agencies that you can rely on for help with problems that you are facing as a result of the disaster?
3. To help identify prior alcohol or drug use ask:
   - Has your use of alcohol, prescription medication, or drugs increased since the disaster?
   - Have you had any problems in the past with alcohol or drug use?
   - Are you currently experiencing withdrawal symptoms from drug use?

Note. From *Psychological First Aid: Field Operations Guide* (2nd ed.), p. 60–61, by M. Brymer et al., 2006, Los Angeles: NCTSN. Copyright 2006 by National Child Traumatic Stress Network and National Center for PTSD. Adapted with permission.

intervener will need to be *directive* (i.e., we will talk, but I will act on your behalf). The contract for action might include a student's family and other community resources. Directive actions range from mobilizing resources to directly controlling the situation. It is important to recognize that such a directive stance may look nothing like a counseling session. If, for example, a student is homicidal or suicidal, an appropriate ICI response would be to take as much control of the situation as is possible (and safe). Table 15.6 provides sample questions that might be asked to determine the potential for independent action (including the presence and degree of any lethality) and the need for the crisis intervener to become directive.

Evaluating and Concluding the ICI Session

As the intervention concludes, the crisis intervener should obtain identifying information, make certain that the crisis survivor has ongoing access to providers of social support, and encourage the use of readily available support systems. To this end, Brymer et al. (2006) suggested the following statements be made to students. To adolescents interveners could state: "When something really upsetting like this happens, even if you don't feel like talking, be sure to ask for what you need." To children they could state: "You are doing a great job of letting grown-ups know what you need. It is important to keep letting people know how they can help you. The more help you get, the more you can make things better. Even grown-ups need help at times like this" (p. 72). Before concluding, the crisis intervener should specify a contract for reconnecting with the crisis survivor to ensure that the student is making the necessary progress toward addressing crisis-generated problems.

This last ICI step involves critically evaluating whether or not immediate coping has been reestablished. To the extent that the crisis survivor has obtained necessary physical and emotional support (and any lethality has been reduced), crisis-generated problems have been identified and

Table 15.7. Sample Individual Crisis Intervention Dialogue

This crisis situation begins with a grade student, Chris, crying in a corner of a school yard, just out of view of the playground. Two days earlier, Chris had witnessed a school-yard shooting.

1. *Establish Psychological Contact*	
Counselor:	Hi. I'm Mr./Ms. Sanchez. What's your name?
Chris:	Chris.
Counselor:	Are you cold, Chris? Can I get you a jacket?
Chris:	No, I'm okay.
Counselor:	Chris, I'm here to try to help the kids at your school deal with the shooting. You look sad. Can you tell me what's wrong?
Chris:	(Through silent tears Chris quietly says) I'm scared.
Counselor:	I think I know why, but do you think you are able to tell me why you're scared?
Chris:	I'm afraid of being shot.
Counselor:	It is frightening to be shot at. (The counselor places an arm around Chris's shoulder.) I understand why you are crying. Would it be okay if we talked? I would like to help.
Chris:	(Chris stops crying and looks at the counselor.) Okay.
Counselor:	Chris, before we talk about the shooting, is there anything you need right now? Are you sure you don't need your jacket? (It is a cold January day.) Are you thirsty or hungry?
Chris:	Yes, I guess I would like to get my jacket.
Counselor:	Before we talk about this, Chris, I need to let you know that as long as it does not appear that anyone, including you, is in immediate danger, I will be able to keep what you tell me between the two of us. However, it is usually a good idea to share what we talk about with your parents and/or teacher. Is that okay with you.
Chris:	It's okay if you talk to my mom.
2. *Verify Emotional Readiness to Begin Problem Identification and Problem Solving*	
	(As Chris and Mr. Sanchez go to get Chris's jacket it becomes clear that Chris is able to begin the problem-solving process. He is responsive to questioning and, while very scared, appears to have his or her emotions under control.)
3. *Identify and Prioritize Crisis Generated Problem*	
Counselor:	Do you think you could tell me about what happened to you the other day?
Chris:	Yes. I was standing right over there (Chris looks around the corner and points to the kickball field). I was waiting my turn when the shooting started. At first I didn't know what was happening. Then I saw all the kids screaming and falling to the ground. My friend Sam was bleeding from the foot. (Chris begins to cry again.)

Table 15.7. (continued)

Counselor:	That sounds scary. So the reason you are not going on the playground is that you are afraid, right?
Chris:	Yes.
Counselor:	You know you're not alone. A lot of kids feel the same way you do. Before now, have you told anyone about being afraid to go out to play?
Chris:	No.
Counselor:	Are there people who you can talk to?
Chris:	Yes. I would like to talk to Sam.
Counselor:	Sam was bleeding from the foot, right?
Chris:	Yes, and I really need to see Sam. Is Sam okay? Can I talk to her?
Counselor:	So you are also worried about your friend, right?
Chris:	Yes.
Counselor:	I don't know Sam, but I can find out how she is doing right after recess. For now, however, we need to decide what we are going to do about recess. We need to make sure you are safe, and we can't do that if you hide during recess. Is there anyone else who might be able to help you not be scared of the playground?
Chris:	My mom, my teacher, my other friends (pause), and you. (Chris looks up at the counselor as the crying begins to subside again.)
Counselor:	Yes, I think I can help. Before the shooting, what was the playground like for you?
Chris:	Fun. I was great at kickball. My friends and I would always play right there (Chris again looks around the corner and points to the kickball field).
Counselor:	Where are your friends now?
Chris:	Right there. (Chris points to a group of eight children playing kickball.) Except Sam. Sam's at home. Sam's foot was bleeding. I miss Sam. Sam is my best friend. Can I talk to Sam?
4. *Address Crisis-Generated Problems*	
Counselor:	We can look into talking to Sam after recess. But for now, what can we do about your recess time? What have you done so far about being scared to play?
Chris:	I've hid in here or in the restroom. Once I stayed in class with my teacher.
Counselor:	Look out on the playground and tell me what you see.
Chris:	(Chris looks around the corner and at the playground.) Kids are playing.
Counselor:	Are they having fun?
Chris:	Yes. (A tentative smile briefly flashes across Chris's face.)

Table 15.7. (continued)

Counselor:	Who are those people over there and there? (The counselor points in the direction of the two police officers that have been temporarily assigned to the school after the shooting.)
Chris:	Police.
Counselor:	I think that it is safe to go out on the playground today. And your friends look like they can still have fun playing kickball. Do you think that anyone will hurt you on the playground today?
Chris:	No.
Counselor:	So if it's safe and still fun, why not try going out and playing again?
Chris:	But I'm still scared. (Chris's eyes become teary.)
Counselor:	Okay. Let's see what we can do to help you not be scared. What if your friends helped you? What if I stayed on the playground and watched you?
Chris:	That might help. (Chris's tears subside.)
Counselor:	I'll go talk to your friends and see what I can do about getting them to include you in their kickball game. (The counselor approaches Chris's friends and explains the problem to them. They readily agree to invite Chris to play. One member of the group walks over to talk to Chris.)
Friend:	Chris, kickball is still fun. Will you please come and play with us?
Chris:	Okay. (The friend puts an arm on Chris's shoulder and begins to walk toward the playground.)
5. *Evaluate and Conclude*	
Counselor:	Before you go, Chris, can you give me your last name and your classroom? I'd like to be able to check up on you to make sure you are okay.
Chris:	Sure. My last name is Smith, and I'm in Mrs. Wong's classroom.
Counselor:	I'll be standing right over there. (The counselor points to an area just off the playground within view of the kickball field.) I'll be there during the rest of today's recess. When the bell rings in a few minutes come over and see me and we can look into how Sam is doing.
Chris:	Okay. (Chris has stopped crying and is smiling as she/he walks with the group of friends out onto the playground.)
Counselor:	One last thing, Chris. I just want you to know that you have done a great job of thinking through and addressing this problem. I'm very hopeful that with time you will be able to not be nearly as scared. Good work!

Note. From *Preparing for Crises in the Schools* (2nd ed.), pp. 171–173, by S. E. Brock, J. Sandoval, and S. Lewis, 2001, New York: Wiley. Copyright 2001 by John Wiley & Sons. Adapted with permission.

addressed, and links have been made to the appropriate helping resources, the ICI session may be concluded. If these goals have not been achieved, the process should be repeated. As the session is ended, it will be important to leave the crisis survivor with a sense of hope and optimism that they will recover from their trauma exposure (Hobfoll et al., 2007). The individual should be complimented on his or her problem-solving efforts and given the expectation that with time they will be able to cope with the trauma.

CONCLUSION

Many of the different elements of ICI described above are illustrated in a sample script in Table 15.7. As the script illustrates, before the crisis intervention begins to move ahead with this basic problem-solving strategy, the intervener must first make psychological contact, address basic needs, clarify confidentiality, and ensure that the crisis-affected individual has the emotional stability required to problem solve. The combination of the emotional stability provided by the crisis intervener's presence, and the identification and prioritization of crisis-generated problems is sometimes all that is needed to reestablish immediate coping. To the extent possible, the crisis survivor should be allowed to engage in independent problem solving. However, crisis interveners should never hesitate to be highly directive and active in the identification and implementation of solutions to crisis problems. This is especially true whenever the crisis survivor is engaging in homicidal or suicidal ideation as a possible problem-solving strategy. Finally, the ICI concludes with an examination of the degree to which adaptive independent coping has been reestablished and strives to leave the individual with a sense of hope that recovery from their trauma exposure will be realized.

Chapter 16

PSYCHOTHERAPEUTIC TREATMENTS

Although psychotherapeutic treatment is not part of the immediate school crisis intervention response, it may be necessary for a minority of crisis-affected students who will experience adverse reactions and develop psychopathology. Therefore it is critical for school-based mental health professionals to have a basic understanding of the psychopathological consequences of, and psychotherapeutic treatments for, severe psychological injury, in order to make appropriate referrals and treatment decisions. This chapter provides an overview of the psychotherapeutic treatments that are most effective for children and adolescents who have been traumatized by a crisis, and briefly reviews psychopharmacological interventions. Because many of these treatments are beyond the role and expertise of the school-based mental health professional, the chapter explores issues relevant to making referrals to outside mental health agencies. Finally, the chapter reviews cultural considerations relevant to treatment referrals.

COGNITIVE–BEHAVIORAL THERAPIES

Cognitive–behavioral therapies (CBTs) are the most widely studied and promising interventions for posttraumatic stress disorder (PTSD; Cohen, Mannarino, Berlinger, & Deblinger, 2000; Feeny, Foa, Treadwell, & March, 2004; March, Amaya-Jackson, Murray, & Schulte, 1998). Because PTSD is relatively unique among DSM-IV-TR diagnoses, in that its criteria require exposure to a traumatic event (American Psychiatric Association, 2000), discussions of treatment for individuals with PTSD are relevant. CBT has been shown to be the most effective treatment for other disorders that may develop in individuals following a crisis, such as depression, anxiety, and behavior problems (see e.g., Kazdin & Weisz, 2003; Prout & Prout, 1998; Weisz, Weiss, Han, Grander, & Morton, 1995). Specific interventions with empirical support include imaginal and in vivo exposure, eye-movement desensitization and reprocessing (EMDR), anxiety management training, group-delivered CBTs, parent training, and psychoeducation.

Imaginal and In Vivo Exposure

Repeated exposure techniques are designed to help individuals confront feared objects, situations, memories, and images. The core components are typically imaginal exposure (repeated recounting of the traumatic memory) and in vivo exposure (repeated prolonged confrontation with trauma-related situations and objects that evoke excessive anxiety). Exposure has been found to be a critical treatment component for adults with PTSD (Foa et al., 1999). Exposure can be intense and prolonged, as practiced in the flooding technique, or more gradual, which involves ongoing exposure to stimuli that represent certain aspects of the traumatic event (Cohen, Mannarino, et al., 2000). Exposure decreases the hyperarousal and negative affect that accompany traumatic reminders (American Academy of Child and Adolescent Psychiatry, 1998; Cohen, Mannarino, et al., 2000). Following exposure, the thoughts of the trauma are no longer paired with the overwhelming negative emotion; in turn, the intensity of intrusive reminders is reduced, minimizing the need for avoidant behavior (Cohen, Mannarino, et al.).

Research shows preliminary support for the use of exposure in treating children with PTSD. However, its use requires a strong therapeutic alliance, excellent rapport building, and treatment conducted at the child's pace (Feeny et al., 2004). It has been argued that in vivo exposure and direct exploration of the trauma are inappropriate for school settings because the intervention can lead to extreme anxiety reactions, such as heightened arousal and reexperiencing of the trauma (Cook-Cottone, 2004; Merrell, 2001; Pfefferbaum, 1997). If the decision is made to use exposure techniques led by a qualified professional in the school setting, the emotional impact needs to be planned for carefully. For example, sending a child back to class prematurely (after he or she has responded significantly to a particular aspect of a psychotherapeutic session) can be problematic. If exposure therapy is conducted outside of school, it is helpful if the school-based mental health professional is aware of this so that behaviors and emotions that may arise from this treatment can be addressed and supported during school hours (Nickerson, Reeves, Brock, & Jimerson, 2008).

Given concerns about the use of exposure techniques with children, particularly the very young, professionals recommend that play, art, or storytelling be used to help children express their feelings about the trauma (Pfefferbaum, 1997). Research has shown that using artwork and free writing with elementary school children is associated with increased expression of feelings (Klingman, 1985; Schwarz, 1982). These techniques may be helpful in encouraging children to be exposed to aspects of the event, and their feelings about it, without doing it in a direct and purposeful way that may be inappropriate for the school setting.

Eye-Movement Desensitization and Reprocessing

Eye-movement desensitization and reprocessing (EMDR) seeks to change unhealthy perceptions that result from traumatic experiences by discussing and reprogramming memories, identifying and desensitizing anxiety-provoking stimuli, and promoting positive social functioning (Shapiro, 2002). In one technique, EMDR therapists rapidly move their finger back and forth and instruct the client to focus on the finger while they visualize the anxiety-provoking situation (Lilienfeld & Arkowitz, 2007). Research on EMDR with children has shown that it decreases avoidance and reexperiencing symptoms and improves functioning (Ahmad, Larsson, & Sundelin-Wahlsten, 2007; Oras, de Ezpeleta, & Ahmad, 2004). Although superior to a wait-list control condition (Ahmad et al., 2007), EMDR and other CBT methods have been found equally effective in treating PTSD (Lilienfeld & Arkowitz, 2007; Siedler & Wagner, 2006).

Anxiety Management Training

There is some initial support for anxiety management training's (AMT's) effectiveness in reducing PTSD, anxiety, and depression (Feeny et al., 2004). In AMT, individuals are taught skills for managing anxiety. Techniques used include education about affect, restructuring of dysfunctional cognitions, and relaxation exercises. These skills are applied to trauma-related, anxiety-provoking situations through role-play and in vivo exposure exercises.

Two specific aspects of AMT that have been researched are restructuring cognitive distortions and stress inoculation. Restructuring cognitive distortions about the crisis event is a core element of cognitive–behavioral treatments such as AMT (American Academy of Child and Adolescent Psychiatry, 1998; Cohen, Mannarino, et al., 2000). It is common for traumatized children to develop distortions such as self-blame (e.g., "I did something to cause this"), survivor guilt ("It should have been me"), or overgeneralized feelings of threatened safety (e.g., "The world is not safe"). When using cognitive restructuring, the therapist asks the child about his or her thoughts and attributions about the event and then identifies any distortions. The therapist and child examine the child's reasoning for the distortions, which leads to replacing the distortion with more accurate thoughts about the event (Cohen, Mannarino, et al., 2000).

Stress inoculation involves teaching coping skills such as relaxation and thought stopping to manage trauma-related anxiety (Cohen, Mannarino, et al., 2000; Foa et al., 1999). This often involves teaching progressive muscle relaxation. Although stress inoculation, alone and in combination with exposure, has been found to be superior to a control condition in treating PTSD in women, exposure alone was superior to stress inoculation and the combined exposure and stress inoculation treatment because there were fewer dropouts, greater reduction in symptoms, lower anxiety, and greater social adjustment (Foa et al., 1999). Research is needed to explore the effects of stress inoculation with children.

Group-Delivered Cognitive–Behavioral Interventions

There is strong support for the effectiveness of group-administered CBT for the treatment of PTSD (Feeny et al., 2004). Group-administered CBT approaches typically consist of exposure to trauma narratives and stress inoculation interventions such as psychoeducation, problem solving, relaxation, and cognitive restructuring. A specific 10-session cognitive–behavioral group intervention has been found to significantly decrease symptoms of PTSD and depression among youth who were exposed to violence (Saltzman, Pynoos, Layne, Steinberg, & Aisenberg, 2001; Stein et al., 2003).

Notable in some of the studies of the group-administered CBT research is that the interventions were implemented by school-based mental health professionals in the field. For example, Stein et al. (2003) demonstrated that a group intervention called Cognitive Behavioral

Intervention for Trauma in Schools (CBITS), delivered by school-based mental health professionals in the school setting, resulted in reductions in PTSD symptoms compared with a wait-list control group. It is significant that the study had no exclusionary criteria (e.g., comorbidity, symptom severity), suggesting that the treatment was effective even with complex problems seen in school settings. Similarly, Kataoka et al. (2003) also showed reductions in PTSD and depressive symptoms for children with clinically significant levels of PTSD or depression following an 8-week CBT group, as compared with the wait-list control condition. This intervention was implemented by school-based mental health professionals with Latino participants. These studies not only demonstrate treatment effectiveness, but also support the portability of group-administered CBT.

Parent Training

Treatment with children often involves a parent or caregiver component. As discussed in detail in chapter 12, parents are the primary providers of support for children, and a parent's own reaction to the trauma may affect his or her ability to provide the support the child needs. Helping parents reframe their cognitive distortions and learn skills to help their children cope is therefore important. Parent involvement in treatment may be especially warranted for children whose traumatic responses include externalizing behavior problems (Cohen, Berlinger, & Mannarino, 2000), as ecological interventions are most effective for these types of problems.

Some evidence suggests that adding a parent component to a child's CBT treatment does not appear to directly affect children's PTSD symptomatology (Deblinger, Lippmann, & Steer, 1996; King et al., 2000), although it has other beneficial effects for the parent and child (Deblinger et al., 1996; Deblinger, Stauffer, & Steer, 2001). For example, Deblinger et al. (2001) implemented a cognitive–behavioral parent group for caregivers whose children had been sexually abused. The group, which assisted caregivers in managing their emotional reactions, provided education about open parent–child communication and taught behavior management skills. The group led to reductions in parents' intrusive thoughts about their children's abuse and less emotional distress compared with a nondirective parent-support group. Another study by Deblinger et al. (1996) found that the parent CBT component resulted in benefits of reduced child depression and behavior problems.

Psychological Education

When used in combination with several of the other interventions described above, psychological education is also supported by the empirical literature. As described by Carr (2004), the purpose of this treatment element, when used as an immediate crisis intervention, is to help reduce children's and parents' fears that they are "going crazy." These strategies are intended to help the child and his or her parents further understand traumatic stress reactions and the need and rationale for exposure-based therapies. Similar to the psychological education approaches described in chapter 13, this approach consists of other elements that may include emphasizing the importance of maintaining a normal daily living routine and the importance of social support systems, along with other adaptive coping strategies.

PSYCHOPHARMACOLOGICAL TREATMENTS

Although psychopharmacological treatments should be used in combination with ongoing psychotherapy (Donnelly, Amaya-Jackson, & March, 1999; Foa et al., 1999), some children and adolescents do not respond to psychosocial and therapeutic interventions for PTSD, making pharmacological interventions the next best treatment (Cohen, 2001; Friedman, 1988). These interventions should be tailored to the needs and symptoms of the individual. Individuals who have been traumatized may exhibit a number of symptoms representative of PTSD, major depression, panic, anxiety, inattention or hyperactivity, or psychoses (Mellman, David, & Barza, 1999; Seedat et al., 2002). Each type of drug targets a limited number or range of symptoms. Selective serotonin reuptake inhibitors (SSRIs), which have been shown to reduce anxious and depressive symptoms in children and young adults, may also reduce symptoms of reexperiencing, numbing, avoidance, and hyperarousal, which are thought to relate to serotonin disturbances (Donnelly, 2003; Seedat, Lockhart, Kaminer, Zungu-Dirwayi, & Stein, 2001; Seedat et al., 2002).

REFERRALS FOR COMMUNITY-BASED TREATMENT

Many of the treatments described above require expertise beyond that typically held by the school-based mental health professional. Even if a school-based mental health professional has the expertise to implement these interventions, his or her workload, the availability of supervision and consultation, and the philosophy of the school administrator and teachers regarding offering this type of service to students may be barriers to providing such treatment in schools (Burrows-Horton & Cruise, 2001).

The first step in making appropriate referrals for community-based treatment is knowing when a referral should be made, based on an understanding of trauma risk related to the child's developmental level. Discussions in chapters 10 and 11 about how to evaluate psychological trauma risk will help; for example, when making referrals for psychotherapeutic treatment, it is important to understand how a child's developmental level influences the expression of traumatic stress. Proposals to modify the DSM-IV-TR criteria for preschool-age children suggest that PTSD should be considered present when only one of the three core symptoms is documented, and suggest that diagnosis should allow some symptoms (e.g., flashbacks) to be identified from behavior alone. Furthermore, constricted play and developmental regression in language and toileting skills have been proposed as additional indications of avoidance symptoms. Finally, a new cluster of symptoms has also been proposed that includes aggression, separation anxiety, and fear of the dark (Carr, 2004). These are just some of the different behaviors and symptoms that should indicate the need to refer a younger child for psychotherapeutic treatment (compared with older youth).

A second consideration in making referral decisions is the nature of the crisis event. For example, relatively brief psychotherapeutic interventions involving three to seven sessions may be indicated for the student who develops PTSD following a single-incident accident or disaster (referred to as Type 1 PTSD; Terr, 1991). On the other hand, the student who develops PTSD following exposure to multiple traumatic stressors (Type 2 PTSD) may require longer psychotherapeutic interventions of up to 25 sessions (Carr, 2004).

Knowing when to refer a student for additional intervention, although critical, is only part of the challenge for school-based mental health professionals. They also need to know where to refer these students. As discussed in chapter 11, the crisis team should develop and maintain a referral list of experienced mental health professionals and agencies who provide treatment for traumatized children and families. This list can be built by consulting with colleagues, contacting local agencies, reviewing the phone book, contacting state and local professional associations, searching the Internet, consulting the United Way's list of community resources in cities and suburban areas (United Way, n.d.), and locating a psychologist through the American Psychological Association at http://locator.apa.org/ or 1 (800) 964-2000 (Nickerson et al., 2008). Chapter 11 includes a Private Practitioner Referral Questionnaire that can be distributed to the resources identified to find out more about the services provided. It is also important to include treatment providers who are from diverse backgrounds and who speak a language other than English (Nickerson & Heath, 2008).

Simply providing a child's family with the name and phone number of a provider is unlikely to lead to treatment. When making a referral to an outside service provider, the school-based mental health professional should meet with the child's parents or caregivers to discuss the concerns and determine if they are willing and able to consider such a referral (Merrell, 2001). If the parents decide to pursue a referral and provide the proper consent, it can also be helpful for the school-based mental health professional to write a one- to two-page letter to the outside professional to describe concerns and provide a brief history (Burrows-Horton & Cruise, 2001; Merrell). Alternatively, the document used in the psychological referral processes (described in chapter 11) might also provide this information. These referral procedures should be developed in collaboration with the school administrator in light of growing concerns about parents asking schools to pay for recommended services (Merrell). Under no circumstance can the child's education be contingent on the parents obtaining such services. It is prudent to use language such as "It may be helpful for you to look into CBT by a community provider to assist your child in coping with his or her feelings and behaviors surrounding the crisis."

If a child is receiving treatment in a community setting, the school-based mental health professional can collaborate with the community-based provider to ensure continuity in services. For this to happen, the student's parent or guardian must sign separate releases for the school to provide information to the community-based mental health professional and to receive information from the mental health professional. The release should detail the specific type of information to be shared, the length of time for which the release is valid, and how the information is to be used. If a parent is uncomfortable with this, creating a release limited to obtaining information related only to the student's needs in school or arranging for a three-way phone call between the school, the parent or guardian, and the community-based mental health professional may be helpful (Cole et al., 2005). Services still may be provided in the school, as long as they are not redundant or in conflict with outside services (Burrows-Horton & Cruise, 2001). For example, a school-based mental health professional might provide anxiety management training to teach skills the student can use when feeling anxious, whereas a community-based mental health professional may use exposure and engage in more direct exploration of the trauma.

CULTURAL CONSIDERATIONS

Cultural beliefs and practices should be considered when selecting treatment options. Chapter 12 reviewed many cultural issues relevant for obtaining support and healing after a crisis. In particular, many individuals from culturally and linguistically diverse backgrounds cope with crises by banding together with family, and they often distrust outside help (Canada et al., 2007; Horowitz, McKay, & Marshall, 2005). Consequently, attempts to offer mental health services may be viewed as forceful or meddling.

To address the issue of mistrust, the crisis response team should find people who are trusted by families in diverse ethnic groups to convey the message about services. A cultural broker may be used to assess needs and tell the families about interventions that may be helpful (Klingman & Cohen, 2004). The school's ability to convey information to students and parents, while showing sensitivity to cultural groups' diversity when considering referrals for psychotherapeutic treatments, can help foster recovery (Sandoval & Lewis, 2002).

CONCLUSION

CBT represent the most well-studied and effective psychotherapeutic treatments for disorders that are most likely to affect children who have been exposed to a crisis event (e.g., PTSD, depression, and anxiety). In some cases, psychopharmacological interventions may be indicated. These interventions are rarely provided by school-based mental health professionals, so it is imperative that schools know the resources available in the surrounding community. Cultural considerations must also be taken into account when recommending additional treatment.

Section 5

EXAMINE

The final element of PREPaRE includes strategies designed to examine the effectiveness of crisis prevention and intervention. As indicated in Figure 1.2, these activities may take place during each of Raphael and Newman's (2000) and Valent's (2000) phases of a crisis event (i.e., preimpact, impact, recoil, postimpact, and recovery and reconstruction). The one chapter in this section (Chapter 17) is designed to promote examination of the effectiveness of the various crisis prevention, preparedness, response, and recovery strategies advocated by PREPaRE. The examination approaches advocated in this chapter may also prove helpful to the school crisis intervention researchers who conduct systematic research on the PREPaRE model.

Chapter 17

EXAMINING THE EFFECTIVENESS OF CRISIS PREVENTION, PREPAREDNESS, RESPONSE, AND RECOVERY

PREPaRE emphasizes that it is crucial to examine the implementation and effectiveness of crisis prevention, preparedness, response, and recovery efforts. Within this chapter, the term *examination* refers to the multifaceted processes necessary to examine these efforts. The chapter begins with a discussion of the importance of examination and a brief overview of three strategies: needs assessment, process analysis, and outcome evaluation. The subsequent sections consider how the three strategies are used for the examination of crisis prevention, preparedness, response, and recovery.

THE IMPORTANCE OF EXAMINATION

Given the current emphasis on evidence-based strategies and accountability, the importance of examining crisis prevention, preparedness, response, and recovery results should not be underestimated. Examination of crisis-related efforts serves seven general purposes: (a) assessing effectiveness, (b) improving implementation and enhancing effectiveness, (c) better managing limited resources, (d) documenting accomplishments, (e) justifying required resources, (f) supporting the need for increased levels of funding, and (g) satisfying ethical responsibilities to demonstrate positive and negative effects of program participation.

There are numerous practical reasons underlying the importance of such examination. First, the examination of prevention efforts is important to discern the effectiveness of programs and strategies implemented to promote healthy student behaviors and reduce the number and intensity of crisis events. As discussed in chapters 3, 4, and 5, each school should assess its unique needs and develop comprehensive and systematic approaches to crisis prevention. Thus, the examination of the effectiveness of prevention efforts provides essential information regarding the degree to which the stated goals and objectives, and the targeted needs of students, have been successfully addressed. Pending the outcomes of such examination, some programs or strategies may be sustained (i.e., those generating desirable outcomes), whereas other programs or strategies may be discontinued or additional efforts may be required to address persistent areas of need.

Second, the examination of preparedness efforts is vital to the annual systematic reviews of school crisis teams and school crisis plans. As discussed in chapters 3, 4, and 5, the development of school crisis teams and plans is considered to be a dynamic process that requires annual evaluation to determine whether the infrastructure and processes are optimal given the contextual considerations and are informed by recent research. For instance, the examination of preparedness efforts (e.g., in the form of drills, readiness checks, or systematic reviews of plans) may reveal that the plans require all staff members to have basic foundational knowledge. However, many new staff members may not have this knowledge, revealing the need for targeted professional development (e.g., in-service workshops to communicate this knowledge).

Third, the examination of response and recovery efforts can offer the school crisis team valuable lessons. With appropriate school crisis plans and preparations, it is anticipated that the examination of response and recovery efforts would reaffirm that both the immediate and longer-term needs of school community members were met. However, in most instances, the examination of the response efforts may also reveal areas that warrant further preparation, planning, or personnel. Overall, examination provides an opportunity to reinforce effective strategies, as well as further improve and enhance crisis prevention, preparedness, response, and recovery efforts. Given the importance of examination, Pagliocca, Nickerson, and Williams (2002) have recommended that systematic examination procedures be included in all aspects of crisis prevention, preparedness, response, and recovery.

To coordinate the examination efforts, the school crisis team must (a) identify an individual (i.e., a school crisis examination leader operating within the ICS's intelligence section) who will provide leadership to assess crisis-related activities and (b) ensure that school crisis plans delineate the processes that will be used to complete the examination tasks. The school crisis examination leader coordinates appropriate methods and organizes data collection to assess the effectiveness of crisis prevention, preparedness, response, and recovery efforts. Examples of such methods include (a) developing pre- and post-crisis measures to assess prevention strategies targeting specific needs (see chapter 4); (b) conducting drills, simulations, and readiness checks to assess preparedness efforts (discussed in chapter 7); and (c) designing questionnaires and interviews to assess response efforts (including both the processes and the outcomes). The school crisis examination leader is also responsible for ensuring that program goals and objectives are clearly articulated and measurable. Essential knowledge of the school crisis examination leader would include program evaluation, basic research design and methodology, and measurement (a skill set often found among school-based mental health professionals). In addition, numerous texts are available that may be valuable resources for the school crisis examination leader (e.g., Berk & Rossi, 1990; Guba & Lincoln, 1989; Patton, 1990; Posavac & Raymond, 1989; Rossi & Freeman, 1993; Short, Hennessy, & Campbell, 1996).

TYPES OF EXAMINATION

In examining crisis prevention, preparedness, response, and recovery efforts, questions to consider include (a) What are the needs of the school and students? (b) What are the key components or processes, and are the strategies implemented with integrity? and (c) What are the objectives, and what do the data reveal regarding whether the stated objectives are accomplished? Three types of examination strategies can be used to address these questions: needs assessment, process analysis, and outcome evaluation. The following sections briefly review each of these examination types, with the subsequent section providing further information regarding each type of examination as it relates to crisis prevention, preparedness, response, and recovery.

Needs Assessment

The primary purpose of the needs assessment is to identify areas to be addressed, so that plans and strategies may be developed to focus on these needs. The needs assessment is particularly valuable because it focuses on information in the local context. Thus, there is an emphasis on specific contextual considerations. For instance, systematically gathering information from teachers, students, staff, and parents and reviewing school files can inform crisis prevention, preparedness, response, and recovery efforts. Files that can be reviewed include discipline trends, student support referrals, attendance records, conduct ratings on report cards, suspensions, weapons violations, and visits to the nurse's office for treatment of injuries. School-wide screeners, surveys, or questionnaires may provide valuable information regarding the prevalence of behavior problems, mental health problems, bullying and victimization, student engagement, and perceptions of safety.

Process Analysis

The primary purpose of process analysis is to understand what was done and by whom, and to assess whether these activities were consistent with established plans. Sometimes referred to as procedural integrity, treatment integrity, or formative assessment, process analysis emphasizes obtaining information about the specific activities implemented. Methods to obtain process information commonly involve questionnaires, surveys, focus groups, or systematic observations regarding the implementation of strategies. Process analysis may yield valuable information about areas needing further professional development. Information from the process analysis is also very important because it helps to interpret the results of the outcome evaluation.

Outcome Evaluation

The purpose of the outcome evaluation, sometimes referred to as summative evaluation, is to assess the effectiveness of stated objectives of crisis prevention, preparedness, response, and recovery activities. Thus, each objective must be clearly articulated and measurable. Methods commonly include questionnaires, surveys, focus groups, systematic observations, and review of archival records to obtain specific information to examine outcomes. It is often optimal to obtain baseline information, for instance, using data available in the school's archival records (e.g., attendance, disciplinary referrals, reports of student-inflicted injuries) or from school-wide screeners that are used for the needs assessment. The school's crisis plan must outline the objectives for each of the crisis prevention, preparedness, response, and recovery activities so they are specifically delineated and measurable. Knowledge and skills to complete data management and data analysis (e.g., basic statistics), and to develop summary tables, charts, and figures, are important for assessing the outcomes in this form of examination.

EXAMINATION AND CRISIS PREVENTION

Examinations that inform crisis prevention efforts include each of the three strategies mentioned above, that is, needs assessment, process analysis, and outcome evaluation.

Needs Assessment and Crisis Prevention

A crisis prevention needs assessment identifies areas of greatest need. For example, systematically obtaining information about teacher, student, and parent concerns provides an opportunity to develop strategies that address issues most important to a given school. Areas of concern noted through a general needs assessment may warrant further systematic data collection. For example, if concerns regarding the school climate are noted, it may be appropriate to administer a school climate survey to better understand the presenting concerns (see Austin & Duerr, 2007a, 2007b, 2007c).

Given schools' finite resources, needs assessment is an essential component of crisis prevention. Results provide the basis for identifying strengths, concerns, target populations, outcomes, and programs or strategies used to address concerns. As noted in chapter 4, in selecting prevention programs or strategies, schools need to consider the fit between their needs and the program. Thus, selection of appropriate programs or strategies must consider several factors, including (a) the needs of the school identified by a needs assessment (Elliott et al., 2002; Strein & Kohler, 2008); (b) the target population, such as students, teachers, and parents; age; and race or ethnicity (Elliott et al.); and (c) available implementation resources, such as financial resources, program knowledge, and competencies of the staff (Elliott et al.; Strein & Kohler).

Process Analysis and Crisis Prevention

After areas of greatest need have been identified and specific programs or strategies selected, the next step in the process is preparation and implementation of the selected programs or strategies. Prior to implementation, it is necessary to identify the key components of the programs or strategies to obtain the information needed for examining the degree to which these key components were systematically implemented. In some instances, it is possible to develop a brief checklist delineating key components; often such checklists are valuable during implementation to develop procedural integrity as well as to provide useful information for the process analysis.

Understanding what was done and by whom during prevention efforts is also essential in interpreting the results of the outcome evaluation, in that outcomes may be linked to the fidelity of implementation. For example, if the process analysis reveals that specific teachers or staff did not implement key components of the programs or strategies, it may be possible to factor this in when interpreting the outcomes of students with whom they worked; that is, these students could be removed from outcome analyses, or outcomes could be compared among students who received all key components relative to those who received only some of the key components.

Outcome Evaluation and Crisis Prevention

The outcome evaluation is important for assessing whether the objectives of the prevention activities have been accomplished. The crisis plan should have identified the specific outcomes and appropriate measures before prevention activities are implemented. Common outcomes that may be related to prevention efforts include problem behaviors, aggression, delinquency, violence, student attendance, school grades, discipline visits to the principal's office, social competence, or social skills. As noted in the previous section, in some instances the process analysis data reveal that not all students received the core components of the prevention activities. Thus, it would be important to consider only the outcomes of students who received the key components or, if there are sufficient numbers, compare the outcomes of students who received the key components with those who did not. Depending on the results of the outcome analysis, subsequent prevention efforts may (a) focus on other areas of need, (b) continue to sustain positive outcomes, or (c) indicate further professional development to address issues related to implementation integrity.

EXAMINATION AND CRISIS PREPAREDNESS

Types of examination that provide critical information to inform crisis preparedness efforts may also include needs assessment, process analysis, and outcome evaluation. Given that PREPaRE emphasizes the importance of school crisis teams being informed by data, the ongoing examination of the plan is critical.

Needs Assessment and Crisis Preparedness

The needs assessment informs what specific crisis events should be addressed in the school crisis plan (e.g., specific natural disasters such as tornadoes, earthquakes, hurricanes, and floods are more or less likely to affect various schools). Common data collection procedures include interviews, surveys, focus groups, reviews of school database information (e.g., discipline referrals, attendance), and reviews of established school crisis plans and exemplary crisis preparedness resources or models (see chapters 4 and 5 for further discussion of plans and resources).

The school crisis team should use information obtained through needs assessment to inform professional development. For example, if a school is located near a site that may release toxic chemicals, this would warrant specific plans, procedures, and professional preparation in understanding chemical monitors and using safety equipment such as oxygen masks. Similarly, if a school is situated in a rural, urban, or suburban context, there are professional development implications related to collaboration with emergency response personnel (National Association of School Psychologists, 2004). For instance, in rural areas it is often necessary for school-based professionals to obtain additional training so that they may offer a breadth of support services, whereas in urban areas there may be many professionals with whom collaborative relationships may be developed to contribute specific skills and services following a crisis. In addition, the school crisis team will use needs assessment data to develop culturally responsive plans. For example, if a school has a large population of students and families who speak a specific language, identifying bilingual responders, accessing interpreters, and possessing translated materials should be identified in the needs assessment. The needs assessment process should also identify established partnerships with local emergency response agencies and professionals, as well as identify nonpartner community agencies and professionals that require further collaboration and communication.

Process Analysis and Crisis Preparedness

The process analysis regarding crisis preparedness helps to determine whether school crisis plans are clear and whether all of the participants (e.g., teachers, students, and crisis team members) understand their responsibilities. As discussed in chapters 4 and 5, a fundamental component of crisis preparedness is the development of a school crisis plan. The plan must detail the specific strategies and key components to be used during a response. One aspect of process analysis regarding crisis preparedness is the systematic review of the school crisis plan. Figure 17.1 is a sample questionnaire or interview form to use when examining school crisis plans.

Another means of completing a process analysis in advance of an actual crisis event is to conduct formal exercises or drills (see chapter 7 for a detailed description).

Outcome Evaluation and Crisis Preparedness

In examining crisis preparedness, it is important to systematically assess the school crisis plans and the crisis team infrastructure that is established—two examples of outcomes of crisis preparedness activities—to determine if they are consistent with best practice recommendations (see, for instance, chapters 3, 4, and 5). The outcome evaluation must also include annual reviews of all crisis preparedness materials, including plans, policies, procedures, and drafts of communication documents and handouts to ensure readiness. Resources available online through the National Association of School Psychologists (www.nasponline.org), the American Psychological Association (www.apa.org), the U.S. Department of Education (www.ed.gov), and the National Institutes of Mental Health (www.nimh.nih.gov) should be accessed annually to update crisis preparedness materials.

EXAMINATION AND CRISIS RESPONSE AND RECOVERY

Needs assessment, process analysis, and outcome evaluation each provide critical information to the examination of crisis response and recovery efforts.

Figure 17.1. Questionnaire or interview form to use when examining school crisis plans.

Examining Crisis Plan Preparedness

1. Was the crisis plan developed in cooperation with all stakeholders? ___ police ___ fire ___ rescue ___ community agencies ___ parents ___ students ___ hospitals ___ community members		
Does the Plan ...	Circle "Yes" or "No"	
2. Include a mission statement?	Yes	No
3. Include clear discipline codes with consistent reinforcement?	Yes	No
4. Provide sufficient communication during emergencies (e.g., walkie-talkies, multiple phone lines)?	Yes	No
5. Require staff to have emergency numbers posted by their phones?	Yes	No
6. Clearly state the chain of command (Incident Command System)?	Yes	No
7. Clearly identify leaders that fulfill positions within the ICS?		
a. Incident commander	Yes	No
b. Planning & intelligence section	Yes	No
c. Operations section	Yes	No
d. Logistics section	Yes	No
e. Finance section	Yes	No
8. Require regular crisis drills?	Yes	No
9. Include a fully stocked and updated crisis box/cart that can be immediately accessed?	Yes	No
10. Require an annual review of physical safety of the building(s)?	Yes	No
11. Allow for other responders outside the school to access blueprints and floor plans?	Yes	No
12. Include requirements for responding to the needs of special needs students?	Yes	No
13. Identify area(s) where students, staff, parents, and caregivers should reunite in an emergency?	Yes	No
14. Provide clear bus routes and an adequate fleet of buses for transporting students to reunion areas or other necessary locations?	Yes	No
15. Consider how to obtain and effectively use volunteer support?	Yes	No
16. Include a policy on verifying facts before releasing them to the public?	Yes	No
17. Include timely and effective means for informing parents and the community of new information?	Yes	No
18. Include a defined policy and system for swiftly and reliably responding to media queries that is managed by two or fewer individuals?	Yes	No
19. Consider alternative sites for conducting school if the school building is destroyed or unusable?	Yes	No
20. Designate safe areas for staff and students to receive help before, during, and after school?	Yes	No
21. Allow students to obtain assistance from additional support staff and community-based professionals?	Yes	No
22. Have policies/procedures for responding to requests for memorials or anniversaries of an event?	Yes	No
23. Have policies/procedures for responding to suicide and suicide contagion issues?	Yes	No

Needs Assessment and Crisis Response and Recovery

The needs assessment process identifies resources necessary to provide crisis response and recovery services. For example, it identifies the specific materials or specific skills, training, and knowledge necessary to provide the immediate crisis response and ensure long-term crisis recovery (e.g., psychological triage screening tools, immediate school-based crisis intervention resources,

Figure 17.2. Questionnaire for examining the crisis team's immediate response and longer-term recovery efforts.

Crisis Response and Recovery Evaluation

School/District ______________________________ **Date** ______________

Crisis Event ____

____

Evaluating Team ____

Use the following scale to estimate the extent to which you feel components of the crisis plan were implemented.

1	2	3	N/A
Not implemented according to plan	Implemented according to plan, but the outcome was not effective/optimal	Implemented according to plan and the outcome was optimal	Not applicable to this situation

Task	**Rating** 1, 2, 3, or N/A
1. Leaders appointed to fulfill positions within the Incident Command System (ICS): a. Incident commander b. Intelligence section c. Operations section d. Logistics section e. Finance section	 a. ___ b. ___ c. ___ d. ___ e. ___
2. Response in each of the ICS sections was: a. Incident commander b. Intelligence section c. Operations section d. Logistics section e. Finance section	 a. ___ b. ___ c. ___ d. ___ e. ___
3. Responders outside the school were readily able to access blueprints and floor plans?	
4. The immediate needs of special needs students were met?	
5. The longer-term needs of special needs students were met?	
6. Students, staff, parents, and caregivers were able to reunite in the location designated by the school?	
7. Buses were able to transport students to necessary locations?	
8. Volunteer support was efficiently coordinated and utilized?	
9. Facts were verified before released to the public?	
10. Parents were informed within a reasonable time frame as new information became available?	
11. Media queries were managed by two or fewer individuals?	
12. Alternative sites were accessed for support and triage?	
13. Staff and students received support before, during, and after school?	
14. School community members were referred for additional assistance from community-based professionals and resources?	
15. Adequate psychotherapy referral resources were available?	
16. Memorials and/or anniversaries of an event were responded to?	
17. Suicide and contagion issues were intervened with?	

Additional comments:

Response/recovery strengths:

Areas that need immediate attention or revision:

knowledge of traumatic stress risk factors, and long-term community-based psychotherapy resources). Many elements of PREPaRE described in this book provide such knowledge and resources (e.g., chapter 10's discussion of the process of psychological triage).

Process Analysis and Crisis Response and Recovery

The process analysis gathers information to determine to what degree crisis response and recovery efforts were consistent with preestablished crisis plans and other process-related considerations. When possible, it is optimal to have an individual who is designated to document the response and recovery efforts or develop materials for each crisis responder to document daily response and recovery activities. These materials provide an opportunity to systematically review the crisis response and recovery process. These data are often collected during crisis response debriefings, individual interviews with school community members, and focus groups following the immediate crisis response (these procedures should be practiced during the simulations and exercises as part of the preparedness efforts). Figure 17.2 provides an example of a questionnaire that can be used when examining the process of implementing the crisis plan and response and recovery activities. Table 17.1 offers some sample questions to consider asking during focus groups or individual interviews.

Outcome Evaluation and Crisis Response and Recovery

The primary purpose of the outcome evaluation is to examine the effectiveness of crisis response and recovery activities in accomplishing targeted objectives. Outcomes that may be appropriate to assess include student adjustment, staff adjustment, and student access to support services. Table 17.2 includes additional outcomes that reflect crisis response and recovery effectiveness. It is essential that key objectives and outcomes be identified in advance so that strategies may be developed to accomplish each of the objectives. Figure 17.3 provides a form to assess the effectiveness of the school crisis intervention response, including questions about reconnecting students and parents and meeting the needs of students with special needs, plus outcomes such as student behavior, attendance, and adjustment. Figure 17.4 offers a teacher survey form to examine the effect of a crisis event on academic functioning.

Table 17.1. Interview or Focus Group Questions Used to Evaluate the Process of Crisis Response and Recovery Implementation

- Which interventions were the most successful and why?
- What were the positive aspects of staff crisis response debriefings and why?
- What immediate response and longer-term recovery strategies would you change and why?
- Do other professionals need to help with future crises?
- What training is necessary to prepare for future crises?
- What equipment is needed to support response and recovery efforts?
- What other planning actions will facilitate future response and recovery efforts?

Table 17.2. Sample Crisis Response Outcomes

1. Crisis interventions indicated by psychological triage were provided.
2. Individuals with psychopathology were provided with or referred for appropriate treatment.
3. Individuals with maladaptive coping behaviors (e.g., suicidal or homicidal ideation) have been referred to the appropriate professionals and lethality was reduced.
4. School behavior problems (i.e., aggressive, delinquent, and criminal behavior) occur at or below precrisis levels.
5. Students attend school at or above precrisis attendance rates.
6. Student academic functioning is at or above precrisis level.

Figure 17.3. Sample form to evaluate the effectiveness of the school crisis intervention response.

Examining the School Crisis Intervention

School/District ______________________ **Date** __________

Crisis Event ______________________

Evaluator(s) ______________________

School Crisis Interventions Provided:

- ☐ Reconnection with parents
- ☐ Reconnection with teachers
- ☐ Caregiver training(s)
- ☐ Individual crisis intervention(s)
- ☐ Reconnection with peers
- ☐ Psychoeducational group(s)
- ☐ Classroom-based crisis intervention(s)
- ☐ Referral(s) for psychotherapy
- ☐ Other (describe): ______________________

Intervention Evaluation Questions: (Circle "Yes" or "No")

1. Psychological Triage Summary Sheet data indicate that all students have been provided with the appropriate school crisis intervention.	Yes No
2. Individuals with a psychopathology have been provided with and/or referred for appropriate treatment(s).	Yes No
3. Individuals with maladaptive coping behaviors (e.g., thoughts of suicide, homicide) have been referred to the appropriate professional(s) and lethality has been reduced.	Yes No
4. Students attend school at or above precrisis attendance rates. a. School attendance rates in the ____ weeks prior to the crisis. b. School attendance rates in the ____ weeks after crisis resolution.	Yes No ______% ______%
5. School behavior problems (i.e., aggressive, delinquent, and criminal behavior) occur at or below precrisis levels. a. Office discipline referrals in the ____ weeks prior to the crisis event. b. Office discipline referrals in the ____ weeks after the crisis event has ended.	Yes No N = ____ N = ____
6. Student academic functioning returns to precrisis levels (from Teacher Survey Form) a. Average of teacher reports of instructional time currently spent talking about the crisis. b. Average of teacher reports of time engaged in academic instruction prior to the crisis. c. Average of teacher reports of time currently engaged in academic instruction. d. Average rating (on a 1 to 5 scale) of the extent to which students have returned to precrisis levels of academic functioning. e. Average of teacher reports of percentage of assignments completed by students in the week prior to the crisis event. f. Average of teacher reports of percentage of assignments currently completed by students in the past week.	______% ______% ______% m = ____ ______% ______%

Figure 17.4. Teacher survey form to examine the effect of a crisis event on academic functioning.

The Effect of a Crisis Event on Academic Functioning: Teacher Survey Form

School/District ____________________ **Date** __________

Crisis Event ______________________________

____

Teacher(s) ______________________________

1. As of today's date, estimate the percentage of instructional time that is devoted to discussion of the crisis event.
__________%

2. Estimate the percentage of instructional time that found students engaged in academic instruction during the 4 weeks *prior* to the crisis event.
__________%

3. Estimate the percentage of instructional time that finds students *currently* engaged in academic instruction.
__________%

4. Use the following scale to estimate the extent to which you feel your students have returned to their precrisis levels of academic functioning. Circle the appropriate number.

1	2	3	4	5
All of my students have returned to precrisis levels of academic functioning		*Half of my students have returned to precrisis levels of academic functioning*		*None of my students have returned to precrisis levels of academic functioning*

5. From your grade book, what percentage of assignments had your students completed during the week *prior to* the crisis event?
__________%

6. From your grade book, what percentage of assignments have your students completed *in the past week*?
__________%

The school crisis team should discuss and identify the desired outcomes and then develop appropriate data collection materials to efficiently obtain the necessary information immediately following a crisis response. Given the short-term and long-term objectives commonly identified, it is optimal to include follow-up assessments to provide further information regarding the long-term outcomes associated with crisis team activities. Previous research examining outcomes associated with crisis team efforts provides additional information regarding potential outcomes and measurements that may be appropriate (for reviews of related research see Croft, 2005; Nickerson & Osborne, 2006; Pagliocca et al., 2002).

CONCLUSION

Overall, there is a lack of research demonstrating the effectiveness of school crisis prevention, preparedness, response, and recovery. Clearly, more systematic research is needed (Brock et al., 2001; Nickerson & Zhe, 2004; Pagliocca & Nickerson, 2001; Pagliocca et al., 2002). However, systematic data collection to examine school crisis plans presents numerous challenges, and it is understood that often school crisis teams face these same challenges, including (a) the unpredictable and infrequent nature of crises; (b) the naturalistic in vivo contexts of schools; (c) the difficulty of analyses to reveal causality of specific intervention strategies given the multifaceted nature of crisis prevention, preparedness, response, and recovery; and (d) the ethical and professional concerns raised by conducting controlled research studies with populations in crisis. Thus, much of the existing research consists of anecdotal accounts describing the steps taken and lessons learned following actual crisis events (Pagliocca & Nickerson, 2001; Petersen & Straub, 1992).

As discussed in this chapter, PREPaRE emphasizes the necessity of examining the implementation and effectiveness of crisis prevention, preparedness, response, and recovery. Each school crisis team's intelligence section must have a school crisis examination leader whose responsibilities include the design, development, and collection of data for use in refining crisis prevention, preparedness, response, and recovery efforts. Through the use of multiple strategies, it is anticipated that this examination will purposefully inform crisis prevention, preparedness, response, and recovery activities by (a) assisting in identifying areas of need (i.e., needs assessment); (b) helping to understand what was done and by whom, and the degree to which these efforts were consistent with specific crisis team programs or response strategies (i.e., process analysis); and (c) determining whether the stated objectives of the activities were accomplished (i.e., outcome evaluation). These objectives demonstrate the importance of planning and obtaining data to examine and inform crisis prevention, preparedness, response, and recovery activities.

Section 6

FINAL CONSIDERATIONS

This book concludes by emphasizing two important considerations: first, the fact that school crisis intervention work can be extremely stressful and potentially have serious consequences for all crisis intervention team members, and second, that systematic research must be conducted to further validate PREPaRE. Chapter 18 addresses the importance of caring for the caregiver and promotes the need for every school crisis responder to develop both professional and personal self-care practice. Chapter 19 highlights the importance of gaining and sustaining a commitment by school-based mental health professionals to improving and strengthening all aspects of school crisis prevention, preparedness, response, and recovery.

Chapter 18

CARING FOR THE CAREGIVER

The previous chapters of this book have focused on a multitude of tasks that crisis interveners should perform to meet the needs of others; however, it is also critical for crisis interveners to care for themselves. Crisis response is difficult, and all school-based mental health professionals are challenged to perform crisis-related activities while fulfilling other demanding job responsibilities and maintaining existing caseloads. School staff members who provide crisis-related services must prepare for the potential consequences of that work and the impact it might have on their health, family, and peer relationships. In addition, they must be protected from revisiting their own losses and traumatic experiences, or from exacerbating previous mental illnesses during the course of providing school crisis services.

The goal of this chapter is to assist school-based mental health professionals in developing a *care for the caregiver* plan. It begins with a brief discussion of resilience, and then addresses the potential consequences of crisis response by providing definitions, symptomatology, prevalence, severity, and measurement of secondary traumatic stress (STS, also known as compassion fatigue and vicarious traumatization). Prevention and intervention strategies are then suggested, and ethical principles of self-care for crisis team members are explored. The chapter concludes by identifying standards for establishing and maintaining wellness. Suggestions are offered so each crisis team member can develop a professional and personal inventory of self-care practices.

RESILIENCE AND PROTECTIVE FACTORS

Resilience is the ability to adapt to difficult, challenging, stressful, or traumatic life experiences, and chapter 7 has already discussed this topic as it relates to students (Eppler, 2008). Resilience as it pertains to school crisis team members is an ongoing process that can be learned and developed. It can be enhanced by accessing social supports, being self-aware, recognizing professional challenges, providing self-care, and, for many, connecting to something larger than themselves. This could include religious or spiritual activities, volunteerism, or an affirmation of

Table 18.1. Risk and Protective Factors

Risk Factors	*Protective Factors*
Individual	
• Mental illness: depression, anxiety, bipolar personality disorders • Substance and alcohol abuse • Losses/failures • Younger age • Female gender	• Active coping and problem-solving skills • Support through ongoing health and mental health care relationships • Resiliency, self-esteem, mission, optimism, empathy, determination • Cultural and religious beliefs
Peer/Family	
• History of interpersonal violence, conflict, abuse, bullying • Isolation and social withdrawal • Exposure to suicide	• Family cohesion • Sense of social support • Interconnectedness
Community/Societal	
• Barriers to mental and health care • Social stigma • Economic instability and unsettling times • Social disintegration • Rural or remote environment	• Access to mental health care • Bond with school • Social supports, caring adults, and gatekeeper (peer, school staff) awareness • Positive media influence • Cultural values that affirm life

Note. Source *World Report on Violence and Health*, by E. G. Krug, L. L. Dahlberg, J. A. Mercy, A. B. Zwi, & R. Lozano (Eds.), 2002, Geneva: World Health Organization.

humanitarian values (Saakvitne, Stamm, & Barbanel, 2003). Factors that protect the school crisis team member from the risks of STS can be viewed from an ecological model that possesses individual, peer/family, community, and societal components (Krug, Dahlberg, Mercy, Zwi, & Lozano, 2002). Table 18.1 contrasts risk factors that contribute to vulnerability and protective factors that protect an individual from harm.

CONSEQUENCES OF RESPONDING TO SCHOOL CRISES

School-based mental health professionals are increasingly being called upon to assist survivors of child abuse, violent crime, disasters, war, and terrorism. At the same time, it has become increasingly apparent that participating in a school crisis intervention has an effect on caregivers. For example, Bolnik and Brock (2005), who surveyed 400 Northern Californian school psychologists, reported that of those who had previously participated in a crisis intervention, over 90% reported one or more reactions to their crisis intervention work. Physical reactions in

Figure 18.1. Signs of the overextended crisis responder.

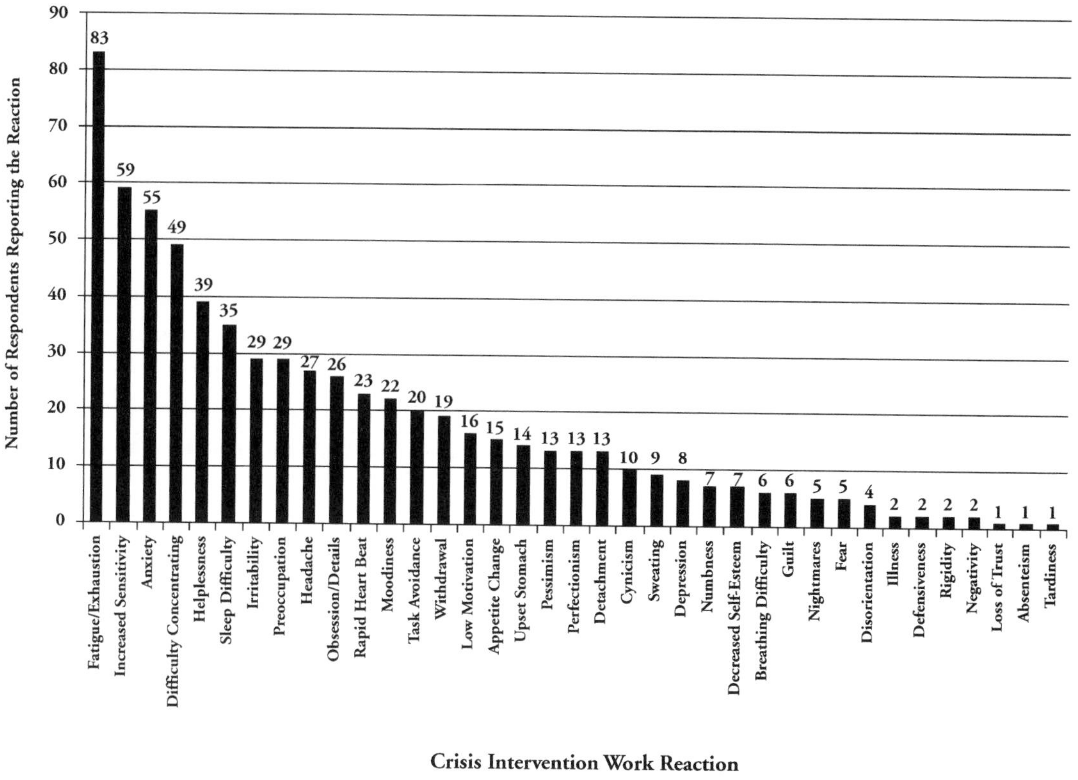

Note. Source "The Self-Reported Effects of Crisis Intervention Work on School Psychologists," by L. Bolnik and S. E. Brock, 2005, *The California School Psychologist, 10,* 117–124.

general, and fatigue and exhaustion in particular, were the most frequently reported. Figure 18.1 offers additional detail regarding these consequences of crisis intervention work. Many of these reactions could be considered "burnout," which refers to the negative consequences of chronic job stress. In addition to physical exhaustion, burnout symptoms among school personnel include emotional exhaustion, depersonalization (negative, detached responses to students), and a reduced sense of personal accomplishment (Huebner, Gilligan, & Cobb, 2002).

Many studies have provided empirical evidence that individuals who provide services to traumatized populations are at risk of experiencing symptoms of traumatic stress (Bride, 2007). The phenomenon of learning about another's traumatic ordeal and in the process experiencing traumatic stress has been referred to as *secondary traumatic stress* (STS; Figley, 1995). Figley (1999) defined STS as the "natural, consequent behaviors and emotions resulting from knowledge about a traumatizing event experienced by a significant other. It is the stress resulting from helping or wanting to help a suffering person" (p. 10). Furthermore, Figley (1999) recognized that individuals who are exposed to traumatized children, such as school personnel, are particularly vulnerable to STS. The contagion, apparently, is in the details. Mental health professionals who are exposed to graphic description of violent events, realities of people's cruelty to one another, and trauma-related reenactments may suffer from vicarious traumatization (Pearlman & Saakvitne, 1995).

Meyers and Cornille (2002) reviewed the literature in the area of secondary trauma, and provided several generalizations: (a) professionals who work with traumatized individuals can exhibit the same range of symptoms as victims, (b) the longevity and severity of these symptoms will vary with the individual, (c) professionals working with trauma victims are more likely to exhibit symptoms if they have been personally traumatized, and (d) female trauma workers are more likely to exhibit STS than are their male colleagues.

As is the case for primary trauma victims (as discussed in chapter 10), some crisis reactions to being a caregiver during school crisis intervention are typical and to be expected. However, others signal that the crisis team member has truly been overwhelmed and is potentially suffering secondary traumatic stress reactions. In the literature, STS is described as a syndrome of symptoms identical to those of posttraumatic stress disorder (American Psychiatric Association, 2000), and long-term reactions generally include intrusive thoughts, hypervigilance, and avoidant behaviors (Bride, 2007; Chrestman, 1999; Figley, 1995). Table 18.2 summarizes the extreme stress reactions of STS and the stressors unique to school crisis responders that might exacerbate certain symptoms.

MEASUREMENT OF SECONDARY TRAUMATIC STRESS

The theory and practice of screening for psychological trauma among crisis-exposed individuals has been explored in chapters 10 and 11. In many respects the measures offered in Table 11.2 parallel the screening tools discussed here. However, the current discussion reviews those measures that are unique to the evaluation of the psychological injury generated by *being a school crisis intervener.*

One of the problems of secondary trauma research is the relative lack of psychometrically sound instruments available for measuring this form of traumatization (compared to the number of instruments for measuring PTSD). Nevertheless, Bride, Radey, and Figley (2007) described and evaluated the leading assessments of STS in terms of their reliability and their validity. They discussed three factors in selecting a measure: the assessment domain or aspect of STS to be measured, simultaneous measurement, and the timeframe of what is being measured. The following scales might be appropriate for school crisis team members as they distinguish between differences in what may be characteristics of STS versus those of burnout.

Compassion Fatigue Scale

The Compassion Fatigue Scale (CFS; Gentry, Baranowsky, & Dunning, 2002) was originally developed from clinical experience and designed to assess both compassion fatigue and job burnout. Figley (2002) was one of the first to suggest that although secondary trauma and burnout are central and critical clinical features of STS, they are not the same, and each should be treated as having a unique effect on a professional's well-being. Adams, Boscarino, and Figley (2006) assessed the psychometric properties of the CFS and examined the scale's predictive validity in a multivariate model. They concluded that the 30-item scale reliably measured two key separate and distinct underlying dimensions, secondary trauma and job burnout.

Table 18.2. Warning Signs, Extreme Stress Reactions, and Exacerbating Variables

Cognitive

- Recurrent, intrusive thoughts about the crisis event, or distressing dreams
- Constant replaying of the event though not actually present
- Confusion, lack of attention, and difficulty making decisions

Somatic

- Hypervigilance or heightened startle response
- Chronic fatigue, exhaustion
- Disturbance in sleep and eating habits

Affective

- Compassion fatigue: demoralization, alienation, resignation
- Numbing, depersonalization
- Extreme anger at coworkers or loved ones
- Extreme depression accompanied by hopelessness and suicidal thoughts
- Excessive anxiety about crisis victims

Behavioral

- Serious difficulties in interpersonal relationships with loved ones (domestic violence); withdrawal from contact
- Attempts to overcontrol in professional situations at work or to act out a rescuer complex; compulsion to be part of every crisis situation
- Self-injury, reliance on substances and alcohol, or unnecessary risk-taking

Exacerbating variables

- Heavier prior trauma caseload; long assignments
- Less professional experience within educational system
- More time with child clients who have suffered physical injury as a result of physical/sexual trauma, witnessed death or threat to physical well-being of self or loved one, or discussed morbid details of the event
- Recent loss, family strife, or secondary media wounds

Note. Sources Bride (2007), Chrestman (1999), Creamer and Liddle (2005), and Figley (1995).

Professional Quality of Life Scale (ProQOL)

The ProQOL (Stamm, 2005) is a structured, 30-item self-report measure and a revision of Figley's (1995) Compassion Fatigue Self Test. The ProQOL is composed of three discrete subscales. The first subscale measures compassion satisfaction, defined as the pleasure derived from being able to do one's work (helping others) well. The second subscale measures burnout, or feelings of hopelessness and difficulties in dealing with work or in doing one's job effectively. The third subscale measures compassion fatigue/STS, with higher scores representing greater levels of compassion fatigue/STS.

Secondary Traumatic Stress Scale

The Secondary Traumatic Stress Scale (STSS; Bride, Robinson, Yegidis, & Figley, 2004) is a 17-item instrument designed to measure intrusion, avoidance, and arousal symptoms associated with indirect exposure to traumatic events via one's professional relationships with traumatized clients. Bride et al. found that the STSS fills a need for a reliable and valid instrument that would be specifically designed to measure the negative effects of social work practice with traumatized populations, and may be used to undertake empirical investigation into the prevention and amelioration of STS among mental health professionals. Motta, Chirichella, Maus, and Lombardo (2004) determined the levels at which the STSS would be associated with clinically meaningful levels of anxiety and depression. The availability of STSS cutoff scores facilitates clinical decision-making in that it allows professionals to judge whether secondary trauma symptoms may be associated with significant emotional difficulties or whether the secondary trauma reactions are of a transient nature.

Impact of Events Scale – Revised

The Impact of Events Scale – Revised (IES-R; Weiss, 2004) is a 22-item self-report measure that assesses subjective distress caused by traumatic events. The revised scale contains new items related to the hyperarousal symptoms of PTSD not included in the original IES. Items correspond directly to 14 of the 17 DSM-IV-TR symptoms of PTSD. The IES-R yields scores for intrusion, avoidance, and hyperarousal subscales. Although the IES-R is not used primarily to diagnose PTSD, cutoff scores for a preliminary diagnosis of PTSD have been cited in the literature (Orsillo, 2001).

PREVENTION AND INTERVENTION

School district administration can play a critical role in reducing the risk of STS among the school-based mental health professionals they use for crisis intervention services by establishing supports and policies *before* crises occur. Prevention and intervention strategies for those who supervise school crisis team members are provided in Table 18.3.

Ethical Principles of Self-Care

Everall and Paulson (2004) discussed the issues of burnout and STS and its potential impact on ethical practice. Clearly, a diminished ability to function professionally may constitute a serious violation of the ethical principles, as they may place students at risk. Everall and Paulson also suggested three major areas of prevention, which include (a) self-monitoring (knowing when to say "no" to a request for crisis response), (b) obtaining supervision, and (c) obtaining intervention and support from colleagues and administrators.

Figley (1995, 2002) has proposed standards of self-care for professionals who work with traumatized clients. These standards propose that it is unethical to not attend to one's own self-care,

Table 18.3. Prevention and Intervention Strategies for Administrators of School Crisis Responders

Prevention

- Identify enough crisis interveners to address all aspects of the school crisis intervention plan.
- Establish supervision, case conferencing, and staff appreciation events.
- Conduct training in secondary traumatic stress and stress management practices.
- Encourage peer partners and consultation.
- Form alliances with employee assistance program (EAP) providers and community mental health agencies; site-based personnel may not be in the best position to provide such assistance.
- Discuss with school administrators the circumstances under which a staff member may need to be removed from a caregiving situation.
- Discuss with school administrators how to remove a staff member from an inappropriate caregiving situation.

Intervention

- Limit shifts so that responders do not provide services beyond 12 hours.
- Rotate responders from the highest-impact assignments to those with lower levels of stress.
- Monitor responders who meet certain high-risk criteria such as:
  - Survivor of crisis or disaster.
  - Those having regular exposure to severely affected individuals.
  - Those with preexisting conditions.
  - Those who have responded to many crises in a short period of time.

Note. Sources *Psychological First Aid: Field Operations Guide* (2nd ed.), by M. Brymer et al., 2006, Rockville, MD: National Child Traumatic Stress Network and National Center for PTSD (Appendix C, Provider Care); and *Treating Compassion Fatigue*, by C. R. Figley, 2002, New York: Brunner-Routledge.

as such care is necessary to providing effective services and avoiding harm to clients. These standards include acknowledging the importance of (a) respecting the dignity and worth of oneself (violation lowers your integrity and trust), (b) taking responsibility for self-care (ultimately it is the professional's responsibility to take care of oneself, and no situation or person can justify neglecting it), and (c) acknowledging the relationship between self-care and duty to perform (there must be recognition that the duties to perform as a crisis intervener can not be fulfilled in the absence of a duty to care for oneself, which includes knowing when to say "no" to a request to provide services).

Professional and Personal Self-Care Practice

The school crisis team member must make a formal commitment to both professional and personal self-care and establish an individual plan for each. Professional self-care has several components, the first of which is finding a balance between work and home and devoting sufficient time and attention to both without compromising either. A second element of self-care is setting firm time, therapeutic, and personal boundaries to deal with multiple roles in the community. A third element is realism in differentiating between things one can change in the system and accepting those one cannot. A fourth element involves seeking ways to gain recognition for, and taking joy in, the achievements of one's work. Finally, getting help and support at work is important. This includes (a) obtaining supervision, consultation, and/or therapy, and debriefing with other crisis team members; (b) working in teams, such as school and district crisis teams; and (c) seeking out mentor–mentee relationships. Finally, a personal self-care plan consists of three components: physical, psychological, and social or interpersonal care. Strategies for such care are summarized in Table 18.4.

Table 18.4. Personal Self-Care Practice

Physical

- Get adequate sleep and avoid extended periods of work without colleagues and breaks.
- Ensure proper nutrition (crisis responders often forget to eat) and limit excess use of alcohol and tobacco
- Exercise regularly (an essential component to any self-care plan).
- Regularly use the stress management techniques of meditation, visualization, relaxation, and diaphragmatic breathing.

Psychological

- Self-monitor and become aware of the signs of secondary traumatic stress.
- Seek out a professional who is knowledgeable about trauma if the signs of secondary traumatic stress last for longer than 2–3 weeks.
- Seek help with your own trauma history, which can make you vulnerable to vicarious traumatization.
- Develop better skills for assertiveness, time management, cognitive reframing, and interpersonal communication.

Social/Interpersonal

- Plan for family and home safety, including child and pet care.
- Identify social supports of at least five people (including two at work) whom you can depend on to be supportive.
- Engage in social activism and advocacy, the key factor in healing and helping victims turn into survivors.
- Practice your religious faith and spirituality.
- Explore a passion for creative self-expression such as writing, drawing, painting, or teaching.
- Find humor everywhere; it has been a key to survival for all oppressed people in history.

Note. From *Psychological First Aid: Field Operations Guide* (2nd ed.), by M. Brymer et al., 2006, Rockville, MD: National Child Traumatic Stress Network and National Center for PTSD (Appendix C, Provider Care); *Compassion Fatigue: Coping With Secondary Traumatic Stress Disorder*, by C. R. Figley (Ed.), 1995, New York: Brunner/Mazel; *Treating Compassion Fatigue*, by C. R. Figley, 2002, New York: Brunner-Routledge.

CONCLUSION

The goal of this chapter was to emphasize the importance of school crisis team members establishing and implementing both a professional and personal self-care plan. Ideally, this is done early in one's career. This chapter has explored resilience, protective factors, and the consequences of working with traumatized populations, and provided prevention and intervention strategies for the caregiver. It has also emphasized that school crisis team members have an ethical obligation to tend to personal self-care so that they are not at risk of harming the very school community members they seek to help.

Chapter 19

CONCLUDING COMMENTS

As discussed throughout the chapters of this book, PREPaRE is designed for educators and other school-based mental health professionals who are committed to improving and strengthening all aspects of school crisis prevention, preparedness, response, and recovery. As highlighted in this book, the need for PREPaRE is emphasized by the fact that schools play a critical role in crisis prevention and intervention, meeting not just the needs of students, but often those of the entire school community.

School crisis teams must be adequately prepared to address a range of crisis events, understand the systems and procedures that need to be in place to respond to crises, and address the unique mental health needs generated by crisis exposure. School crisis plans must also be fully integrated into community-based emergency response efforts, including law enforcement, fire and rescue, and community and mental health service providers. Furthermore, plans must be clearly communicated to staff, parents, and community leaders.

Important issues emphasized in PREPaRE include (a) promotion of the mental health, resiliency, and coping capacity of individuals affected by a crisis, particularly students; and (b) the unique opportunities and challenges presented to schools when preventing, preparing for, responding to, and recovering from crises. As such, the chapters in this book emphasized that school crisis teams must address crises as a mental health risk, as well as a physical health and safety risk. Finally, an important goal of successful crisis prevention, preparedness, response, and recovery is to support academic functioning.

The *PREPaRE School Crisis Prevention and Intervention Training Curriculum* was developed to offer guidance regarding best practices in school crisis prevention, preparedness, response, and recovery (Brock, 2006a, 2006c; Reeves, Nickerson, & Jimerson, 2006a, 2006b). As summarized in the preceding chapters, this model was developed after a careful review of the empirical literature, and as such it offers evidence-informed crisis prevention and intervention practices. Furthermore, as noted in the preface, pilot testing of this curriculum revealed that the PREPaRE workshops have a high degree of consumer satisfaction, have a positive effect on participant attitudes in terms of their ability to participate on a school crisis team, and result in significant changes in crisis prevention, preparedness, response, and recovery knowledge (Brock, 2006b; Nickerson, 2006). However, it is important to acknowledge that at this point in time, no one community- or school-based crisis prevention, preparedness, response, and recovery protocol has been validated by careful research (Vernberg et al., 2008). Thus, a need for systematic research addressing the effectiveness of the PREPaRE workshops and the specific elements of the PREPaRE model and its curriculum remains.

Specific questions designed to evaluate the effects of *Workshop 1 – Crisis Prevention and Preparedness: The Comprehensive School Crisis Team* (Reeves et al., 2006a) can be based on the workshop's objectives. These questions should determine to what extent individual workshop participants (and the schools and school districts that participants serve) are able to identify and demonstrate knowledge of the following: (a) the characteristics of a crisis event, (b) the key concepts associated with the PREPaRE acronym, (c) the activities of the comprehensive school crisis team, (d) the importance of a hierarchical crisis team structure and response, (e) the five major functions of the Incident Command System, (f) strategies for communicating with school boards when trying to create or sustain teams, (g) the three concepts related to crime prevention through environmental design, (h) the guiding principles in crisis plan development, and (i) the essential elements of crisis plans, including examination of their effectiveness.

Specific questions designed to evaluate the effects of *Workshop 2 – Crisis Intervention and Recovery: The Roles of School-Based Mental Health Professionals* (Brock, 2006a) can also be based on the workshop's objectives. These questions should include the degree to which workshop participants report positive attitudes regarding their ability to provide crisis intervention services (both short-term and long-term). Such research should also explore the degree to which individual workshop participants (and the schools and school districts that participants serve) are able to identify and demonstrate knowledge of (a) the variables that determine the traumatizing potential of a crisis event, (b) the range of school crisis interventions indicated by the PREPaRE acronym, (c) how school crisis interventions fit into the larger school crisis response, (d) factors that are critical to evaluating psychological trauma risk, and (e) how to match psychological trauma risk to a range of appropriate school crisis interventions.

In addition to addressing the degree to which PREPaRE workshop objectives are achieved, future research should perhaps most importantly examine the effects of specific PREPaRE elements on crisis-exposed students. These questions might include the degree to which (a) schools employing a PREPaRE crisis team model are better able to prevent crises and prepare for those that cannot be prevented; (b) PREPaRE strategies help to reaffirm student security and safety; (c) PREPaRE protocols accurately classify student risk for traumatic stress; and (d) PREPaRE crisis intervention strategies (i.e., the reestablishment of social support, psychological education, classroom-based crisis intervention, and individual crisis intervention) are able to promote adaptive coping, identify students at risk for traumatic stress reactions, and facilitate the treatment of students whose crisis reactions are psychopathological (e.g., PTSD).

Possible tools for conducting such research were presented in chapter 17's discussion on examining the effectiveness of crisis prevention, preparedness, response, and recovery. In addition, Vernberg et al. (2008) reported that the National Child Traumatic Stress Network's Terrorism and Disaster Working Committee has formed a subcommittee to develop measures to evaluate how psychological first-aid interventions are used and what effects these interventions have on individuals exposed to crisis events.

In conclusion, the authors of the PREPaRE model and its curriculum enthusiastically support and look forward to collaborating with other scholars regarding the evaluation of this model. Those interested in conducting such research, and who feel that contact with the PREPaRE workgroup would be helpful, are encouraged to contact Dr. Stephen E. Brock (brock@csus.edu) or Dr. Amanda Nickerson (anickerson@uamail.albany.edu).

REFERENCES

Adams, R. E., Boscarino, J. A., & Figley, C. R. (2006). Compassion fatigue and psychological distress among social workers: A validation study. *American Journal of Orthopsychiatry, 76*, 103–108.

Adams, C. M., & Kritsonis, W. A. (2006). An analysis of secondary schools' crisis management preparedness: National implications. *National Journal for Publishing and Mentoring Doctoral Student Research, 1*, 1–7.

Adamson, A. D., & Peacock, G. G. (2007). Crisis response in the public schools: A survey of school psychologists' experiences and perceptions. *Psychology in the Schools, 44*, 749–764.

Ahern, J., Galea, S., Resnick, H., Kilpatrick, D., Bucuvalas, M., Gold, J., et al. (2002). Television images and psychological symptoms after the September 11 terrorist attack. *Psychiatry, 65*, 289–300.

Ahern, J. A., Galea, S., Resnick, H., & Vlahov, D. (2004). Television images and probable posttraumatic stress disorder after September 11. *The Journal of Nervous and Mental Disease, 192*, 217–226.

Ahmad, A., Larsson, B., & Sundelin-Wahlsten, V. (2007). EMDR treatment for children with PTSD: Results of a randomized controlled trial. *Journal of Nordic Psychiatry, 61*, 349–354.

Allen, M., & Ashbaker, B. (2004). Strengthening schools: Involving paraprofessionals in crisis prevention and intervention. *Intervention in School and Clinic, 39*, 139–146.

Allen, S. F., Dlugokinski, E. L., Cohen, L. A., & Walker, J. L. (1999). Assessing the impact of a traumatic community event on children and assisting with their healing. *Psychiatric Annals, 29*, 93–97.

Allen, J. P., & Land, D. (1999). Attachment in adolescence. In J. Cassidy & P. R. Shaver (Eds.), *Handbook of attachment: Theory, research, and clinical applications* (pp. 319–335). New York: Guilford Press.

Allen-Heath, M., Ryan, K., Dean, B., & Bingham, R. (2007). History of school safety and psychological first aid for children. *Brief Treatment and Crisis Intervention, 7*, 206–233.

American Academy of Child and Adolescent Psychiatry. (1998). Practice parameters for the assessment and treatment of children with posttraumatic stress disorder. *Journal of the American Academy of Child and Adolescent Psychiatry, 37*(10 Suppl.), 4S–26S.

American Psychiatric Association (APA). (2000). *Diagnostic and statistical manual of mental disorders* (4th ed., Rev. ed.). Washington, DC: Author.

American Psychiatric Association (APA). (2003). Practice guidelines for the assessment and treatment of patients with suicidal behavior. Retrieved June 18, 2008, from http://www.med.umich.edu/depression/suicide_assessment/APA%20Suicide%20Guidelines.pdf

American Red Cross. (1991). *Disaster services regulations and procedures.* (ARC Document 3050M). Washington, DC: Author.

Amstadter, A. B., McCart, M. R., & Ruggiero, K. J. (2007). Psychosocial interventions for adults with crime-related PTSD. *Professional Psychology: Research and Practice, 38*, 640–651.

Andrews, B., Brewin, C. R., Philpott, R., & Stewart, L. (2007). Delayed-onset posttraumatic stress disorder: A systematic review of the evidence. *American Journal of Psychiatry, 16*, 1319–1326.

Annandale, N. O. (2007). States' school crisis planning materials: An analysis of cross-cultural considerations and sensitivity to student diversity. *Dissertation Abstracts International: Section B: The Sciences and Engineering, 67*(8-B), 4698.

Appleyard, K., Egeland, B., & Sroufe, L. A. (2007). Direct social support for young high-risk children: Relations with behavioral and emotional outcomes across time. *Journal of Abnormal Child Psychology, 35*, 443–457.

Applied Research and Consulting, Columbia University Mailman School of Public Health, & New York Psychiatric Institute. (2002, May 6). *Effects of the World Trade Center attack on NYC public school students: Initial report to the New York City Board of Education.* New York: New York City Board of Education.

Armstrong, K. H., Massey, O. T., & Boroughs, M. (2006). Implementing comprehensive safe school plans in Pinellas County Schools, Florida: Planning, implementation, operation, sustainability, and lessons learned. In S. R. Jimerson & M. Furlong (Eds.), *Handbook of school violence and school safety: From research to practice* (pp. 525–536). Mahwah, NJ: Erlbaum.

Armstrong, M. (1990, April). Emotional reactions to Stockton. In F. Busher (Chair), *Tragedy in Stockton schoolyard.* Symposium conducted at the annual meeting of the National Association of School Psychologists, San Francisco, CA.

Arnold, M. E., & Hughes, J. N. (1999). First do no harm: Adverse effects of grouping deviant youth for skills training. *Journal of School Psychology, 37*, 99–115.

Aseltine, R. H., & DeMartino, R. (2004). An outcome evaluation of the SOS suicide prevention program. *American Journal of Public Health, 94*, 446–451.

Athey, J., & Moody-Williams, J. (2003). *Developing cultural competence in disaster mental health programs: Guiding principles and recommendations.* Washington, DC: U.S. Department of Health and Human Services.

Austin, G., & Duerr, M. (2007a). *Guidebook for the California Healthy Kids Survey: Part I. Administration.* San Francisco: WestEd.

Austin, G., & Duerr, M. (2007b). *Guidebook for the California Healthy Kids Survey: Part II. Data use & dissemination.* San Francisco: WestEd.

Austin, G., & Duerr, M. (2007c). *Guidebook for the California Healthy Kids Survey: Part III. School climate survey for teachers and other staff.* San Francisco: WestEd.

Ayers, T. S., Sandler, I. N., West, S. G., & Roosa, M. W. (1996). A dispositional and situational assessment of children's coping: Testing alternative models of coping. *Journal of Personality and Social Psychology, 51*, 1173–1182.

Azarian, A., & Skriptchenko-Gregorian, V. (1998a). Children in natural disasters: An experience of the 1988 earthquake in Armenia. Commack, NY: American Academy of Experts in Traumatic Stress. Retrieved March 1, 2008, from http://www.aaets.org/article38.htm

Azarian, A., & Skriptchenko-Gregorian, V. (1998b). Traumatization and stress in child and adolescent victims of natural disasters. In T. W. Miller (Ed.), *Children of trauma: Stressful life events and their effects on children and adolescents* (pp. 77–118). Madison, CT: International Universities Press.

Bailey, K. A. (2006). Legal knowledge related to school violence and school safety. In S. R. Jimerson & M. Furlong (Eds.), *Handbook of school violence and school safety: From research to practice* (pp. 31–49). Mahwah, NJ: Erlbaum.

Baisden, B., & Quarantelli, E. L. (1981). The delivery of mental health services in community disasters: An outline of research findings. *Journal of Community Psychology, 9,* 195–203.

Baranowsky, A. B., Young, M., Johnson-Douglas, S., Williams-Keeler, L., & McCarrey, M. (1998). PTSD transmission: A review of secondary traumatization in Holocaust survivor families. *Canadian Psychology, 39,* 247–256.

Barenbaum, J., Ruchkin, V., & Schwab-Stone, M. (2004). The psychosocial aspects of children exposed to war: Practice and policy initiatives. *Journal of Child Psychology and Psychiatry, 45,* 41–62.

Berk, R. A., & Rossi, P. H. (1990). *Thinking about program evaluation.* Newbury Park, CA: SAGE.

Berkowitz, S. J. (2003). Children exposed to community violence: The rationale for early intervention. *Clinical Child and Family Psychology Review, 6,* 293–302.

Berman, A. L., Jobes, D. A., & Silverman, M. M. (2006). *Adolescent suicide: Assessment and intervention* (2nd ed.). Washington, DC: American Psychological Association.

Berman, S. L., Kurtines, W. M., Silverman, W. K., & Serafini, L. T. (1996). The impact of exposure to crime and violence on urban youth. *American Journal of Orthopsychiatry, 66,* 329–336.

Bernat, J. A., Ronfeldt, H. M., Calhoun, K. S., & Arias, I. (1998). Prevalence of traumatic events and peritraumatic predictors of posttraumatic stress symptoms in a nonclinical sample of college students. *Journal of Traumatic Stress, 11,* 645–664.

Bischof, N. L. (2007). School psychology and crisis intervention: A survey of school psychologists' involvement and training, *Dissertation Abstracts International Section A: Humanities and Social Sciences, 67*(11-A), 4091.

Bisson, J. I., Jenkins, P. L., Alexander, J., & Bannister, C. (1997). Randomised controlled trial of psychological debriefing for victims of acute burn trauma. *British Journal of Psychiatry, 171,* 78–81.

Bisson, J. I., McFarlane, A. C., & Rose, S. (2000). Psychological debriefing. In E. B. Foa, T. M. Keane, & M. J. Friedman (Eds.), *Effective treatments for PTSD: Practice guidelines from the International Society for Traumatic Stress Studies* (pp. 39–59, 317–319). New York: Guilford Press.

Bitney, J., & Title, B. B. (2001). *No-bullying program, preventing bullying at school: Program director's manual.* Center City, MN: Hazelden Foundation.

Black, S. (2004). Revising school attack protections since 9/11. *American School Board Journal, 191,* 36–38.

Blanchard, E. B., Kuhn, E., Rowell, D. L., Hickling, E. J., Wittrock, D., Rogers, R. L., et al. (2004). Studies of the vicarious traumatization of college students by the September 11th attacks: Effects of proximity, exposure and connectedness. *Behaviour Research and Therapy, 42,* 191–205.

Blom, G. E. (1986). A school disaster: Intervention and research aspects. *Journal of American Academy of Child Psychiatry, 25,* 336–345.

Blom, G. E., Etkind, S. L., & Carr, W. J. (1991). Psychological intervention after child and adolescent disasters in the community. *Child Psychiatry and Human Development, 21,* 257–266.

Bolnik, L., & Brock, S. E. (2005). The self-reported effects of crisis intervention work on school psychologists. *The California School Psychologist, 10*, 117–124. Retrieved May 2, 2008, from http://education.ucsb.edu/school-psychology/CSP-Journal/index.html

Borges, G., Angst, J., Nock, M. K., Ruscio, A. M., & Kessler, R. C. (2008). Risk factors for the incidence and persistence of suicide-related outcomes: A 10-year follow-up study using the national comorbidity surveys. *Journal of Affective Disorders, 105*, 25–33.

Boulton, M. J. (1994). Understanding and preventing bullying in the junior school playground. In P. K. Smith & S. Sharp (Eds.), *School bullying: Insights and perspectives* (pp. 132–159). London: Routledge.

Bourduin, C. M., Mann, B. J., Cone, L. T., Henggeler, S. W., Fucci, B. R., Blaske, D. M., et al. (1995). Multisystemic treatment of serious juvenile offenders: Long-term prevention of criminality and violence. *Journal of Consulting and Clinical Psychology, 63*, 569–578.

Bowis, J. (2007). Mass violence and mental health. *International Review of Psychiatry, 19*, 297–301.

Boyle, G. J. (2003). Review of the Trauma Symptom Checklist for Children. In B. S. Plake, J. C. Impara, & R. A. Spies (Eds.), *The fifteenth mental measurements yearbook*. Lincoln, NE: Buros Institute of Mental Measurements.

Bradburn, S. I. (1991). After the earth shook: Children's stress symptoms 6–8 months after a disaster. *Advances in Behavior Research and Therapy, 13*, 173–179.

Bremner, J. D., Southwick, S. M., Johnson, D. R., Yehuda, R., & Charney, D. S. (1993). Childhood physical abuse and combat-related posttraumatic stress disorder in Vietnam veterans. *American Journal of Psychiatry, 150*, 235–239.

Breslau, N. (1998). Epidemiology of trauma and posttraumatic stress disorder. In R. Yehuda (Ed.), *Psychological trauma* (pp. 1–29). Washington, DC: American Psychiatric Press.

Brewin, C. R., Andrews, B., & Rose, S. (2000). Fear, helplessness, and horror in posttraumatic stress disorder: Investigating DSM–IV criterion A2 in victims of violent crime. *Journal of Traumatic Stress, 13*, 499–509.

Brewin, C. R., Andrews, B., & Valentine, J. D. (2000). Meta-analysis of risk factors for posttraumatic stress disorder in trauma-exposed adults. *Journal of Consulting and Clinical Psychology, 68*, 748–766.

Brickman, H. K., Jones, S. E., & Groom, S. E. (2004, May). Evolving school crisis management since 9/11. *Education Digest, 69*(9), 29–35.

Bride, B. E. (2007). Secondary traumatic stress among social workers. *Social Work, 52*, 63–70.

Bride, B. E., Radey, M., & Figley, C. R. (2007). Measuring compassion fatigue. *Journal of Clinical Social Work, 35*, 155–163.

Bride, B. E., Robinson, M. M., Yegidis, B., & Figley, C. R. (2004). Development and validation of the Secondary Traumatic Stress Scale. *Research on Social Work Practice, 14*, 27–35.

Briere, J. (1996). *Trauma Symptoms Checklist for Children (TSCC): Professional manual.* Odessa, FL: Psychological Assessment Resources.

Brislin, R. W. (1970). Back-translation for cross-cultural research. *Journal of Cross-Cultural Psychology, 1*, 185–216.

Brock, S. E. (1998) Helping classrooms cope with traumatic events. *Professional School Counseling, 2*, 110–116.

Brock, S. E. (1999). School crisis intervention mutual aid: A county level response plan. In A. S. Canter & S. A. Carroll (Eds.), *Crisis prevention and response: A collection of NASP resources* (pp. 91–94). Bethesda, MD: National Association of School Psychologists.

Brock, S. E. (1999, Summer). The crisis of youth violence: Dangers and opportunities. *CASP Today: A Quarterly Magazine of the California Association of School Psychologists, 48*(4), 18–20.

Brock, S. E. (2000). Development of a school district crisis intervention policy. *California School Psychologist, 5*, 53–64.

Brock, S. E. (2002a). Crisis theory: A foundation for the comprehensive school crisis response team. In S. E. Brock, P. J. Lazarus, & S. R. Jimerson (Eds.), *Best practices in school crisis prevention and intervention* (pp. 5–17). Bethesda, MD: National Association of School Psychologists.

Brock, S. E. (2002b). Estimating the appropriate crisis response. In S. E. Brock, P. J. Lazarus, & S. R. Jimerson (Eds.), *Best practices in school crisis prevention and intervention* (pp. 355–366). Bethesda, MD: National Association of School Psychologists.

Brock, S. E. (2002c). Group crisis intervention. In S. E. Brock, P. J. Lazarus, & S. R. Jimerson (Eds.), *Best practices in school crisis prevention and intervention* (pp. 385–399). Bethesda, MD: National Association of School Psychologists.

Brock, S. E. (2006a). *Crisis intervention and recovery: The roles of school-based mental health professionals.* (Available from National Association of School Psychologists, 4340 East West Highway, Suite 402, Bethesda, MD 20814)

Brock, S. E. (2006b). *Crisis intervention and recovery: The roles of school-based mental health professionals. Workshop evaluation/test summaries and workshop modification suggestions.* (Available from National Association of School Psychologists, 4340 East West Highway, Suite 402, Bethesda, MD 20814)

Brock, S. E. (2006c). *Trainer's handbook. Workshop 2. Crisis intervention and recovery: The roles of school-based mental health professionals.* Bethesda, MD: National Association of School Psychologists.

Brock, S. E., & Davis, J. (2008). Best practices in school crisis intervention. In A. Thomas & J. Grimes (Eds.), *Best practices in school psychology V* (Vol. 3, pp. 781–798). Bethesda, MD: National Association of School Psychologists.

Brock, S. E., & Jimerson, S. R. (2004). School crisis interventions: Strategies for addressing the consequences of crisis events. In E. R. Gerler (Ed.), *Handbook of school violence* (pp. 285–332). Binghamton, NY: Haworth Press.

Brock, S. E., Jimerson, S. R., & Hart, S. R. (2006). Preventing, preparing for, and responding to school violence with the National Incident Management System. In S. R. Jimerson & M. J. Furlong (Eds.), *Handbook of school violence and school safety: From research to practice* (pp. 443–458). Mahwah, NJ: Erlbaum.

Brock, S. E., Jimerson, S. R., Lieberman, R., Zatlin, R., & Huff, L. (2002). *School crisis intervention workshop.* Sacramento, CA: California Association of School Psychologists.

Brock, S. E., Navarro, L., & Teran, E. (2008, March). *The English to Spanish translation of psycho-educational materials for use during school crisis intervention.* Poster presented at the annual meeting of the California Association of School Psychologists, Burlingame, CA.

Brock, S. E., Nickerson, A. B., O'Malley, M. D., & Chang, Y. (2006). Understanding children victimized by their peers. *Journal of School Violence, 5*(3), 3–18.

Brock, S. E., Nickerson, A. B., Reeves, M. A., & Jimerson, S. R. (2008). Best practices for school psychologists as members of crisis teams: The PREPaRE Model. In A. Thomas & J. Grimes (Eds.), *Best practices in school psychology V* (Vol. 4; pp. 1487–1504). Bethesda, MD: National Association of School Psychologists.

Brock, S. E., & Poland, S. (2002). School crisis preparedness. In S. E. Brock, P. J. Lazarus, & S. R. Jimerson (Eds.), *Best practices in school crisis prevention and intervention* (pp. 273–288). Bethesda, MD: National Association of School Psychologists.

Brock, S. E., Sandoval, J., & Hart, S. R. (2006). Suicidal ideation and behaviors. In G. Bear & K. Minke (Eds.), *Children's needs III: Understanding and addressing the developmental needs of children* (pp. 225–238). Bethesda, MD: National Association of School Psychologists.

Brock, S. E., Sandoval, J., & Lewis, S. (1996). *Preparing for crises in the schools: A manual for building school crisis response teams.* Brandon, VT: Clinical Psychology Publishing Company.

Brock, S. E., Sandoval, J., & Lewis, S. (2001). *Preparing for crises in the schools: A manual for building school crisis response teams* (2nd ed.). New York: Wiley.

Broughton, D. D., Allen, E. E., Hannemann, R. E., & Petrikin, J. E. (2006). Reuniting fractured families after a disaster: The role of the National Center for Missing and Exploited Children. *Pediatrics, 117*, S442–S445.

Brown, E. J., & Bobrow, A. L. (2004). School entry after a community-wide trauma: Challenges and lessons learned from September 11th, 2001. *Clinical Child and Family Psychology Review, 7*, 211–221.

Bryant, R. A., Salmon, K., Sinclair, E., & Davidson, P. (2007). A prospective study of appraisals in childhood posttraumatic stress disorder. *Behaviour Research and Therapy, 45*, 2502–2507.

Brymer, M., Jacobs, A., Layne, C., Pynoos, R., Ruzek, J., Steinberg, A., et al. (2006). *Psychological first aid: Field operations guide* (2nd ed.). Rockville, MD: National Child Traumatic Stress Network and National Center for PTSD. Retrieved March 3, 2008, from http://www.nctsn.org/nccts/nav.do?pid=typ_terr_resources_pfa

Buka, S. L., Stichick, T. L., Birdthistle, I., & Earls, F. J. (2001). Youth exposure to violence: Prevalence, risks, and consequences. *American Journal of Orthopsychiatry, 71*, 298–310.

Burling, W. K., & Hyle, A. E. (1997). Disaster preparedness planning: Policy and leadership issues. *Disaster Prevention and Management, 6*, 234–244.

Burrows-Horton, C., & Cruise, T. K. (2001). *Child abuse and neglect: The school's response.* New York: Guilford Press.

Caffo, E., & Belaise, C. (2003). Psychological aspects of traumatic injury in children and adolescents. *Child & Adolescent Psychiatric Clinics of North America, 12*, 493–535.

California Governor's Office of Emergency Services. (1998, June). *School emergency response: Using SEMS at districts and sites. Guidelines for planning and training in compliance with the standardized emergency management system.* Sacramento, CA: Author.

California Governor's Office of Emergency Services. (2007). *State of California Exercise Program.* State of California. Retrieved May 1, 2008, from http://www.oes.ca.gov/Operational/OESHome.nsf/Operational/OESHome.nsf/ALL/4AB87F7567265B76882572B3005D4D38?OpenDocument

Campfield, K. M., & Hills, A. M. (2001). Effect of timing of critical incident stress debriefing (CISD) on posttraumatic symptoms. *Journal of Traumatic Stress, 14*, 327–339.
Canada, M., Heath, M. A., Money, K., Annandale, N., Fischer, L., & Young, E. L. (2007). Crisis intervention for students of diverse backgrounds: School counselors' concerns. *Brief Treatment and Crisis Intervention, 7*, 12–24.
Caplan, G. (1964). *Principles of preventive psychiatry.* New York: Basic Books.
Caplan, G. (1974). *Support systems and community mental health: Lectures on concept development.* New York: Behavioral Publications.
Capewell, E. (2000). *When tragedy strikes: Guidelines for effective critical incident management in schools.* United Kingdom: Irish National Teachers Union.
Carlson, E. B. (1997). *Trauma assessments: A clinician's guide.* New York: Guilford Press.
Carr, A. (2004). Interventions for post-traumatic stress disorder in children and adolescents. *Pediatric Rehabilitation, 7*, 231–244.
Carrion, V. G., Weems, C. F., Ray, R., & Reiss, A. L. (2002). Toward an empirical definition of pediatric PTSD: The phenomenology of PTSD symptoms in youth. *Journal of the American Academy of Child and Adolescent Psychiatry, 41*, 166–173.
Cauce, A. M., Felner, R. D., & Primavera, J. (1982). Social support in high risk adolescents: Structural components and adaptive impact. *American Journal of Community Psychology, 10*, 417–428.
Centers for Disease Control and Prevention. (2008, June 6). Youth risk behavior surveillance – United States, 2007. *Morbidity and Mortality Weekly Report, 57*, SS-4. Retrieved August 29, 2008, from http://www.cdc.gov/HealthyYouth/yrbs/pdf/yrbss07_mmwr.pdf
Charuvastra, A., & Cloitre, M. (2008). Social bonds and posttraumatic stress disorder. *Annual Review of Psychology, 59*, 301–328.
Chemtob, C., Thomas, S., Law, W., & Cremniter, D. (1997). Postdisaster psychosocial interventions: A field study of the impact of debriefing on psychological distress. *American Journal of Psychiatry, 154*, 415–417.
Chrestman, K. R. (1999). Secondary exposure to trauma and self-reported distress among therapists. In B. H. Stature (Ed.), *Secondary traumatic stress: Self-care issues for clinicians, researchers, & educators* (2nd ed., pp. 29–36). Lutherville, MD: Sidran Press.
Christopher, R. (2007). Review of the Children's PTSD Inventory: A structured interview for diagnosing posttraumatic stress disorder. In K. F. Geisinger, R. A. Spies, J. F. Carlson, & B. S. Plake (Eds.), *The fifteenth mental measurements yearbook.* Lincoln, NE: Buros Institute of Mental Measurements.
Cobb, S. (1976). Social support as a moderator of life stress. *Psychosomatic Medicine, 38*, 300–314.
Cohen, J. A. (2001). Pharmacologic treatment of traumatized children. *Trauma, Violence, & Abuse, 2*, 155–171.
Cohen, J. A., Berlinger, L., & Mannarino, A. P. (2000). Treating traumatized children: A research review and synthesis. *Trauma, Violence, and Abuse, 1*, 29–46.
Cohen, J. A., Mannarino, A. P., Berlinger, L., & Deblinger, E. (2000). Trauma-focused cognitive behavioral therapy for children and adolescents: An empirical update. *Journal of Interpersonal Violence, 15*, 1202–1223.

Cohen, S., Gottlieb, B. H., & Underwood, L. G. (2001). Social relationships and health: Challenges for measurement and intervention. *Advances in Mind-Body Medicine, 17*, 129–142.

Cohen, S., & Wills, T. A. (1985). Stress, social support, and the buffering hypothesis. *Psychological Bulletin, 98*, 310–357.

Cole, S. F., O'Brien, J. G., Gadd, M. G., Ristuccia, J., Wallace, D. L., & Gregory, M. (2005). *Helping traumatized children learn: Supportive school environments for children traumatized by family violence.* Boston: Advocates for Children. Retrieved July 2, 2007, from http://www.massadvocates.org/uploads/images/203/Help_Tram_Child-Med.pdf

Collaborative for Academic, Social, and Emotional Learning. (2007). *Background of social and emotional learning (SEL).* Retrieved June 18, 2008, from http://www.casel.org/downloads/SEL&CASELbackground.pdf

Conduct Problems Prevention Research Group. (1999). Initial impact of the Fast Track Prevention Trial for Conduct Problems: II. Classroom effects. *Journal of Consulting and Clinical Psychology, 67*, 648–657.

Conlon, L., Fahy, T. J., & Conroy, R. (1999). PTSD in ambulant RTA victims: A randomized controlled trial of debriefing. *Journal of Psychosomatic Research, 46*, 37–44.

Cook-Cottone, C. (2004). Childhood posttraumatic stress disorder: Diagnosis, treatment, and school reintegration. *School Psychology Review, 33*, 127–139.

Cornell, D., Dorman, S., Hurley, G., Kanan, L., Sharkey, J., Sievering, K., et al. (2005). *Essential core knowledge regarding threat assessment and threat management in the schools.* Bethesda, MD: National Association of School Psychologists. Retrieved December 4, 2008, from http://www.nasponline.org/prepare/crisispresentations.aspx

Cornell, D. G., & Sheras, P. L. (1998). Common errors in school crisis response: Learning from our mistakes. *Psychology in the Schools, 35*, 297–307.

Cornell, D., Sheras, P. L., Kaplan, S., McConville, D., Douglass, J., Elkon, A., et al. (2004). Guidelines for student threat assessment: Field-test findings. *School Psychology Review, 33*, 527–546.

Cotton, K. (2001). *New small learning communities: Findings from recent literature.* Portland, OR: Northwest Regional Educational Laboratory.

Creamer, T. L., & Liddle, B. J. (2005). Secondary traumatic stress among disaster mental health workers responding to the September 11 attacks. *Journal of Traumatic Stress, 18*, 89–96.

Croft, I. A. (2005). Effectiveness of school-based crisis intervention: Research and practice (Doctoral dissertation, University of Maryland, 2005). *Dissertation Abstracts International, 66*(12), 4296.

Deblinger, E., Lippmann, J., & Steer, R. (1996). Sexually abused children suffering posttraumatic stress symptoms: Initial treatment outcome findings. *Child Maltreatment, 1*, 310–321.

Deblinger, E., Stauffer, L. B., & Steer, R. A. (2001). Comparative efficacies of supportive and cognitive behavioral group therapies for young children who have been sexually abused and their nonoffending mothers. *Child Maltreatment, 6*, 332–343.

Demaray, M. K., & Malecki, C. K. (2002). Critical levels of perceived social support associated with student adjustment. *School Psychology Quarterly, 17*, 213–241.

Demaray, M. K., & Malecki, C. K. (2003). Importance ratings of socially supportive behaviors by children and adolescents. *School Psychology Review, 32*, 108–131.

Demaray, M. K., & Malecki, C. K. (2006). A review of the use of social support in anti-bullying programs. *Journal of School Violence, 5*, 51–70.

Demaray, M. K., Malecki, C. K., Davidson, L. M., Hodgson, K. K., & Rebus, P. J. (2005). The relationship between social support and student adjustment: A longitudinal analysis. *Psychology in the Schools, 42*, 691–706.

Demaree, M. A. (1994, May). *Responding to violence in their lives: Creating nurturing environments for children with post-traumatic stress disorder.* Newton, MA: Education Development Center.

Dempsey, M., Overstreet, S., & Moely, B. (2000). "Approach" and "avoidance" coping and PTSD symptoms in inner-city youth. *Current Psychology: Developmental, Learning, Personality, Social, 19*, 28–45.

Denson, T. F., Marshall, G. N., Schell, T. L., & Jaycox, L. H. (2007). Predictors of posttraumatic distress 1 year after exposure to community violence: The importance of acute symptom severity. *Journal of Consulting and Clinical Psychology, 75*, 683–692.

Devilly, G. J., & Annab, R. (2008). A randomized controlled trial of group debriefing. *Journal of Behavior Therapy and Experimental Psychiatry, 39*, 42–56.

Devilly, G. J., & Varker, T. (2008). The effect of stressor severity on outcome following group debriefing. *Behavior Research and Therapy, 46*, 130–136.

Devilly, G. J., Varker, T., Hansen, K., & Gist, R. (2007). An analogue study of the effects of psychological debriefing on eyewitness memory. *Behavior Research and Therapy, 45*, 1245–1254.

DeVoe, J. F., Peter, K., Noonan, M., Snyder, T. D., & Baum, K. (2005). *Indicators of school crime and safety: 2005* (NCES 2006-001/NCJ 210697). Washington, DC: U.S. Government Printing Office.

de Wilde, E. J., & Kienhorst, C. W. M. (1998). Life events and adolescent suicidal behavior. In T. W. Miller (Ed.), *Children of trauma: Stressful life events and their effects on children and adolescents* (pp. 161–178). Madison, CT: International Universities Press.

Dinkes, R., Cataldi, E. F., & Lin-Kelly, W. (2007). *Indicators of school crime and safety: 2007* (NCES 2008-021/NCJ 219553). Washington, DC: National Center for Education Statistics, Institute of Education Sciences, U.S. Department of Education and Bureau of Justice. Retrieved July 10, 2008, from http://www.ojp.usdoj.gov/bjs/abstract/iscs07.htm

Doll, B., & Lyon, M. A. (1998). Risk and resilience: Implications for the delivery of educational and mental health services in schools. *School Psychology Review, 27*, 348–363.

Doll, B., & Osborn, A. (2007). Review of the Children's PTSD Inventory: A structured interview for diagnosing posttraumatic stress disorder. In K. F. Geisinger, R. A. Spies, J. F. Carlson, & B. S. Plake (Eds.), *The fifteenth mental measurements yearbook.* Lincoln, NE: Buros Institute of Mental Measurements.

Donnelly, C. L. (2003). Pharmacologic treatment approaches for children and adolescents with posttraumatic stress disorder. *Child and Adolescent Psychiatry in the Clinics of North America, 12*, 251–259.

Donnelly, C. L., Amaya-Jackson, L., & March, J. S. (1999). Psychopharmacology of pediatric posttraumatic stress disorder. *Journal of Child and Adolescent Psychopharmacology, 9*, 203–220.

Dulmus, C. N. (2003). Approaches to preventing the psychological impact of community violence exposure on children. *Crisis Intervention, 6*, 185–201.

Duncan, R. D. (2004). The impact of family relationships on school bullies and victims. In D. L. Espelage & S. M. Swearer (Eds.), *Bullying in American schools: A social-ecological perspective on prevention and intervention* (pp. 227–244). Mahwah, NJ: Erlbaum.

Dyregrov, A., & Yule, W. (2006). A review of PTSD in children. *Child and Adolescent Mental Health, 11*, 176–184.

Dwyer, K., & Jimerson, S. R. (2002). Enabling prevention through planning. In S. E. Brock, P. J. Lazarus, & S. R. Jimerson (Eds.), *Best practices in school crisis prevention and intervention* (pp. 23–46). Bethesda, MD: National Association of School Psychologists.

Ebata, A., & Moos, R. (1994). Personal, situational, and contextual correlates of coping in adolescence. *Journal of Research on Adolescence, 4*, 99–125.

Ehlers, A., & Clark, D. M. (2000). A cognitive model of posttraumatic stress disorder. *Behaviour Research and Therapy, 38*, 319–345.

Ehlers, A., Mayou, R. A., & Bryant, B. (1998). Psychological predictors of chronic posttraumatic stress disorder after motor vehicle accidents. *Journal of Abnormal Psychology, 107*, 508–519.

Ehlers, A., & Clark, D. M. (2000). A cognitive model of posttraumatic stress disorder. *Behaviour Research and Therapy, 38*, 319–345.

Eksi, A., Braun, K. L., Ertem-Vehid, H., Peykerli, G., Saydam, R., Toparlak, D., et al. (2007). Risk factors for the development of PTSD and depression among child and adolescent victims following a 7.4 magnitude earthquake. *International Journal of Psychiatry in Clinical Practice, 11*, 190–199.

Elias, M. J., Zins, J. E., Weissberg, R. P., Frey, K. S., Greenberg, M. T., Haynes, N. M., et al. (1997). *Promoting social and emotional learning: Guidelines for educators.* Alexandria, VA: Association for Supervision and Curriculum Development.

Elkit, A. (2002). Victimization and PTSD in a Danish national youth probability sample. *Journal of the American Academy of Child and Adolescent Psychiatry, 41*, 174–181.

Elliott, D. S., Grady, J. M., Heys, L., Bell, H., Woodward, B., & Williams, S. (2002). *Safe communities–safe schools guide to effective program selection: A tool for community violence prevention efforts.* Boulder, CO: University of Colorado, Center for the Study and Prevention of Violence.

Ellis, B. H., Lhewa, D., Charney, M., & Cabral, H. (2006). Brief report. Screening for PTSD among Somali adolescent refugees: Psychometric properties of the UCLA PTSD Index. *Journal of Traumatic Stress,19*, 547–551.

Environmental Protection Agency. (2005). *Emergency response tabletop exercises.* Retrieved May 1, 2008, from http://www.epa.gov/ogwdw000/watersecurity/tools/trainingcd/printable/introduction-p.html

Eppler, C. (2008). Exploring themes of resiliency in children after the death of a parent. *Professional School Counseling, 11*, 189–196.

Erikson, K. T. (1976). *Everything in its path.* New York: Simon & Schuster.

Evans, W. P., Marte, R. M., Betts, S., & Silliman, B. (2001). Adolescent suicide risk and peer-related violent behaviors and victimization. *Journal of Interpersonal Violence, 16*, 1330–1348.

Everall, R. D., & Paulson, B. L. (2004). Burnout and secondary traumatic stress: Impact on ethical behavior. *Canadian Journal of Counseling, 38*, 25–35.

Everly, G. S. (1999). Toward a model of psychological triage: Who will most need assistance? *International Journal of Emergency Mental Health, 3*, 151–154.

Everly, G. S. (2003). Early psychological intervention: A word of caution. *International Journal of Emergency Mental Health, 5*, 179–184.

Everly, G. S., Lating, J. M., & Mitchell, J. T. (2005). Innovations in group crisis intervention. In A. R. Roberts (Ed.), *Crisis intervention handbook: Assessment, treatment, & research* (pp. 221–245). New York: Oxford University Press.

Family Education Rights and Privacy Act of 1974 (FERPA). 20 U.S.C. § 1232g; 34 CFR Part 99.

Federal Emergency Management Agency (FEMA). (2003, March). *Emergency management institute independent study: Exercise design.* Washington, DC: Author.

Federal Emergency Management Agency (FEMA). (2007a). *IS-120.A: An introduction to exercises.* Retrieved April 3, 2008, from http://training.fema.gov/EMIWeb/IS/is120.asp

Federal Emergency Management Agency (FEMA). (2007b). *IS-139: Exercise design.* Retrieved April 3, 2008, from http://www.training.fema.gov/emiweb/IS/is139.asp

Feeny, N. C., Foa, E. B., Treadwell, K. R. H., & March, J. (2004). Posttraumatic stress disorder in youth: A critical review of the cognitive and behavioral treatment outcome literature. *Professional Psychology: Research and Practice, 35*, 466–476.

Fein, R. A., Vossekuil, F., Pollack, W. S., Borum, R., Modzeleski, W., & Reddy, M. (2002). *Threat assessment in schools: A guide to managing threatening situations and to creating safe school climates.* Washington, DC: U.S. Secret Service and U.S. Department of Education.

Figley, C. R. (1995). *Compassion fatigue: Coping with secondary traumatic stress disorder.* New York: Brunner/Mazel.

Figley, C. R. (1999). Compassion fatigue: Towards a new understanding of the costs of caring. In B. H. Stamm (Ed.), *Secondary traumatic stress: Self-care issues for clinicians, researchers, & educators* (2nd ed., pp. 3–28). Lutherville, MD: Sidran Press.

Figley, C. R. (2002). *Treating compassion fatigue.* New York: Brunner-Routledge.

Fleming, K. (2006). Resiliency in severely abused children. *Dissertation abstracts international section A: Humanities and social sciences, 66*(12-A), 4307.

Foa, E. B. (2002). *The Child PTSD Symptom Scale (CPSS).* (Available from the author, Center for the Treatment and Study of Anxiety, University of Pennsylvania School of Medicine, Department of Psychiatry, 3535 Market Street, Sixth Floor, Philadelphia, PA 19104)

Foa, E. B., Dancu, C. V., Hembree, E. A., Jaycox, L. H., Meadows, E. A., & Street, G. P. (1999). A comparison of exposure therapy, stress inoculation training, and their combination for reducing posttraumatic stress disorder in female assault victims. *Journal of Consulting and Clinical Psychology, 67*, 194–200.

Foa, E. B., Johnson, K. M., Feeny, N. C., & Treadwell, K. R. H. (2001). The Child PTSD Symptoms Scale: A preliminary examination of its psychometric properties. *Journal of Clinical Child Psychology, 30*, 376–384.

Frazier, P., Steward, J., & Mortensen, J. (2004). Perceived control and adjustment to trauma: A comparison across events. *Journal of Social and Clinical Psychology, 23*, 303–324.

Frazier, P., Tashiro, T., Berman, M., Steger, M., & Long, J. (2004). Correlates of levels and patterns of positive life changes following sexual assault. *Journal of Consulting and Clinical Psychology, 72*, 19–30.

Frey, C. U., & Rothlisberger, C. (1996). Social support in healthy adolescents. *Journal of Youth and Adolescence, 25*, 17–31.

Friedman, M. J. (1988). Toward rational pharmacotherapy for posttraumatic stress disorder: An interim report. *American Journal of Psychiatry, 145*, 281–285.

Frommberger, U. H., Stieglitz, R., Nyberg, E., Schlickewei, W., Kuner, E., & Gerger, M. (1998). Prediction of posttraumatic stress disorder by immediate reactions to trauma: A prospective study in road traffic accident victims. *European Archives of Psychiatry & Clinical Neuroscience, 248*, 316–321.

Froschl, M. J., Sprung, B., & Mullin-Rindler, N. (1998). *Quit it! A teacher's guide on teasing and bullying for use with students in grades K–3*. New York: Educational Equity Concepts.

Furlong, M. J., Chung, A., Bates, M., & Morrison, R. L. (1995). Who are the victims of school violence? A comparison of student non-victims and multi-victims. *Education and Treatment of Children, 18*, 282–298.

Furman, W., & Buhrmester, D. (1992). Age and sex differences in perceptions of networks of personal relationships. *Child Development, 63*, 103–115.

Galea, S., Ahern J., Resnick, H., Kilpatrick, D., Bucuvalas, M., Gold, J., et al. (2002). Psychological sequelae of the September 11 terrorist attacks in New York City. *New England Journal of Medicine, 346*, 982–987.

Galea, S., Brewin, C. R., Gruber, M., Jones, R. T., King, D. W., King, L. A., et al. (2007). Exposure to hurricane-related stressors and mental illness after Hurricane Katrina. *Archives of General Psychiatry, 64*, 1427–1434.

Galea, S., Vlahov, D., Resnick, H., Ahern, J., Susser, E., Gold, J., et al. (2003). Trends of probable post-traumatic stress disorder in New York City after the September 11 terrorist attacks. *American Journal of Epidemiology, 158*, 514–524.

Gentry, J. E., Baranowsky, A. B., & Dunning, K. (2002). ARP: The accelerated recovery program (ARP) for compassion fatigue. In C. R. Figley (Ed.), *Treating compassion fatigue* (pp. 123–137). New York: Brunner-Routledge.

Giannopoulou, I., Strouthos, M., Smith, P., Dikaiakou, A., Galanopoulou, V., & Yule, W. (2006). Post-traumatic stress reactions of children and adolescents exposed to the Athens 1999 earthquake. *European Psychiatry, 21*, 160–166.

Gil, S. (2005). Coping style in predicting posttraumatic stress disorder among Israeli students. *Anxiety, Stress, and Coping, 18*, 351–359.

Gil, S., & Caspi, Y. (2006). Personality traits, coping style, and perceived threat as predictors of posttraumatic stress disorder after exposure to a terrorist attack: A prospective study. *Psychosomatic Medicine, 68*, 904–909.

Gil-Rivas, V., Holman, E. A., & Silver, R. C. (2004). Adolescent vulnerability following the September 11th terrorist attacks: A study of parents and their children. *Applied Developmental Science, 8*, 130–142.

Gist, R., & Lubin, B. (Eds.) (1999). *Response to disaster: Psychosocial, community, and ecological approaches*. Philadelphia, PA: Brunner/Mazel.

Goals 2000 Educate America Act, Pub. L. 103-227, §101–102, 20 USC 58115812 (1994). Retrieved September 11, 2008, from http://www.ed.gov/legislation/GOALS2000/TheAct/index.html

Gordon, R. S. (1983). An operational classification of disease prevention. *U.S. Department of Health and Human Services Public Health Report 1983, 98*, 107–109.

Gottfredson, D. (1997). School-based crime prevention. In L. W. Sherman, D. Gottfredson, D. MacKenzie, J. Eck, P. Reuter, & S. Bushway (Eds.), *Preventing crime: What works, what doesn't, what's promising: A report to the United States Congress.* Washington, DC: Department of Justice, Office of Justice Programs.

Gracie, A., Freeman, D., Green, S., Garety, P. A., Kuipers, E., Hardy, A., et al. (2007). The association between traumatic experience, paranoia and hallucinations: A test of the predictions of psychological models. *Acta Psychiatrica Scandinavica, 116*, 280–289.

Graham, J., Shirm, S., Liggin, R., Aitken, M. E., & Dick, R. (2006). Mass-casualty events at schools: A national preparedness survey. *Pediatrics. 117*, 8–15.

Green, B. L. (1994). Psychosocial research in traumatic stress: An update. *Journal of Traumatic Stress, 7*, 341–361.

Green, B. L., Korol, M., Grace, M. C., Vary, M. G., Leonard, A. C., Gleser, G. C., et al. (1991). Children and disaster: Age, gender, and parental effects on PTSD symptoms. *Journal of the American Academy of Child and Adolescent Psychiatry, 30*, 945–951.

Green, W. G., III (2002, August). *The incident command system for public health disaster responders.* Paper presented at the meeting of the Public Health Task Group, Richmond Metropolitan Medical Response System, Richmond, VA.

Greenberg, M. T., & Kusché, C. A. (2006). Building social and emotional competence: The PATHS curriculum. In S. R. Jimerson & M. J. Furlong (Eds.), *Handbook of school violence and school safety: From research to practice* (pp. 395–412). Mahwah, NJ: Erlbaum.

Greenwald, R., & Rubin, A. (1999). Brief assessment of children's post-traumatic symptoms: Development and preliminary validation of parent and child scales. *Research on Social Work Practice, 9*, 61–75.

Grieger, T. A., Fullerton, C. S., & Ursano, R. J. (2003). Posttraumatic stress disorder, alcohol use, and perceived safety after the terrorist attack on the Pentagon. *Psychiatric Services, 54*, 1380–1382.

Groome, D., & Soureti, A. (2004). Post-traumatic stress disorder and anxiety symptoms in children exposed to the 1999 Greek earthquake. *British Journal of Psychology, 95*, 387–397.

Grosse, S. J. (2001, September). Children and post traumatic stress disorder: What classroom teachers should know. ERIC Clearinghouse on Teaching and Teacher Education (Report No. ED460122). Retrieved May 30, 2007, from http://www.eric.ed.gov/ERICDocs/data/ericdocs2sql/content_storage_01/0000019b/80/19/9d/e5.pdf

Guba, E. G., & Lincoln, Y. S. (1989). *Fourth generation evaluation.* Newbury Park, CA: SAGE.

Gurwitch, R. H., Sitterle, K. A., Yound, B. H., & Pfefferbaum, B. (2002). The aftermath of terrorism. In A. M. La Greca, W. K. Silverman, E. M. Vernberg, & M. C. Roberts (Eds.), *Helping children cope with disasters and terrorism* (pp. 327–357). Washington, DC: American Psychological Association.

Haden, S. C., Scarpa, A., Jones, R. T., & Ollendick, T. H. (2007). Posttraumatic stress disorder symptoms and injury: The moderating role of perceived social support and coping for young adults. *Personality and Individual Differences, 42*, 1187–1198.

Halikias, W. (2005). Assessing youth violence and threats of violence in schools: School-based risk assessments. In S. H. McConaughy (Ed.), *Clinical interviews for children and adolescents: Assessment to intervention* (pp. 200–223). New York: Guilford Press.

Harrison, A. O., Wilson, M. N., Pine, C. J., Chan, S. Q., & Briel, R. (1990). Family ecologies of ethnic minority children. *Child Development, 61*, 347–367.

Harvey, A. G., & Bryant, R. A. (1998). The relationship between acute stress disorder and posttraumatic stress disorder: A prospective evaluation of motor vehicle accident survivors. *Journal of Consulting and Clinical Psychology, 66*, 507–512.

Haskett, M. A., Scott, S. S., Nears, K., & Grimmett, M. A. (2008). Lessons from Katrina: Disaster mental health service in the Gulf Coast region. *Professional Psychology: Research and Practice, 39*, 93–99.

Hawkins, N. A., McIntosh, D. N., Silver, R. C., & Holman, E. A. (2004). Early responses to school violence: A qualitative analysis of students' and parents' immediate reactions to the shootings at Columbine High School. *Journal of Emotional Abuse, 4*, 197–223.

Hazler, R. J., & Carney, J. V. (2000). When victims turn aggressors: Factors in the development of deadly school violence. *Professional School Counseling, 4*, 105–112.

Heath, M. A., & Sheen, D. (2005). *School-based crisis intervention: Preparing all personnel to assist.* New York: Guilford Press.

Henggeler, S. W., Schoenwald, S. K., Rowland, M. D., & Cunningham, P. B. (2002). *Serious emotional disturbance in children and adolescents: Multisystemic therapy.* New York: Guilford Press.

Herrick, C. A., & Brown, H. N. (1998). Underutilization of mental health services by Asian-Americans residing in the United States. *Issues in Mental Health Nursing, 19*, 225–240.

Hester, J. P. (2003). *Public school safety: A handbook, with a resource guide.* Jefferson, NC: McFarland & Company.

Hilarski, C. (2004). The relationship between perceived secondary trauma and adolescent comorbid posttraumatic stress and alcohol abuse: A review. *Stress, Trauma, and Crisis, 7*, 119–132.

Hill, M. S., & Hill, F. W. (1994). *Creating safe schools: What principals can do.* Thousand Oaks, CA: Corwin Press.

Hobbs, M., Mayou, R., Harrison, B., & Warlock, P. (1996). Randomised controlled trial of psychological debriefing for victims of road traffic accidents. *British Medical Journal, 313*, 1438–1439.

Hobfoll, W. E., Watson, P., Bell, C. C., Bryant, R. A., Brymer, M. J., Friedman, M. J., et al. (2007). Five essential elements of immediate and mid-term mass trauma intervention: Empirical evidence. *Psychiatry, 70*, 283–315.

Horner, R. H., Sugai, G., Todd, A. W., & Lewis-Palmer, T. (2005). School-wide positive behavior support. In L. M. Bambara & L. Kern (Eds.), *Individualized supports for students with problem behaviors: Designing positive behavior support plans* (pp. 359–390). New York: Guilford Press.

Horowitz, K., McKay, M., & Marshall, R. (2005). Community violence and urban families: Experiences, effects, and directions for intervention. *American Journal of Orthopsychiatry, 75*, 356–368.

House, J. S. (1981). *Work stress and social support.* Reading, MA: Addison-Wesley.

Hoven, C. W., Duarte, C. S., Wu, P., Erickson, E. A., Musa, G. J., & Mandell, D. J. (2004). Exposure to trauma and separation anxiety in children after the WTC attack. *Applied Developmental Science, 8*, 172–183.

Howard, J. M., & Goelitz, A. (2004). Psychoeducation as a response to community disaster. *Brief Treatment and Crisis Intervention, 4*, 1–10.

Huebner, E. S., Gilligan, T. D., & Cobb, H. (2002). Best practices in preventing and managing stress and burnout. In A. Thomas & J. Grimes (Eds.), *Best practices in school psychology IV* (pp. 173–182). Bethesda, MD: National Association of School Psychologists.

Imanaka, A., Morinobu, S., Toki, S., & Yamawaki, S. (2006). Importance of early environment in the development of post-traumatic stress disorder-like behaviors. *Behavioural Brain Research, 173*, 129–137.

Imich, A. J. (1994). Exclusions from school: Current trends and issues. *Educational Research, 36*, 3–11.

Improving America's Schools Act of 1994, H.R. 6. Retrieved September 11, 2008, from http://www.ed.gov/legislation/ESEA/toc.html

Jacob, S., & Feinberg, T. (2002). Legal and ethical issues in crisis prevention and response in schools. In S. E. Brock, P. J. Lazarus, & S. R. Jimerson (Eds.), *Best practices in school crisis prevention and intervention* (pp. 709–732). Bethesda, MD: National Association of School Psychologists.

Jacobs, J., Horne-Moyer, H. L., & Jones, R. (2004). The effectiveness of critical incident stress debriefing with primary and secondary trauma victims. *International Journal of Emergency Mental Health, 6*, 5–14.

Jeney-Gammon, P., Daugherty, T. K., Finch, A. J., Belter, R. W., & Foster, K. Y. (1993). Children's coping styles and report of depressive symptoms following a natural disaster. *Journal of Genetic Psychology, 154*, 259–267.

Jimerson, S. R., & Brock, S. E. (2004). Threat assessment, school crisis preparation, and crisis response. In M. J. Furlong, M. P. Bates, D. C. Smith, & P. M. Kingery (Eds.), *Appraisal and prediction of school violence: Methods, issues and contents* (pp. 63–82). New York: Nova Science.

Jimerson, S. R., Brock, S. E., & Cowan, K. (2003). *Helping children after a wildfire: Tips for parents and teachers.* Retrieved September 7, 2008, from http://www.nasponline.org/resources/crisis_safety/wildfire_teachers.pdf

Jimerson, S. R., Brock, S. E., & Cowan, K. (2007). *Ayudando A Los Niños Después De Los Incendios Forestales: Consejos Para Los Padres y Maestros* (L. Navarro, E. Terán, & M. Muñoz, Trans.). California State University, Sacramento, CA.

Jimerson, S., Brock, S. E., Greif, J., & Cowan, K. (2004). Threat assessment at school: A primer for educators. In A. S. Canter, S. A. Carroll, L. Paige, & I. Romero (Eds.), *Helping children at home and school: Handouts from your school psychologist* (pp. S9, 49–53). Bethesda, MD: National Association of School Psychologists.

Jimerson, S. R., & Huff, L. (2002). Responding to a sudden, unexpected death at school: Chance favors the prepared professional. In S. E. Brock, P. J. Lazarus, & S. R. Jimerson (Eds.), *Best practices in school crisis prevention and intervention* (pp. 451–488). Bethesda, MD: National Association of School Psychologists.

Johns, B. H., & Keenan, J. P. (1997). *Techniques for managing a safe school.* Denver, CO: Love Publishing.

Johnson, K. (1993). *School crisis management: A hands-on guide to training crisis management teams.* Alameda, CA: Hunter House.

Johnson, K. (2000). *School crisis management: A hands-on guide to training crisis management teams* (2nd ed.). Alameda, CA: Hunter House.

Jones, J. M. (2007). Exposure to chronic community violence: Resilience in African American children. *Journal of Black Psychology, 33,* 125–149.

Jones, R. T., Fletcher, K., & Ribbe, D. R. (2002). *Child's Reaction to Traumatic Events Scale-Revised (CRTES-R): A self-report traumatic stress measure.* (Available from the author, Department of Psychology, Stress and Coping Lab, 4102 Derring Hall, Virginia Tech University, Blacksburg, VA 24060)

Joseph, S. (1999). Social support and mental health following trauma. In W. Yule (Ed.), *Post-traumatic stress disorders, concepts and therapy* (pp. 71–91). New York: Wiley.

Joshi, P. T., & Lewin, S. M. (2004). Disaster, terrorism and children. *Psychiatric Annals, 34,* 710–716.

Kano, M., & Bourke, L. B. (2007). Experiences with and preparedness for emergencies and disasters among public schools in California. *NASSP Bulletin, 91*(3), 201–218.

Kartez, J. D., & Kelley, W. J. (1988). Research-based disaster planning: Conditions for implementation. In L. K. Comfort (Ed.), *Managing disasters: Strategies and policy perspectives* (pp. 126–146). Durham, NC: Duke University Press.

Kassai, S. C., & Motta, R. W. (2006). An investigation of potential Holocaust-related secondary traumatization in the third generation. *International Journal of Emergency Mental Health, 8,* 35–48.

Kaštelan, A., Frančišković, T., Moro, L., Rončević-Gržeta, I., Grković, J., Jurcan, V., et al. (2007). Psychotic symptoms in combat-related post-traumatic stress disorder. *Military Medicine, 172,* 273–277.

Kataoka, S. H., Stein, B. D., Jaycox, L. H., Wong, M., Escudero, P., Tu, W., et al. (2003). A school-based mental health program for traumatized Latino immigrant children. *Journal of the American Academy of Child and Adolescent Psychiatry, 42,* 311–318.

Kazdin, A. E. (1987). Treatment of antisocial behavior in children: Current status and future directions. *Psychological Bulletin, 102,* 187–203.

Kazdin, A. E. (2003). Problem-solving skills training and parent management training for conduct disorder. In A. E. Kazdin & J. R. Weisz (Eds.), *Evidence-based psychotherapy for children and adolescents* (pp. 241–262). New York: Guilford Press.

Kazdin, A. E., Bass, D., Siegel, T., & Thomas, C. (1989). Cognitive-behavioral therapy and relationship therapy in the treatment of children referred for antisocial behavior. *Journal of Consulting and Clinical Psychology, 57,* 522–535.

Kazdin, A. E., Esveldt-Dawson, K., French, N. H., & Unis, A. S. (1987). Problem-solving skills training and relationship therapy in the treatment of antisocial child behavior. *Journal of Consulting and Clinical Psychology, 55,* 76–85.

Kazdin, A. E., & Weisz, J. R. (Eds.). (2003). *Evidence-based psychotherapies for children and adolescents.* New York: Guilford Press.

Keppel-Benson, J. M., Ollendick, T. H., & Benson, M. J. (2002). Post-traumatic stress in children following motor vehicle accidents. *Journal of Child Psychology and Psychiatry and Allied Disciplines, 43*, 203–212.

Kilic, Z. K., Özgüven, H. D, & Sayil, I. (2003). The psychological effects of parental mental health on children experiencing disaster: The experience of Bolu earthquake in Turkey. *Family Process, 42*, 485–495.

Kim, H. K., & McKenry, P. (1998). Social networks and support: A comparison of African Americans, Asian Americans, Caucasians, and Hispanics. *Journal of Comparative Family Studies, 29*, 313–334.

King, D. A., King, L. A., Foy, B. W., & Gudanowski, D. M. (1996). Prewar factors in combat-related posttraumatic stress disorder: Structural equation modeling with a national sample of female and male Vietnam veterans. *Journal of Consulting and Clinical Psychology, 64*, 520–531.

King, L. A., King, D. W., Fairbank, J. A., Keane, T. M., & Adams, G. A. (1998). Resilience-recovery factors in post-traumatic stress disorder among female and male Vietnam veterans: Hardiness, postwar social support, and additional stressful life events. *Journal of Personality and Social Psychology, 74*, 420–434.

King, N. J., Tongue, B. J., Mullen, P., Myerson, N., Heyne, D., Rollings, S., et al. (2000). Treating sexually abused children with posttraumatic stress symptoms: A randomized clinical trial. *Journal of the American Academy of Child and Adolescent Psychiatry, 39*, 1347–1355.

Kinzie, J. D., Sack, W. H., Angell, R. H., Manson, S., & Rath, B. (1986). The psychiatric effects of massive trauma on Cambodian children: I. The children. *Journal of the American Academy of Child Psychiatry, 25*, 370–376.

Kline, M., Schonfeld, D., & Lichtenstein, R. (1995). Benefits and challenges of school-based crisis response teams. *Journal of School Health, 65*, 245–249.

Klingman, A. (1985). Free writing: Evaluation of a preventive program with elementary school children. *Journal of School Psychology, 23*, 167–175.

Klingman, A. (1986). Emotional first aid during the impact phase of a mass disaster. *Emotional First Aid, 3*, 51–57.

Klingman, A. (1987). A school-based emergency crisis intervention in a mass school disaster. *Professional Psychology: Research and Practice, 18*, 205–216.

Klingman, A. (1989). School-based emergency intervention following an adolescent's suicide. *Death Studies, 13*, 263–274.

Klingman, A. (1996). School-based intervention in disaster and trauma. In M. C. Roberts (Ed.), *Model programs in child and family mental health* (pp. 149–172). Mahwah, NJ: Erlbaum.

Klingman, A. (2001). Stress responses and adaptation of Israeli school-age children evacuated from homes during massive missile attacks. *Anxiety, Stress, and Coping, 14*, 149–172.

Klingman, A., & Ben Eli, Z. (1981). A school community in disaster: Primary and secondary prevention in situational crisis. *Professional Psychology: Research and Practice, 12*, 523–533.

Klingman, A., & Cohen, E. (2004). *School-based multisystemic interventions for mass trauma.* New York: Kluwer Academic/Plenum.

Kneisel, P. J., & Richards, G. P. (1988). Crisis intervention after the suicide of a teacher. *Professional Psychology: Research and Practice, 19*, 165–169.

Knox, K. S., & Roberts, A. R (2005). Crisis intervention and crisis team models in schools, *Children and Schools, 27,* 93–100.

Kolaitis, G., Kotsopoulos, J., Tsiantis, J., Haritaki, S., Rigizou, R., Zacharaki, L., et al. (2003). Posttraumatic stress reactions among children following the Athens earthquake of September 1999. *European Child & Adolescent Psychiatry, 12,* 273–280.

Koopman, C. C., Catherine, S., & David, A. (1994). Predictors of posttraumatic stress symptoms among survivors of the Oakland/Berkeley, Calif., firestorm. *American Journal of Psychiatry, 151,* 888–894.

Kratochwill, T. R., & McGivern, J. E. (1996). Clinical diagnosis, behavioral assessment, and functional analysis: Examining the connection between assessment and intervention. *School Psychology Review, 25,* 342–355.

Krause, E. D., Kaltman, S., Goodman, L. A., & Dutton, M. A. (2008). Avoidant coping and PTSD symptoms related to domestic violence exposure: A longitudinal study. *Journal of Traumatic Stress, 21,* 83–90.

Krug, E. G., Dahlberg, L. L., Mercy, J. A., Zwi, A. B., & Lozano, R. (Eds.). (2002). *World report on violence and health.* Geneva: World Health Organization.

Kutz, I., & Dekel, R. (2006). Follow-up of victims of one terrorist attack in Israel: ASD, PTSD and the perceived threat of Iraqi missile attacks. *Personality and Individual Differences, 40,* 1579–1589.

La Greca, A. M., & Prinstein, M. J. (2002). Hurricanes and earthquakes. In A. M. La Greca, W. K. Silverman, E. M. Vernberg, & M. C. Roberts (Eds.), *Helping children cope with disasters and terrorism* (pp. 107–138). Washington, DC: American Psychological Association.

Landolt, M., Vollrath, M., Timm, K., Gnehm, H. E., & Sennhauser, F. H. (2005). Predicting posttraumatic stress symptoms in children after road traffic accidents. *Journal of the American Academy of Child and Adolescent Psychiatry, 44,* 1276–1283.

Laubmeier, K. K., & Sakowski, S. G. (2004). The role of objective versus perceived life threat in the psychological adjustment to cancer. *Psychology and Health, 19,* 425–437.

Lawyer, S. R., Resnick, H. S., Galea, S., Ahern, J., Kilpatrick, D. G., & Vlahov, D. (2006). Predictors of peritraumatic reactions and PTSD following the September 11th terrorist attacks. *Psychiatry, 69,* 130–141.

Lecic-Tosevski, D., Gavrlovic, J., Knezevic, G., & Priebe, S. (2003). Personality factors and posttraumatic stress: Associations in civilians one year after air attacks. *Journal of Personality Disorders, 17,* 537–549.

Leinhardt, M. C., & Willert, H. J. (2002, June). Involving stakeholders in resolving school violence. *NASSP Bulletin, 86,* 32–43.

Levitt, M. J., Guacci-Franco, N., & Levitt, J. L. (1993). Convoys of social support in childhood and early adolescence: Structure and function. *Developmental Psychology, 29,* 811–818.

Levitt, M. J., Levitt, J., Bustos, G. L., Crooks, N. A., Santos, J. D., Telan, P., et al. (2005). Patterns of social support in the middle childhood to early adolescent transition: Implications for adjustment. *Social Development, 14,* 398–420.

Levy, M. S. (2008). The impact of Katrina: Shedding light on things forgotten. *Professional Psychology: Research and Practice, 39,* 31–36.

Lewinsohn, P. M., Rohde, P., & Seeley, J. R. (1996). Adolescent suicidal ideation and attempts: Prevalence, risk factors, and clinical implications. *Clinical Psychology: Research and Practice, 3*, 25–46.

Lewis, S. J. (2003). Do one-shot interventions for PTSD work? A systematic research synthesis of psychological debriefings. *Aggression and Violent Behavior, 8*, 329–343.

Liang, B., & Bogat, G. A. (1994). Culture, control, and coping: New perspectives on social support. *American Journal of Community Psychology, 22*, 123–147.

Lieberman, R., Poland, S., & Cassel, R. (2008). Best practices in suicide intervention. In A. Thomas & J. Grimes (Eds.), *Best practices in school psychology V* (Vol. 4; pp. 1457–1472). Bethesda, MD: National Association of School Psychologists.

Lilienfeld, S. O., & Arkowitz, H. (2007). EMDR: Taking a closer look. *Scientific American Special Edition, 17*, 10–11.

Litz, B. T., Gray, M. J., Bryant, R. A., & Adler, A. (2002). Early intervention for trauma: Current status and future directions. *Clinical Psychology: Science and Practice, 9*, 112–134.

Lochman, J. E. (1992). Cognitive-behavioral intervention with aggressive boys: Three-year follow-up and preventive effects. *Journal of Consulting and Clinical Psychology, 60*, 426–432.

Lochman, J. E., Burch, P. R., Curry, J. F., & Lampron, L. B. (1984). Treatment and generalization effects of cognitive-behavioral and goal-setting interventions with aggressive boys. *Journal of Consulting and Clinical Psychology, 52*, 915–916.

Lochman, J. E., Curry, J. F., Dane, H., & Ellis, M. (2001). The anger coping program: An empirically-supported treatment for aggressive children. *Residential Treatment for Children and Youth, 18*, 63–73.

Lochman, J. E., Lampron, L. B., Burch, P. R., & Curry, J. F. (1985). Client characteristics associated with behavior change for treated and untreated aggressive boys. *Journal of Abnormal Child Psychology, 13*, 527–538.

Lockyer, B., & Eastin, D. (2000). *Crisis response box: A guide to help every school assemble the tools and resources needed for a critical incident response.* Sacramento, CA: California Department of Education.

Lonigan, C. J., Phillips, B. M., & Richey, J. A. (2003). Posttraumatic stress disorder in children: Diagnosis, assessment, and associated features. *Child & Adolescent Psychiatric Clinics of North America, 12*, 171–194.

Lonigan, C. J., Shannon, M. P., Finch, A. J., Daughtery, T. K., & Taylor, C. M. (1991). Children's reactions to a natural disaster. *Advanced Behavior & Research Therapy, 13*, 135–154.

Lord, J. H. (1990). *Death at school: A guide for teachers, school nurses, counselors, and administrators.* Dallas, TX: Mothers Against Drunk Driving.

Los Angeles Unified School District (1994, Spring). *A handbook for crisis intervention* (Rev. ed.). (Available from the Los Angeles Unified School District, Mental Health Services, 6520 Newcastle Ave., Reseda, CA 91335-6230)

Lukens, E. P., & McFarlane, W. R. (2004). Psychoeducation as evidence-based practice: Considerations for practice, research, and policy. *Brief Treatment and Crisis Intervention, 4*, 205–225.

Luthar, S. S. (1991). Vulnerability and resilience: A study of high-risk adolescents. *Child Development, 62*, 600–616.

Malecki, C. K., & Demaray, M. K. (2002). Measuring perceived social support: Development of the Child and Adolescent Social Support Scale. *Psychology in the Schools, 39,* 1–18.

Malecki, C. K., & Demaray, M. K. (2003). What type of support do they need? Investigating student adjustment as related to emotional, informational, appraisal, and instrumental support. *School Psychology Quarterly, 18,* 231–252.

March, J. S., Amaya-Jackson, L., Murray, M. C., & Schulte, A. (1998). Cognitive-behavioral psychotherapy for children and adolescents with PTSD after a single incident stressor. *Journal of the American Academy of Child and Adolescent Psychiatry, 37,* 585–593.

March, J. S., Amaya-Jackson, L., Terry, R., & Costanzo, P. (1997). Posttraumatic symptomatology in children and adolescents after an industrial fire. *Journal of the American Academy of Child and Adolescent Psychiatry, 36,* 1080–1088.

Marshall, R. D., Bryant, R. A., Amsel, L., Suh, E. J., Cook, J. M., & Neria, Y. (2007). The psychology of ongoing threat. *American Psychologist, 62,* 304–316.

Martin, A., & Marchand, A. (2003). Prediction of posttraumatic stress disorder: Peritraumatic dissociation, negative emotions and physical anxiety among French-speaking university students. *Journal of Trauma & Dissociation, 4,* 49–63.

Matsakis, A. (1994). *Post-traumatic stress disorder: A complete treatment guide.* Oakland, CA: New Harbinger.

May, P. A., Serna, P., Hurt, L., & DeBruyn, L. M. (2005). Outcome evaluation of a public health approach to suicide prevention in an American Indian tribal nation. *American Journal of Public Health, 95,* 1238–1244.

Mayou, R. A., Ehlers, A., & Hobbs, M. (2000). Psychological debriefing for road traffic accident victims: Three-year follow-up of a randomised controlled trial. *British Journal of Psychiatry, 176,* 589–593.

McFarlane, A. C. (1988). The longitudinal course of posttraumatic morbidity: The range of outcomes and their predictors. *The Journal of Nervous and Mental Disease, 176,* 30–39.

McFarlane, A. C., & Yehuda, R. (1996). Resilience, vulnerability, and the course of posttraumatic reactions. In B. A. van der Kolk, A. C. McFarlane, & L. Weisaeth (Eds.), *Traumatic stress: The effects of overwhelming experience on mind, body, and society* (pp. 155–181). New York: Guilford Press.

McIntyre, M., & Reid, B. (1989). *Obstacles to implementation of crisis intervention programs.* Unpublished manuscript, Chesterfield County Schools, Chesterfield, VA.

McNally, R. J., Bryant, R. A., & Ehlers, A. (2003). Does early psychological intervention promote recovery from posttraumatic stress? *Psychological Sciences in the Public Interest, 4,* 45–80.

Mellman, T. A., David, D., & Barza, L. (1999). Nefazodone treatment and dream reports in chronic PTSD. *Depression and Anxiety, 9,* 146–148.

Meraviglia, M. G., Becker, H., Rosenbluth, B., Sanchez, E., & Robertson, T. (2003). The Expect Respect Project: Creating a positive elementary school climate. *Journal of Interpersonal Violence, 18,* 1347–1360.

Merrell, K. W. (2001). *Helping students overcome depression and anxiety: A practical guide.* New York: Guilford Press.

Metzler, C. W., Biglan, A., Rusby, J. C., & Sprague, J. R. (2001). Evaluation of a comprehensive behavior management program to improve school-wide positive behavior support. *Education and Treatment of Children, 24*, 448–479.

Meyers, T. W., & Cornille, T. A. (2002). The trauma of working with traumatized children. In C. R. Figley (Ed.), *Treating compassion fatigue* (pp. 39–55). New York: Brunner-Routledge.

Miller, D. N., & McConaughy, S. H. (2005). Assessing risk for suicide. In S. H. McConaughy (Ed.), *Clinical interviews for children and adolescents: Assessment to intervention* (pp. 184–199). New York: Guilford Press.

Mitchell, J. T., & Everly, G. S. (1996). *Critical incident stress debriefing: An operations manual for the prevention of traumatic stress among emergency services and disaster workers* (2nd ed., Rev.). Ellicott City, MD: Cheveron.

Möhlen, H., Parzer, P., Resch, F., & Brunner, R. (2005). Psychosocial support for war-traumatized child and adolescent refugees: Evaluation of a short-term treatment program. *Australian and New Zealand Journal of Psychiatry, 39*, 81–87.

Molock, S. D., Puri, R., Matlin, S., & Barksdale, C. (2006). Relationship between religious coping and suicidal behavior among African American adolescents. *Journal of Black Psychology, 32*, 366–389.

Monahon, C. (1993). *Children and trauma: A guide for parents and professionals.* San Francisco: Jossey-Bass.

Montgomery County Public Schools. (n.d.). *Emergency preparedness.* Retrieved May 21, 2008, from http://www.montgomeryschoolsmd.org/info/emergency/preparedness/index.aspx.

Moos, R., & Billings, A. (1984). Conceptualizing and measuring coping resources and processes. In L. Goldberger & S. Breznitz (Eds.), *Handbook of stress: Theoretical and clinical aspects* (pp. 109–145). New York: Macmillan.

Morgan, K. E., & White, P. R. (2003). The functions of art-making in CISD with children and youth. *International Journal of Emergency Mental Health, 5*, 61–76.

Morrison, G. M., & D'Incau, B. (1997). The web of zero tolerance: Characteristics of students who are recommended for expulsion from school. *Education and Treatment of Children, 20*, 316–335.

Morrison, G. M., Laughlin, J., Miguel, M., San Smith, S., & Widaman, K. (1997). Sources of support for school-related issues: Choices of Hispanic adolescents varying in migrant status. *Journal of Youth and Adolescence, 26*, 233–252.

Motta, R., Chirichella, D., Maus, M., & Lombardo, M. (2004). Assessing secondary trauma. *Behavior Therapist, 27*, 54–57.

Nader, K., & Muni, P. (2002). Individual crisis intervention. In S. E. Brock & P. J. Lazarus (Eds.), *Best practices in school crisis prevention and intervention* (pp. 405–428). Bethesda, MD: National Association of School Psychologists.

Nader, K., & Pynoos, R. (1993). School disaster: Planning and initial interventions. *Journal of Social Behavior and Personality, 8*, 1–22.

Nader, K., Pynoos, R., Fairbanks, L., & Frederick, C. (1990). Children's post-traumatic stress disorder reactions one year after a sniper attack at their school. *American Journal of Psychiatry, 147*, 1526–1530.

National Adolescent Health Information Center. (2006). Fact sheet on suicide: Adolescents & young adults. San Francisco: Author, University of California, San Francisco.

National Association of School Psychologists. (2004). *Culturally competent crisis response: Information for school psychologists and crisis teams.* Bethesda, MD: Author.

National Center for Education Statistics (NCES). (2004). *Crime and safety in America's public schools: Selected findings from the school survey on crime and safety.* Retrieved August 1, 2008, from http://nces.ed.gov/pubs2004/2004370.pdf

National Consortium of School Violence Prevention Researchers and Practitioners (2006, November). *Fall 2006 school shootings position statement.* Retrieved May 7, 2007, from http://education.ucsb.edu/netshare/c4sbyd/csbyd-web/NCSVPRP/School%20Shootings%20Position%20Statement-Nov-2-FINAL.pdf

National Crime Victimization Survey (1992–2005). Retrieved June 20, 2008, from http://www.ojp.usdoj.gov/bjs/cvict.htm

National Education Association (NEA) Health Education Network. (2007a). *School crisis guide: Help and healing in a time of crisis.* Retrieved May 24, 2008, from http://www.neahin.org/crisisguide/before/districtelements.html

National Education Association (NEA) Health Education Network. (2007b). *School crisis guide. How local, state and federal laws may affect a school or district plan.* Retrieved May 24, 2008, from http://www.neahin.org/crisisguide/before/laws.html

National Institute of Mental Health (NIMH). (2001). *Mental health and mass violence: Evidence-based early psychological intervention for victims/survivors of mass violence. A workshop to reach consensus on best practices.* Washington, DC: U.S. Government Printing Office.

Nemeroff, C. B. (2004). Neurobiological consequences of childhood trauma. *Journal of Clinical Psychiatry, 65*(Suppl. 1), 18–28.

Nemeroff, C. B., Bremner, J. D., Foa, E. B., Mayberg, H. S., North, C. S., & Stein, M. B. (2006). Posttraumatic stress disorder: A state-of-the-science review. *Journal of Psychiatric Research, 40,* 1–21.

Newman, D. A., Horne, A., & Bartolomucci, C. L. (2000a). *Bully busters: A teacher's manual for helping bullies, victims, and bystanders, grades K–5.* Champaign, IL: Research Press.

Newman, D. A., Horne, A., & Bartolomucci, C. L. (2000b). *Bully busters: A teacher's manual for helping bullies, victims, and bystanders, grades 6–8.* Champaign, IL: Research Press.

Nickerson, A. B. (2006, August). *Crisis prevention and preparedness: The comprehensive school crisis team. Workshop evaluation/test summaries and workshop modification suggestions.* (Available from National Association of School Psychologists, 4340 East West Highway, Suite 402, Bethesda, MD 20814)

Nickerson, A. B., Brock, S. E., & Reeves, M. A. (2006). School crisis teams within an incident command system. *California School Psychologist, 11,* 51–60.

Nickerson, A. B., & Heath, M. A. (2008). Developing and strengthening crisis response teams. *School Psychology Forum, 2*(2), 1–16. Retrieved April 3, 2008, from http://www.nasponline.org/publications/spf/issue2_2/nickerson.pdf

Nickerson, A. B., & Nagle, R. J. (2005). Parent and peer attachment in late childhood and early adolescence. *Journal of Early Adolescence, 25,* 223–249.

Nickerson, A. B., & Osborne, K. M. (2006). Crisis preparedness, response, and management: Surveys of school professionals. In S. R. Jimerson & M. J. Furlong (Eds.), *Handbook of school violence and school safety: From research to practice* (pp. 89–101). Mahwah, NJ: Erlbaum.

Nickerson, A. B., Reeves, M. A., Brock, S. E., & Jimerson, S. R. (2009). *Identifying, assessing, and treating posttraumatic stress disorder at school.* New York: Springer.

Nickerson, A. B., & Slater, E. D. (2008). School and community violence and victimization as predictors of suicidal behavior for adolescent males and females. Manuscript submitted for publication.

Nickerson, A. B., & Zhe, E. J. (2004). Crisis prevention and intervention: A survey of school psychologists. *Psychology in the Schools, 41*, 777–788.

No Child Left Behind Act of 2001, Pub. L. 107–110, 115 Stat. 1425 (2002). Retrieved September 11, 2008, from http://www.ed.gov/policy/elsec/leg/esea02/index.html

Norris, F. H., Byrne, C. M., Diaz, E., & Kaniasty, K. (2002). *Psychosocial resources in the aftermath of natural and human-caused disasters: A review of the empirical literature.* Retrieved June 2, 2008, from http://www.ncptsd.va.gov/ncmain/ncdocs/fact_shts/fs_resources.html?opm=1&rr=rr51&srt=d&echorr=true

Norris, F. H., Friedman, M. J., Watson, P. J., Byrne, C. M., Diaz, E., & Kaniasty, K. (2002). 60,000 disaster victims speak: Part I. An empirical review of the empirical literature, 1981–2001. *Psychiatry, 65*, 207–239.

O'Donnell, J., Hawkins, D., Catalano, R. F., Abbott, R. D., & Day, E. (1998). Preventing school failure, drug use, and delinquency among low-income children: Long-term intervention in elementary schools. *American Journal of Orthopsychiatry, 65*, 87–100.

Oflaz, F., Hatipoğlu, S., & Aydin, H. (2008). Effectiveness of psychoeducational intervention on post-traumatic stress disorder and coping styles of earthquake survivors. *Journal and Clinical Nursing, 17*, 677–687.

Ohan, J. L., Myers, K., & Collett, B. R. (2002). Ten-year review of rating scales. IV: Scales assessing trauma and its effects. *Journal of the American Academy of Child and Adolescent Psychiatry, 41*, 1401–1422.

Olff, M., Langeland, W., & Gersons, B. P. R. (2005). The psychobiology of PTSD: Coping with trauma. *Psychoneuroendocrinology, 30*, 974–982.

Olweus, D. (1993). *Bullying at school: What we know and what we can do.* Malden, MA: Blackwell.

Oras, R., de Ezpeleta, S. C., & Ahmad, A. (2004). Treatment of traumatized refugee children with Eye Movement Desensitization and Reprocessing in a psychodynamic context. *Journal of Nordic Psychiatry, 58*, 199–203.

Orsillo, S. M. (2001). Measures for acute stress disorder and posttraumatic stress disorder. In M. M. Antony & S. M. Orsillo (Eds.), *Practitioners guide to empirically based measures of anxiety* (pp. 255–307). New York: Kluwer Academic/Plenum.

Osher, D., Dwyer, K., & Jimerson, S. R. (2006). Safe, supportive, and effective schools: Promoting school success to reduce school violence. In S. R. Jimerson & M. Furlong (Eds.), *Handbook of school violence and school safety: From research to practice* (pp. 51–71). Mahwah, NJ: Erlbaum.

Ostrowski, S. A., Christopher, N. C., & Delahanty, D. L. (2007). Brief report: The impact of maternal posttraumatic stress disorder symptoms and child gender on risk for persistent posttraumatic stress disorder symptoms in child trauma victims. *Journal of Pediatric Psychology, 33*, 338–342.

Otto, M. W., Henin, A., Hirshfeld-Becker, D. R., Pollack, M. H., Biederman, J., & Rosenbaum, J. F. (2007). Posttraumatic stress disorder symptoms following media exposure to tragic events: Impact of 9/11 on children at risk for anxiety disorders. *Journal of Anxiety Disorders, 21*, 888–902.

Oxley, D. (2001). Organizing schools into small learning communities. *NASSP Bulletin, 85*(625), 5–16.

Oxley, D. (2004). *Small learning communities: A review of the research.* The Mid-Atlantic Regional Educational Laboratory at Temple University Center for Research in Human Development and Education. Retrieved June 10, 2008, http://www.temple.edu/lss/

Ozer, E. J., Best, S. R., Lipsey, T. L., & Weiss, D. S. (2003). Predictors of posttraumatic stress disorder and symptoms in adults: A meta-analysis. *Psychological Bulletin, 129*, 52–73.

Pagliocca, P. M., & Nickerson, A. B. (2001). Legislating school crisis response: Good policy or just good politics? *Law & Policy, 23*, 373–407.

Pagliocca, P. M., Nickerson, A. B., & Williams, S. (2002). Research and evaluation directions in crisis intervention. In S. E. Brock, P. J. Lazarus, & S. R. Jimerson (Eds.), *Best practices in school crisis prevention and intervention* (pp. 771–790). Bethesda, MD: National Association of School Psychologists.

Patton, M. Q. (1990). *Qualitative evaluation and research methods* (2nd ed.). Newbury Park, CA: SAGE.

Pearlman, L., & Saakvitne, K. (1995). *Trauma and the therapist: Counselor transference and vicarious traumatization in psychotherapy with incest survivors.* New York: Norton.

Pepin, E. N., & Banyard, V. L. (2006). Social support: A mediator between child maltreatment and developmental outcomes. *Journal of Youth and Adolescence, 35*, 617–630.

Petersen, S., & Straub, R. L. (1992). *School crisis survival guide: Management techniques and materials for counselors and administrators.* West Nyack, NY: Center for Applied Research in Education.

Pfefferbaum, B. (1997). Posttraumatic stress disorder in children: A review of the past 10 years. *Journal of the American Academy of Child and Adolescent Psychiatry, 36*, 1503–1511.

Pfefferbaum, B., Nixon, S. J., Tucker, P. M., Tivis, R. D., Moore, V. L., Gurwitch, R. H., et al. (1999). Posttraumatic stress responses in bereaved children after the Oklahoma City bombing. *Journal of the American Academy of Child and Adolescent Psychiatry, 38*, 1372–1379.

Pfefferbaum, B., Nixon, S. J., Tivis, R. D., Doughty, D. E., Pynoos, R. S., Gurwitch, R. H., et al. (2001). Television exposure in children after a terrorist incident. *Psychiatry, 64*, 202–211.

Pfefferbaum, B., Seale, T. W., McDonald, N. B., Brandt, E. N., Rainwater, S. M., Maynard, B. T., et al. (2000). Posttraumatic stress two years after the Oklahoma City bombing in youths geographically distant from the explosion. *Psychiatry: Interpersonal & Biological Processes, 63*, 358–370.

Phinney, A. (2004). *Preparedness in America's schools: A comprehensive look at terrorism preparedness in America's twenty largest school districts.* New York: America Prepared Campaign.

Phipps, A. B., & Byrne, M. K. (2003). Brief interventions for secondary trauma: Review and recommendations. *Stress and Health, 19*, 139–147.

Phoenix, B. J. (2007). Psychoeducation for survivors of trauma. *Perspectives in Psychiatric Care, 48*, 123–131.

Pine, D. S., & Cohen, J. A. (2002). Trauma in children and adolescents: Risk and treatment of psychiatric sequelae. *Biological Psychiatry, 51*, 519–531.

Pitcher, G. D., & Poland, S. (1992). *Crisis intervention in the schools*. New York: Guilford Press.

Poland, S. (1994). The role of school crisis intervention teams to prevent and reduce school violence and trauma. *School Psychology Review, 23*, 175–189.

Poland, S., & Lieberman, R. (2002). Best practices in suicide intervention. In A. Thomas & J. Grimes (Eds.), *Best practices in school psychology IV* (pp. 1151–1165). Bethesda, MD: National Association of School Psychologists.

Poland, S., & McCormick, J. S. (1999). *Coping with crisis: Lessons learned.* Longmont, CO: Sopris West.

Posavac, E. J., & Raymond, G. C. (1989). *Program evaluation: Methods and case studies* (3rd ed.). Englewood Cliffs, NJ: Prentice Hall.

Prinstein, M. J., La Greca, A. M., Vernberg, E. M., & Silverman, W. K. (1996). Children's coping assistance: How parents, teachers, and friends help children cope after a natural disaster. *Journal of Clinical Child Psychology, 25*, 463–475.

Prout, S. M., & Prout, H. T. (1998). A meta-analysis of school-based studies of counseling and psychotherapy: An update. *Journal of School Psychology, 36*, 121–136.

Pynoos, R. S., Frederick, C., Nader, K., Arroyo, W., Steinberg, A., Eth, S., et al. (1987). Life threat and posttraumatic stress in school-age children. *Archives of General Psychiatry, 44*, 1057–1063.

Pynoos, R. S., Goenjian, A., Tashjian, M., Karakashian, M., Manjikian, R., Manoukian, G., et al. (1993). Post-traumatic stress reactions in children after the 1988 Armenian earthquake. *British Journal of Psychiatry, 163*, 239–247.

Pynoos, R., Rodrigues, N., Steinberg, A., Stuber, M., & Frederick, C. (1998). *The UCLA PTSD Reaction Index for DSM IV* (Rev. 1). Los Angeles: UCLA Trauma Psychiatric Program.

Qouta, S., Punamäki, R. L., & El Sarraj, E. (2003). Prevalence and determinants of PTSD among Palestinian children exposed to military violence. *European Child & Adolescent Psychiatry, 12*, 265–272.

Qouta, S., Punamäki, R. L., & El Sarraj, E. (2005). Mother-child expression of psychological distress in war trauma. *Clinical Child Psychology and Psychiatry, 10*, 135–156.

Quallich, K. (2005). Crisis management research summary: Television images and psychological symptoms after the September 11 terrorist attacks. *Communiqué, 33*(5), 32.

Quinn, K. P., & McDougal, J. L. (1998). A mile wide and a mile deep: Comprehensive interventions for children and youth with emotional and behavioral disorders and their families. *School Psychology Review, 27*, 191–203.

Ramsay, R. F., Tanney, B. L., Lang, W. A., & Kinzel, T. (2004). *Suicide Intervention Handbook* (10th ed.). Calgary, AB: LivingWorks.

Raphael, B. (2007). The human touch and mass catastrophe. [Commentary on the report "Five essential elements of immediate and mid-term mass trauma intervention: empirical evidence" by Hobfoll, Watson et al.]. *Psychiatry, 70*, 329–336.

Raphael, B., & Meldrum, B. (1993). The evolution of mental health responses and research in Australian disasters. *Journal of Traumatic Stress, 6*, 65–89.

Raphael, B., & Newman, L. (2000). *Disaster mental health response handbook: An educational resource for mental health professionals involved in disaster management.* North Sydney, New South Wales: NSW Health.

Raywid, M. (1996). *Taking stock: The movement to create mini-schools, schools-within-schools, and separate small schools.* New York: Columbia University, Teachers College, ERIC Clearinghouse on Urban Education.

Reeves, M. A., Nickerson A. B., & Jimerson, S. R. (2006a). *Crisis prevention and preparedness: The comprehensive school crisis team.* (Available from National Association of School Psychologists, 4340 East West Highway, Suite 402, Bethesda, MD 20814)

Reeves, M. A, Nickerson A. B., & Jimerson, S. R. (2006b). *Trainer's handbook. Workshop 1. Crisis prevention and preparedness: The comprehensive school crisis team.* Bethesda, MD: National Association of School Psychologists.

Richards, D. (2001). A field study of critical incident stress debriefing versus critical incident stress management. *Journal of Mental Health, 10*, 351–362.

Rigby, K. (2000). Effects of peer victimization in schools and perceived social support on adolescent well-being. *Journal of Adolescence, 23*, 57–68.

Rigby, K., & Slee, P. (1999). Suicidal ideation among adolescent school children, involvement in bully-victim problems, and perceived social support. *Suicide and Life-threatening Behavior, 29*, 119–130.

Ritchie, E. C. (2003). Mass violence and early intervention: Best practice guidelines. *Primary Psychiatry, 10*, 43–48.

Rosenbaum, S. (2006). U.S. health policy in the aftermath of Hurricane Katrina. *JAMA, 295*, 437–440.

Rossi, P. H., & Freeman, H. E. (1993). *Evaluation: A systematic approach* (5th ed.). Newbury Park, CA: SAGE.

Ruzek, J. L., Brymer, M. J., Jacobs, A. K., Layne, C. M., Vernberg, E. M., & Watson, P. J. (2007). Psychological first aid. *Journal of Mental Health Counseling, 29*, 17–49.

Saakvitne, K., Stamm, B., & Barbanel, L. (2003). *Fostering resilience among mental health workers* (APA Task Force on Resilience in Response to Terrorism). Washington, DC: American Psychological Association. Retrieved December 6, 2008, from www.apa.org/psychologists/pdfs/mentalhealthworkers.pdf

Saigh, P. A. (2004). *Children's PTSD Inventory™: A structured interview for diagnosing posttraumatic stress disorder.* San Antonio, TX: PsychCorp.

Saigh, P. A., Mroueh, M., & Bremner, J. D. (1997). Scholastic impairments among traumatized adolescents. *Behavior Research & Therapy, 35*, 429–436.

Saigh, P. A., Yasik, A., Oberfield, R., Green, B., Halamandaris, P., Rubenstein, H., et al. (2000). The Children's PTSD Inventory. Development and reliability. *Journal of Traumatic Stress, 13*, 369–380.

Saigh, P. A., Yasik, A. E., Sack, W. H., & Koplewicz, H. S. (1999). Child-adolescent posttraumatic stress disorder: Prevalence, risk factors, and comorbidity. In P. A. Saigh & J. D. Bremner (Eds.), *Posttraumatic stress disorder: A comprehensive text* (pp. 18–43). Needham Heights, MA: Allyn & Bacon.

Saltzman, W. R., Pynoos, R. S., Layne, C. M., Steinberg, A. M., & Aisenberg, E. (2001). Trauma- and grief-focused intervention for adolescents exposed to community violence: Results of a school-based screening and group treatment protocol. *Group Dynamics: Theory, Research, and Practice, 5*, 291–303.

Sandler, I. N., Wolchik, S. A., MacKinnon, D., Ayers, T. S., & Roosa, M. W. (1997). Developing linkages between theory and intervention in stress and coping processes. In S. A. Wolchik & I. N. Sandler (Eds.), *Handbook of children's coping: Linking theory and intervention* (pp. 3–41). New York: Plenum.

Sandoval, J., & Brock, S. E. (2009). Managing crisis: Prevention, intervention, and treatment. In C. R. Reynolds & T. B. Gutkin (Eds.), *The handbook of school psychology* (pp. 886–904). New York: Wiley.

Sandoval, J., & Lewis, S. (2002) Cultural considerations in crisis intervention. In S. E. Brock, P. J. Lazarus, & S. R. Jimerson (Eds.), *Best practices in school crisis prevention and intervention* (pp. 293–308). Bethesda, MD: National Association of School Psychologists.

Saylor, C. R. (2002). *The Pediatric Emotional Distress Scale (PEDS).* (Available from the author, Department of Psychology, The Citadel, 171 Moultrie Ave., Charleston, SC 29409)

Saylor, C. F., Belter, R., & Stokes, S. J. (1997). Children and families coping with disaster. In S. A. Wolchik & I. N. Sandler (Eds.), *Handbook of children's coping: Linking theory and intervention* (pp. 361–383). New York: Plenum.

Saylor, C. R., Cowart, B. L., Lipovsky, J. A., Jackson, C., & Finch, A. J. (2003). Media exposure to September 11: Elementary school students' experiences and posttraumatic symptoms. *American Behavior Scientist, 46*, 1622–1642.

Saylor, C. F, Swenson, C. C., Reynolds, S. S., & Taylor, M. (1999). The Pediatric Emotional Distress Scale: A brief screening measure for young children exposed to traumatic events. *Journal of Clinical Child Psychology, 28*, 70–81.

Schäfer, I., Barkmann, C., Riedesser, P., & Schulte-Markwort, M. (2004). Peritraumatic dissociation predicts posttraumatic stress in children and adolescents following road traffic accidents. *Journal of Trauma & Dissociation, 5*, 79–92.

Scheeringa, M. S., Wright, M. J., Hunt, J. P., & Zeanah, C. H. (2006). Factors affecting the diagnosis and prediction of PTSD symptomatology in children and adolescents. *American Journal of Psychiatry, 163*, 644–651.

Scheeringa, M. S., & Zeanah, C. H. (2001). A relational perspective on PTSD in early childhood. *Journal of Traumatic Stress, 14*, 799–815.

Schneider, T., Walker, H., & Sprague, J. (2000). *Safe school design: A handbook for educational leaders: Applying the principles of crime prevention through environmental design.* Eugene, OR: ERIC Clearinghouse on Educational Management.

Scholes, C., Turpin, G., & Mason, S. (2007). A randomized controlled trial to assess the effectiveness of providing self-help information to people with symptoms of acute stress disorder following a traumatic injury. *Behaviour Research and Therapy, 45*, 2527–2536.

School and Staffing Survey (1993–1994, 1999–2000, and 2003–2004). Retrieved June 20, 2008, from http://nces.ed.gov/surveys/sass/

School Anti-Violence Empowerment Act of 2000, H.R. 1895 (May 20, 1999). Retrieved September 11, 2008, from http://frwebgate.access.gpo.gov/cgi-bin/getdoc.cgi?dbname=106_cong_bills&docid=f:h1895ih.txtpdf

School Crime Supplement to the National Crime Victimization Survey. (1995, 1991, 2001, 2003, and 2005). Retrieved June 20, 2008, from http://nces.ed.gov/programs/crime/surveys.asp

School Health Policy and Programs Study (SHPPS). (2007). Crisis preparedness, response and recovery. *Journal of School Health, 77,* 385–397.

School Safety Alliances. (2004). *Anatomy of a school crisis management program.* Retrieved April 7, 2008, from http://www.schoolsafetyalliance.org/documents/Anatomy%20of%20a%20Comprehensive%20School%20Crisis%20Management%20Program1.doc

Schools Safety Enhancement Act of 1999, H.R. 1898 (May 20, 1999). Retrieved September 11, 2008, from http://www.govtrack.us/data/us/bills.text/106/h/h1898.pdf

School Survey on Crime and Safety. (1999–2000, 2003–2004, and 2005–2006). Retrieved June 20, 2008, from http://nces.ed.gov/surveys/ssocs/

Schwarz, E. D., & Kowalski, J. M. (1991). Malignant memories: PTSD in children and adults after a school shooting. *Journal of the American Academy of Child & Adolescent Psychiatry, 30,* 936–944.

Schwarz, J. H. (1982). Guiding children's creative expression in the stress of war. In C. D. Spielberger, I. G. Sarason, & N. A. Milgram (Eds.), *Stress and anxiety* (Vol. 7, pp. 351–354). Washington, DC: Hemisphere.

Seedat, S., Lockhart, R., Kaminer, D., Zungu-Dirwayi, N., & Stein, D. J. (2001). An open trial of citalopram in adolescents with post-traumatic stress disorder. *International Clinical Psychopharmacology, 16,* 21–25.

Seedat, S., Nyamai, C., Njenga, F., Vythilingum, B., & Stein, D. J. (2004). Trauma exposure and post-traumatic stress symptoms in urban African schools. *British Journal of Psychiatry, 184,* 169–175.

Seedat, S., Stein, D. J., Ziervogel, C., Middleton, T., Kaminer, D., Emsley, R. A., et al. (2002). Comparison of response to a selective serotonin reuptake inhibitor in children, adolescents, and adults with posttraumatic stress disorder. *Journal of Child and Adolescent Psychopharmacology, 12,* 37–46.

Serketich, W. J., & Dumas, J. E. (1996). The effectiveness of behavioral parent training to modify antisocial behavior in children: A meta-analysis. *Behavior Therapy, 27,* 171–186.

Servaty-Seib, H. L., Peterson, J., & Spang, D. (2003). Notifying individual students of a death loss: Practical recommendations for schools and school counselors. *Death Studies, 27,* 167–186.

Shalev, A. Y., & Freedman, S. (2005). PTSD following terrorist attacks: A prospective evaluation. *American Journal of Psychiatry, 162,* 1188–1191.

Shalev, A. Y., Tuval-Mashiach, R., & Hadar, H. (2004). Posttraumatic stress disorder as a result of mass trauma. *Journal of Clinical Psychiatry, 65*(Suppl. 1), 4–10.

Shapiro, F. (2002). EMDR 12 years after its introduction: Past and future research. *Journal of Clinical Psychology, 58,* 1–22.

Sharan, S. (1980). Cooperative learning in small groups: Recent methods and effects on achievement, attitudes and ethnic relations. *Review of Educational Research, 50,* 241–271.

Shaw, J. A. (2003). Children exposed to war/terrorism. *Clinical Child and Family Psychology Review, 6*, 237–246.

Short, L., Hennessy, M., & Campbell, J. (1996). Tracking the work: A guide for communities in developing useful program evaluations. In *A guide for communities: Building an integrated approach for reducing family violence* (pp. 59–72). Chicago: American Medical Association.

Siedler, G., & Wagner, F. (2006). Comparing the efficacy of EMDR and trauma-focused cognitive-behavioral therapy in the treatment of PTSD: A meta-analytic study. *Psychological Medicine, 36*, 1515–1522.

Sijbrandij, M., Olff, M., Reitsma, J. B., Carlier, I. V. E., & Gersons, B. P. R. (2006). Emotional or educational debriefing after psychological trauma: Randomised controlled trial. *British Journal of Psychiatry, 189*, 150–155.

Silva, R. R., Alpert, M., Munoz, D. M., Singh, S., Matzner, F., & Dummit, S. (2000). Stress and vulnerability to posttraumatic stress disorder in children and adolescents. *American Journal of Psychiatry, 157*, 1229–1235.

Silver, R. C., Holman, E. A., McIntosh, D. N., Poulin, M., & Gil-Rivas, V. (2002). Nationwide longitudinal study of psychological responses to September 11. *JAMA, 288*, 1235–1244.

Silverman, W. K., & La Greca, A. M. (2002). Children experiencing disasters: Definitions, reactions, and predictors of outcomes. In A. M. La Greca, W.K. Silverman, E. M. Vernberg, & M. C. Roberts (Eds.), *Helping children cope with disasters and terrorism* (pp. 11–33). Washington, DC: American Psychological Association.

Simeon, D., Greenberg, J., Knutelska, M., Schmeidler, J., & Hollander, E. (2003). Peritraumatic reactions associated with the World Trade Center disaster. *American Journal of Psychiatry, 160*, 1702–1705.

Singer, M. I., Flannery, D. J., Guo, S., Miller, D., & Leibbrandt, S. (2004). Exposure to violence, parental monitoring, and television viewing as contributors to children's psychological trauma. *Journal of Community Psychology, 32*, 489–504.

Sjostrom, L., & Stein, N. (1996). *Bullyproof: A teacher's guide on teasing and bullying for use with fourth and fifth grade students.* Wellesley, MA: Wellesley College Center for Research on Women.

Skiba, R. J. (2000). *Zero tolerance, zero evidence: An analysis of school disciplinary practice* (Policy Research Report No. SRS2). Bloomington, IN: Indiana University, Indiana Education Policy Center.

Skiba, R., & Peterson, R. (1999). The dark side of zero tolerance. *Phi Delta Kappa, 80*, 372–379.

Skiba, R. J., Peterson, R. L., & Williams, T. (1997). Office referrals and suspension: Disciplinary intervention in middle schools. *Education and Treatment of Children, 20*, 295–315.

Slaikeu, K. A. (1990). *Crisis intervention: A handbook for practice and research* (2nd ed.). Newton, MA: Allyn & Bacon.

Smith, P. K., Boulton, M. J., & Cowie, H. (1993). The impact of cooperative group work on ethnic relations in middle school. *School Psychology International, 14*, 21–42.

Smith Harvey, V. (2007, November). Resiliency: Strategies for parents and educators. *NASP Communiqué, 36*(3). Retrieved September 19, 2008, from http://www.nasponline.org/publications/cq/mocq363resiliency_ho.aspx

Speier, A. H. (2000). *Psychosocial issues for children and adolescents in disasters* (2nd ed.), Washington, DC: U.S. Department of Health and Human Services.

Sprague, J. R., & Horner, R. H. (2006). School-wide positive behavioral supports. In S. R. Jimerson & M. J. Furlong (Eds.), *Handbook of school violence and school safety: From research to practice* (pp. 413–427). Mahwah, NJ: Erlbaum.

Sprague, J., & Walker, H. (2000). Early identification and intervention for youth with antisocial and violent behavior. *Exceptional Children, 66*, 367–379.

Sprague, J. R., & Walker, H. M. (2005). *Safe and healthy schools: Practical prevention strategies.* New York: Guilford Press.

Sprague, J., Walker, H., Golly, A., White, K., Myers, D. R., & Shannon, T. (2001). Translating research into effective practice: The effects of a universal staff and student intervention on indicators of discipline and school safety. *Education and Treatment of Children, 24*, 495–511.

Stallard, P., & Salter, E. (2003). Psychological debriefing with children and young people following traumatic events. *Clinical Child Psychology and Psychiatry, 8*, 445–457.

Stallard, P., & Smith, E. (2007). Appraisals and cognitive coping styles associated with chronic post-traumatic symptoms in child road traffic accident survivors. *Journal of Child Psychology and Psychiatry, 48*, 194–201.

Stallard, P., Velleman, R., Salter, E., Howse, I., Yule, W., & Taylor, G. (2006). A randomized controlled trial to determine the effectiveness of an early psychological intervention with children involved in road traffic accidents. *Journal of Child Psychology and Psychiatry, 47*, 127–134.

Stamm, B. H. (2005). *The ProQOL Manual: The Professional Quality of Life Scale: Compassion satisfaction, burnout & compassion fatigue/secondary trauma scales.* Baltimore: Sidran Press.

Stein, B. D., Jaycox, L. H., Kataoka, S. H., Wong, M., Tu, W., Elliot, M. N., et al. (2003). A mental health intervention for school children exposed to violence: A randomized controlled trial. *JAMA, 290*, 603–611.

Steinberg, A. M., Saltzman, W. R., & Brymer, M. (n.d.). *Administration and scoring of the UCLA PTSD Reaction Index for DSM-IV (Revision 1).* Retrieved April 12, 2008, from http://www.nctsnet.org/nctsn_assets/video/ptsdproducer_files/intro.htm

Strand, V. C., Sarmiento, T. L., & Pasquale, L. E. (2005). Assessment and screening tools for trauma in children and adolescents. *Trauma, Violence & Abuse, 6*, 55–78.

Strein, W., & Koehler, J. (2008). Best practices in developing prevention strategies for school psychology practice. In A. Thomas & J. Grimes (Eds.), *Best practices in school psychology V* (Vol. 4; pp. 1309–1322). Bethesda, MD: National Association of School Psychologists.

Suckling, A., & Temple, C. (2002). *Bullying: A whole-school approach.* London: Jessica Kingsley Publishers.

Sugai, G., & Horner, R. (2002). The evolution of discipline practices: School-wide positive behavior supports. *Child and Family Behavior Therapy, 24*, 23–50.

Sullivan, M., Harris, E., Collado, C., & Chen, T. (2006). Noways tired: Perspectives of clinicians of color on culturally competent crisis intervention. *Journal of Clinical Psychology: In Session, 62*, 987–999.

Susan, M. (in press). Crisis prevention, response, and recovery: Helping children with special needs. In A. Canter & L. Paige (Eds.), *Helping children at home and school III: Handouts for families and educators.* Bethesda, MD: National Association of School Psychologists.

Sutherland, K. S., & Wehby, J. H. (2001). Exploring the relationship between increased opportunities to respond to academic requests and the academic and behavioral outcomes of students with EBD. *Remedial and Special Education, 22*, 113–121.

Swahn, M. H., Simon, T. R., Hertz, M. F., Arias, I., Bossarte, R. M., Ross, J. G., et al. (2008). Linking dating violence, peer violence, and suicidal behavior among high-risk youth. *American Journal of Preventative Medicine, 34*, 30–38.

Swick, S. D., Dechant, E., & Jellinek, M. S. (2002). Children or victims of September 11th: A perspective on the emotional and developmental challenges they face and how to help meet them. *Journal of Developmental and Behavioral Pediatrics, 5*, 378–384.

Tatum, E. L., Vollmer, W. M., & Shore, J. H. (1986). Relationship of perception and mediating variables to the psychiatric consequences of disaster. In J. J. Shore (Ed.), *Disaster stress studies: New methods and findings* (pp. 100–121). Washington, DC: American Psychiatric Press.

Taylor, M. (2006, September). *Conducting effective table tops, drills and exercises.* Presentation of the Office of Safe and Drug-Free Schools, Santa Monica, CA.

Terr, L. C. (1981). Psychic trauma in children: Observations following the Chowchilla school-bus kidnapping. *American Journal of Psychiatry, 138*, 14–19.

Terr, L. C. (1983). Chowchilla revisited: The effects of psychic trauma four years after a school bus kidnapping. *American Journal of Psychiatry, 140*, 1543–1550.

Terr, L. C. (1991). Childhood traumas: An outline and overview. *American Journal of Psychiatry, 148*, 10–20.

Thabet, A. A., Vostanis, P., & Karim, K. (2005). Group crisis intervention for children during ongoing war conflict. *European Child & Adolescent Psychiatry, 14*, 262–269.

Tichenor, V., Marmar, C. R., Weiss, D. S., Metzler, T. J., & Ronfeldt, H. M. (1996). The relationship of peritraumatic dissociation and posttraumatic stress: Findings in female Vietnam theater veterans. *Journal of Consulting and Clinical Psychology, 64*, 1054–1059.

Tobin, T., & Sugai, G. (1996). Patterns in middle school discipline records. *Journal of Emotional and Behavioral Disorders, 4*, 82–95.

Toubiana, Y. H., Milgram, N. A., Strich, Y., & Edelstein, A. (1988). Crisis intervention in a school community disaster: Principles and practices. *Journal of Community Psychology, 16*, 228–240.

Tramonte, M. R. (1999). *School psychology in the new millennium: Constructing and implementing a blueprint for intervening in crisis involving disasters and/or violence.* Annual Convention of the National Association of School Psychologists, Las Vegas, NV.

Tremblay, C., Hebert, M., & Piche, C. (1999). Coping strategies and social support as mediators of consequences in child sexual abuse. *Child Abuse & Neglect, 23*, 929–945.

Trump, K. S. (2000). *2002 NASRO school resource officer survey.* Cleveland, OH: National School Safety and Security Services.

Trump, K. (2003). *School safety threats persist, funding decreasing: NASRO 2003 national school-based law enforcement survey.* Retrieved August 1, 2008, from http://www.schoolsecurity.org/resources/2003NASROSurvey%20NSSSS.pdf

Tucker, P., Pfefferbaum, B., Nixon, S. J., & Dickson, W. (2000). Predictors of post-traumatic stress symptoms in Oklahoma City: Exposure, social support, peri-traumatic responses. *Journal of Behavioral Health Services and Research, 27*, 406–416.

Udwin, O., Boyle, S., Yule, W., Bolton, D., & O'Ryan, D. (2000). Risk factors for long-term psychological effects of a disaster experienced in adolescence: Predictors of post-traumatic stress disorder. *Journal of Child Psychology and Psychiatry and Allied Disciplines, 41*, 969–979.

United Way. (n.d.). *United Way: America's number 1 charity*. Retrieved June 7, 2007, from http://national.unitedway.org/about/index.cfm

University of the State of New York. (2001). *Project SAVE. Guidance document for school safety plans*. Albany, NY: University of the State of New York, State Education Department. Retrieved June 1, 2008, from http://www.emsc.nysed.gov/sss/SAVE/

U.S. Department of Education. (2003). *Practical information on crisis planning: A guide for schools and communities*. Washington, DC: Author.

U.S. Department of Education, REMS Technical Assistance Center. (2006a). Emergency exercises: An effective way to validate school safety plans. *ERCMExpress, 2*(3), 1–4. Retrieved September 15, 2008, from http://rems.ed.gov/index.cfm?event=express

U.S. Department of Education, REMS Technical Assistance Center. (2006b). Integrating students with special needs and disabilities into emergency response and crisis management planning. *REMSExpress, 2*(1), 1–4. Retrieved September 15, 2008, from http://rems.ed.gov/index.cfm?event=express

U.S. Department of Education. (2007, October). *Balancing student privacy and school safety: A guide to the Family Educational Rights and Privacy Act (FERPA) for elementary and secondary schools*. Washington, DC: Author. Retrieved October 3, 2008, from http://www.ed.gov/policy/gen/guid/fpco/brochures/elsec.html

U.S. Department of Homeland Security (DHS). (2003, March). *Paige, Ridge, Unveil new Web resource to help schools plan for emergencies*. Retrieved February 29, 2008, from http://www.dhs.gov/xnews/releases/press_release_0107.shtm

U.S. Department of Homeland Security (DHS). (2004, March). *National incident management system*. Retrieved February 29, 2008, from http://www.fema.gov/pdf/nims/nims_doc_full.pdf

U.S. Department of Homeland Security. (2006, February). *Homeland security exercise and evaluation program. Vol. IV: Sample exercise documents*. Washington, DC: Author. Retrieved December 4, 2008, from https://hseep.dhs.gov/pages/1001_HSEEP7.aspx

U.S. Department of Homeland Security. (2007a, February). *Homeland security exercise and evaluation program. Vol. I: HSEEP overview and exercise program management*. Washington, DC: Author. Retrieved December 4, 2008, from https://hseep.dhs.gov/pages/1001_HSEEP7.aspx

U.S. Department of Homeland Security. (2007b, February). *Homeland security exercise and evaluation program. Vol. II: Exercise planning and conduct*. Washington, DC: Author. Retrieved December 4, 2008, from https://hseep.dhs.gov/pages/1001_HSEEP7.aspx

U.S. Department of Homeland Security. (2007c, February). *Homeland security exercise and evaluation program. Vol. III: Exercise evaluation and improvement*. Washington, DC: Author. Retrieved December 4, 2008, from https://hseep.dhs.gov/pages/1001_HSEEP7.aspx

Vaiva, G., Brunet, A., Lebigot, F., Boss, V., Ducrocq, F., Devos, P., et al. (2003). Fright (effroi) and other peritraumatic responses after a serious motor vehicle accident: Prospective influence on acute PTSD development. *Canadian Journal of Psychiatry, 48*, 395–401.

Valent, P. (2000). Disaster syndromes. In G. Fink (Ed.), *Encyclopedia of stress* (Vol. 1; pp. 706–709). San Diego, CA: Academic Press.

Valle, R., & Bensussen, G. (1985). Hispanic social networks, social support, and mental health. In W. Vega & M. Miranda (Eds.), *Stress and Hispanic mental health: Relating research to service delivery* (pp. 147–173). Rockville, MD: National Institute of Mental Health.

van Emmerik, A. A. P., Kamphuis, J. H., Hulsbosch, A. M., & Emmelkamp, P. M. G. (2002). Single session debriefing after psychological trauma: A meta-analysis. *Lancet, 360*, 766–771.

VanTassel-Baska, J. L., Olszewski-Kubilius, P. O., & Kulieke, M. (1994). Self concept and social support in advantaged and disadvantaged seventh and eighth grade gifted students. *Roeper Review, 16*, 186–191.

Vernberg, E. M., LaGreca, A. M., Silverman, W. K., & Prinstein, M. J. (1996). Predictors of children's postdisaster functioning following Hurricane Andrew. *Journal of Abnormal Psychology, 105*, 237–248.

Vernberg, E. M., Steinberg, A. M., Jacobs, A. K., Brymer, M. J., Watson, P. J., Osofsky, J. D., et al. (2008). Innovations in disaster mental health: Psychological first aid. *Professional Psychology: Research and Practice, 39*, 381–388.

Vijayakumar, L., Kankan, G. K., Ganesh Kumar, B., & Devarajan, P. (2006). Do all children need intervention after exposure to tsunami. *International Review of Psychiatry, 18*, 515–522.

Virginia Board of Education. (1999). *Model school crisis management plan.* Richmond, VA. Retrieved August 28, 2008, from http://www.doe.virginia.gov/VDOE/Instruction/model.html

Virginia Department of Emergency Management. (2001). *School crisis management exercise development guide.* Richmond, VA: Author. Retrieved December 4, 2008, from www.vaemergency.com/library/handbooks/schoolcrisisguide.pdf

Viswesvaran, C. (2003). Review of the Trauma Symptoms Checklist for Children. In B. S. Plake, J. C. Impara, R. A. Spies (Eds.), *The fifteenth mental measurements yearbook.* Lincoln, NE: Buros Institute of Mental Measurements.

Vogel, J. M., & Vernberg, E. M. (1993). Children's psychological responses to disasters. *Journal of Clinical Child Psychology, 22*, 464–484.

Vossekuil, B., Fein, R. A., Reddy, M., Borum, R., & Modzeleski, W. (2002). *The final report and findings of the Safe School Initiative: Implications for the prevention of school attacks in the United States.* Washington, DC: U.S. Secret Service and U.S. Department of Education.

Warda, G., & Bryant, R. A. (1998). Cognitive bias in acute stress disorder. *Behaviour Research and Therapy, 36*, 1177–1183.

Watson, T. S., & Steege, M. W. (2003). *Conducting school-based functional behavioral assessments: A practitioner's guide.* New York: Guilford Press.

Weaver, T. L., & Clum, G. A. (1995). Psychological distress associated with interpersonal violence: A meta-analysis. *Clinical Psychology Review, 15*, 115–140.

Weems, C. F., Watts, S. E., Marsee, M. A., Taylor, L. K., Costa, N. M., Cannon, M. F., et al. (2007). The psychosocial impact of Hurricane Katrina: Contextual differences in psychological symptoms, social support, and discrimination. *Behaviour Research and Therapy, 45*, 2295–2306.

Weinberg, R. B. (1990). Serving large numbers of adolescent victim survivors: Group interventions. *Professional Psychology: Research and Practice, 21*, 271–278.

Weiss, D. S. (2004). The Impact of Event Scale – Revised. In J. P. Wilson & T. M. Keane (Eds.), *Assessing psychological trauma and PTSD* (2nd ed., pp. 168–189). New York: Guilford Press.

Weiss, D. S., Marmar, C. R., Metzler, T. J., & Ronfeldt, H. M. (1995). Predicting symptomatic distress in emergency services personnel. *Journal of Consulting and Clinical Psychology, 63*, 361–368.

Weisz, J. R., Weiss, B., Han, S. S., Grander, D. A., & Morton, T. (1995). Effects of psychotherapy with children and adolescents revisited: A meta-analysis of treatment outcome studies. *Psychological Bulletin, 117*, 450–468.

Wellisch, D., Kawaga-Singer, M., Reid, S. L., Lin, Y., Nishikawa-Lee, S., & Wellisch, M. (1999). An exploratory study of social support: A cross-cultural comparison of Chinese-, Japanese-, and Anglo-American breast cancer patients. *Psycho-Oncology, 8*, 207–219.

Widom, C. S. (1999). Posttraumatic stress disorder in abused and neglected children grown up. *American Journal of Psychiatry, 156*, 1223–1229.

Wilson, D. B., Gottfredson, D. C., & Najaka, S. S. (2001). School-based prevention of problem behaviors: A meta-analysis. *Journal of Quantitative Criminology, 17*, 247–272.

Wilson, J. P., Raphael, B., Meldrum, L., Bedosky, C., & Sigman, M. (2000). Preventing PTSD in trauma survivors. *Bulletin of the Menninger Clinic, 64*, 181–196.

Wintre, M., Hicks, R., McVey, G., & Fox, J. (1988). Age and sex differences in choice of consultant for various types of patterns. *Child Development, 59*, 1046–1055.

Wollman, D. (1993). Critical incident stress debriefing and crisis groups: A review of the literature. *Group, 17*, 70–83.

Wright, K. M., Ursano, R. J., Bartone, P. T., & Ingraham, L. H. (1990). The shared experience of catastrophe: An expanded classification of the disaster community. *American Journal of Orthopsychiatry, 60*, 35–42.

Yap, M. B. H., & Devilly, G. J. (2004). The role of perceived social support in crime victimization. *Clinical Psychology Review, 24*, 1–14.

Yehuda, R., & Hyman, S. E. (2005). The impact of terrorism on brain, and behavior: What we know and what we need to know. *Neuropsychopharmacology, 30*, 1773–1780.

Yorbik, O., Akbiyik, D. I., Kirmizigul, P., & Söhmen, T. (2004). Post-traumatic stress disorder symptoms in children after the 1999 Marmara earthquake in Turkey. *International Journal of Mental Health, 33*, 46–58.

Youth Risk Behavior Survey (1993, 1995, 1997, 1999, 2001, 2003, and 2005). Retrieved June, 20, 2008, from http://www.cdc.gov/YRBS/

Young, B. H., Ford, J. D., Ruzek, J. I., Friedman, M., & Gusman, F. D. (1998). *Disaster mental health services: A guide for clinicians and administrators.* Palo Alto, CA: National Center for Post Traumatic Stress Disorder.

Young, M. A. (1998). The *community crisis response team training manual* (2nd ed.). Washington, DC: National Organization for Victim Assistance.

Yule, W. (1998). Posttraumatic Stress Disorder in children and its treatment. In T. W. Miller (Ed.), *Children of trauma: Stressful life events and their effects on children and adolescents* (pp. 219–244). Madison, CT: International Universities Press.

Zayas, L., Lester, R., Cabassa, L., & Fortuna, L. (2005). "Why do so many Latina teens attempt suicide?" A conceptual model for research. *American Journal of Orthopsychiatry, 75*, 275–287.
Zionts, P., Zionts, L., & Simpson, R. L. (2002). *Emotional and behavioral problems: A handbook for understanding and handling students.* Thousand Oaks, CA: Corwin Press.

INDEX

A

B

C

D

E

F

G

H

I

K

L

M

R

S